Editor's Note

It was with joy that I undertook the first and second French editions of the present volume.

The author, Father Gilleman, after the brilliant recognition accorded his thesis by the Institut Catholique of Paris, was sent to India as professor of dogmatic theology and so was unable to do himself the considerable work of revision, completion, and even recomposition that he judged necessary for the publication of his work. I performed this work of revision in full agreement with him—agreement made easy by friendship and a profound kinship of thought.

The success of the French edition and the importance of the subject for a positive presentation of properly Christian morality stimulated me to prepare an English translation.

In Fathers William F. Ryan, S.J., and André Vachon, S.J., both Canadians, I found translators as competent as I could desire. In their work together they drew not only on a common knowledge of their two mother tongues, but on a long preparatory study of the primacy of charity, so that they approached their difficult task with deep understanding.

As the translation progressed, the English text was sent to the author himself and was carefully examined by him. Finally, it was the author who corrected the proofs.

From all this the reader will no doubt conclude that not many translations can show such guarantees of faithfulness.

I take this occasion to thank enthusiastically the two translators for their long and patient labor.

RENE CARPENTIER, S.J.

Louvain, January 1959.

Preface

While presenting this translation from the second edition of *Le primat de la charité en théologie morale* (Brussels-Paris, Desclée De Brouwer, 1954), we wish to thank sincerely all those who have made possible this publication.

Our deep and warm gratitude goes first of all to Father R. Carpentier, S.J., not only as to the master whose teaching and guidance have provided the inspiring atmosphere for the composition of this work, but also as to the dearly revered friend whose fatherly devotedness has assumed the burden of publishing the two French editions, after he had revised and, in several places, substantially deepened the thought of the original.

In close contact with him and in answer to his wishes, two of his disciples and collaborators at St. Albert's Theological College, Louvain, Fathers William F. Ryan, S.J., and André Vachon, S.J., have kindly undertaken the labor of the present translation. For their selfless and skillful work and for the faithfulness of their rendering, we thank them most heartily.

We again express our deep appreciation of how much the original work owed to Fathers G. de Broglie, S.J., and E. Tesson, S.J., who guided us in the elaboration of this book at the Institut Catholique of Paris.

We also express our gratitude to the Newman Press for having accepted to publish the present translation and for having made it a fine piece of work according to their best traditions.

Any suggestions from our readers which may improve upon a work requiring the common effort of many will be most gladly accepted by us.

G. GILLEMAN, S.J.

St. Mary's Theological College,
Kurseong, N.F.Ry, India,
Feast of the Purification of Our Lady, 1959.

Acknowledgments

We wish to thank the following publishers for the permission to quote from their publications.

BURNS, OATES & WASHBOURNE, LTD., London, and Benziger Brothers, New York
The "Summa Theologica" and *The "Summa Contra Gentiles" of St. Thomas Aquinas*, literally translated by the Fathers of the English Dominican Province, 25 vols., 1920–1929.

B. HERDER BOOK COMPANY, St. Louis
The Theology of the Mystical Body by E. MERSCH, S.J., translated by C. Vollert, S.J., 1951.

LONGMANS, GREEN & COMPANY, New York
Psychoanalytical Method and the Doctrine of Freud by R. Dalbiez, Translated by T. F. Lindsay, 2 vols., 1941.

RANDOM HOUSE, New York
Basic Writings of St. Thomas Aquinas, edited and annotated, with an Introduction, by A. C. PEGIS, 2 vols., 1944.

Contents

SECOND PART

Toward a Charity-Centered Moral Theology
(*Methodological and Speculative Part*)

Contents

THIRD PART

Outline of a Charity-Centered Moral Theology
(*Practical Part*)

Contents

Contents

Abbreviations

AAS	*Acta apostolicae sedis.* Rome.
ACW	*Ancient Christian Writers.* Westminster, Md., and London.
Ang	*Angelicum.* Rome.
APASTh	*Acta Pontificiæ Academiæ Sancti Thomæ Aquinatis et Religionis Catholicæ.* Rome.
BT	*Bulletin thomiste.* Le Saulchoir, Etiolles (S.-et-Oise).
DB	Denzinger-Bannwart, *Enchiridion symbolorum, definitionum et declarationum de rebus fidei et morum.* Ed. 26 by Umberg-Rahner, Freiburg i. Breisgau.
DSAM	*Dictionnaire de spiritualité ascétique et mystique.* Paris.
DTC	*Dictionnaire de théologie catholique.* Paris.
Et	*Études.* Paris.
ETL	*Ephemerides theologicæ Lovanienses.* Louvain.
Greg	*Gregorianum.* Rome.
NRT	*Nouvelle revue théologique.* Louvain.
Per	*Periodica de re morali, canonica, liturgica.* Rome.
PG	*Patrologia, series graeca.* Migne, Paris.
PL	*Patrologia, series latina.* Migne, Paris.

RAM	*Revue d'ascétique et de mystique.* Toulouse.
RCIF	*Revue catholique des Idées et Faits.* Brussels.
RNP	*Revue néo-scholastique de philosophie.* Louvain.
RSPT	*Revue des sciences philosophiques et théologiques.* Paris.
RSR	*Recherches de science religieuse.* Paris.
RSRUS	*Revue des sciences religieuses de l'Université de Strasbourg.* Strasbourg.
RT	*Revue thomiste,* St Maximin (Var).
RTAM	*Recherches de théologie ancienne et médiévale.* Louvain.
Schol	*Scholastik.* Freiburg and Eupen.
StZ	*Stimmen der Zeit.* Freiburg i. Breisgau.
Sum. th.	St. Thomas, *Summa theologica.*
ThQ	*Theologische Quartalschrift.* Tübingen.
ThR	*Theologische Revue.* Münster.
TS	*Theological Studies.* Woodstock, Md.
ZKT	*Zeitschrift für katholische Theologie.* Vienna.

Introduction

§I. CHRISTIAN TRADITION AND MORAL THEOLOGY

On reading certain of our textbooks in moral theology, one gathers the impression that there is a notable difference of perspective between their exposition and the Christian revelation of moral life as found in the Gospel and Tradition. Doubtless we should not look in Scripture for the elaborate theology we find in our manuals; theological methodology was determined only in the Middle Ages; but we can draw from the New Testament and Tradition a core of teachings and of practical attitudes which reveal a certain spirit, a vital moral choice, the source of all further systematization. This very soul of the moral life expressed in the fundamental law of love—*plèrôma nomou hè Agapè* (Rom. 13:10)—does not obviously appear to be reflected in our classical treatises on morals. But this requires a brief explanation.

I. CHRISTIAN TRADITION

a) Scripture. In order to understand the meaning of moral life, it is necessary to pentrate the mystery of man himself, for action follows being. The philosophers had long tried to build an ethics patterned on what man could know about himself by studying his own nature: at best this would be an ethics based on the notion of a creature depending on a

personal God known as perfect Being. Some of these efforts
do not lack a certain stoic grandeur, the grandeur proper to
justice: *in justitia, virtutis splendor est maximus, ex qua
boni viri nominantur*—admirable but cold splendor of the
starry sky.[1] Some even perceived that human action was
deeply rooted in "an appetite for being," seeing there a
trace of the divine, yet failing to understand its full natural
import, just as a child watching the flowing water in a
stream knows not from what source it runs, nor to what
ocean it is heading.

In fact, until the moment of the Incarnation, man remained for himself a baffling mystery, mainly because of
the inheritance of egoism which he carried within himself
since the original fall. When God Himself revealed what
man is in virtue of divine election, and what the exigencies
of his supernatural moral life were, it was for human consciousness as novel and striking as new wine breaking old
bottles (Mt. 9:17), or as a blinding light in the darkness
(Jn. 1:5). It was the very structure of this morality that
was new, for it contained the germ of an ontology of man
and his actions of which philosophers could never dream.
The core of the "good news" was this: God is charity; and
we no longer are merely His creatures or participations,
but we are really His sons, invited *in Filio* to communion
with the Father. With this the whole world was renewed;
man could no longer live as before. It was only a matter of
time before the message would be spread throughout the
universe and leaven it. No wonder that it roused opposition, for it touched on human egoism as a hot poker on an
open wound. It was a fire, and had to burn (Lk. 12:49); a
light, and had to shine before all (Mt. 5:15); but the darkness would not receive it (Jn. 1:5): egoism felt the challenge and hugged the dark (Jn. 3:20). The first preachers
of the message of love were condemned to death as Christ
Himself, just as He had predicted (Mt. 20:26). The early

Christians lived so close to the generosity of Christ's sacrifice that martyrdom was their ideal.[2] What is more, this new spirit found in each convert something to destroy and mortify[3]: the old inheritance of human egoism. To follow the new gospel is to carry one's cross each day (Lk. 9:23); it is dying to the old, in order to live to the new. A new man (2 Cor. 5:17; Col. 3:10), reborn (Jn. 3:3; 1 Pet. 1:23), must replace the old man (Rom. 6:6), and they will war against one another (Mt. 10:34). One must test one's own sincerity, just as a man who desires to build must decide whether he is willing to pay the price (Lk. 14:28–30), to take it or leave it: one cannot adhere to, and at the same time, reject the gospel of charity (Mt. 12:30). Only he that shall lose his old life shall find the new (Mt. 10:39). To pay the full price of the treasure-field, one must sell all his goods (Mt. 13:44); he must even pluck out his eye to save this new life (Mt. 5:29). How terribly exacting are the requirements of the gospel!

That is why the gospel for the early Christians was obviously real *news*. Though dramatic, it was nevertheless good news, a message of joy so overwhelming (2 Cor. 7:4) that it entails a duty of continuous joy (Phil. 4:4), and makes him exult who realizes his good fortune (Lk. 6:23; Col. 3:15).

What then is this novelty which so takes hold of a man that he is willing to die for it and can smile even in the face of death?

We have already pointed out that it is the revelation of love. St. John insists that *God is Agapè* (1 Jn. 4:8, 16). But, after all, is there anything astonishing in this revelation? Is not love an essential attribute of the Supreme Being, just as wisdom and goodness?[4] But we learn from the gospel that God possesses His own essence in the intimate communications of a Trinitarian life. This is, then, a revelation of a radically new kind of love.

If God should decide, *liberrimo consilio*, to bring into being a spiritual creature, it would evidently be necessary that its nature be a certain participation of the divinity and that, right from the beginning, love be its very fabric. What else could it be, since there was nothing but love—that is, Being—to be participated? More than that, God elevated this diluted love to the gratuitous communication of the *Agapè* wherein man partakes of the intimate life of the Trinity.

It was Jesus Christ's mission to reveal the wonderful meaning of this new way of being: that we are of a divine family (Mt. 18:3; Rom. 8:15), little children who can say "Father" to God (Gal. 4:6; Mt. 6:9), for we are possessed of the same Spirit as He (Eph. 4:4), and the Trinity dwells in us (Jn. 14:23), for we are united in the total Christ, branches of the same tree (Jn. 15:4), members of the same body (1 Cor. 12:27). Sanctifying grace is nothing but the communication of the *Agapè* that is God's being. In the soul which it divinizes it gives birth to a new reality which we might call "charity-love" in first act. So much for the aspect of being.

It follows, therefore, that Christian action will necessarily consist in transferring this particular way of being—which is loving—into second act. Adopting this perspective, we see at once all the commandments and, in fact, the whole of gospel morals converging toward charity. God being love, His greatest and first commandment will be the obligation of loving (Mt. 22:38); everything is contained in this one point (Mt. 22:40), for it recapitulates every precept whatsoever (Rom. 13:9); it is the link of perfection (Col. 3:12–14), "binding in one bundle all of the virtues."[5] Though each virtue retains its proper character, we must not forget that virtue is the "ordering of love," as Augustine puts it.[6] To love is a way more sublime than all charisms (1 Cor. 12:31–14:1); it is the beginning of eternal life (1 Jn. 3:14).

Now, whom must we love? Obviously enough, God. But the same movement of love must attain all those who are related to God (Mt. 22:37–39); did He not include us all in Himself, loving us all right from the beginning (1 Jn. 4:10), so that His own love is now loving in us and through us. In other words, Christian society is nothing less than a society pervaded by Trinitarian love. That is why the distinctive mark of Christians is charity toward others (Jn. 13:37) considered as concrete images of Christ and of God invisible (1 Jn. 4:20). Taken as a society, the Church is, in a certain sense, a witness: the mutual union of her members is a living testimony of the intimate unity of the divine Persons (Jn. 17:20–23).*

Now, if we ask what should be the intensity of Christian love, the answer is that we must adopt the divine

---

* L. CERFAUX, in a very stimulative article, attempts to show the relation between the "new commandment" and the absence of Christ until His "second coming":

"Charity is the normal occupation of Christians while they wait and prepare themselves for the judgment of the 'parousia'" ("La charité fraternelle et le retour du Christ," ETL, 24 [1948], 326).

And he adds: "St. John developed the theological notion of charity as St. Paul had done before him: 'In this is the love, not that we have loved God, but that he has first loved us, and sent his Son a propitiation for our sins. Beloved, if God has so loved us, we also ought to love one another' (1 Jn. 4:10–12).

"'This is,' says O. CULLMANN, 'the catechism of the ethics of the New Testament; in no other place does it receive more classic expression' (*Christ and Time*, translated by F. V. FILSON [London, 1952], p. 230). And it is at the same time a résumé of St. John's theology. The relation between God's charity for us and fraternal charity is more strongly underlined here than in Pauline theology. The movement of charity, or the river of charity, takes its source in the Eternal Godhead and finds its completion in the fraternal charity of Christians who thus identify themselves with divine unity. . . . The formula, 'new commandment,' seems to signify that charity is specifically Christian in the sense that it is a celestial reality already manifested by God here below and consequently proper to the new times in which we live" (L. CERFAUX, *art. cit.*, pp. 329–30).

habits, the habits of *Agapè*, with all their drastic demands.
But this revelation of love was not merely conceptual.
Being the way (Jn. 14:6), Jesus gave us an example of it
(Jn. 13:15); being the life (Jn. 6:51), He gave us the
strength to live it (Jn. 15:5). An authentic love is an all-
consuming fire (Lk. 12:49). It is exclusive: we must love
with our whole heart, our whole soul, and our whole mind
(Mt. 22:37). Without the example of Jesus, we would
never have dared to believe that love can even mean the
sacrifice of life itself (Jn. 15:13). Without His grace, we
would never have had the strength to accomplish it. Having
put on Christ by baptism (Gal. 3:27), we must adopt His
manners and grow to the stature of perfect manhood (Eph.
4:13–15) so that we can say, "I live, now not I, but Christ
lives in me" (Gal. 2:20). The moral life of Jesus Christ is
the pattern of our own conduct.[7] Our life will be an imitation of His (Lk. 9:23), a *Nachfolge Christi*, according to
the very significant title of F. Tillmann's moral theology.[8]

Our activity finds its full Christian meaning only by
translating this love which infinitely exceeds the capacity
of our earthly and sinful nature. To love as God loves
means the shattering of our limits. Old bottles break under
the pressure of new wine (Mt. 9:17). The labor of bringing forth a son of God is bound to be painful to the old
man. In its very structure, the Christian life is a beloved
cross, a cross carried in the wake of love. Here again we
find the demands which appeared so drastic (Mt. 5:29).
But love transforms them into joy.[9] Jesus Christ crucified is
the most perfect translation in human terms of a love-
natured God. Humanly speaking, He could not do more,
even though His thirst for giving Himself was far from
being quenched. No finite manifestation can exhaust infinite love.[10]

In a world sunk in egoism, charity appeared as a new
commandment (Jn. 13:34), a *metanoia* (Mt. 4:17), a

profound transformation of life. It leavened (Mt. 13:33) the whole moral life, giving it a new soul.

b) Tradition. From the first days of the Church, of this Church which St. Ignatius of Antioch called *Agapè*,[11] Christian life was lived on intimate terms of fraternal charity (Acts 4:32) which fed on the Eucharist (Acts 2:42). To the churches, Ignatius recommends again and again "union in faith and charity above all."[12] Then, too, there is the beautiful chapter, so Pauline in inspiration, which Clement of Rome wrote to the Corinthians.[13] The commandment of love is so generally accepted and unquestioned that the Fathers do not even think of writing treatises about it. They will praise it occasionally in their commentaries on Scripture, insisting rather on how one must love and why.[14] Martyrdom, "the imitation of true charity,"[15] is considered as the perfection of Christian life, for it is a perfect imitation of Christ[16] in His supreme act of giving.[17]

Between the councils of Nicæa and Chalcedon, the Fathers continued to work out moral doctrine, bringing into brighter light the excellency of the theological virtues.[18] St. Augustine, in his *De moribus ecclesiæ catholicæ*,[19] outlines a short but comprehensive treatise of Christian moral theology. In the first section, he develops the idea that our ultimate happiness consists in possessing God and that the revealed means of attaining it is humble love. In the second section, the essence of virtue appears as the sovereign love of God.[20] In the final section, Augustine shows how the love of God and of neighbor is a universal law embracing all human relations whether they be social, familial, or pedagogical.

Following Augustine, Gregory,[21] and Bernard, from whom the early Middle Ages drew their inspiration,[22] St. Thomas remains faithful to the traditional Catholic doctrine when he states that the substance and perfection of Christian life consists in charity:

A man may be said to be perfect in two ways. First, simply: and this perfection regards that which belongs to a thing's nature; for instance, an animal may be said to be perfect when it lacks nothing in the disposition of its members and in such things as are necessary for an animal's life. Secondly, a thing is said to be perfect relatively: and this perfection regards something connected with the thing externally, such as whiteness or blackness or something of the kind. Now the Christian life consists chiefly in charity whereby the soul is united to God: Wherefore it is written (1 Jn. 3:14): *He that loveth not abideth in death.* Hence the perfection of the Christian life consists simply in charity, but in the other virtues relatively. And since that which is simple is paramount and greatest in comparison with other things, it follows that the perfection of charity is paramount in relation to the perfection that regards the other virues.[23]

The dominant theme of charity was endlessly varied by the different schools of spirituality, each contributing a particular nuance;[24] and the lives of the saints are nothing but a vivid orchestration of it.

In brief, the substance of Christian morality, committed to us by the tradition and life of the Church, is a love springing "with joy out of the Saviour's fountains" (Is. 12:3),[25] with a dynamic spontaneity reaching unto the infinity of God's own perfection (Mt. 5:48). What Christian love finally encounters is a Person (Jn. 14:21). That is why it fosters a spirit of deep interior life rather than a mere observance of the letter of the law.

2. MORAL THEOLOGY

Our manuals of moral theology, at least at first glance, do not seem to be written in the same perspective. Law rather than love is their dominant theme. Where there should be a spiritual impulse, we find a fixed body of doctrine. Even inspiration and liberty are precisely codified.

To speak plainly, our treatises have systematized into a science the pulsing vitality of concrete Christian life. It was inevitable. Great theologians like St. Thomas succeeded in keeping unity between moral theology and dogma. The intuition of a genius and a mystic breathed a soul into this admirable body of doctrine and injected life into the Aristotelian method by giving it a Christian and Augustinian finality. But later theologians let the intuition gradually fade away, allowing philosophy to outweigh revelation more and more.[26]

But another tendency also favored this preponderance of body over soul, of law over love. Two main currents contributed to the elaboration of moral doctrine. The first, which we have just described, had its golden age in patristic times; intimately connected with dogma, it was truly theological. Its foremost representative was Augustine. This current continued throughout the age of the scholastics, when philosophy was systematizing theology, and found its most perfect expression in the Thomistic synthesis. It was further enriched in the time of Suárez when the Roman code was being used to solve economic and social problems. But in accepting the indispensable influence of philosophy and law, certain commentators ran the risk of obscuring the revealed aspect of moral theology. Moreover, from the middle of the fifteenth century, morals tended to become an autonomous discipline separated from dogma.[27] In 1419, St. Antonine wrote the first *Summa theologiæ moralis* devoted exclusively to moral questions.

The second main current, besides the canonical collections,[28] the decretals (1243), and the *Summæ de casibus pœnitentialibus* of Raymond of Peñafort (thirteenth century), carried along a heavy accumulation of *Libri pœni-*

tentiales (St. Columban, seventh century), of *Summæ confessionales* (St. Antonine, fifteenth century), of *Directoria confessariorum* (Busenbaum, *Medulla theologiæ moralis*, 1650), of *Collectiones casuum conscientiæ* (Diana, † 1663). After the period of Rationalism and Jansenism extending from the middle of the seventeenth to the middle of the eighteenth century, this current ended in the commentaries of St. Alphonsus Liguori on Busenbaum's *Medulla* (1748) and in his monumental *Theologia moralis* (1753–1755), which marked the beginning of a complete renewal in moral theology. But it is important to note that it was casuistry more than theology that brought about this renewal. That is why the manuals written at the end of the past century did not always escape the danger of restricting the object of their study to the consideration of sin, thus elaborating a moral theology far too negative and concerned chiefly with minimal obligations; virtues were passed over in favor of commandments and law.* They were summaries adapted to the needs of confessors and hence partly indispensable. But their theological content was so scanty that they scarcely merited the name of *Theologiæ morales*; *Summæ pastorales* would have been a more apt title.[29]

This brief historical survey explains the general aspect of moral teaching at the end of the nineteenth century: the first trend ended in its separation from dogma; the second, more casuistic, brought it under the domination of canon law.[30] But already in the latter half of the nineteenth century, moralists began to follow Ballerini[31] in his search for a more doctrinal foundation.[32]

Starting from this point, the return to a more thoroughly Christian morality required two successive

---

* The adversaries of Christian morality have often used these objections; cf. A. BAYET, *La morale laïque et ses adversaires* (Paris, 1925); P. BERT, *La morale des Jésuites* (Paris, 1880).

steps. The first and more urgent task for moral theologians was to reintegrate their moral teaching with dogma; it would thus become a discipline animated by a decidedly positive, supernatural, theological spirit, though retaining a limited choice of casuistic decisions and ever remaining open to modern needs.[33] Successively, the manuals of J. Lehmkuhl, s.j.;[34] A. Tanquerey;[35] D. M. Prümmer, o.p.;[36] A. Vermeersch, s.j.;[37] J. Mausbach;[38] O. Schilling;[39] B. H. Merkelbach, o.p.,[40] ripened as the choice fruits of this first effort.

A second effort is now possible. It is even necessary. Much has already been accomplished in re-establishing the contact between moral and dogma. But have moralists in fact rediscovered the dominant theme of charity, the soul of Christian tradition? Only this rediscovery can restore their teaching to its true vocation of being the *Schola caritatis Christi*.

In most of the best manuals, charity is treated in a chapter among other chapters and does not appear as the nourishing substance of all virtues. For example, in our traditional treatise on justice one does not find much more than in a course on natural law. Again, our treatise on moral principles draws its most fundamental tenets from moral philosophy and remains above all oriented toward the solution of cases and the determination of sins. This is, and will remain, necessary. But love, the inner soul of moral theology, has not yet come into its own in our manuals, if we except the works of F. Tillmann,* and a few others like the remarkable book by B. Häring.[41]

---

* Cf. note 30, *supra*. This author remained faithful to the tradition of Sailer and Hirscher. Cf. J. M. Sailer, *Handbuch der christlichen Moral*, 3 vols. (Munich, 1817); cf. also DTC, "Sailer." Cf. J. B. Hirscher, *Die christliche Moral als Lehre von der Verwirklichung des göttlichen Reiches in der Menschheit*, 3 vols. (Tübingen, 1835–1837); Hirscher's pioneer work, written at the time of the "Aufklärung," presents many shortcomings, but it marked a considerable progress in the teaching of

It is true that all the elements of revelation can be found in our manuals, but they are scattered here and there and are studied separately. Thus the task we would like to undertake is methodological rather than doctrinal in character, although doctrine is always intimately connected with methodology. Our purpose is to establish a method of formulating moral teaching and of molding it faithfully on Revelation and true Christian life. In this way, moral theology would find in each moral act the innermost and universal presence of charity.

§II. VITAL NEEDS AND MORAL THEOLOGY

The parallel which we have just drawn between Christian tradition and moral theology suggests another comparison. In spite of an apparent divorce between modern aspirations and the traditional formulation of morals, the spiritual tendencies of our Catholic elite and true Christian morals are in basic agreement.

I. MODERN ASPIRATIONS

Among the best of our contemporaries, moral aspirations tend to become more and more interior. These people are attracted by the mystery of the spiritual personality and love. With new techniques of thought—in which the objective and the abstract give way before the subjective, the psychological, and the existential[42]—they are trying to sound the depth of this fascinating abyss. Is an atmosphere not often as important as sharp outlines? Is letter always to prevail over spirit? This profound understanding of the meaning of the interior life requires authentic generosity. The engagement of one's entire being demands much more than moral conformity to law. This new importance given

---

moral theology and prepared its renewal. On this latter point, see E. HOCEDEZ, s.j., *Histoire de la théologie au XIXe siècle* (Brussels-Paris, 1947), I, 221-226; and E. MANGENOT, "Hirscher," in DTC.

to the interior life, far from isolating men from one another, rather compels each of them to discover, on a more profound level, something which he has in common with other men. The last few centuries did not experience that social drive which is so characteristic of our day.[43]

The counterpart of this attitude is also obvious: it is a crisis of obedience; men loathe to obey commands whose vital significance is somewhat obscure. They wait for an inner justification of the command which will give it its rightful place in a scale of values. Legal decisions are despised and passed over as formalisms. The urgency of a return to reality[44] is often advocated, and nerveless supernaturalism denounced.[45] For supernaturalism can very well engender naturalism; a body abandoned by its spirit can fall very low indeed, and give itself over to the fatal influence of a mechanical, materialistic civilization.[46]

2. HOW TO FORMULATE MORAL THEOLOGY

Perhaps too many present textbooks overstress the objective and individualistic bearings of moral theology; they keep harping, with a casuistic bias, on minimum obligation and sin. That is why they fail to satisfy those modern cravings for interior fulfillment and for a personal generosity reaching out to all men; nor do they satisfy the human need for a subjective, psychological, and synthetic explanation. All these shortcomings of our manuals stem from the fact that they do not formulate morality with sufficient reference to the interior life, which is left to a special branch of theology called spirituality. Thus there is present in modern thought, just as in Christian tradition, a group of values which are, unfortunately, lacking in our manuals.

It is our contention that by introducing charity as the pivot of its formulation, moral theology will not only come into closer contact with Christ but will also meet the best aspirations of the modern conscience.[47] For among all other values love is most able to bring together the living subject and the moral object. By its insatiable demands it liberates all the generous impulses of the individual without minimizing precise duties; without diminishing the importance of his own person, it drives a man into the society of other men.[48]

Let us explain exterior precepts as the claims of love, and we shall give them their highest intelligibility, uncover the true root of their unity, and, at the same time, make them powerfully attractive; we shall also reconcile law and love and be well on the way to reconciling more deeply body and soul, nature and supernature, as they should be in the order of Redemption. For Christian love is the love of a Person in whom natural and supernatural, body and soul are united in the mystery of the Incarnation.

In this way charity would safeguard the true values of modern aspirations and at the same time reveal the treasure hidden in the formulas of our moral theology. Then Christians would no longer be tempted to say: "Indeed we love Jesus Christ, but nothing in the world can ever make us love moral precepts."[49]

§III. Modern Thought and Moral Theology

There is a third factor encouraging us to undertake this study. Might not the recent trends of existentialism and the philosophy of value be able to contribute some help to our research? Evidently we are referring to an existentialism which admits the reality of essence and of God. For an existentialism which denies Supreme Existence can only see moral effort as a tendency to self-annihilation, thus effectively killing the love for the last end which is the soul of moral life.

The philosophy of value, especially that of M. Le Senne,[50] acquires a special moral bearing by the fact that it presents its object not only under its aspect of knowledge but also as worthy of being desired by the will, faculty of the absolute good. His merit is that he presents truth itself as the good of an intelligence which also has its dynamism.

Our purpose is to show that morality is everywhere connected with love, that in all its details it refers to some good, to some "value" worthy of being loved because it is already the fruit of an active love. Henceforward the question can be raised whether the proper "value" of Christian morality is not charity.

Obviously, neither theology nor the *philosophia perennis* prevents us from adopting a modern philosophical notion if we find it capable of aptly expressing a fundamental thesis of Thomistic ethics. Though it has always been contained in the heritage which we received from Christian revelation and traditional theology, this thesis has been largely neglected. The works of J. Maréchal, s.j.,[51] have already made explicit the notion of the dynamism of the intelligence which was latent in Thomism and is a fundamental point of the philosophy of value.

The sole intent of the present work is to better the formulation traditionally used in the teaching of moral theology. This task is explicitly encouraged by the encyclical *Humani generis*. It would be a mistake to see in our work an attempt to borrow a doctrinal novelty from modern philosophy. On the contrary, our only aim is to highlight the most fundamental truth of Christian tradition, namely, the primacy of charity. If we succeed, moral theology will only become more kerygmatic; and this would be in harmony with the wishes of many.[52]

On the other hand, the existential, concrete, and dynamic character of moral reality, a commonplace in Thomistic writings, may find happy expression in the structures of certain modern philosophies, at least to the extent that they do not reject the objectivity of thought.

From spiritualistic philosophers, such as Bergson, R. Le Senne, and Gabriel Marcel, we will not ask doctrinal content, but we will gladly accept their suggestions on how to formulate our doctrine. It is clear that the thought of a J.-P. Sartre cannot offer us any positive help, since he has deliberately repudiated the communion of love.*

§IV. Purpose of This Study

After the preceding observations it is easy to determine the purpose of our study. It will be to look for a method that will permit us to apply to the formulation of each and every question of moral theology the universal principle of St. Thomas: *Caritas forma omnium virtutum*. In other words, our aim is to work out a method of exposition in which charity will play the role of a vital principle, just as it does in the message of Christ and in Christian life. If each concrete virtue and action is in fact ultimately animated by charity, then charity should also be the soul of moral theology.

Thus our study is mainly methodological. Obviously enough, the primacy of charity as such does not need to be proved. But it is urgent to devise a method capable of highlighting this fundamental fact at each step of the exposition. Yet an important part of our work will be doctrinal:

* Cf. R. Troisfontaines, *Le choix de Jean-Paul Sartre* (Paris, 1945). A parallel effort was presented at the congress of Christian philosophical studies at Gallarate in 1949. The *Bulletin thomiste* summarizes the general tendencies of the report as follows: "There seem to be two parallel tendencies manifested: one maintains the intellectualist aspect of moral theology by emphasizing the role of the metaphysical and epistemological assumption on which it is certainly based; but the other current vigorously recalls, with De Raeymaeker, De Corte, and Jolivet, the existential character which confers on moral theology its status of 'practical' science. Finally, we mention the effort of Dom Bengoecha to integrate certain elements of the philosophy of 'value' in an ethic of the good." Cf. BT, 8 (1947–1953), 632, reviewing *Fondazione della morale. Atti del Vᵒ convegno de studi filosofici cristiani tra professori universitari Gallarate, 1949* (Padua, 1950).

method must be based on doctrine, for it is nothing but a way of approaching doctrine itself.

Our effort is therefore directed toward a formulation of Christian morality which will always be kept under the primacy of charity. We do not have to rediscover the theological method but to set out systematically what theology itself reveals to be most fundamental in Christian morality, namely, the all-pervading influence of charity in the life of a son of God.

§V. General Outline

The first part, "Charity and Morality in St. Thomas," is historical. It will be a brief sketch of the Thomistic position on the role played by charity in moral activity, a position which can be summarized in the following formula: charity is the form of all the virtues. The richness of the traditional doctrine will then clearly appear, opening the way for research in expressing this doctrine.

The second part, strictly methodological, will establish the main features of our proposed method by explaining how moral acts "mediate" our fundamental spiritual tendency (ch. 1), which is charity-love (ch. 2), and the role of virtue in this process (ch. 3). This method will be a positive orientation "Toward a Charity-centered Moral Theology."

In the third part, "Outlines of a Charity-centered Moral Theology," the method will be applied to the different branches of moral theology. Starting from the fundamental attitudes which charity communicates to the will (ch. 1), we will extend this application to general (ch. 2) and then to special moral theology (ch. 3).

Let it be clear that this work is not intended to be a manual and will, therefore, not enter into casuistic determinations, otherwise very necessary in the teaching of moral theology and in pastoral work.

§VI. THOMISTIC PERSPECTIVE OF THE WORK

St. Thomas has formulated the primacy of charity in the supernatural moral life. On the other hand, a close study of his writings suggests that natural moral life is dominated by the primacy of love. Acts and objects are moral insofar as they are oriented toward the ultimate end by the will,[53] and the proper act of the will is love;[54] hence it is the influence of love which causes an act or object to be moral. In each act there is, corresponding to its supernatural informing by charity in the just, and underlying it, a natural informing by love. The perspective of this work is decidedly supernatural; while considering, with St. Thomas, all things from the supernatural angle, we will, nevertheless, be constantly aware of the presence of a love-powered will in each moral act of the pagan as well as the Christian. The reader should always keep in mind this supernatural perspective wherein charity and natural love are so closely associated, though remaining clearly distinct.*

To talk of charity as the form of the virtues grants its universal role of animation and makes it *the* general virtue par excellence. This peculiar influence has been recognized by theologians for a long time.[55] We must distinguish between this general implicit presence and the explicit act of charity when this virtue terminates in its own proper act.

Since the perspective of this study is decidedly Thomistic, we will not expressly repeat at each step the distinction between the general implicit and the general explicit activity of charity.

---

* Cf. V. WARNACH, *Agapè, Die Liebe als Grundmotiv der neutestamentlichen Theologie* (Düsseldorf, 1951). We believe that this observation will satisfy the reservation which V. WARNACH expressed in his study (p. 466, n. 1), where he refers to our articles which appeared in NRT, 72 (1950), 3–26; 113–133, esp. 129 ff.

Obviously, he was unable to place them in the context of the present work, from which they were taken, for it was still unpublished; they expressed only summarily this distinction and the point of view which we underline here; these things will be developed more clearly in the following pages, e.g., pp. 7, 11 f., 16.

The Primacy of Charity in Moral Theology

FIRST PART

Charity and Morality in St. Thomas

(*Historical Part*)

INTRODUCTION

Very few manuals of moral theology care to study the question of the influence of charity on moral life taken as a whole. The doctrine of the influence of charity on the virtuous life, as Cardinal Van Roey deplores, has almost fallen into disuse in the manuals of moral and dogmatic theology and has been left to ascetical and mystical theology.[1]

Most authors recognize, at least implicitly, the primacy of "the precept which contains the whole law," but very seldom do they try to explain how the "recapitulation" of all the precepts in the law of love is accomplished. But all the moralists who touch on the problem[2] adopt the solution of St. Thomas as condensed in the formula: *Caritas est forma virtutum.*

Our investigation will then take this formula as its starting point. To avoid any misunderstanding, let it be clear that this study does not pretend to be a self-sufficient critical and historical study. Such a study, to be at all complete, would require a thorough investigation of Scripture and Tradition. Research in the Augustinian background of St. Thomas would also be indispensable. The limits which we

3

must impose on this work do not permit us to undertake such an immense survey.

What influence does St. Thomas attribute to charity in the moral activity of the Christian? This question will be the starting point of our research in methodology and will provide it with a solid doctrinal basis. And we will at the same time be led to this other question: How is it that a thesis so fundamental in Thomism has received so little attention in the exposition of moral theology?

Starting from the key notions of moral act, virtue, and intention, we will see in a first chapter, "Charity and the Moral Act," why St. Thomas attributes to charity a real constitutive influence in all the activity of the just.

The second chapter, "Charity, Form of the Virtues," will determine the mode of this influence and hence the meaning of the expression "form of the virtues" which St. Thomas applies to charity.

In the conclusion, we will explain why modern authors have paid less attention to this problem, even though it is fundamental in moral theology.

CHAPTER I

Charity and the Moral Act

First of all, let us describe briefly the whole field of activity which charity is to integrate. The ultimate goal of our moral life is to glorify God by possessing Him in an act of vision and of love. There, all our moral activity finds its reason for being; and only in effectively approaching this goal does it acquire some value. Action has meaning insofar as it tends to the ultimate end;[1] the mere structure of the second part of the *Summa theologica* already suggests this Augustinian perspective.

§I. Subject of the Moral Act

In order to attain this end, man has at his disposal a certain number of faculties all proceeding from the essence of the soul in hierarchical order.

In things which proceed from one according to a natural order, just as the first is the cause of all, so that which is nearer to the first is, in a way, cause of those which are more remote. Now it has been shown above that among the powers of the soul there are several kinds of order. Therefore one power of the soul proceeds from the essence of the soul by the medium of another. But since the essence of the soul is compared to the powers both as an active and a final principle, either separately by itself, or together with the body; and since the agent and the end are more perfect, while the receptive principle, as such,

5

is less perfect, it follows that those powers of the soul which precede the others, in the order of perfection and nature, are the principle of the others, after the manner of an end and an active principle. For we see that sense is for the sake of the intellect, and not the other way about. Sense, moreover, is a certain imperfect participation of the intellect, and therefore, according to its natural origin, it proceeds from the intellect as the imperfect from the perfect.[2]

In the same way, the appetitive powers find their efficient and final cause in the will. Our body is entirely ordered to our soul: right from the beginning it is the soul which presides over the development of the body. Hence, the will, a spiritual appetitive power,[3] is ontologically at the origin of our other tendential faculties.[4]

So much for the ontological hierarchy of our faculties. A similar order governs their exercise: some faculties are concerned with the end itself, while others merely dispose the means.

. . . the will moves the other powers of the soul to their acts, for we make use of the other powers when we will. For the ends and perfections of every other power are included under the object of the will as particular goods; and the art or power, to which the universal end belongs, always moves to their acts the acts or powers to which belong the particular ends included in the universal end.[5]

Thus the hierarchy in the being and exercise of the tendential faculties depends on the will.

§II. THE MORAL ACT

We will not delay here on the mystery of action, which is the mystery of being itself.[6] Action is always heavy with an ontological weight since it is always an actuation; it causes us to exist more fully, making us pass from what we were to what we want to be. The grandeur of human action appears in that it is a step in our assimilation to God and an actual participation of divine creative activity.

But we will rather insist on the psychological and moral aspects of the human act. To prevent any misunderstanding, let us insist that we are not forgetting the psychology of natural love underlying the supernatural plane on which our analysis will be developed.

The concrete human act proceeding under the light of the conscience[7] is normally made up of an act of will together with acts of the other powers, for our spirit, as we have just said, is closely linked with the sensitive part of our being. The *imperium* of the will[8] and the *actus imperati* form one total human act[9] in which the act of the will plays the role of form and the act of a lower power that of matter.[10]

The commanded acts receive their first specification, their *prima bonitas*, from their proper object, which is not the exterior thing as such, but an intentional and moral reality perceived by the reason and seen in its proportion to action. For example, it will be "to accept suffering" or "to pardon an offense." In the order of action, this object is the equivalent of what form is in the order of being. The moral object is the form of the moral act and hence bestows on it the fullness of being that is proper to it. Just as this flower is called a rose, so my act is said to be one of accepting suffering or pardoning an offense.

As for the act of the will, considered in itself, it receives its first specification from its object; but here the proper object is the end, the good known as such.[11] The will recognizes as intermediate ends those objects which are presented to it by the other powers.[12]

In one and the same act, the intention of the will can aim at the final end and simultaneously at several intermediate ends. This is possible because the intellect can

think of many things in a single act, provided there is a
certain unity among them, as in the case of premises and
conclusion. Hence, the will can direct itself toward its
proper object and, in the same movement, toward the
object of the lower powers.[13] Such is the case with all
concrete human actions, for they are all finally willed for
one and the same ultimate end.* Thus St. Thomas is fully
aware that the intermediate ends can very well set the
intention of the will in motion.[14] He goes even further and
says that the same intention can be directed toward several
ends which are not subordinated to one another, but merely
coordinated. This happens, for example, when we choose
one line of action because it opens on many ends,[15] or when
we choose two different means leading to the same end, for
example, two remedies to cure the same illness.[16]

We had to recall this principle of the multiplicity of
ends or of objects in a single act, for we will need it later
to interpret the internal unity of an act which depends on
charity and some other virtue at the same time.

Man, as a moral agent, is driven by a spiritual impulse,
the craving of his will for the ultimate end which he
glimpses in the intermediate ends themselves. Only this
deep-seated tension, which is free, though it has a definite
structure, confers morality on our acts, for it alone conforms them to the norm of good, which is their proportion
to the end, God. Let us note in passing that the will is a
function: that which wills is not the will itself, but the
subject.

This spiritual dynamism toward God is not pure will,

---

* Cf. 1-2, q. 1, a. 6. In maintaining, with St. Thomas, this specific influence of the ultimate end, God, in every human act, we do not say that
the human will explicitly desires God in each of its acts. We are obviously only speaking of the morally good act and, especially, of an implicit
presence and love of the ultimate end. This presence is, however, actual
and actively "informs" in the sense in which St. Thomas uses this expression; without it, there is no morality for men.

for it assumes the auxiliary dynamism of the other active powers. Although these powers have their own finality, yet they draw it from the energy of the will. They are real participations of the will in the sensible order. On the other hand, their particular finality is specified by their proper object, which is not the object of the total impulse.

We can, then, for the sake of analysis, distinguish between voluntary acts and commanded acts; it is even indispensable and conformed to the nature of the moral act to distinguish a *bonitas prima* or a *bonitas objectiva* which the commanded act draws from its own particular object, such as giving alms, doing penance, rendering justice. But we should not lose sight of the fact that this commanded act is moral in the concrete only in virtue of the real finality which the will communicates to it in carrying it along toward the ultimate end. The act of a lower power is human only when it is an actual participation of an act of will, just as the lower power is an ontological participation of the will as a faculty.

The whole of this complex act, St. Thomas tells us, is a single act entirely from the will and entirely from the subordinate powers as well as from their proper objects. Thus the commanded act is specified by its moral object (for this object is the formal cause of the act and gives it its *bonitas prima*) and becomes formally moral by being assumed by the will (for the will, by involving the object in its own finality, confers on it the form of moral object). The commanded act is human insofar as it is one with the act of the will.

§III. THE MORAL OBJECT

An act is moral in virtue of its link with the will that is tending toward the ultimate end. Of course, we can conceive of a pure act of will which would be nothing but love of the ultimate end. But generally the will commands moral acts in the lower powers. For example, the act of feeding oneself is complex and one at the same time: although there are several faculties and hence several subordinate ends involved in it, nevertheless, its unity is essentially guaranteed by the free will which elevates all these elements to its own order, that of the ultimate end.

Now how can we judge of the moral value of the concrete act? On this particular point there are two interpretations of Aquinas' thought.

The first interpretation abstracts from the voluntary aspect which characterizes the human act, thus isolating the commanded act in a separate representation. For example, the rules of temperance will be determined according to the objective link which must exist between the physical act of eating and its immediate end, the sustaining of the body. The same is applied to the other moral acts. The resulting ethics will consider each of its objects separately, abstracting from their mutual relations. Every act, in order to be honest, will have to correspond to its immediate end. This immediate end in turn will be determined by examining each natural faculty or each theological virtue. That is why there will be question of an objective abstract morality and of an abstract object conferring the *bonitas prima;* nevertheless, the act will receive the full form of moral act when it concretely takes place under the influence of the will. At this moment, the ultimate end confers on the act its concrete morality and only then also does charity, the infused love of the ultimate end, give supernatural value to the Christian act. Thus it will be possible to build a purely objective moral doctrine without taking into account the informing of charity or supernatural morality except in the chapters on the theological virtues—in a word, without ever using the principle of St. Thomas: *Caritas forma.*

But we think there is another way of interpreting the

thought of St. Thomas without forcing it. The moral object which confers the *bonitas prima* does not spring from a purely representative relation which abstracts from the ultimate end, and only links the physical act to its immediate end (e.g., the act of eating as related to the sustaining of the body). Such a relation, if it is merely representative, reveals nothing of the morality of the act. In reality, it includes the perception of a duty, and no duty can exist without the influence of the ultimate end under the form of love.* As soon as I perceive a moral object, I will my ultimate end; I cannot not will it, and I will it freely in the present act. Such is the meaning of duty. Thus in the moral or human act of taking food, the moral object necessarily contains, besides the specification by the particular end, a relation to the ultimate end, which is love, and for the Christian, charity. The same is true of all other moral acts and so must be taken into consideration in formulating their rules. In each act, the constitutive element of these moral objects is distinct from the others by its physical object and its particular end; nevertheless, they are united in the love of the end which animates all of them.

Is it possible to maintain that the second interpretation is genuinely Thomistic? First of all, Aquinas considers nothing but infused charity, which is the only real and efficacious love of the ultimate supernatural end. Now the influence of charity on the moral act requires a supernatural cause, and does not necessarily manifest itself explicitly on the level of the moral object or of synderesis. In any case, it is surely not as explicit as the orientation of the simply human act toward the ultimate end. In other words, we have here two different problems; the first is that of the conscious relationship between the moral act and the ultimate supernatural end;[17] the second is that of the orientation of every moral object, capable of specifying

---

* This love is, at least, implicit. See *supra*, p. 8 n.

the free human act, toward the ultimate end. But the fact remains that God infuses charity in a will whose proper act is love. The two problems are thus intimately connected and, in the texts which we will refer to, St. Thomas always takes them as one whole. In Thomistic thought, each natural virtue is elevated to the supernatural order by a corresponding infused virtue; in the same way, charity, the queen of supernatural virtues, corresponds to the natural love of the ultimate end, which, being the proper act of the will, is not itself a virtue.

Furthermore, the difference between these two interpretations strictly involves the very formulation of moral theology. Even if the texts were to force the first interpretation on us, yet nothing would prevent us from maintaining that St. Thomas held firmly all that the second interpretation implies. The thinkers of the thirteenth century used some synthetic concepts which had not yet been divided by analysis. But we would misinterpret the texts if we pretended that the impregnation of the moral object by love and supernatural charity did not, even at that time, need to be explicitly formulated. We will develop this point further later on. In St. Thomas' time, moral theology was not separated from dogma, nor ethics from supernatural morality. We have already insinuated, in the introduction, why the absence of the formulation of charity-love later came to be gravely felt in moral theology. Today we are very much aware of the danger faced by a love-deficient morality. Since this danger scarcely existed in the time of St. Thomas, he is no more responsible for the separation of moral theology from charity than he is responsible for the nominalistic trend which later influenced some scholastic interpreters of his doctrine of knowledge.

It is now possible to point out some difficulties that might arise from the first interpretation. In this perspective the moral object is considered in the abstract and thus can be good, bad, or, as it is said, "indifferent." Such is, for instance, walking. In any case, Thomists hold that this object ceases to be indifferent as soon as it is concretely willed. Then, indeed, and only then, according to the first interpretation, is it put in relation with the ultimate end.

Is there not a certain optical illusion at the origin of this opinion? If an object is formally considered in the abstract, that is, as separated from its relation to a concrete will, is it not by that very fact cut off from its relation to the ultimate end? Thus, reduced to its merely representative elements, could it be called the object of the human act; would it really be a moral object? In this position, one could admit the possibility of moral acts which would not be human, and of indifferent human acts; but then it would be difficult to understand the Thomistic thesis. Once we talk of an act being human, the only thing with which moral theology is concerned, can there be any question of an object being indifferent? An object is only indifferent insofar as it is not willed nor related to the ultimate end. But then it is not a moral, but merely a physical object, which lies outside the subject matter of ethics. Walking, considered as a human act, is a good object and cannot be indifferent. That an act is morally specified by its object is a genuinely Thomistic principle. If we hold that concrete acts are never indifferent and at the same time admit the possibility of indifferent moral objects, then we are forced to conclude that some concrete acts are not specified by the *prima bonitas* of the moral object, but only by their end— an exception to the essential principle of objective morality. We think that there also could be found the fissure through which in past years the laxist wave invaded moral theology.

St. Thomas would say that the recognition of a moral object is not a work of pure intelligence, but that it always involves synderesis. I must recognize the concrete agree-

ment between this object and my judgment of synderesis
which points out to the will its own object, the good to be
done in order to satisfy its love of the ultimate end. In
recognizing a moral object, the intelligence implicitly ap-
prehends a tendency and the objective link which relates to
it this particular act. Hence, this objective link perceived in
each moral object is in no way abstract, as if it were separated from the concrete influence of love. It is rather an
echo of the love of the ultimate end produced in my cognitive faculty by synderesis. (Let us remember that the
presence of supernatural charity in me is a related, though
different, problem.) The first interpretation conceives this
objective link as an acquired image which would abstract
from synderesis and love, and yet the whole of moral value
comes from love. The second interpretation attempts to
describe the moral object just as it is concretely in terms of
synderesis, love, and finality. An object at the same time
moral and indifferent is inconceivable. The *bonitas prima*
of the moral object, as understood in the second interpretation, can alone explain the morality of the act.

Do we find this last conclusion explicitly formulated by
St. Thomas? As our study is not properly historical, we are
content to say that such a conclusion is perfectly in line
with his thought as expressed in some fundamental texts
which we will analyze later. It is probably the only manner
of correctly understanding the Thomistic principle: *Caritas
forma virtutum.*

§IV. Acquired Virtue

A complex spiritual being, tending to its ultimate end
through the diversity of intermediate ends, will be greatly
helped if reason imposes on each power an ideal of action
conformed to the good, a partial end for particular action.

Each power becomes so possessed by the particular ideal toward which it tends that it receives a habitual direction facilitating the performance of its acts. Our action is creative: it leaves in the faculty an ontological trace, a quality[18] growing with the repetition of the same act.[19] This quality which fosters the perfection of action—*habitus operativus bonus*—is virtue.

Thus virtue is not a thing glued on to a faculty. It is a *qualitas*, a way of being of this faculty, a functional attitude, just as the faculty itself, which is not a thing but a function of our spiritual being. In our virtuous activity, the virtue does not elicit an act different from that of the faculty; that which elicits the act is the faculty bettered by the virtuous quality. And, in its turn, the faculty is but an instrument of the will and, finally, of the soul.

In the psychology of St. Thomas, it is possible for a single act of the will to aim at several ends. We can thus conclude that this same act can aim at several ideals or partial ends, provided these *fines virtutum* are subordinated to one another or at least coordinated. Such spiritual realities, more than others, can be embraced in a single act of the intelligence, and, so unified, they can be willed as a whole. Nothing prevents the will from commanding in one act many acts elicited by virtue-perfected faculties. These commanded acts of virtue become subordinated as soon as the end or ideal of one of them is more general or nearer the total end of the will. Therefore, one virtue can eventually command another virtue. The will sets these acts in hierarchical order and thus unifies them by drawing them all into its own finality. The resulting complex, though it contains particular specifications arising from the diversity of objects, remains nevertheless a single act of the will and of the virtue (or virtues). In the act of caring for a patient, a doctor at the same time can intend to earn his

living, perform his professional duty, pay a debt due in
justice, show his pity, and do a genuine act of charity
toward a member of Christ. Thus at the same time and in
the same act he practices several virtues.

§V. Infused Virtues

We have just considered the acquired virtues and their
ideals as driven by a finality which did not exceed the
natural resources of the will. But we live in a supernatural
order—which St. Thomas always considers. In order to
proportion the will to this end, God infuses in it the theological virtue of charity.

That which is elevated is the will with the whole complexity of its faculties of action and their corresponding
acquired virtues; the infused moral virtues form an admirable supernatural system exactly patterned on our psychological organism.[20] These infused moral virtues achieve in
the powers and in the natural virtues a partial elevation, just
as charity achieves a total elevation in the will.[21] It is quite
clear, then, that the infused moral virtues are all subordinated to the theological virtue of charity.

Neither are the supernatural virtues things added to the
faculties, but supernatural qualities of those faculties; they
are those faculties inasmuch as they are elevated and supernaturalized. When we say that an act proceeds from an
infused virtue, we mean that it proceeds from the faculty
elevated by that virtue: it springs entirely from the faculty
and entirely from the virtue. Thus we can say of the infused virtues what we said of the acquired virtues and the
faculties: a single act of the elevated will can aim at the
ends of several subordinated infused virtues. In other
words, charity and the other virtues can be exercised at the
same time in one indivisible, though complex, act.

§VI. THE INFLUENCE OF CHARITY IN VIRTUOUS ACTS

We must now raise the last and most important question: Does charity play an effective role in the production of an act springing from a virtue which is itself subordinate to charity? For the sake of clarity we will examine the problem in two different cases.

First of all, let us examine the case of an act in which charity is explicitly exercised along with other virtues. The preceding study permits us to assert that, in this complex act, charity commands the acts of the other virtues, whether they be natural or supernatural, and constitutes with them a single indivisible act. Just as the active faculties are participations of the will and their acts are participations of its acts, so the infused virtues are participations of the will divinized by charity and their acts are participations of the act of charity. Therefore, the act proceeds entirely from charity and entirely from the subordinate virtues. Let us recall that Augustine defined virtue as *ordo amoris*.[22] St. Thomas adopts this definition because he recognizes that every virtue depends in some way on love.[23] And, so, if I perform an act of patience with the explicit intention of making it an act of love of God, such an act stands indivisible, even though it proceeds from both patience and charity.

Now let us examine a second case, in fact, the case most often considered by St. Thomas: Does charity have an effective influence on every act of virtue performed in the state of grace even if it is not an explicit act of charity?

The answer to this question will indicate what importance St. Thomas attributes to charity in our moral activity. Again, the interpretation and formulation of this role of charity constitutes the main problem to be solved in this study.

Let us first recall the different types of influence that an act of will can exert on any other activity. This will prepare the way for a better understanding of the influence of charity on any virtuous activity.[24]

The influence of the will on an act is actual when the attention of the intellect bears on this act. This influence may be explicit or implicit. It is explicit when the good willed is itself directly present to the attention of the intellect. It is implicit when the presence of the good actually willed is felt only through its connection with another good explicitly willed.

This influence is virtual in the *strict* sense when it proceeds from an act of will which is no longer present to the attention, but nevertheless continues to exercise an effective influence on the act whose existence depends on this *intentio causans*. Now what is this effective influence? If the actual influence of will contains an element of volition and an element of attention, we must say that in its virtual influence only the first element is present. A mass-production worker can repeat indefinitely without the least attention the same mechanical gesture, and yet we cannot say that his present action is no longer positively influenced by his first explicit act of will commanding this action.

This virtual influence in the strict sense can be termed explicitly virtual. There can also be an implicitly virtual influence which arises from an end which has been implicitly willed in the past.

At times, St. Thomas calls habitual intention[25] that virtual intention which we termed explicit or implicit. Hence the danger of ambiguity in interpreting many of his texts.

The influence which is virtual in the *wider* sense is nothing but a former actual intention persisting in a merely negative way because it never was retracted, and so does not positively affect the present action. Here the influence does not play the role of a true cause in the present, but only persists as an attitude adopted in the past. Let us consider the case of two pagans who are in danger of death and unconscious. If one of them has at one time explicitly expressed his desire for baptism, he will be better disposed than the other who would have rejected this same suggestion.* If every action leaves a trace in our psychological being, then it is legitimate to speak of the persistence of a former "ordination." Since this "ordination" no longer influences the present act, it somewhat resembles the possession of a habit. It is then understandable that some authors name this intention "habitual in the wider sense." Suárez calls it "objective" and puts it as an intermediate intention between the virtual and the habitual, both understood in the strict sense.

Now an act of infused virtue performed in the past is bound to leave in present activity a still bolder trace. In fact, such an act builds up or even implants the infused virtue: think of the first explicit act of faith or charity. The trace which it leaves behind is, by reason of divine intervention, the infused virtue itself implanted or maintained. It will then influence future acts. However, this influence is not sufficient where the act requires in the present the persisting influence of a past act of the will, as in the case of the minister conferring a sacrament. The virtual intention in the wider sense, though not very remote from a habitual intention, nevertheless involves a real "ordination" of the faculty which will elicit the future acts. It will

* But even in this last case, it is possible for a man, under the influence of grace, to change his disposition when he can no longer express it.

color, so to say, all the activity of the faculty. A will which under the influence of grace has implanted in itself the habit of charity by an initial act of perfect love will be, in all its activity, a virtuous and charitable will. If it performs an act of penance, even without explicitly renewing its intention of charity, the value of this act will be really different from that of a will deprived of charity.

It will be necessary to further investigate whether the virtual intention in the wider sense does not also suppose an implicit actual influence. We will examine this point later.

Finally, the habitual intention in the strict sense is the simple presence of a habit in the agent at the moment of the act, without any actual or virtual influence of a preceding act of this habit.

2. THE POSITION OF ST. THOMAS

Among theologians we find a great variety of explanations concerning the influence of charity required to assure the supernatural merit of good acts.[26]

St. Thomas, as we know, holds as meritorious all good acts performed in the state of grace and, for the essentials, attributes this value to the influence of charity.[27] "Habentibus caritatem omnis actus est meritorius vel demeritorius."[28] We still have to explain in what this influence consists when there is no explicit act of charity.

On the one hand, St. Thomas formally denies that the mere habitual presence of charity is sufficient to confer merit; it must effectively influence the virtuous act: "Non sufficit omnino habitualis ordinatio actus in Deum, quia ex hoc quod est in habitu nullus meretur, sed ex hoc quod actu operatur."[29] On the other hand, he does not require an explicit actual intention, and this is stated in the very same passage.

Thus, the problem lies between these two extremes and can be formulated in the following alternative: Does St. Thomas require an actual though implicit influence of charity, that is, without any conceptual presentation of its proper motive? Or does he merely require the effective virtual influence of a former explicit act?

Most of the texts incline us to think that he requires both these influences at the same time. Nevertheless, we think that his authentic position retains only the first: the actual, though implicit, influence of charity is always required and suffices, as the following discussion will demonstrate.

On the one hand, according to our analysis, the implicit and actual activity of charity is always supposed in any virtuous act of the just, for the moral act must necessarily proceed from the will and be drawn into its ultimate finality. Even when the will tends to an intermediate end, it does so only because it recognizes there a participation of the ultimate end. This influence of the ultimate end is implied everywhere in moral activity. In the moral act of the just there will, therefore, necessarily be an actual collaboration of charity. Now how can this influence be real, though implicit, that is without any psychological representation of the specific motives of charity? And how can these be implicit in the motives of all the other virtues? Is it not precisely because the objects of the different virtues, which the will takes as intermediate ends, are objective participations or, so to say, diffracted rays of the ultimate end? The will is not attracted to them unless it recognizes there, in some way, the charm of its proper object, the good. In this perspective the following text of St. Thomas is quite clear:

The acts of any man in the state of grace have to be meritorious or demeritorious; . . . for, as charity commands all the other virtues and the will all the other powers, it is necessary that all that is ordered to the end of some virtue be also ordered to the end of charity; and since every [human] act is ordered to the end of some virtue, it will also be ordered to the end of charity, and hence be meritorious.[30]

We have already proposed an interpretation of the moral object which conforms to this explanation. We will later propose a parallel interpretation of the Thomistic doctrine on virtue.

On the other hand, it seems that St. Thomas normally understands this implicit activity of charity as a virtual prolongation of an explicit act performed in the past.

Immediately after the text just quoted, Thomas continues: "And so the acts of eating and drinking with temperance are meritorious in him who has charity, by which he makes God the ultimate end of his life."[31] And here are two other texts which emphasize this same point:

When a man orders himself to God as to his end, the intention of the ultimate end, which is God, remains virtual [*virtute*] in all that he does for himself; so that if he has charity he can merit in all his activity.[32]

It is clear that he who has charity has ordered himself and all that he possesses to God, to whom he is attached as to his ultimate end. So that each time he orders an act either to himself or to some end that is his, he acts meritoriously, even if he is not actually thinking of God, unless the merit be prevented by some disorder in the act, which makes it incapable of being referred to God. But this cannot happen unless some sin, at least venial, is committed. Thus every act of a man possessing charity is either meritorious or sinful: no act is indifferent.[33]

These texts[34] make it quite clear that the existence of merit is necessarily linked to the possession of charity. But they also seem to say that charity itself has been implanted in us by an explicit act: man "has ordered himself" to his end. This seems all the more likely when we consider that St. Thomas supposes at the beginning of each moral life, and right from the age of reason, an act in which man accepts or rejects the ultimate end, an act of charity or a mortal sin. We will come back later on to this initial act of the moral life.

But what exactly is the influence of such a past act on all present meritorious acts? How often in the course of one's life must this explicit act be renewed? "In a certain way," says St. Thomas, "this question amounts to asking when must the habit of charity be exercised in act."[35] It seems, therefore, that to assure the influence of charity required for merit, it would suffice to produce an explicit act when the precept of charity so commands. Such acts would be relatively frequent, but not enough, however, to exercise on all acts a virtual influence in the strict sense, that is to say, an effective causality emanating from an *intentio causans* which would persist in the agent. It would rather be a virtual influence in the wider sense, the persistence, not of an effective impulse on the acts, but a disposition remaining in the faculty in virtue of a former explicit act. With this disposition, the faculty is different from what it was before, for now its acts are differently colored from a supernatural viewpoint. It is an ordering of the faculty in its ontological dynamism, but it is also an ordering of its psychology, a general atmosphere of assent and offering.

Must we not then conclude that the simple presence of charity in the will, independently of any former explicit act, necessarily produces this ontological ordering and this general atmosphere of which we are confusedly conscious? Thus St. Thomas would require explicit acts of charity not so much to assure merit but rather to maintain the very existence of charity, for it is sure that if charity is not explicitly expressed it will soon perish.

It would follow from this that the true influence of

charity on merit consists in this implicit actual efficacy. Moreover, is it not always supposed as underlying the virtual influence in the wider sense? Indeed, what could the virtual influence of a general disposition of charity in the will mean, if, even though implicit, it did not actually exercise itself on the present act? If it is true that merit results from an implicit actual influence of charity, then the virtual influence in the wider sense, due to former explicit acts, would only be a normal and usual complement of the implicit actual influence.

Must we add, with some authors, that this normal complement is also necessary? Before answering this question, we must solve two difficulties. First, does not moral life begin with the awakening of reason and before any act of perfect charity? Such an act, just as any mortal sin, requires the full possession of conscience and liberty, which some authors deny to the first moral acts. For them, a child can begin his moral life and judge at least in some elementary manner whether his concrete actions are good or bad before being fully conscious of his own tendency to the ultimate end. On the other hand, since he is justified by baptism, the child is fundamentally ordered to the ultimate end; this ordering is also confusedly present in his awakening conscience, and its explicit ratification will come only gradually.* As soon as he possesses this initial morality, the child can perform human acts which are the fruit of charity in his will and so are meritorious, even though he is perhaps incapable of an explicit act of perfect love.

* On this question of the first moral act, see *Sum. th.*, 1-2, q. 89, a. 6. Cf. P. DE BLIC, "La théorie de l'option morale initiale," RSRUS, 13 (1933), 325-352. St. Thomas generally works from a hypothesis different from our own, since he mainly considers the case of unbaptized children. Cf. also: G. DE RHODEZ, S.J., "L'âge de raison," NRT, 48 (1921), 232-246; P. CLAEYS-BOUUAERT, S.J., "Tous les athées sont-ils coupables?" *ibid.*, 172-179; J. ERNST, *Über die Notwendigkeit der guten Meinung* (Freiburg im Breisgau, 1905), p. 202.

But there is a still more serious difficulty. It is the case of the sinner who recovers the state of grace, that is, the state of charity, by the sacrament of penance and by simple attrition. Must all supernatural merit be denied to his morally good acts before he has performed an explicit act of perfect charity? In any case, this would seem to be an exception to the general principle of St. Thomas: "In him who has charity, every act is meritorious or demeritorious."[36]

Some solve the difficulty by saying that at the moment of justification the *attritus* becomes *contritus.*[37] But this formula is not to be understood as if attrition was transformed into contrition. This is impossible for two reasons. First, because attrition is an act and not a habit: it is already past when charity is infused into the soul. Attrition cannot be conceived as a kind of "formless virtue" which is waiting to be informed by charity. Much less is it a supernatural virtue, for then it would be already informed by charity and could not exist in the sinner as a condition previous to the remission of sin.[38] The second reason is that justification requires not only the transformation of one habit into another, but acts distinct from attrition, which turns the will toward God and away from sin.[39] In justification, says St. Thomas,

there is not only infusion of grace and forgiveness of sin, but also a movement of the free will toward God, which is an act of faith quickened by charity, and a movement of the free will against sin, which is the act of penance. Yet these human acts are there as the effects of operating grace, and are produced at the same time as the forgiveness of sin. Consequently the forgiveness of sin does not take place without an act of the virtue of penance . . .[40]

This act of the virtue of penance is an effect inseparable from grace, by which sin is chiefly forgiven.[41] There is nothing surprising in the fact that God can infallibly produce this movement of the free will at the moment that He infuses sanctifying grace, for He can move each being according to its proper nature. Thus He will move the sinner provided the latter freely offers his will to the influence of grace.[42] This movement of the free will takes place *in instanti*, for the infinite power of God need not pass through successive transformations.[43]

Now here a new question arises. It is clear that the will begins to act at the instant grace is infused.[44] On the other hand, St. Thomas holds that conceptual knowledge, because it is linked to the phantasm, does not take place *in instanti*.[45] Are we not compelled, then, to say that this instantaneous act of the free will performed under the influence of grace does not reach conceptual consciousness? And since we have defined explicit intention by the conceptual presence of the end in the intelligence,[46] we must conclude that the act of charity, or the act of faith formed by charity which St. Thomas requires for justification, is not necessarily an explicit act of charity. This would resolve the very real problem which arises if we require an explicit act of perfect charity at the very instant of sacramental justification, since experience does not confirm the presence of this act in every case.[47] If our reasoning is true, here is still another proof that St. Thomas strictly requires for merit nothing but the implicit actual influence of charity. This influence does not necessarily presuppose a former explicit act of charity.

However, in the last case, if we search for some explicit activity of charity, could we not find it in attrition itself? In order to do so, we should consider attrition not as an act, for such an act is already past when charity is infused, nor as an infused habit, for charity alone is the source of these habits. We should rather conceive attrition as an atti-

tude of soul, something like an initial act of love, which,
under the influence of grace and at the moment of justification, tends to flower into perfect love, at least if this attrition presents the *signa contritionis* required by St. Thomas
for absolution.*

Our solution to a relatively frequent case does not belie
the fact that merit normally requires the double influence
of charity, the implicit actual and the implicit virtual in the
wider sense, each time the latter is psychologically possible
as a conscious repercussion of ontological reality. However,
it still remains true that only actual charity, at least implicit,
is ontologically required.†

In any case, even if we were compelled to recognize
that implicit virtual charity were necessary, one conclusion
is certain: St. Thomas does not attribute to charity an
extrinsic influence on moral acts in order to make them
meritorious. On the contrary, with him charity stands as
the most fundamental and radical element of our acts. The
question which naturally arises here is rather: Why not call
any act of any virtue an act of charity? Such a confusion,
we will see later, is completely foreign to the mind of St.
Thomas.[48]

* Cf. P. DE LETTER, s.j., "Two Concepts of Attrition and Contrition,"
TS, 11 (1950), 3–33; H. DONDAINE, o.p., *L'attrition suffisante* (Paris, 1943),
pp. 52–57; P. DE VOOGHT, o.s.b., "La justification dans le sacrement de
pénitence," ETL, 5 (1928), 225–256; *idem*, "A propos de la causalité du
sacrement de pénitence," ETL, 7 (1930), 663–675; *idem*, "Le théologie
de sacrement de pénitence," ETL, 25 (1949), 77–82; M. FLICK, s.j., *L'at-
timo della giustificazione secondo S. Tommaso* (Rome, 1947). For the
opposite interpretation, see P. GALTIER, s.j., "L'amour de Dieu et l'attrition," Greg, 9 (1928), 373–416. Consequently, from a pastoral viewpoint,
it is of the utmost importance to rouse the penitent who is still incapable
of making a perfect act of contrition to an attrition that longs to become
true contrition and charity. Hence, this explicit psychological disposition
may bridge the gap between attrition and contrition.

† For a thorough treatment of the liberty of the act at the moment
of justification, see BUCHBERGER, *Die Wirkungen des Busssakraments* . . .
(Freiburg im Breisgau, 1901), pp. 181–195. We have relied on this work
throughout the preceding paragraphs.

§VII. ANTICIPATIONS

In formulating the ethics of any virtue, we will again be faced with two possible interpretations. The first sees in each virtue a particular object which is abstract, being cut off from the act of the will animated by charity. The latter informs and renders it meritorious only at the moment of action. Thus each virtue will have its peculiar ethics and the informing by charity-love does not enter into its formulation. The second interpretation affirms that the object of any virtue springs essentially from a judgment of value, from a duty formulated at the level of synderesis, embodying the moral attraction inscribed in the will by the Creator. Each virtue translates in a particular area the rules dictated by the love of the good, and, for the Christian, the supernatural rules of the gospel dictated by charity. The value of this second interpretation will appear clearly in the following chapter.

CHAPTER II

Charity the Form of the Virtues

In the preceding chapter we have affirmed the real intrinsic influence of the virtue of charity on the moral activity of the just. We must now determine, always following the mind of St. Thomas, the mode of this influence.

First, let us cite a very enlightening text from the *Summa:*

In morals the form of an act is taken chiefly from the end. The reason for this is that the principle of moral acts is the will, whose object and form, so to speak, are the end. Now the form of an act always follows from the form of the agent. Consequently, in morals, that which gives an act its order to the end, must needs give the act its form. Now, it is evident, in accordance with what has been said [a. 7], that it is charity which directs the acts of all other virtues to the last end, and which, consequently, also gives the form to all other acts of virtue: and it is precisely in this sense that charity is called the form of the virtues, for these are called virtues in relation to "formed" acts.*

To render the meaning of this passage more explicit, we shall proceed in two steps: we will show first that charity is the form of virtuous acts; and then, that it is the form of

---

* *Sum. th.*, 2-2, q. 23, a. 8. The second last word of the text seems to us to refer to "complete" acts of virtue, taken as such; cf. the case of *fides informis.* On the natural level, a purely exterior act of politeness, "without any love," would not be "virtuous." See the text from the *De veritate*, q. 14, a. 5, ad 3, cited on p. 36, where faith is said to derive all its perfection from charity.

virtues themselves. Hence the titles of the first two sections. In a third section we shall link this doctrine with the theory of merit. This last development will at the same time confirm our whole interpretation of the text and thought of St. Thomas.

§I. CHARITY, THE FORM OF VIRTUOUS ACTS

The text just quoted can be summarized in the following syllogism:

That which orders the moral act to its end also gives it its form.

But charity is the virtue which orders all virtuous activity to its end.

Therefore, it also gives all this activity its form.

No special difficulty arises from the major. Let us observe, however, that the word "form," in the mind of St. Thomas, does not here refer to the formal cause. In fact, in the same article,[1] he expressly denies this when he applies the word to charity. The moral form is nothing but the voluntary ordering of the "moral reality" to the ultimate end.

In the minor, this principle is transferred to the supernatural plane, where it remains susceptible of the two interpretations explained above.

The first interpretation distinguishes the formal goodness of the commanded act from the objective *bonitas prima*, abstractly considered, which constitutes the formal cause of each particular act. The formal goodness confers on the act, at the moment of its concrete realization, its effective ordering to the ultimate end. This ordering can be called a form, for the word "form" designates a principle of perfection and can be applied to any concrete or abstract specification. In the present case, this supreme ordering gives to the act its highest formality or perfection, for an act has no meaning if it does not point to an end, and finally to the ultimate end. In the Christian, the act will reach the ultimate end under the influence of charity. Thus, charity gives to the act, on the supernatural plane, its highest concrete moral specification or, in other words, the ultimate formal goodness of an effectively performed act.

If we accept this interpretation, we have to admit that charity is not an integral part of the act of virtue, considered in its abstract essence. And this would account for the fact that charity does not replace other virtues, that it is not an element of their particular goodness as such, nor of their formal cause; for the abstract object can be conceived without including charity.

In this perspective, charity certainly plays a major role in actual moral activity, for every action derives its ultimate formal goodness from this virtue. Because of the internal unity of the human act,[2] this informing does not come from the outside: it is both an act of virtue and an act of charity at the same time.

However, this interpretation presents several difficulties parallel to those we encountered in our discussion on the moral object. Is this abstract essence of the virtuous act still an authentic moral reality when we conceive it separately from its concrete ordination to the ultimate end? If charity is only present in the moral object at the moment of the act, then the definition of supernatural virtuous activity does not seem much different from a non-Christian definition of natural moral activity. St. Thomas requires an implicit actual activity of charity in every virtuous act of the just. Does not this presence suppose, as we have already suggested,[3] that all the particular motives of the virtues are participations of the ultimate end? This distinction between abstract essence and concrete reality may well be responsible for the major divorce which we meet everywhere in the exposition of moral acts. With this separation of abstract goodness and concrete goodness into two worlds, cut off from each other, does the abstract essence not risk being reified and is not charity in danger of being reduced to the role of an extrinsic accident?

In the course of this study, we shall have to examine whether the "essence" of all virtuous activity does not require a concrete definition, explicitly taking into account the influence of the formal goodness which morally specifies the act and thus constitutes the very substance of morality. With this intention in mind, we propose another interpretation, which in no way abandons the informing by charity at the moment of the concrete act, but finds it already in the object of the act. Let us then apply this second interpretation to the minor of the syllogism in which we have summarized the text of St. Thomas.

Without the formal goodness derived from the ordering to the end, the object would be no more than a physical thing void of any moral value. As we have already said, there is no moral object where there is no intrinsic ordering to the ultimate end as testified by synderesis. We shall now show that there is no virtue without an intrinsic ordering by love to the ultimate end. The first moral goodness, as the formal cause of the act of virtue, is a concrete essence. It derives its formal goodness from the objective informing by the love of the end, and, on the supernatural plane, by charity. In this perspective, the word "form," used by St. Thomas, is all the more justified, since the ordering to the ultimate end is already verified on the level of objects before presenting itself on the level of action.

In this interpretation, therefore, charity becomes an essential element of the first objective goodness of the act of the infused virtue, just as love is an essential element of the natural virtuous act. But it is obvious that charity-love, though necessarily animating all supernatural acts, does not constitute their whole objective goodness. In calling charity a form, we are refusing to consider, in the virtuous act, an abstract essence, and are, at the same time, affirming that charity does not alone constitute the whole of morality. It is the moral object informed by charity-love which is the formal cause of the moral act and its corresponding virtue. Charity does not replace the particular moral object, but confers on it its supernatural morality. This interpretation will be more fully justified in the course of this study. But already it seems to correspond more naturally to the essential principles of Thomistic thought. In this interpretation, we do not run the risk of defining infused virtuous activity without explicitly taking into account charity, the queen of the virtues, or of defining natural virtue without its explicit reference to love. That Christian morality requires concrete definitions of virtuous acts will become more and more evident.

What we have said of the moral object, the moral form, and the end of the virtuous act, takes on a very special meaning when these are applied to the act of the will itself, the act of charity. The will is the faculty whose proper object is the good as such.[4] This object extends to every aspect of the good that may be found in the end or in the means.[5] But in its moral act, the will tends formally toward the end, and all that is not the end is not willed for itself but for the end.[6] It cannot be moved to the means, as such, unless it is moved to the end.[7] It is clear then that by tending to the ultimate end the will attains its proper perfection. Thus the will acquires its specifying form which confers on it its first goodness. Therefore, in the proper act of the will, the moral object, the end, and the moral form (both that of the object and that of its actuation)—all coincide. The formal goodness, the orientation toward and the actual attainment of, God, is identical with the objective goodness, the realization of the idea of attaining God; and the end, which is the attainment of God, is also the "formal cause" which first intrinsically specifies this act. Thus the object, the end, and the proper form of the pure act of charity are, all three, union with God, in Himself and in the neighbor. And when we say that charity gives to all the commanded acts its own proper form, we mean that it makes them participate in its own specific perfection, that of touching God; in this also consists the supernatural perfection of the human act of the just. But this does not mean at all that the perfection of charity-love deprives the acts of virtue of their particular specifications which they derive from their particular objects. For example, the paying of a debt, although intrinsically an act of charity-love, remains a true act of justice.

With this last remark we meet again the thought of St. Thomas expressed in the text which we are analyzing. "It is charity which directs the acts of all the virtues to the last end."[8] We knew this already from the fact that the will is elevated by charity and that it alone attains the end, while the other powers attain only the means.[9] Now St. Thomas holds that the hierarchy of virtues—and even of infused virtues—is parallel to that of the faculties which they elevate. "The habit which concerns the end always commands the habits which concern the means."[10] And again:

Although the essence is the root of all the powers, yet they do not all derive from the essence in the same degree (*ex æquo*), since some of them have natural priority over others and move these others. This is why it is necessary that the habits of the lower powers be informed by those of the higher powers; and thus the informing of the lower virtues must come from some higher virtue and not immediately from grace.[11]

Among the theological virtues, this higher virtue is charity:

Among the theological virtues themselves, the first place belongs to that which attains God most. . . . But faith and hope attain God indeed insofar as we derive from Him the knowledge of truth or the acquisition of good, whereas charity attains God Himself that it may rest in Him, but not that something may accrue to us from Him. Hence charity is more excellent than faith or hope, and, consequently, than all the other virtues.[12]

We can conclude that, for St. Thomas, the influence of the habit of charity on the virtuous acts consists in an *informing*, wherein charity gives these acts, really and intrinsically, their supernatural moral perfection, their concrete moral form, by ordering them to its own end. Charity is called the form of all virtuous acts, not as being their exemplar or their essential form, but rather as an efficient cause, insofar as it sets the form on all. But in commanding[13] and moving,[14] this efficient causality is completely subordinated to a final causality, for charity moves the other virtuous acts to its own end.[15] Furthermore, this informing by charity-love seems all the more intelligible if we conceive it as being already active in the moral object of virtuous acts.

As we have said, this interpretation will be fully justified in the course of our study.

§II. CHARITY, FORM OF THE VIRTUES

After having proved, with St. Thomas, that charity "gives the form to all other acts of virtue," there is no difficulty in taking a further step and adding with him "that charity is called the form of the virtues, for there is question of virtues only in relation to 'formed' acts."[16]

Indeed, virtues have no other value and purpose than to make us apt for their corresponding acts, and for acts ever more perfect. If the function of one virtue is to confer on our acts their moral and supernatural perfection as such, we must recognize it as a perfective, and thus a formal principle of all the other virtues.

Here again, charity does not suppress the proper specification of the virtues, any more than it did for the acts. Its presence does not produce in us what the other virtues are destined to confer. If this were true, charity would replace the other particular virtues, or these would not be really distinct from it. Such a supposition is completely contrary to the thought of St. Thomas, for he expressly denies that in the other virtues charity plays the role of a formal cause in the proper sense.* According to Jerome and Augustine, if charity enters into the definition of every virtue, "it is not because every virtue is essentially charity, but because they all depend on it in some way."[17]

But if the informing by charity does not go as far as suppressing the other virtues, nevertheless, strictly speaking, without it there is no authentic virtue.

Virtue is ordered to the good. . . . Now the good is chiefly an end, for things directed to the end are not said to be good except in relation to the end. Accordingly, just as the end is twofold, the last end, and the proximate end, so also is good twofold, one, the ultimate and universal good, the other, proximate and particular. The ultimate and principal good of man is the enjoyment of God, . . . and to this good, man is ordered by charity. Man's secondary and, as it were, particular good may be twofold: one is truly good, because, considered in itself, it can be directed to the principal good, which is the last end; while the other is good apparently and not truly, because it leads us away from the final good. Accordingly, it is evident that simply true virtue is that which is directed to man's principal good; . . . and in this way, no true virtue is possible without charity. . . . We may speak of virtue being where there is no charity, insofar as it is directed to some particular

---

* *Sum. th.*, 2–2, q. 23, a. 8, ad 1. Here "form" is taken in the proper sense of substantial form, which has nothing in common with a purely accidental "form" or "formal causality" (as, for example, the whiteness of a white wall), which could be attributed to charity inasmuch as it gives to the virtues their supernatural character. The role of charity is more profound, as can be shown from 2–2, q. 23, a. 7.

good. But if this particular good is not a true, but an apparent, good, it is not a true virtue that is ordered to such a good, but a counterfeit virtue. . . . If . . . this particular good be a true good, it will indeed be a true virtue, imperfect, however, unless it be referred to the final and perfect good. Accordingly, no strictly true virtue is possible without charity.[18]

Again:

Since the end is in practical matters what the principle is in speculative matters, just as there can be no strictly true science, if a right estimate of the first indemonstrable principle be lacking, so there can be no strictly true justice, or chastity, without that due ordering to the end, which is effected by charity, however rightly a man be affected about other matters.[19]

In the mind of St. Thomas, the particular virtues are related to charity by an intimate link of participation. For example, with regard to faith, he says, "What perfection there is in faith is derived from charity (*a caritate deducitur*), so that while charity possesses this perfection essentially, faith and the other virtues only participate in it."[20] And if we take the word "participation" in its true sense, the particular virtues and their acts are analogically so many acts and virtues of charity, though in an inferior degree, just as the sensible powers are imperfect participations of the intellect.[21]

St. Thomas recognizes that legal justice and prudence also play the role of general virtues. In legal justice there is a higher motive, the common good, which can be added to any particular good.[22] And prudence is necessarily the general rule of the other virtues.[23] Nevertheless, St. Thomas finds no difficulty in affirming that both are special virtues and that they do not prevent other virtues from having their proper essence. Now it is obvious that charity does not exactly give a motive or a rule to the other virtues. Its role is much more fundamental and yet leaves even more intact the proper rules and motives of each virtue. The very presence of the ultimate end in virtuous activity constitutes its moral goodness (which St. Thomas always considers on the all-embracing supernatural plane).

In the following text from the *Commentary on the Sentences* it clearly appears that charity gives to the virtues their perfective principle, their moral being. This text presents a synthesis of the various properties of charity influencing the other virtues in their concrete activity: efficient and final causality, participation, and informing.

In agents ordered [to an end], the ends of the secondary agents are ordered to the end of the principal agent, just as the whole universe is ordered to the good which is God . . . and this is why the action of the first agent is at once first and subsequent. It is first inasmuch as it gives movement [to the others], for the actions of all secondary agents are founded on the action of the first agent; since the latter is one and gives consistency to all the others, its effect is specified, in such and such a secondary agent, according to the exigencies of this agent, just as in response to a single order of the chief commanding the war, one man takes up the sword, the other prepares his horse, etc. On the other hand, this action of the first agent is subsequent in the use which it makes of the other agents for its own proper end; and hence all the actions of the other agents are modified by the action of the first agent. Therefore, since among the powers of the soul the will plays the role of first mover, its act is, in some way, first in relation to the acts of the other powers, inasmuch as it commands them in view of the ultimate end and uses them in order to attain it. And this is why the powers moved by the will receive from it two things. First, a certain form of the will itself, for every mover and agent impresses its likeness in that which is moved by it. This form is either according to the form of the will itself, inasmuch as all the powers moved by the will participate in its liberty, or it is according to the habit which perfects the will, that is, charity. Hence all the habits, which are in the powers moved by the will thus perfected, participate in the form of charity. However, since this form in which the powers moved by will participate is common to all, besides this form, the habits perfecting the powers have their own special forms which correspond to the special needs of these powers in relation to their acts and objects. Secondly, they receive from the will their perfect accomplishment in the end, and thus charity is called the end of the other virtues inasmuch as it unites all of them to the ultimate end.[24]

Virtues are, therefore, complex entities in which the participation of charity is diversified by the special forms proper to each virtue.

Now we will come back to the question we raised at the end of the first chapter. In view of the texts which we have just quoted, can there be two interpretations of the thought of St. Thomas regarding the animation of all infused virtues by charity, and, on the natural plane, of acquired virtues by the informing of love?

The first interpretation introduces the informing by charity-love only at the moment when the virtue passes into act and therefore does not include in its essence, and thus in its definition, the orientation to the ultimate end under the influence of charity-love. In the second interpretation, charity-love, and thus the ultimate end, is already present in the essence and definition of the particular virtues which, nevertheless, preserve their proper nature.

The problem of exegesis which arises here is outside the scope of our study, for it would require a more thorough discussion of the thought of St. Thomas. However, we think that the texts already quoted can be fully understood only in the second interpretation. St. Thomas states clearly that the presence of the orientation to the ultimate end is indispensable to the determination and definition of virtue.

If he places the participation of, and the informing by, charity-love on the level of particular virtuous habits, it is difficult to accept an interpretation which admits the informing of virtue by charity-love only at the moment of the act.

Indeed, one could see in the presence of charity a mere condition of supernatural merit, and conceive it as being added over and above the habit which would already possess all its determinations, its complete *form*, and, in itself, have no intrinsic need of charity-love. In this case, virtue itself would have no objective supernatural being, for the informing by charity would be purely extrinsic. Besides, the two governing ideas of the Thomistic argumentation would hardly be justified: the necessary reference of genuine virtue to the ultimate end, and the agent of this reference, which is charity-love. The unequivocal affirmation that the essence of virtue participates in charity-love would strengthen our position that charity-love is also present in the moral object. As for the relation between charity and supernatural merit, we will discuss it in the next section.

We find a still more subtle but rather involved interpretation of the informing by charity among the Salmanticenses. In their *Cursus theologicus* they touch on this question when treating of charity and of merit.[25] They teach explicitly that the informing of virtue by charity is in the order of intrinsic causality,[26] for even if the final cause is extrinsic, "yet the proper proportion and relation to this end is inherent in the action (*inhæret actioni*)."[27] Thus they try to solve the problem by having recourse to a modal quality, a particular participation of charity which informs each virtue, elevates it intrinsically, and makes it capable of attaining the end of charity and of producing intrinsically supernatural acts.

The virtues and their acts must be formed by something real, intrinsic, and derived from charity. Virtue must be formed, in itself, by some intrinsic principle by reason of which it already contains the ordering to the end of charity later found in its acts; and since this form does not belong to the inferior virtue by reason of itself, but by reason of charity which is properly related to the end, it follows that the inferior virtues are intrinsically formed by something real deriving from charity. . . . We maintain that this intrinsic element which affects the powers and the virtues, and which can truthfully be called virtual charity, is not purely transitory, or passing with the operation, but something habitual and permanent. . . . This intrinsic element is an incomplete quality deriving from the commanding virtue (*de linea virtutis operantis*) and directed toward the same object: it not only brings into operation the virtue which it moves, but elevates this virtue, enabling it to act otherwise than it could by its own proper nature.[28]

This "quality deriving from charity is not a complete but a modal quality . . . and, *per se primo*, the virtues remain ordered to their own specific acts."[29] It is produced by way of emanation quite in the same way that "virtues derive from grace and properties from nature."[30]

St. Thomas has no need of this modal quality which seems to betray the unity of virtue in its activity by overemphasizing the role of the strictly proper acts of the virtues. For him, the infused virtues are not merely modal, but essential, participations of charity. The same is true for the acquired virtues, whose acts are commanded by the corresponding infused virtues: the infused virtues, being inseparable from charity, extend the influence of the latter to the acquired virtues.

Let us now summarize the results we have so far acquired from our investigation.

We will now give definite precision to our interpretation by returning to the expression of St. Thomas[31] which we have already quoted several times. It answers the most natural objection to the doctrine that charity is the form of the virtues. Are these then going to be replaced by charity? No, for it is not a form *"essentialiter aut exemplariter, sed magis effective."* What is the exact meaning of this distinction? And have we given it sufficient consideration in our second interpretation?

St. Thomas has exposed at length in his *De caritate* and *De veritate* the universal informing of charity. When we bring together the various elements of his thought contained in these two treatises, it seems impossible to mistake the real meaning of the role of charity.*

---

* In this résumé, as earlier in this chapter, we make use of texts of St. Thomas written at different periods. So one has every right to ask us whether we have taken into account the evolution of the Angelic Doctor's thought. The question is to know whether the texts reveal a real evolution on the precise point that concerns us. Now, our analysis seems to discover a very coherent pattern of thought. In the four works studied (*III Sent., De veritate, De caritate, Sum. th.*), we find everywhere a similar effort to surmount the conflict between two terminologies, the one, traditional in the theology of the Middle Ages—the *caritas forma* of Ambrose and Jerome—the other, Aristotelian, wherein "form" normally means *causa formalis* or *causa essentialis.* But this latter sense is unacceptable as an explanation of the universal role of charity in the virtues, for it is certain that charity does not replace the virtues. When St. Thomas says more briefly in the *Summa* that charity is not the form *essentialiter aut exemplariter, sed magis effective,* he does not contradict himself; he merely takes up his thought of the *De caritate* where charity is called the *forma exemplaris* of all the virtues, but in the sense of an *exemplar effectivum* (a. 3, ad 8). Neither in his earlier writings does he take the *forma exemplaris* in its full sense, as if charity was going to engender in its peculiar likeness all the other virtues, nor in the *Summa* does he deny all exemplarity, as if efficient causality (*effectiva*) were going to produce no likeness in the term of its action. Again, in the *Summa,* he does not contradict but presupposes the distinction of the *De caritate* and the *De veritate* between the *forma specialis* (the proper essence which specifies each virtue) and the *forma generalis* (charity which informs all the virtues) as we have explained in the text. Hence, charity is neither the essential, nor the formal, nor the exemplary cause of chastity, for example; and, nevertheless, it plays a principal role in this virtue: it is the *forma formæ*, since, without this general higher informing by charity-love

Charity is the exemplary form of all virtue, but it is an effective exemplar producing the virtues.[32] It is an exemplary form, indeed, for it gives orientation to the end.[33] But, on the other hand, the influence of this end is implicit rather in the way of an efficient cause.[34]

It is the intrinsic form of the virtue taken in its ontological totality, even though it remains extrinsic to the particular form of each virtue.[35] Without the informing of charity the act will not be an act of virtue in the supernatural order.[36]

For example, what faith or any other virtue receives from charity "is accidental to it in the order of nature," but is "essential to it in the order of morality (*quantum ad genus moris*)."[37] Again, the end which directs the act of eating is accidental to the physical act, but essential in relating it to the moral order.

We can truly say, "with St. Jerome and St. Augustine, that charity enters into the definition of every virtue" as its *causa motiva*.[38] It does not follow, however, that it is "part of the essence,"[39] nor "the intrinsic form."[40] If charity were a formal cause in the sense which opposes it to material cause, then charity would be the only real virtue.

In every virtue there is a special form which accounts for its particular nature, and a general form which properly makes it a virtue.[41] These two forms cannot be extrinsic to one another, otherwise virtue would be intrinsically divided. St. Thomas adopts the expression *forma formæ* to characterize the role of charity, for charity is the higher form,[42] and is formal in relation to the particular form of

---

which relates it to the ultimate end, chastity would not be a (Christian) virtue.—This persevering effort of St. Thomas, which always terminates in the same nuanced formulation of the primacy of charity, seems to indicate, on his part, not a mere external fidelity to the traditional formula, but a conviction that this formula represents a capital truth, an integral element of his synthesis in moral theology.

each virtue. What charity possesses by essence, it communicates to the other virtues by way of participation.[43] Charity produces in the particular virtue "a perfection,"[44] and even more, it produces "whatever perfection there is in this virtue."[45] The *fides informis* no longer has its principal form[46] and thus is not a true virtue, for its particular form made it a true virtue only inasmuch as it was itself informed by charity.

We will now summarize our second section by bringing together all these remarkably converging elements:

1. On the supernatural plane, charity orders all the other virtues to the ultimate end.

2. But in the moral order, the form of an act or of a virtue derives principally from its end.

3. Charity does not enter into an act or a virtue as a *finis operantis* explicitly added. Rather it is the intrinsic end of all moral activity and its implicit orientation to the ultimate end. This orientation enters implicitly into the *finis operis*, and thus into the moral object.

4. Charity communicates itself to the concrete essence of each virtue by way of participation as its general but principal form, and because it informs the specific elements of the special forms; it does not in the least replace them, just as the essence of any concrete animal necessarily includes the life-element, without which it would be nothing but a particular anatomical system.

5. On the level of nature, the natural love of the ultimate end plays the same role, for it gives form to all the acquired virtues. Thus the sinner, even though he loses the supernatural virtues, can still retain the acquired virtues and perform their corresponding acts.*

* Cf. *De veritate*, q. 14, a. 5, *corpus*, where this role of the will appears under that of charity. Suppose two principles ordered to one another acting together in the same object: "The effect produced by the superior

6. Charity-love is the principal, even though implicit, element of supernatural morality. Therefore, moral theology, being the practical science of Christian duty, must make it explicit in its formulation.

§III. CHARITY AND THE MERIT OF VIRTUOUS ACTS

The doctrine of the supernatural merit of virtuous acts follows immediately from the teaching of St. Thomas on the informing of these acts by charity. It will serve here as a confirmation of the preceding analysis.

The notion of merit, in St. Thomas, has two distinct though inseparable aspects. One is ontological and the other juridical.

According to its first aspect, merit resides principally in charity, because it is the obtaining of the ultimate end to which man is supernaturally ordered. Now charity concerns the supernatural end, while the other infused virtues concern the supernatural means, and only by charity are they ordered to the end. "Thus it belongs primarily to charity to merit eternal life, and secondarily, though indispensably, to the other virtues, inasmuch as their acts are commanded by charity."[47] In this ontological aspect of merit, charity is, in a way, the seed which virtually contains the fruit ultimately to be picked in the divine land.[48]

In the second, more juridical, aspect, charity again plays

---

agent plays the role of the formal element, the effect of the inferior agent, that of the material element." In the complex act of faith, the fruit of the will, "the cognitive element proper to faith is as the material element in relation to the will; from the latter derives the *formatio* of faith. Now, charity is the "perfection of the will." Thus it is by charity that faith is "informed," and so too for all the [supernatural] virtues "which the theologian considers"; for "no act can be meritorious [supernaturally good], if it is not voluntary." Hence, all the virtues considered by the theologian exist "in the vital forces of the soul to the extent that they spring from the will."

the first role in merit. If we conceive merit as the reward due in justice for good works accomplished *in statu viatoris*, it is all too clear that there is no proportion between the action proceeding from our liberty and the heavenly reward. But from the moment that our work proceeds from a divine infused activity, namely from charity, which is participation of the charity of Christ, it becomes, in justice, meritorious *de condigno*.

> If, however, we speak of a meritorious work, inasmuch as it proceeds from the grace of the Holy Ghost moving us to life everlasting, it is meritorious of life everlasting condignly. . . . The worth of the work depends on the dignity of grace, whereby a man, being made a partaker of the Divine Nature, is adopted as a son of God, to whom the inheritance is due by right of adoption. . . .[49]

Moreover, if it is true that the more acts are voluntary, the more they are worthy of reward, then acts accomplished out of love are the most meritorious of all, for they are also the most voluntary of all. Hence, once again, merit must be attributed principally to charity.[50]

In his work, *De ratione meriti secundum Sanctum Thomam*, P. De Letter shows that the ontological and juridical aspects of merit, far from excluding one another, are complementary, since neither exhausts the richness of this reality. The juridical aspect must be founded on a supernatural ontological relation. But this relation does not give full value to the personal import of merit, which appears in better light in the juridical aspect—even though juridical relations between persons are by no means the most personalizing. The most profound bonds between spiritual persons are formed by love-relations.[51]

If "the merit of life everlasting pertains first to charity, and secondly to the other virtues, inasmuch as their acts are commanded by charity";[52] if the diversity of substantial merit comes, not from the diversity of virtuous works (the generosity of the martyr, or the perfection of the confessor), but from the diversity of charity;[53] and if the specific reward of the virtues is only accidental merit (the satisfaction in work well done or the personal glory of the doctors, virgins, and martyrs),[54] are we then to accuse St. Thomas, as J. Ernst does,[55] of denying meritorious value to the acts of virtue themselves in order to attribute it to charity alone? In the light of what we have tried to establish concerning the act of virtue and the act of charity constituting one indivisible act, we believe there is no foundation to this reproach. St. Thomas distinguishes several formalities or ends in one and the same act of the will; in the same way, he can distinguish in the act of virtue a higher formality, that of ordering to the ultimate end, and attribute it to charity. He can rightly say that, if an act is meritorious, it is not insofar as it proceeds from man or from a particular virtue, as such, but insofar as it proceeds from charity and the Holy Spirit in us. This does not prevent the act from being one and indivisible, nor from being meritorious by its whole indivisible reality. This distinction of formalities does not divide the act into isolated pieces, but merely reflects the various aspects of a dynamic reality which is altogether one and complex. Thus we can distinguish in our activity that which makes it worthy of essential reward (insofar as it proceeds from charity), and that by which it merits accidental reward (insofar as it proceeds from particular virtues). It is our whole act taken in its complex unity that merits both one and the other. But it is necessary to recall to what formality of the act essential merit is due, for this is of great importance to the ascetic life and to the work of sanctification in general. Since our psychology also is complex, we must know what aspect of our activity is to be emphasized. Some authors, failing to understand the Thomistic conviction that reality cannot be exhausted by one single formality, accuse St. Thomas of overdividing the moral activity of the just. On the contrary, he preserves the unity of this activity in all its richness, though often approaching it from different angles.

Conclusion of the First Part

§I. Formulation of Moral Theology

This brief survey shows clearly what a prominent role St. Thomas attributes to charity in moral life.[1] For him charity is, in a very real sense, the soul of moral life; it is everywhere present in our activity. Since charity elevates the act of the will, which is fundamentally love of the ultimate end, we have been able to affirm that the moral act and virtue are informed by love, on the natural plane, and by charity, on the supernatural plane. Then we discussed an interpretation of St. Thomas according to which the informing by charity-love is present and already discernible in the moral object and in the essence of each particular virtue. Hence the necessity of expressing this presence in the very definition of moral objects and virtues throughout the whole exposition of moral theology. This simple conclusion is of great importance, for it relates the present study to authentic Thomistic theology.

But how is it that theologians coming after St. Thomas, especially the moderns, have not progressed as steadily in this direction? How is it that they give so little attention to the informing by charity-love in their formulation of Christian morals? How is it that for them charity occupies but a modest place alongside the other virtues? First we will explain how this tendency crept into modern treatises. Then we will explain what elements in the writings of St. Thomas could have encouraged this tendency among later scholastics. More particularly, we will point out why the exposition of moral virtues in the *Secunda Secundæ* does

49

not emphasize the informing by charity-love, and why the whole of the *Secunda* could be written before the *Tertia*, that is, before Christology.[2]

Historically, modern treatises are merely a systematic development of an examination of conscience in preparation for confession. Confessors and penitents are chiefly preoccupied with the exact recognition of sins, the solution of cases, the verification of guilt, the enumeration of faults according to their species and number. But if charity-love is everywhere present in moral life, it is its very absence that is sin. Sin, considered as a human act, owes its whole ontological reality to love of the ultimate end, but by choosing a particular good which contradicts this love, it renounces grace and infused charity and so does not lead to the ultimate end. Hence a moral theology which takes sin as its starting point does not feel any need of relating its object to charity-love. In this perspective, a good action will be characterized merely as being the contrary of some particular sin, and because some moral objects, considered in their physical nature, are not opposed to any sin, they will be called indifferent.

In the long run this negative formulation has revealed its most serious deficiency, the absence of love, of that which is the very heart of Christ's message. That is why contemporary moralists feel acutely the need for a positive, and hence a more supernatural, charity-centered moral theology.

Again, in the determination of sins, this negative approach not only omits the informing by charity-love but, by that very fact, limits itself to the consideration of the abstract elements of the act as separated from the concrete tendency to the ultimate end.[3] Here one considers only the material aspect of acts while neglecting the form of morality, "which is either according to the form of the will . . . or according to the habit which perfects the will, that is, charity."[4] In brief, one attends only to the object of the acts, that is, to an object rigorously separated from the intellect that thinks it and the will that wills it, to an object thus reduced to its purely representative elements.

This method, when applied to particular duties and virtues, results in a moral theology made up of independent chapters, each governed by its own proper principles, which at times seem opposed to one another, as, for example, the principles of strict justice and charity. It is easy to be content with such a formulation, for the determination of particular duties is a very necessary aspect of morality, and even appears self-sufficient until it is realized that these determinations, cut off from the love of the ultimate end, lack the driving power that would lead the soul to God. Paradoxically enough, moral theology becomes the science of strictly minimum obligations and leaves to spiritual theology the duty of fostering love and charity, thus renouncing the very principle of its strength and value.

As a result, many moralists have called for a formulation of morals which would pay more attention to the subject. But this does not mean merely introducing some notions from normal and abnormal psychology. Just as an object in thought owes its intentional form no less to the intelligence than to its proper intelligibility, in the same way the moral object owes its moral form both to the subject that wills and loves it and to its conformity to the ultimate end. In conceiving and formulating the content of the moral object, we must take into account the role of synderesis, this innate habit of the practical reason which grasps the good at the same time as it commands and imposes it. This is even more manifest on the supernatural plane, where charity elevates our judgments and desires both subjectively and objectively, since the motives and measure of the good now are found in God Himself supernaturally revealed and communicated to the sons of God. Hence an approach to morals which takes the subject into consideration is not subjective in a pejorative sense, but rather succeeds in integrating in itself the objective values of the natural and supernatural tendency to the ultimate end.

There is a third reason why theologians have not followed the orientation contained in the Thomistic thesis of the primacy of charity: it is the inevitable difficulty which arises whenever one tries to formulate scientifically a tendential element in moral theology. This difficulty is both methodological and theological.

The difficulty that arises from methodology is obvious, for a reality as dynamic as love cannot easily be forced into strictly scientific formulas. And even among authors who agree that charity is at the origin of the whole supernatural moral order, we find great differences of opinion on the structure of this order. A number of them deny the existence of infused moral virtues affirmed by St. Thomas. Some admit infused virtues only where objects are concerned which do not seem to have any counterpart in a purely natural order; this would be the case, for example, of humility and mortification. Others admit with St. Thomas the perfect parallelism of infused and natural virtues, but they hold in practice that an infused virtue cannot have a definition which would distinguish it from its corresponding natural virtue, so that it can be questioned whether supernatural virtue can be objectively recognized by motives and acts proper to itself. All these different positions arise from the difficulty of expressing the essentially dynamic element of our tendency to the supernatural ultimate end.

In fact, this difficulty is inherent in the very concept that has to be formulated. Just as our concept of God is imperfect and always remains, so to say, "open," for it exceeds the sensible representation which supports it, so, in the same way, though analogically, our moral concept is essentially "open," for it always carries within itself the connotation of love for the ultimate end from which it derives all its force. What is generally referred to as the "sense" of moral life or of any virtue is precisely this love-driven tendency, and thus it must necessarily find its way into the formulation of all moral concepts. The purpose of the present study is to demonstrate the possibility of such a formulation. On the other hand, it is easy to understand why moralists who are chiefly preoccupied with the determination of sins can only with great difficulty tackle this problem.

The second difficulty is of a theological nature. The formulation of the primacy of charity might seem to indulge in quietism. But we will show, against the quietist heresy, that charity stands in need of particular virtues and gives them their highest moral status; it is for this reason only that charity is called the form of the virtues and not because it would replace them. Nevertheless, there remains a certain force in the objection that the universal presence of charity-love might weaken the objectivity and realism essential to Catholic morals. This objection is practically unsolvable for authors used to a process of abstract representation which totally separates from one another the different moral objects and virtues. Thus they make charity an extrinsic form of supernatural morality, for they find no other way of reconciling the informing affirmed by St. Thomas with their tendency to represent the various moral values as entirely autonomous and heterogeneous. For them virtues are just so many things and charity also a mere thing among them.

But how is it that such a traditional position, such a fundamental thesis of St. Thomas, was not correctly understood by his followers? The reason is clear: St. Thomas did not develop all the implications of his thesis. As for all the thinkers of his time, his thought was centered on synthetic concepts which had not yet suffered the abuse of over-analysis. On the other hand, we should not be surprised to witness today a return to synthetic thought in reaction to the present overemphasis on scientific analysis. This craving for unity is a healthy sign, for the human spirit must always defend itself against the danger of disintegration. For only a firm formulation focusing his whole attention on his profound tendency to the ultimate end can prevent a man from scattering his moral energy uselessly.

Although St. Thomas affirmed and demonstrated the informing by charity, he did not apply it in detail in his exposition of morals. In his long exposition of virtues, the complexity of logical connections and the multiplicity of particular notions tend to overshadow the profound onto-logical unity which derives from love. Again, his habitual recourse to sensible illustrations may well have caused his metaphysical thought to be misunderstood. The starting point of his discussions is often taken from common ex-perience and, when speaking of divine activity, merit, or perfection, he often emphasizes their analogy with the sensible world of images. These secondary aspects of the thought of St. Thomas may well have led his immediate followers into an overanalytical and merely representative approach to moral realities. Thus it is not surprising that later commentators, who were less preoccupied than St. Thomas with the synthetic unity of human action, focused their attention rather on the individual pieces of this struc-ture, which they gradually tended to consider as so many separate things. Some of those who defend the extrinsic informing by charity, as well as several of those who are opposed to it, maintain that it can be traced back to St. Thomas himself.*

* "Multis error accidit circa formas ex hoc quod de eis judicant sicut

In our exposition of the Thomistic doctrine of moral acts and virtues, we have considered an interpretation which maintains a purely abstract conception of objects of human acts, and even of the essence of each virtue; therein is perceived nothing but particular representations cut off from the virtual orientation to the ultimate end. We then raised the question, without definitely solving it, whether this interpretation genuinely reflected the over-all thought of St. Thomas, for a good number of texts clearly suggested another interpretation. But the fact remains that the first interpretation has been adopted by very many moralists and has often obscured and even extinguished the essential principle of the informing by charity.

But the main reason for this abandonment cannot be imputed to St. Thomas. It is rather due to the very praiseworthy intention, found in early modern manuals, of solving practical cases and preparing the accusation of sins. Unfortunately, this pastoral preoccupation gradually led theologians to forget the more positive element of moral life, which is the love-powered tendency toward the good.

§II. CONTEMPORARY ATTEMPTS TO FORMULATE MORALS

In its sincere effort to formulate moral values, modern thought has been tempted in an exactly opposite direction. As we saw in the introduction, the interest of modern

---

de substantiis judicatur: quod quidem ex hoc contingere videtur, quod formæ per modum substantiarum signantur in abstracto, ut albedo, vel virtus, aut aliquid hujusmodi; unde aliqui modum loquendi sequentes, sic de eis judicant ac si essent substantiæ" (St. Thomas, *De virtutibus in communi*, a. 11). Cf. P. ROUSSELOT, S.J., "Métaphysique thomiste et critique de la connaissance," RNP, 17 (1910), 476–509, especially p. 478; *idem, The Intellectualism of Saint Thomas*, pp. 11 f. See also, in this last-mentioned passage, the description of the attitude of St. Thomas toward abstraction and intuition. Cf. H. M. FÉRET, O.P., "Creati in Christo Jesu," RSPT, 30 (1941–1942), 105–110.

philosophy has moved from the realm of objects into the subjective, psychological world, from abstract determination to existential description of the conscience. This moral philosophy, in emphasizing the subjective and concrete aspect of knowledge and action, which is perceived in personal experience, tends to neglect the objective structure of thought and objective values of action.† But some modern thinkers, as Le Senne, adopt a more balanced position. They call it "ideo-existential" to show that they admit the role of the idea as sign of the existing being, the role of the determination as mediation of the value.[5] Between this doctrine and our own interpretation of St. Thomas there may well be more affinity than appears at first sight. In the course of our study we will show the advantages of bringing into closer contact the informing by charity-love and the best tendencies of modern philosophy.

These last pages have made clear the task which we are undertaking: first, to give fuller meaning to the implicit, subjective, concrete element of our natural and supernatural moral activity; second, to elaborate a method which will permit us to conceive and formulate this concrete element throughout general and special moral theology, and at the same time to remain fully conscious of the particular objective elements which are essential to any sound moral doctrine.

---

† "One of the crucial characteristics of the modern mentality is—and this in all fields—the weakening of the 'sense of the object.' Oriented toward his interior world, man forgets the universal order of which he is a part and fastens on what can be experienced and felt under the form of subjective vibrations. Of these states of soul he makes 'self-sufficient things' and supreme ends. The subject is king" (G. Thibon, "Propositions sur la douleur," *Études carmélitaines*, 21 [1936], II, 137).

SECOND PART

Toward a Charity-Centered
Moral Theology

(Methodological and Speculative Part)

Introduction

In the preceding preliminary section we have pointed out two interpretations of the role of charity in moral life which can be found among scholastic moralists. Some authors, considering that charity is wholly exterior to the other virtues, will express both these realities in concepts irreducible to one another. Others, in an attempt to remain faithful to the texts of St. Thomas, admit the intrinsic influence of charity; but as long as the moral concept seemed limited to its representative elements, this basic Thomistic intuition could not pervade the whole exposition of moral theology.

For St. Thomas, the moral concept is essentially open because of the tendential form which it receives from both intellect and will and, in the just, from charity; by that tendential form, the concept depends ceaselessly on the subject. In brief, St. Thomas recognized that the moral concept, bearing in itself the trace of the subject, has a subjective aspect and at the same time an implicit and concrete aspect, for it is contained in the affirmation of moral value pronounced by synderesis. As he himself says, that which gives a moral act its *ordinatio* also gives it its form.

In this second part, we attempt to demonstrate the existence and explain the nature of this "trace of subject" in the moral concept. We will first analyze the profound tendency of our moral activity (Chapter I), which will later be recognized as love and charity (Chapter II).

But since the moral activity, wherein charity reveals itself, is only realized through the intermediary of the virtues, we must also establish their role (Chapter III).

CHAPTER I

The Moral Act as Mediation of Our Profound Spiritual Tendency

INTRODUCTION

In our attempt to remain as close as possible to reality, the first step of our analysis will be to consider the moral act as it appears in our individual consciousness.

This moral reality is always expressed in moral concepts. When we speak of moral objects, we mean a moral reality which specifies our acts or virtues and which we express in moral concepts. There is the complete moral object which includes the various ends and circumstances of the concrete moral act. But there is above all the primary moral object which gives to the act or virtue its fundamental specification: it defines the *opus morale* and, therefore, is of utmost importance for moral conscience. It is the aim of this chapter to find clear and adequate expression for these moral objects.

First, we will determine in what measure our conceptual knowledge requires the total context of consciousness in order to express moral reality (Section I). Then we will describe the dynamic reality that appears in the moral concept (Section II). Hence we will be able to see this tendential reality as the mediation of a more profound tendency (Section III).

§I. THROUGH THE CONCEPT TO LIVING KNOWLEDGE

I. THE STRUCTURE OF CONCEPTUAL KNOWLEDGE

Our conceptual knowledge reveals its full meaning only when set in the deep stream of conscious life. A friend returns after a long absence. Will you really have the impression of having expressed all your thoughts and feelings in your first stuttering exclamation of joy? At such moments we often express ourselves best by silence and mere presence. Only effects and signs, not the living reality of friendship, can be conveyed by words. True friendship does not consist in spoken words but in a participated experience.

Before Fra Angelico's "Annunciation" a critic may draw attention to the characteristic features of the artist's technique and describe at length the impression of peace and humble submission which radiates from the Virgin. If he is a true artist, he will realize that his description can in no way replace personal experience, for peace and humility are concepts which, so to say, create in the soul an atmospheric state. Such a state aroused by the work of art cannot be translated into determined notions. A man can study this "Annunciation" and technically describe its qualities without having experienced the artistic ecstasy. Such ecstasy far exceeds any possible conceptual content. Being an experience, it must be lived to be understood.

These facts and many others indicate the structure of our knowledge. If our conceptual thought, inasmuch as it is explicit and communicable to others, remains unable to comprehend our global experience, it is because the act in which we perceive the concept makes us aware of something else beyond it. If the concept, in its representative elements, does not satisfy us, it is because our knowledge exceeds them, embodying and comparing them with another criterion. This criterion is perceived in the very act of forming the concept; it is a direct unformulated grasping, akin to intuition.

Even the most refined artist will always leave unexpressed the main element of his ecstasy, the qualitative atmosphere of his own soul which no duplicate can reproduce. It is a unique personal experience; another may live it, but always with a different affective nuance. Underlying every act of knowledge there is an existential experience. It is even more manifest in our knowledge of spiritual reality than of sensible objects. In our understanding of courage, for example, we can elaborate its definition or picture to ourselves courageous acts or attitudes, but as a state of soul it can only be experienced.

St. Thomas himself holds that the reliability of the concept is derived from its starting point, the vision of first principles in inner experience. "It is proper to these principles that not only is their truth necessary but also that we necessarily see the self-evidence of this truth."*

Even more than in the vision of universal abstract principles, St. Thomas finds the root of all our certitude in the concrete perception of our intellectual nature. He writes in the *De veritate:*

[Truth] is in the intellect as a consequence of the act of the

---

* *In I Post. Anal.*, lect. 19. Is knowledge by connaturality to be interpreted in the same light? Cf. *Sum. th.*, 2–2. q. 45, a. 2 and 1–2, q. 2, a. 3, ad 2. See also ROUSSELOT, *The Intellectualism of Saint Thomas*, pp. 78–80. Father ROUSSELOT himself admitted having, in his thesis, "exaggerated the irrealism of conceptual knowledge" (Unpublished letter to a friend, February 5, 1914). He also wrote: "In the knowledge *per modum naturæ* which I have of my act is contained a certain instinct for reality which is the necessary condition of my attributing being to the object of my act. If you like, I conceive *ens ut nomen*, but I intuitively perceive *ens ut participium, 'realitatem formaliter,'* as the atmosphere common to myself and the other (since I only know myself by and in communion with the other). I would admit the intuition and hence the identity in what concerns the existentiality perceived in my actuation by the exterior thing: *patimur a rebus*" (Unpublished letter to a friend, April 13, 1910).

intellect and as known by the intellect. Truth follows the operation of the intellect inasmuch as it belongs to the intellect to
judge about a thing as it is. And truth is known by the intellect
in view of the fact that the intellect reflects upon its own act—
not merely as knowing its own act, but as knowing the proportion of its act to the thing. Now, this proportion cannot be
known without knowing the nature of the act; and the nature
of the act cannot be known without knowing the nature of the
active principle, that is, the intellect itself, to whose nature it
belongs to be conformed to things. Consequently, it is because
the intellect reflects upon itself that it knows truth.[1]

St. Thomas insists that this process involves a total
reflection (*reditio completa*) of which only intellectual
substances are capable. But this does not mean that he
alludes to a reflex operation in which the intellectual nature
becomes to itself an object of conceptual knowledge. He
simply says that our intellect, when knowing conceptually
any truth, also knows itself directly in that same act; if this
consciousness of the concept had to express itself in a new
concept in order to be perceived, it would imply an infinite
series, which is impossible. Thus St. Thomas recognizes
that, along with the objective content of the concept,
something else is grasped in the intellectual act of knowledge. In other words, in the total intellectual grasp there is
an objective, though nonconceptual, perception of the
subject which founds the value of objective conceptual
knowledge.

Hence it is clear that human knowledge, taken as a
whole, exceeds the explicit content of the concept both by
its objective extension and subjective experience.

Let us first consider the conditions which make the
concept a valid instrument of objective knowledge. We
will see that such conditions imply both the infra- and
supraconceptual.

By means of the phantasm, the concept always preserves

an inescapable affinity with the sensible consciousness. Even our highest flights of intellectual activity have to feed on phantasms, however rudimental they may be. *Nil est in intellectu quod non fuerit in sensu.*[2] The very idea of God as a pure spirit supposes a negative reference to sensible representation.[3]

Likewise our knowledge reaches beyond the explicit content of the concept into the higher levels of consciousness.[4] In grasping the limitation of the concept as limitation, are we not somehow really, though implicitly, conscious of the unlimited? But cannot this implicit content of our daily apprehensions of the limited become explicit in the argument for the existence of God? There is no question here of a mere consciousness of the indefinite, a kind of a priori category capable of recording all possible images because it would be the subjective condition of all perception. Here it is rather a matter of actual infinity. What is perceived together with the limitation of any particular object is not only the possibility of indefinite progression in our inventory of being, it is above all the actual inability of any object to satisfy our appetite for being. In the eyes of our craving intelligence, this shortcoming could only be overcome by the negation of all ontological limitation whatsoever. Every object short of perfect being fails to put an end to our search. What we are searching for is being itself, and every finite object appears to us as participated and not total being. It is by means of this experience of a concrete unlimited, present in our knowledge of finite being, that our intelligence can arrive at demonstrating the existence of God: *Non est procedere in indefinitum.*

The doctrine of participation and of analogy is metaphysically founded on this perception. If every single thing can be grasped by our faculty of being and, whatever be its degree between matter and God, merits the name of being, it is because being is there encountered, not in its divine purity, nor broken down in independent parts, but as at once immanent and transcendent, that is, participated.

The objective scope of our knowledge reaches from matter to God, because we discover our ontological kinship with every element that lies between these two limits. We only know what we are by identity or by analogy.

But subjective experience also exceeds the explicit content of the concept. We discover the relation of human knowledge to God and to the world by analyzing, not the content of particular concepts, taken in their final stage and as though cut off from all their connections, but the total conceptual content, which reveals the transcendental conditions and implications of the concept. We must now add that all this objective richness is attained only in an act concretely perceived as belonging to the subject; its authenticity is guaranteed by its relation to the subject, as noted by St. Thomas in the text from the *De veritate* quoted above. The end toward which the subject aspires by nature or by habitual disposition is always in some way perceived. We must recognize that there is an experimental element not only in self-knowledge, for the subject knows itself in each of its acts, but also in the act of knowing its ends, by reason of the following principle: "The application of the appetitive power to the thing . . . acquires by a kind of likeness the name of sense, since as it were it acquires an experience of the thing to which it cleaves, insofar as it finds satisfaction in it."[5] Hence it follows that the object as conceived and explicitly affirmed always presents itself as exercising a mediating role between the subject and its ends.

We can now determine the type of intuition which we recognized in our spiritual knowledge. Properly speaking, it is not a direct intuition, in which intelligence would totally perceive the intelligible form of the object, as found for example in the vision of God by the elect; but it is rather a tendential intuition, an actual experience, a vital knowledge of our finality and dependence. One might call it a fringe of intuition, for it must always find its starting point in a determined perception which it suffuses with its aura.

Thus far we have considered the internal structure of the concept. But it is just as important to observe that our knowledge is capable of truth or error only through and in the judgment, which synthesizes various possible conceptual contents by affirming that they express one and the same real object. That is why every act of objectifying a concept implies the following affirmative judgment: That *is*. The fact that our intelligence needs an affirmation to become conscious of the real, shows that, before all consideration of the antithesis between object and subject, a certain antithesis is perceived between the ontological unity of the object affirmed and the multiplicity of representations that are thus unified. This natural need protects the mind against the temptation of confusing concept and thing or of believing that only one concept can be formed from a given thing. It is the law and the ideal of the mind to express about one single reality, whose unity has already been affirmed in a concept, many other formally distinct concepts. Such a process is a substitute for an intuition which our human mind cannot achieve.

Thanks to this direct contact between our total knowledge and the concrete, the order of essences arises, right in the stream of existence: each determination—that is, each element of the explicit conceptual content—reveals itself, when taken alone, as at once insufficient and indispensable for putting us in contact with reality. Each of these determinations is but a step on the never-ending journey of our spirit toward being.

We are now led to a new observation. We have already recognized that total consciousness surpasses any explicit determination which arises in it and thus far exceeds the range of representative conceptual content. It will be useful to add that total consciousness also exceeds the actual moment of time in which the explicit contents are grasped. There is a real inner growth of knowledge, for the objects are successively seized by our appetite for being, and then retained and assimilated. To know is to actuate a tendency: in the intellectual operation by which we confer objective being on a concept, we also affirm—and of this we are dimly aware—a dynamism still more radical than our knowledge itself, a dynamism that is the very heart of our being.

Thus concrete consciousness appears as much more vast than the particular reflex consciousness of an isolated object and impregnates the latter with subjective experience: it confers on it the quality of existing. Just as the description of a perfume will never give us its scent, so too the conceptual content corresponding to goodness, joy, and sorrow will remain empty unless they are referred to our moral experience.

This new dimension derived from direct experience is not a sentiment that remains merely on the level of sensibility. The experience of abnegation, of duty, or of virtue cannot be reduced to the sensible, even though it merits the name of sentiment. Its direct perception pertains to the intellectual order.

From all these observations it is evident that, if we isolate the explicit content of the concept, there will remain only one aspect of our objective knowledge, an aspect opposed to profound consciousness as the determined to the indeterminate, the abstract to the existing, the body to its form.

Here is exactly what we mean by the insufficiency of the explicit conceptual content. If one refuses to consider anything beyond the conceptual representation and still takes this as genuine being, while it is separated from the being affirmed in the total concept, then one would let the very existence escape and retain but a partial aspect of the object, as inert as a photograph.

True, the abstract content of the concept is not self-sufficient; it must be supported and penetrated by an existence. Nevertheless, the abstract aspect of the concept is indispensable in order to attain a consciousness of the very existence and of the total atmosphere in which it is set. Complete absence of explicit determination in human consciousness would reduce it to nothingness. If the intellect experiences existence only on the fringe of its objectifying act, then it is necessary that all human knowledge be centered on an element of representation. Besides, only determined ideas can be directly communicated and are really useful in social life.

Human consciousness, therefore, does not consist only in a particular concept, nor in the indeterminate, tendential intuition of existence which informs it. It is rather the actual relation between these two elements, the grasping, through a concept, of the existential tendency. Thus, what we have criticized in the preceding paragraphs is the false attribution of an absolute value to the isolated representative content of the concept. Contrary to this disguised idealism, we recognize that the concept has an unfathomable depth. For if we are willing to pass beyond its immediate surface, it will lead us into the inner recesses of the spirit and finally of being itself. Concept is not an absolute, but it has a certain absolute value by virtue of its unity with profound consciousness. It is not a dry symbol of truth, but an authentic manifestation of it in that zone of consciousness where the spirit is in contact with the senses.

Because its structure is essentially open, because it exceeds objectively and subjectively its explicit content in the act in which it constitutes itself, the concept never loses the character of intrinsic reference to the ontological unity of the objects of which it expresses a particular aspect, and moreover remains a transparent witness of our profound intellectual tendency which is ever reaching out for these objects as so many ends.

II. MEANING AND VALUE OF KNOWLEDGE

Daily experience teaches us that being flows like a current in a definite direction; it is a bipolar reality whose one pole is always valued over the other. But this requires some explanation.

We instinctively prefer to the lightheaded man, always absorbed in trifling exterior happenings, the interior man fully oriented toward the more solid spiritual realities. *Outside* and *inside* are spatial images symbolizing ontological reality: there is in the human being interiority and exteriority. It is a fact of universal human experience that everyone jealously defends the intimacy of his soul. The novelty of the Christian revelation consists in interiorizing morals and religion: God, our Father, sees in secret (Mt. 6:6) and is worshiped in spirit and in truth (Jn. 4:23–24). Therein also lies the meaning of asceticism, which forges the interior life.[6]

Spontaneously we associate the spirit with interiority and matter with exteriority. So too, in the Thomistic vision of the world, being becomes gradually more exterior to itself as it descends from pure spirit to pure matter.

Man is at the juncture of spirit and matter.[7] In him, interiority and exteriority meet and are fused into a single consciousness which experiences, in one and the same act, the unity of the spirit and the dispersion of the spatio-temporal; the intuition of existence comes from the spirit, while the sensible phantasm, to which the concept is always linked, comes from the matter. Our spirit, because it is incarnate, can only know when holding at the same time these two elements in their actual relation. It is obvious that the spirit-element has the greater value; but the concept also plays an essential role: it is the spatio-temporal representation of an intuition of spiritual unity; it is the apparition of this unity on the carnal level of the spirit.

Just as the sunbeam, imperceptible in a pure atmosphere, becomes visible in dust-saturated air, in the same way our spirit, being incarnate, needs, in order to possess itself, a determination or *verbum* in which it expresses itself. The concept is not separated from the intuition, and the intuition itself is perceived only as a context of our determined perceptions. These perceptions direct us toward the intuition and make possible a certain consciousness of it: the concept is the medium which leads us to the knowledge of our spirit under certain determinations. In its turn, this rough intuition gives to the schematized determination of the concept the value which it could never have of itself.

The concept, because of its aspect of explicit determination, would normally accentuate the distinctions, the exteriority, the mutual imperviousness of notions, and the judgments affirming diversities. On the other hand, by its intuitional aspect, the concept fosters unity; it grasps, though inchoatively and imperfectly, the mutual interiority of diverse realities.

The geometrical or the intuitive mind—which are we to prefer? Human consciousness does not consist in either of its aspects, but in their actual relation. We do not have two distinct channels of knowledge, one of which would attain the intimate nature and the other only the phenomenal appearances of reality. Just as our being, so too our act of knowledge has two aspects, interiority and exteriority, and it is by means of this complex knowledge that we attain the real. We have said earlier that our knowledge by way of synthetic judgments created in us the spontaneous conviction that we need many concepts in order to fully seize one single reality. In the concept itself there is an inner exigency which will not permit it to be separated from other concepts or from the total context of concrete consciousness, an exigency for being considered as dynamic and not static or abstract. To affirm that the concept is radically inept to express activity and motion is to ignore the fact that it is deeply rooted in concrete consciousness and to attend only to its representative element. We admit that because of this second element many manuals often seem to be juggling with abstractions and thus cause the concept to be despised. But, as we have seen, this is not the orientation given to the concept in the texts of St. Thomas. In the complex act, which is at once an act of a particular virtue and an act of charity, we can distinguish two concepts whose particular contents are extrinsic to one another; but we should not conclude from this that, in reality, the influence of charity supervenes extrinsically on a virtue which would exist independently of it. In order to determine and express this influence, we must correct, by the unity of the intuition in which the concepts are immersed, the cutting up which would be caused by the spatial aspect of their sensible schema. Since human knowledge of the real does not have the simplicity found in pure spirits, it requires an actual tension from the one to the many. When we speak of the unity of intuitive grasp, we do not mean to suggest that this profound knowledge attains the real as an undivided and compact whole, wherein conceptual distinctions would have no other value than that of illusory phenomena; we do not mean either that reality becomes multiple only when cut up by concepts. Such a metaphysical monism has no attraction for us, for we admit a real ontological dispersion in created being. But, for the moment, we are emphasizing the concrete unity of our spiritual activity; and we are conscious of this unity to the extent that we perceive the unity of our person, of its ideal, and of the concrete duty which imposes itself on us.

In fact, the representative content and the intuition,

found in our total concept, are the faithful messengers of our body and our soul. For we find between them the same opposition and the same unity of relation as between body and soul. Just as the human face at times appears as an impersonal mask, though it should reveal the soul, in the same way the concept can be taken for itself as an opaque thing apart from its true value of sign.

Much in the same way, the body has no value in itself, for it does not exist of itself. It is a point of Catholic faith that the soul is the essential form of the body.[8] Just as consciousness, so too human being involves a relation between two poles: spirit and matter. This relation actually implies God, for the creature exists only as depending each moment on the creative act. But the same relation extends also to the material world, whose energy we feed on.

So then the explicit content of the concept is, so to say, the body of our total knowledge, and profound consciousness is its soul.[9]

The question may now be raised concerning the role played by conceptual knowledge in supernatural life, since the latter occupies the deepest recesses of human being, deeper still than any natural tendency. It is in conceptual terms that we know and express such revealed dogmas as the Incarnation. Our act of faith is the synthesis of two elements. First, there is a direct contact with God, directly lived by our intelligence and distinct from the conceptual representation: the wholehearted assent to the testimony which God bears of Himself in our believing soul. Secondly, there is an adhesion to dogmas, that is, to conceptual formulas explicitly professed because they are proposed on God's authority. It is in one and the same intellectual act that the conceptual enunciation is possessed and this adhesion to God exercised. The apparent difficulty is to explain how a conceptual formulation, using human terms, can contain other than natural elements.

In fact, the representative elements in the explicit act of faith are purely natural and psychological, but the adhesion and the judgment of faith are not. We have already said that conceptual knowledge consists essentially in a judgment. Now the formal object of the judgment of faith is wholly supernatural, for it is none other than Supreme Truth that guarantees the proposition; and we have a direct, exercised consciousness of this specifically supernatural judgment-synthesis. Only the formal object of the conceptual representation as such is natural, even though its material object is supernatural.

Thus the adhesion of faith represents the maximum of interiority in our intellectual life. In the last analysis, it is this adhesion that will be manifested in the concept expressing our supernatural activity. Herein lies the highest dignity of this modest conceptual instrument: it has, in a certain way, the power of putting us in contact with God, not by its purely representative aspect, but by the ontological unity of this aspect with the whole complex of our intellectual act of adhering to God. Hence we must say that, apart from the mediation of the objective concept relative to faith, the Christian has a certain experience, direct though obscure, of his faith in his act of adhesion. This experience may never have been an object of reflection, but it is present in our act of faith in the same way as the dynamic intuition of ourselves is present in our conceptual knowledge.

The experience of mystics, the highest conscious human experience, can well confirm, not only what we have just said of the supernatural, but also our whole argumentation on the nature of knowledge. With them, consciousness of faith becomes more explicit and direct; faith and charity become luminous without the help of concepts.

The progress toward contemplation is a laborious pilgrimage which leads from sensible exteriority to the innermost regions of the soul. After one has passed through the night of the senses, one must undergo the more demanding night of the soul. The closer the mystic approaches this higher knowledge, the more he must rid himself of every determination of consciousness and take refuge in the innermost pole of his incarnate spirit.

Purification consists in letting oneself be despoiled of the excessive tyranny of sensible knowledge. St. John of the Cross requires, above all, the renunciation of the spirit of ownership to which we are constantly lured back by determined objects, for even these can be considered as possessions. Now, in our case, this attention to the concept is already an excessive manifestation of this spirit of owner-ship, unless it is accompanied by a persevering effort to force the limits of the concept and reach out for its spiritual depths. The clarity of the concept is often blinding and thus hides the more profound, obscure, and confused regions of consciousness, as the sun outshines the stars. The conflict becomes crucifying for the mystic because he ex-periences more acutely the abyss of faith in profound consciousness. The soul must consent to the displacing of its center of gravity from clear, easy, sensitive-rational knowledge toward the complete despoilment of the spiritual night. In the active and passive nights of the soul, that long pilgrimage from one pole of our being to the other, it re-quires the utmost human effort as well as God's help.

"Nothingness, nothingness, nothingness," cries St. John of the Cross in order to indicate the void of contemplative consciousness. "Preoccupation with clear and irrelevant knowledge is sufficient to deprive the soul of the com-munication which comes from the abyss of faith."[10] But when the soul "awakens from the dream of natural life to the supernatural reality,"[11] it "sees then in one and the same vision what God is in Himself and in His creatures"[12] and "the vast universe is but an ocean of love"[13] because it is now seen only in its transparency, that is, in its quality of sign and actual relation to God from whom it derives.[14]

Having arrived that far, the soul can come back to the conceptual, because, without lingering there, it will make use only of its value of supernatural transparency. In the spiritual marriage

. . . the soul comes to know how all creatures draw from the Word their life and permanence in being. . . . She sees that, as creatures, all these things are distinct from God and she contemplates them with all their energies and the root of their vigor in Him; and yet she sees that God in His infinite being is all those things in some supremely eminent way, and she knows them better in God's being than in themselves.[15]

This is "knowing creatures through God rather than God through creatures."[16]

These testimonies from mystical experience confirm the preceding observations. Consciousness and being have a definite orientation, and values become all the more worthwhile as they withdraw from the exteriority of the body and approach the intimacy of the soul. In fine, the determinations have no other role than that of transparent signs: we must always accept them only as guides toward spiritual realities. The mystics, on the other hand, come back to these signs, their eyes purified by another light. Nevertheless, words and concepts will ever remain inept to fully translate the aspiration experienced in the depth of the soul.*

III. THE AFFECTIVE ASPECT OF KNOWLEDGE

We will now focus our attention on a third dimension of consciousness and show how the concept is related to it.

From what has already been said we can conclude that

---

* R. Le Senne, *Obstacle et valeur*, p. 182: the value is "bipolar and oriented."

human knowledge has an affective or at least a tendential aspect.

There is no question of knowledge being love. But it is interesting to note that the more we love a person the better we know him. Of course, we are speaking here of a knowledge which is not abstract, mathematical, or logical, but aims at a real understanding of the person. Obviously, there will be a rupture of communication and, hence, no hope of deep understanding between two men who meet one another with antipathy. On the contrary, friendship and love have sensitive antennas which introduce our knowledge into the intimacy of the other person. Love cannot be said to know—its tendency to supplant knowledge is even dangerous—but it presents in a more complete way the object to be known. This simple observation leads us to a more general consideration: just as love for a person fosters a better understanding of him, in the same way, on the level of the ontological tendency, the movement which drives the intellect toward being, its proper good, is an essential condition of the possibility of knowledge. That which, in the case of friendship, favors better understanding, becomes here an essential condition affecting the very being of the faculty of knowledge.

Rational psychology teaches us that, in our intellect, the species becomes objective only when it is the term of a tendency directed toward it and trying to assimilate itself to it, while seeking its own good, namely being, contained in it.

Hence the intellect also has its dynamism. There is no type of knowledge which on close inspection is not, so to speak, the luminosity of a tendency or of an affective activity. Our being, then, appears in consciousness as possessing at once intellectual luminosity and affective tendency. A Thomist would say in other words that, on the level of being, *verum et bonum convertuntur:* being is an object of knowledge and appetition, and what we directly know is our tendential activity, not the depth of our ontological substance. Consciousness and affectivity are two aspects of our being. Though they are irreducible to one another, they are in a relation of reciprocal and complementary causality, and thus one cannot appear without the other. It is as if the very depth of our substance, prior to branching out into intellect and will, were one single intellectual dynamism. When we will something, we become aware that a more profound will has been molded into a conscious determination. In becoming conscious of our act of will, we grasp reflexively our profound dynamism under a given determination of consciousness. In the same way, when we become conscious of our intellectual dynamism, it is always under a determination which reveals it as distinct from the will. The determinations under which intellect and will are known to us can thus very well be opposed to the indeterminate interiority of the spirit, as René Le Senne thinks. Both our faculties, inasmuch as they appear as distinct, are but prolongations of two complementary aspects which are more intimately fused in our substance. In this perspective, the primary dynamism of our being is not to be looked for in our will, but rather in a more radical tendency which is apt to become will and intellect.* We will further develop this point later on.[11]

---

* Cf. J. MARÉCHAL, *Le point de départ de la métaphysique*, "Cinquième cahier," 2nd ed., pp. 405–440. Here again the testimony of the mystics might shed some light on our problem. How often St. John of the Cross talks of this contact of God with "the substance of the soul," which reaches beyond the powers, and of the intimate compenetration of the will and intelligence. "It [this contemplation] is a science and as such belongs to the understanding, but at the same time, it is a science of love; it is, therefore, also savory to the will, since love belongs to the will" (*The Spiritual Canticle*, recension A, stanza 18). "God does not communicate Himself properly speaking . . . through knowledge which she [the soul] has of God, but by the love that is born of this knowledge" (*Ibid.*, stanza 12). The soul "asks for a vision of God's face, that is, an essential communication of the divinity, without any intermediary,

The act of explicit knowledge which produces the concept thus presents itself as but one manifestation, among others, of our dynamism. Besides, its conscious aspect is irreducible to its tendential aspect. Nevertheless, the first aspect forms one single whole with the second and is situated in the larger domain of action. We now see better why the concept, insofar as it is determined and particular, appears to us as a terminal point of our vital act of knowledge. That is why we must necessarily replace the concept in the current of life which it brings to a standstill, for an instant, in order to make it graspable and communicable, while still revealing its more profound dynamic dimension.

If we have insisted at length on the concept and the act of knowledge, it is because we are searching for a method to express moral reality which will not betray its vital content. It is our conviction that an overly exclusive use of the explicit conceptual content may well prevent a full realization of this project. Besides, these epistemological considerations serve as an excellent introduction to the study of moral activity.

§II. FROM MORAL ACTIVITY TO THE PROFOUND TENDENCY

I. INNER STRUCTURE OF THE MORAL ACT

If we define the moral act as one that proceeds from

---

in other words, a contact with God free of all sentiment and accident, wherein the two substances, that of the soul and that of God, touch each other nudely and immediately" (*Ibid.*, stanza 32). The will loves, even though the intellect does not provide it with anything distinct, for this is naturally impossible. "Here God pours something of Himself into this soul. By a single touch, God communicates at once light and love, . . . supernatural knowledge impregnated with love, . . . inflamed light, for in illuminating, it gives birth to love" (*The Living Flame of Love*, stanza 3). All this happens as if the communication took place on a level where the will and the intellect are still not consciously distinct.

deliberate will[18] with reference to a norm of goodness, then every moral act must pass through the field of clear consciousness, where it is the object of a deliberation. By its element of consciousness, the moral act appears to be that part of our activity which falls under determination. This determination comes from the intellect, or rather from the reason; that is why a moral act essentially implies a concept, at least as a schema of action. The portion of the voluntary tendency which constitutes the action is cut out—if we may speak in quantitative and spatial terms—by the representation that accompanies it and is its conscious aspect.

We should not be surprised that the act, thus considered, has a structure very similar to that of the concept. Doubtless, the specifically volitive aspect by which the moral act comes from me as from its responsible author is irreducible to its aspect of determination; but this is not what we are considering here. We have already seen in conceptual knowledge an act wherein tendency and consciousness are intimately fused,[19] the accent always remaining on the knowledge aspect. Now the moral act also possesses these two aspects. The moral act is obviously an active tendency; but it is also conscious, for if it were not elicited in the full light of consciousness, it would be neither moral nor human.

Just as concepts, so too moral acts are partial realizations which emerge from the flowing stream of our profound tendency. Just as the concept is related to a dynamic intuition which founds and envelops it, so too the moral act is related to the moral intuition of synderesis which is its ultimate criterion. Of course, one can isolate the moral act, just as one can consider the conceptual content abstractly, but then its true significance will not be grasped.

Let us fix our attention on a concrete state of consciousness, for example, that of a worker putting the finishing touches on a shaft which he has just turned. The whole process has involved, not only a simple act, but moral virtues and values. Is this a mere mechanical gesture, and does admiration for the precision of the work exhaust its true significance? The principal event that has just happened and lights a spark of joy in the worker's eyes is not the mere fact of holding in his hands a perfect piece of work, nor the power he has exercised over a complex machine, nor the physical effort furnished by his body; all these are exterior and material. What he feels is a more profound reality wherein are mingled pride in his life as a skilled worker, the happiness of being able to support his family, and, if he is a Christian, the satisfaction of having performed his duty in God's service. Behind this ordinary daily action, there lies the more or less conscious presence of love, a profound intention which is realized partially in each daily task. An act should be isolated neither from its source nor from the end whither it tends; even if the explicit goal, such as earning one's living, seems near at hand, nevertheless the true and ultimate intention, that without which the partial intentions would be impossible, moves straight to God. It is very impressive to detect in every human movement the total destiny engaged in it as well as the rich network of relations which link this act to God and to the whole of creation. The human act can be fully understood only if it is seen in this complex. No doubt it is necessary to determine an act by its explicit object, its circumstances, and its immediate ends, but these do not reveal its ultimate meaning and orientation.

Just as total consciousness exceeds explicit consciousness of the concept, so too the concrete moral act exceeds its explicit content. Our total value is greater—and at times it is less—than our explicitly conscious acts.

Such acts do not constitute the whole of our moral activity, but they are an indispensable expression of it. True charity cannot be content with good intentions and refuse to reveal itself in determined acts when circumstances require them. And how could we evaluate the genuineness of our charity if we did not translate it into acts?

When we state that explicit acts express our profound tendency, we do not mean that they have not also a real efficacy and that this belongs exclusively to the profound tendency. This would be to forget that our profound activity together with its moral determination forms a single act of which they are but two aspects. They cooperate together in the efficacy of the action. A human act has necessarily a human structure wherein profound tendency and determination concur in its moral value. That act would be immoral and inhuman which, under pretext of realizing the profound tendency of charity, would involve a contradiction in its objective determination; this would be the case in a suicide or an abortion performed out of would-be love of one's neighbor. We can even go as far as saying that it is to its moral determination that our moral activity owes its formally human and personal character, for only this determination takes place under the full light of consciousness and deliberation. Hence our determined moral activity entails positive enrichment, a real ontological actuation, on condition, however, that it is not opposed nor even separated from its profound context. This total activity is mainly responsible for the shaping of our moral personality.

Any moral doctrine absolutely requires this aspect of essential and objective determination. Without it, moral conscience is deprived of its absolute and universal values and tends to fall into quietism or into "situation ethics,"*

* GRISEBACH, *Gegenwart, Eine kritische Ethik* (Halle, 1928). Pope Pius XII warned against the danger of this "new morality" in his radio message of March 23, 1952 (AAS, 44 [1952], 270–278) and in an address to the members of the international congress of the World Federation of Feminine Youth, April 18, 1952 (*Ibid.*, pp. 413–419). For a commentary on these two documents, see F. HÜRTH in Per, 41 (1952), 223–244. Cf.

where the existential experience of the moment is the only criterion. An existentialism which would deny the concept and the essential determination would not escape still worse dangers. That is why all existentialist thought inevitably has to be harmonized with the traditional doctrine of essence and existence.

II. MEANING OF THE MORAL ACT

Because the moral act is determined, our intellect can be accurately conscious of it, and our will can elicit it as something truly its own, inasmuch as it is responsible for its emission. This fact reveals the exteriority of the moral act, which is nothing but the profound tendency reaching the field of clear consciousness.† Moral acts are our possession rather than our being itself. This is a common sentiment, for our acts are always said to come out from our deliberate will. They do not seem so much to be ourselves as to be possessed by us. In fact, this image is derived from our transient activity. It cannot be fully applied to immanent activity, where the whole fruit of the operation remains interior and even fosters further interiorization; think, for example, of the act by which the intellect assimilates truth, or the act of love intensifying the spiritual life. But even in these cases, the conscious act consists in bringing to a momentary standstill a more profound flow. It requires a certain intervention of our sensibility, at least, in order to reach perceptibility by means of the phantasm. The determination-aspect of the act, appearing as if on the

---

J. FUCHS, *Situation und Entscheidung: Grundfragen christlicher Situationsethik* (Frankfort on the Main, 1952); K. RAHNER, s.j., "Situationsethik und Sünden mystik," StZ, 145 (1949–1950), 330–342.

† It is interesting to compare this mode of expression with that of Father J. DE GUIBERT, s.j., who also underlines the various forms of superficial and profound, rational and intuitive activity found at the two poles of the soul, and the necessity of always taking both into account together with their hierarchy of values. Cf. J. DE GUIBERT, s.j., *Leçons de théologie spirituelle* (Toulouse, 1943), I, 235–236.

surface of our being, is but the visible tip of a much vaster hidden reality. The determined activities constitute the limit of our real activity; they are its exterior aspect or body.[20]

Any progress in the life of the spirit manifests itself by a turning back to an activity which escapes more and more the grasp of multiplied precise acts. It requires an interior unification, which in the mystics goes as far as depriving the will of all determined appetites[21] and plunging all the powers into the void of darkness.[22] The mystic will finally be forced to pass beyond all other particular activity and tend toward loving God in an act as despoiled as possible of all particular specifications, for "all created things, all acts and activities of nature have no relation with God and cannot be joined to Him."[23]

And even when "the rivers of love of the soul are about to enter the ocean and are now so wide and full that they resemble seas,"[24] then, "it is, properly speaking, no longer the soul but the Holy Spirit who produces the acts by His divine motion. Hence it is true to say that all the acts of this soul are divine, for the soul is moved and actuated by God so that it can produce them."[25]

From these observations we can draw two conclusions. First of all, as spiritual beings elevated by grace, we tend to a divinely unified and interiorized activity which ends in a simple act of love; the elect will attain this simplicity in the beatific vision, and the saints will approach it in their experiences of faith and the mystical life. Secondly, our activity is by nature, from its very starting point, diversified and scattered. The moral act is the point where the exigencies of love penetrate into the field of multiplicity; it is the beginning of the return into oneself. The moral act is, so to say, the scene of a battle of frontiers; spiritual interiority is forever striving to conquer a thicker layer of that portion of our activity which is interlocked with sensibility, instinct, and biological forces. This battle will last as long as we are on earth at grips with matter. Interior love cannot do without explicit and diversified moral activity any more than the living person can dispense with his body. Moral life is the continuous victory of spiritual love over multiplicity, instinct, and the exterior. It is the point where the biological is spiritualized and the spiritual takes on spatial and temporal behavior in order to inform matter. By incorporating "carnal" reality in our eternal spirit, the moral act creates a kind of being destined to last forever.

This moral activity reveals its full depth on condition that we consider it only as a steppingstone to something further. Otherwise, there is danger of the letter hardening, as a dry crust, to the prejudice of the spirit; one would risk running into moralism, which could easily degenerate into legalism. In order to remain truly moral, human life must remain in a state of perpetual tension between two poles bearing opposite signs. The relation-aspect of the moral act must never be lost sight of; when reduced to its conceptualizable content, it loses part of its substance and becomes purely static. On the contrary, if we take it together with its value of sign, it gives us an inkling of the more profound act of love that leads unto God. Moral life assumes its full meaning and value only by virtue of its transparency.

As in the case of the concept, the problem now arises of the relations between the explicit moral act and supernatural efficacy. By definition, the moral act includes clear consciousness of its realization or intention and comprises representative elements drawn from the sensible world. Just as in the concept the representative elements are set in a formally supernatural judgment, so too, in the moral supernatural act, they are but an aspect of a voluntary act and a judgment bearing on supernatural ends.

As a result of this, St. Thomas affirms that infused

virtues differ from natural virtues, not only because of the
ultimate end toward which they tend, but also in virtue of
their specific and proximate end or, in other words, in
virtue of their formal object. The ideal of conduct at which
infused virtues aim is not opposed, but simply superior to
that of natural virtues. But it is true that we can often
discover a natural formal object in our supernatural activity. When, for example, a man eats or drinks, keeping in
mind the intention of avoiding excess which would do harm
to his health,[26] then the formal object of his act corresponds
to the proper ideal of the acquired virtue, which ordinarily
arises and grows under the light of synderesis.

In reality, all voluntary acts of the just spontaneously
bear on a supernatural end, unless they are prevented by a
positive contrary intention. The so-called "natural" is but
a piece artificially cut out from concrete reality which is,
in fact, supernatural. But we will come back on this point
later, when we treat of merit.

III. SUMMARY

Let us now summarize the preceding development and
show its consistency with Thomistic thought.

Human being is matter and spirit unified in a single
whole. The soul is the form of the body; soul and body are
two real aspects of the same being; the body itself results
from the embedding of the spirit in matter, time, and space.

But action is shaped on being (*agere sequitur esse*), for
action is a second act whose first act is being. This doctrine
gives to the least of human actions ontological efficacy,
because action is here transformed into being.

Therefore human action contains at once a material and
a spiritual element in the unity of a single act: not two
things, but two aspects of one reality.

But the material determination of the human act is relative to the spiritual activity. For matter is in view of form; it is the act that is first.

By material determination, we mean the aspect of the action appearing in clear consciousness and which sets the action in the coordinates of space and time; this element implies an actual relation to both the phantasm and the determination of the will (psychological moral determination of clear and reflex consciousness). By spiritual activity, we mean the aspect which in one and the same action, because of its relation to intellect and will, emanates from our spiritual depths, inasmuch as the latter is distinct from the aforesaid determination and connotes a certain illimitation, indetermination, and creative liberty, a profound, direct, and confused consciousness.*

The moral determination, as we have understood it thus far, can be defined as follows: it is the determined activity wherein the spiritual being, in contact with its material limit (phantasm and voluntary determination), consciously and freely takes possession of a new particle of itself, spiritualizes it by introducing it into its finality, and thus submits it to the norm of the spirit. For example, an act of mortification forces the spirit to penetrate into sensibility; an act of obedience brings the instinctive or egoistic reactions under the domination of a spiritual will in which a certain presence of divine will is acknowledged; an act of force permits a decision of the spirit to rule over the agitations of sensibility. All these acts positively enrich our being, thus creating in us, in a certain participated but real way, this particular degree of being which constitutes our moral personality; this personality does not differ from our profound spiritual reality, but is a kind of ontological

* J. MONCHANIN opposes the determination-element to the element of spiritual activity as structure and rhythm; cf. his article in *Formes, vie et pensées,* published by the Groupe lyonnais d'études médicales, philosophiques et biologiques (Lyons, 1934), pp. 402–419.

quality by which we become, so to say, our own creation. It is in our moral personality that we ratify and possess ourselves, that we become responsible for ourselves.

St. Thomas also situates this specifically human activity on the frontier between matter and spirit, for he calls this second act an actuation, that is, a passing from potency to act. The spirit becomes the act of a matter in the moral operation, which thus appears as a meeting point for matter and spirit,[27] a passing from relative to absolute.

§III. THE MORAL ACT AS MEDIATION OF OUR PROFOUND SPIRITUAL TENDENCY

We will now attempt to define in a more technical way the function of the moral act in relation to the profound spiritual dynamism from which it emerges. Hitherto we have concentrated on the metaphysical implications of interior experience. It remains for us to formulate the role of determined human activity with precision sufficient to make it usable in the method of exposing moral theology. The existential function of mediation seems to fulfill these requirements. In this section we will first analyze the content and foundation of mediation and then point out a few consequences of its use.

I. CONTENT OF MEDIATION

It goes without saying that the mediation here considered is free of all Hegelian connotations. Thus it does not here mean the synthesis of being and nothingness, of thesis and antithesis as Hegel understands it. Nor is it related to any other idealistic philosophy, unless this expression be taken in the sense in which traditional Christian philosophy is licitly said to be idealistic. Is it not a genuinely Christian conception that a divine idea, in which everything is intelligible, is found at the core of creation? In this sense everything is God's thought. But that does not prevent the mediations from having a true, though relative, reality. In fact, the closest equivalent of this notion of mediation in tradition is rather to be found in the idea of participation and also in the theology of the Mediator, which is as old as the Church herself.*

For us a reality is considered as a mediation to the extent that it is in actual relation and puts us in contact with a more profound reality which it manifests by appearing in the zone of clear consciousness and explicit activity. Its etymology connotes middle position between two terms, between the spiritual depths of the person, source of the profound dynamism of human activity, and the ends to which the subject consciously aspires; between the person that he is and the person that he wants to be; between two states of the person which are the poles of his activity. In other words, a reality is a mediation of another when it appears as a real sign of this other, when we can grasp its full significance only if we see it as revealing by its transparency another reality with which it puts us in mediate contact.†

The word "means" cannot replace "mediation." Means would be likened rather to a corpse than to a soul-impregnated body; it would be lifeless, static mediation, deprived of its actual relation to a more profound reality of which it is the sign. A means, by definition, can be set aside once it has fulfilled its task of putting us in contact

---

* Cf. 1 Tim. 2:5. An attempt to bring together this notion of mediation with that of instrumentality, in the writings of St. Thomas, would no doubt open up some interesting perspectives.

† A. LALANDE, *Vocabulaire technique et critique de la philosophie* (5th ed.; Paris, 1947), pp. 588–589, gives the two following definitions of mediation: "B. Action of serving as intermediary between a term or a being which one takes as a starting point, and a term or a being toward which one tends, this action being productive of the second, or at least a condition of its production. . . . C. The thing itself which exercises or constitutes a mediation, especially in sense B."

with spiritual reality, whereas mediation is an actual reference, an inalienable aspect of our activity as incarnate spirits. Just as the body is one with the soul, mediation is one with what it signifies. In brief, the word "mediation" designates a reality whose existential character consists in mediating intrinsically and actually, whereas the word "means" designates a thing by statically limiting it to the use one makes of it. It is clear then that mediation permits a certain consciousness of the undetermined spiritual existence which underlies our being. The mediation of the moral act, while clearly determined in our will and knowledge, remains, nevertheless, always in contact with the deeper levels that clear consciousness could never attain without it. Mediation witnesses the emergence of the spirit into the limited.

Nor is mediation a useless duplicate of the notion of participation. It is true that the concept is a participated intuition and the moral act a participation of our profound spiritual activity. Participation here is the analogical possession of a mode or quality of being fully possessed by another reality[28] which founds this participation.* Thus every participation supposes that the different analogates actually depend on the principal analogate. But participation in no way includes in its definition an active functional dependence; its dependence is rather ontological. To say that the vegetable world is, in itself, a participation of God, is, philosophically speaking, to determine its degree of being; it does not directly signify its role of putting us in contact with God or of actually manifesting God. This

---

* The fact that the moral act constitutes a single whole with the profound tendency, as the body with the soul, does not prevent one of them from being a participation, in the wide sense, of the other, in the measure that they are considered as distinct levels of being or action. The saint lives on the very life of God and forms a living whole with Him: he remains, nevertheless, a participation of God.

would rather be signified by saying: "This vegetable is for me a mediation of God."

Yet every mediation is founded on the very fact that it is a participation—because the concept participates in the intuition; it can stand for it and invite us to look in its direction—but the inverse is not formally true. Mediation is of the order of action, while participation is of the order of being. But the necessity of recognizing their intimate affinity will soon become evident.

To consider in mediation the emergence of its deeper source is to focus our attention on its function of transparency, its function of knowledge. Under this aspect, one could say that the profound tendency is the soul of the moral object and the moral act, which are both moral mediations.

But on the other hand, we should not neglect the active function of mediation. No doubt, it is the echo of the voice rising out of our spiritual depth. But, in turn, it directs us toward, and centers our moral activity on this profound soul; it also enriches and actuates the latter, ever endowing it with new conquests of spirit over matter. Under this aspect, profound spiritual dynamism gives its meaning and orientation to this mediation which is determined moral activity. And thus moral activity recovers its true soul and meaning when we consider it as a mediation.

The origin and finality of the determined activity—of mediation—situate it between two successive states of spirit in quest of perfection. The moral act is an intervention of the spirit into the realm of space and time, which it gradually spiritualizes. This will appear more clearly when we have given its real name to this tendency and when we have recognized in the moral act a manifestation of love, on the natural plane, and, on the plane of grace, a manifestation of charity.*

* Cf. *infra*, pp. 99 ff. One might attempt to reconcile the notion of medi-

II. FOUNDATION OF MEDIATION

We have already seen that mediation is imposed on us by the very fact that our spirit is embedded in matter. Our being itself is a tension between these two degrees of being.

Our spirit yearns for intuition; but because we are bound to time, this intuition is given us only in the dynamic consciousness of our act. In us two exigencies must be reconciled: that of the explicit content of the concept, which is determined, spatial, temporal, linked to sensibility and thus to the more superficial layers of being; and that of an intuition that would penetrate to the root of existent being.

---

ation with that of "mystery," if the latter is given the full meaning which Father A. PLÉ, O.P., and his collaborators of *La vie spirituelle* restore to it. Cf. A. PLÉ, O.P., "Les mystères de Dieu," *La vie spirituelle*, 72 (1945), 209–226; *idem*, "Un mystère de Dieu, le prochain," *ibid.*, 73 (1945), 225–241; *idem*, "Pour une mystique des mystères," *Supplément de la Vie spirituelle*, 5 (1952), 377–396; see also, L. BOUYER, "Mysterion," *ibid.*, pp. 397–412. Taken in this sense, a "mystery is 'something' which is seen, heard, touched, something human, on which God confers a divine meaning and presence. By it, God *manifests* and *realizes* His plan of salvation on humanity. The mystery is at once this human *sign* and the divine *reality* which it manifests and confers; or, if you like, this salutary divine reality manifested and conferred by this sign. We seem, therefore, to be authorized to call this something . . . which plays the role of *medium* between God and ourselves, a mystery" (A. PLÉ, O.P., "Pour une mystique des mystères," *art. cit.*, p. 386; the italics are our own). The mystery par excellence will be the cross, Christ Himself recapitulating human and cosmic history in the reconciliation of man with God. The central mystery reveals and communicates itself in a thousand different manifestations. Every supernatural action is one of them, for it is a visible appearance of an action of Christ in His members, which is perceptible by faith, or more immediately, it is the "mystery" of charity in each Christian. There will certainly be many an occasion to make use of "mystery" thus defined, for it introduces us into a Christian, ecclesial, and sacramental context. However, what we need here, above all, is a precise philosophical term which can convey the thought of the presence of charity. Moreover, "mediation" is not reserved to the supernatural order, as the term "mystery" seems to be, at least if we are to avoid continual equivocation. "Mystery," then, cannot replace "mediation," no more than it can replace the concept of "participation," however close it may be in meaning.

Never on earth will we be satisfied with conceptual determination alone, because it divides and freezes reality; nor will our tendency to intuition ever become sufficiently concentrated and integral to seize on the total reality of being. By its constitution, our grasp of the real is a compromise between the relation to the sensible contained in the concept and the tendency to the intuition of being; it is a phantasm given life by an existential element. This is precisely what mediation is able to realize in the field of knowledge; on the one hand, it is sufficiently determined and it enters far enough into the zone of explicit concept to be clearly known; on the other hand, it tends sufficiently by an actual reference to existence, toward which it draws the concept, to be itself a revelation of this existence.

The same is true of moral activity. Being spiritual, our action aims at being a simple act of unconditional adhesion; being "carnal," it must scatter itself in a multitude of partial, never radical, never final, adhesions. That is why the moral act satisfies our tendency only to the extent that it is actually referred to this dynamic adhesion which attains its total perfection in the supreme surrender of death and in the afterlife.

III. SOME CONSEQUENCES OF MEDIATION

1. SPECIFICATION OF ACTS

Thus far we have established the relative value of mediation: it always carries us beyond itself. Now does this mean that the moral act taken as a mediation will lose its proper individuality, its moral species, and assume, in some way, the nature of the profound tendency of which it is the sign? This question was raised earlier, under a different aspect, in our analysis of St. Thomas. We then said that the informing of virtues by charity does not destroy their species.[29]

Neither is the species of the moral act destroyed. Using again the same comparison, let us recall that the body is not a thing alongside the soul; they are not adequately distinct, so that the body finds its true meaning and being only by virtue of the soul. Nevertheless, our organic acts do not lose their species by the fact that they are accomplished by a spiritual being. In the same way, the moral act—whether it be an act of justice, of courage, or of any other virtue—preserves its definition intact even when we see in it a mediation leading us to the depth of our Christian activity, where all activity flows from charity-love as from an existential principle which gives it being. We have discovered in our action, as in our being and knowledge, a depth comprising two levels. And it is precisely because virtuous acts and charity-love, which is their root, are not on the same level, that they can coexist without being confused. The total reaction of our being takes place simultaneously on the two levels; each produces its specific reaction, even though one is the soul of the other.

Just as the body is not in itself intelligible, for a corpse without a soul is not a human body, so too the moral acts cannot fully be understood if they are not related to the profound tendency of which they are mediations, for in that case they would be deprived of their soul, their meaning, and, in some way, their natural and supernatural existence. We will see the practical consequence of this doctrine in the third and last part of our study.

It may be useful to recall here that the mediating act can be considered as a participation of our spiritual tendency. They both really and analogically participate in the same being and nevertheless preserve their proper species.

2. THE EXISTENTIAL CONTEXT

Now that we have suggested the method of considering the moral act as the actual mediation of a reality beyond it, we must now analyze the ontological implications and the total context of this "sign-act." If it is true that the act finds its full meaning only when replaced in the current which carries it, we must then take into account this current when we want to qualify the action. If it is true that an act of obedience manifests charity-love, then we must inquire into the nature and exigencies of charity-love in order to pass a sound judgment on the practice of obedience. The method which studies the existential relations as well as the notional determinations of the moral act must have recourse to psychology and other human sciences, but also especially to dogma which teaches us of man, his life in grace and charity, his actual inclusion in the Mystical Body of Christ, and his need of sacraments. For the moral act is related to all these realities; the same is true of the moral object which specifies and reveals the moral act in its first morality. It also is a mediation of all the vital conditions which are indispensable to it. Fundamentally, to consider the human act as a mystery seen through the transparency of mediation permits us to see its deepest root in Christ and through Him in the Trinity. But even if it is true that each moral decision is bound up with a total vision of the world, it is neither necessary nor possible to refer to it at our every movement. After all, our capacity for attention is limited. But a moral theology which outlines the doctrine and shapes the plan of human action requires a total vision wherein landmarks can be found in order to plot, for each object, the moral course of life. Moreover, in practical life, the degree of our moral maturity will be determined according to the measure of our progress in taking consciousness of our total reality.

Mediation will no longer be merely an appearance of our interior life in the world of space; it will also foster a better understanding of our duration, and by repeated touches will gradually reveal our unity in time. It cannot be understood unless it is situated in relation to the whole of moral life. The act of the child does not have the same significance as that of the adult or of the old man, for it is impossible to repeat identically the same gesture in the course of a lifetime. The *homo viator* will first see his determined acts as so many partial mediations of his spiritual soul; but little by little he will also discover that his whole life is but one progressive mediation, a slow process of conversion leading from sensibility-ridden childhood unto a deep-seated, bare, spiritual pole, which is finally fixed in God. Then partial mediations will have been surpassed precisely because they led to something that stood beyond them; the dispersed elements of the person will have at last reached their point of convergence, just as a circle is polarized by its center. That which was determined, explicit, particular gradually blends into an extremely simple, though extremely rich, unity. Death is a point of "immediation"; for it replaces the diversity of acts by pure charity.

The act taken as a mediation should, then, always reveal its own orientation. We cannot be content with a definition which would not reveal this meaning and orientation.

Once again we find the scholastic position very close to our own. Not only does St. Thomas remind us that creation is an ever-present action of God,[30] that every act is animated by divine concursus,[31] and that all merit requires actual grace,[32] but he also teaches that the virtues play a role *per modum naturæ* in man—which means that they have an actual efficacy, a much more ample ontological import than we are conscious of. He holds that faith, and hence the whole content of dogma, plays a fundamental role at the root of all the supernatural virtues. In this perspective, an act cannot be understood unless the complex system of its relations with creation and the order of grace is also grasped. We find here expressed in abstract terms that which the notion of mediation translates in functional terms, and the notion of mystery in Christian terms.

3. VALUE OF MEDIATION

Instead of considering the explicit and representative aspect of the concept which specifies human acts, our method focuses our attention on that which gives the acts their soul and meaning. Seen from this angle, moral realities lose their opacity and thus become for us so many points of contact with spiritual being and, finally, with God.

In so doing, we present the moral objects under their aspect of value, or better, we discover in them the presence of value. The consideration of value emphasizes the fact that the being in which it appears is not only capable of being known but also of being loved. Its goodness is presented to an affective faculty which is, nevertheless, controlled by the intellect,[33] and which can be far removed from the sensible. Value is that which is esteemed and desired, or, more fundamentally, that which is rightly estimable and desirable because it is founded on God, the absolute value. Being has value or is a value only in the measure that it participates God and puts us in contact with Him or, in other words, only in the degree that it mediates the ultimate value. Thus mediation is par excellence the function that valuates the real. We have already said, and will later further explain, that the most profound depth into which we are introduced by the mediation of the moral act corresponds to our contact with God in Christ on whom we are grafted. Thus we can now recognize that the profound tendency mediated by our human action is the real and proper value of Christian moral life.

This perspective is interesting from many points of view. It enhances the dignity of the moral act, instead of lessening it, as might be thought at first sight. Here the act is transparent and reveals a beloved presence; it becomes a living appeal. This theology is essentially personalizing, for it transforms all moral life into an exchange between persons. Nor is there any question of abandoning the mediations to the exclusive profit of the value they disclose. We will have no part with the Beghards and other quietists who maintain that the man perfect in charity has no need of producing virtuous acts.[34] Our ontological and supernatural structure is that of incarnate spirits, and we need to translate in concrete behavior our profound spiritual reactions. Mediation is not a means that can be left aside after use; it is an actual relation, as necessary as body is to soul and concept to thought.

This method also has the merit of presenting traditional moral theology under an aspect most easily understood by modern thought, which is chiefly preoccupied with value and person; moreover it finds its place in the most authentic Christian tradition.

In choosing this approach we have no intention of encouraging moralists to abandon the Thomistic method for a modern one, or to incur the reproach of mixing methods. In fact, we intend to profit by certain aspects of contemporary philosophy, integrating them into the deposit of the *philosophia perennis*. The latter is sufficiently open and receptive to welcome these modern values, allowing them fully to realize their implications in the measure that they permit it better to deliver its perennial message to the modern world and to aid theology in putting across its Christian message.

That is why, during the whole course of this study, we have made use of an authentic Thomistic work, that of J. Maréchal. This work fully exploits the existential values of

Thomism, but is always solicitous to safeguard its essence-values as well as its metaphysical and noetic structure. R. Le Senne can also furnish us with precious aid, for in affirming the ideo-existential value of his philosophy, he intends to preserve both indispensable aspects of our knowledge of the real.

Therefore, even if mediation and other expressions, common in modern philosophy, are not found in St. Thomas, nevertheless we are conscious of remaining faithful to traditional Christian thought in using them.

CONCLUSION

This last point corresponds to the desire expressed in our introduction. We were then searching for a method of expression which would permit us to find in each treatise, and even in every moral activity to be studied, a mystery, a revelation of that which constitutes the soul and substance of Christian moral life: the charity of Christ. The present chapter succeeded in showing in every moral act a mediation which puts us in contact with our most interior tendency. If all moral activity and its very formulation appear as essentially transparent, then it will be much easier to discover the intimate and universal presence of the profound soul.

Even in the material world, the physical phenomenon of transparency is somewhat of a fascinating marvel. Limpid water slipping over a rock, a faultless crystal, a stained glass window in the sun, each of these have the humble and wonderful property of allowing light to pass through them. In looking at them we can see far beyond them; they ravish our eyes, especially because of their astonishing power of being partly invisible; they are light more than they are themselves. Material transparency reminds us of the spirit because it is a perfect analogy of immanence of one being in another, whereas matter is pure exteriority.

What a consolation it would be to see the sun of charity through the transparency of our moral treatises. The most beautiful stained glass of Chartres is but grisaille when seen from the outside; but it is ablaze with color, when from the inside the sun is seen shining through it.

To illuminate the drab greyness of our lives with the warm splendor of profound love, to see there but a vast transparent pane transfigured by charity: is this really possible?

CHAPTER II

Our Profound Spiritual Tendency Is Charity-Love

INTRODUCTION

It will be possible to contemplate charity through the transparency of moral theology, if, having considered all human activity as a mediation of our profound tendency, we can establish that this tendency—as it is found in the actual, gratuitous order of Providence—is love elevated to the plane of charity. Such is the purpose of the present chapter. The whole meaning of our moral life and, finally, of our being, is here at stake. We start straight off on the plane of Christian life and, like St. Thomas, we speak directly of charity, yet without forgetting that the supernatural virtue is infused by God in the will, whose natural act is love. Right from the beginning of this study we have used the expression "charity-love" to signify this concrete dynamic unity consisting in our profound natural tendency elevated by the gratuitous gift of charity.

If our profound tendency, instead of being love, were a force seeking realization through domination, or a blind creative energy channeled by rigid laws, then the scale of moral values would be overturned: the prevailing ideal would be the morality of superman or sheer legalism.

We will develop our thought in three successive steps. First, we will show that interior experience reveals that the depth of our being is tendential (Section I). Secondly, we will establish that this tendency is love. This will enable us to grasp the substance of our morality in all its richness. The problem of love underlies that of charity. It is one and the same Creator who has destined us to love Him and has further elevated us to such a height that He can love Himself in us. Because the fundamental tendency of man is love, in the just it can be gratuitous charity (Section II). Finally, we will see that in the Christian this love does, in fact, become charity (Section III).

§I. Interior Experience Reveals Our Being as a Tendency

From what we have already said of interior experience,[1] it is clear that we become conscious of ourselves only under the form of a dynamism. All our determined acts appear to us as carried along by a stream of life or of consciousness which exceeds each one of them. This is true of the act of knowledge; the concept is a privileged element of a dynamic intuition, for it bears witness of this intuition which envelops it. The same is true of the moral act known in the moral object: it is the field of an ever operating actuation.

But how are we to interpret this testimony arising from our depths? From what we can perceive of our activity, can we conclude that our very being is tendency?

This is a matter of metaphysics. The latter tells us that the operation, of which our consciousness is the direct witness, is but the second act of a substance. Substance itself is first act and in each of these operations is perpetually moving from potency to act. Thus action and being are brought together as close as possible: action is a second, fuller being, while being itself is radically action. If our profound substance cannot be grasped immediately by reflex consciousness, it is because it lacks precise determination, the determination of operation, which alone can be perceived by our imperfect knowledge.

Being and action are thus not heterogeneous. Our active tendency really reveals our profound being.

Just as the whole of creation, our being is in search of Someone whose traces it discovers in every reality. In fact, it could not linger at these partial goods were it not for the glimpse of the ultimate end contained in them. What a marvelous sight to see all beings in their orderly march toward one and the same end.[2] They are all driven by the same appetite for divine goodness; they have in common a vital need of being assimilated to God, of imitating His ontological goodness,[3] and, in their own analogical way, of becoming God Himself.[4] Where are they all heading? To their beatitude, which is to obtain the ultimate end.[5] Among all creatures, man alone can conceive perfect goodness and aspire to it; he alone can tend to his *own* beatitude, a real contact with divine goodness which will take place, says St. Thomas, through intelligence[6] and contemplation,[7] after having been prepared and searched for in the operations of appetitive powers. Nonspiritual beings attain their ontological climax when they possess the perfection of their form. It is only through man that they can come into contact with the ultimate end, and thus find their true meaning.

Man and, through him, the whole universe *are* but one long craving for God. Without the slightest doubt our being is a tendency.

§II. THIS TENDENCY IS LOVE

How will it be possible to identify, under the self-seeking appearance of appetite, a type of love akin to charity?

And, first of all, what is love? In the course of time, there have been two answers to this question. Plato assimilated love to *erôs*, the aspiration for happiness realized in the possession of goodness, which is the finality of our being. On the contrary, Christian revelation, as found in the gospels and in the epistles of St. Paul, affirms that love is *agapè;* it is the spontaneous, gratuitous diffusion of a generosity which, far from being solicited by its object, creates its lovability. God loves because He *is* love, and for no other reason. In his book entitled *Agapè and Eros,*[8] Mr. A. Nygren has developed and interpreted this thesis in a Lutheran perspective.

The opposition between these types of love is all the more sharp when they are realized in two cities: "the terrestrial city, the work of self-love becoming bold enough to despise God, and the celestial, the work of love for God becoming strong enough to despise self."[9]

Medieval thinkers were divided between the partisans of physical love and those of ecstatic love,[10] and in the seventeenth century, Bossuet fought the excesses of pure love.

This age-old ambiguity can again be found in our daily experience. We have only to sound our consciousness to discern there two voices, now alternating, now confused, pronouncing contradictory declarations on love. We are sincere when our better self in a burst of generosity renounces its own interests and gives itself to others and to God; but, on the other hand, the desire to turn to our own interest, praise, and material goods also belongs to ourselves. Life consists in this tension and the victory of one self over the other. If we look beyond our interior experience, we no longer see opposition between two selves but between men, between saints and egoists.

Indeed, it is impossible to forget that our being is stretched and straining between two poles and that our life takes meaning only from our option.

Since our purpose is to discover in love the very fabric of moral life and since the meaning of love is still ambiguous, it will not be surprising that we devote much time to research on this notion. In discovering the meaning of love, we discover that of all our acts. We will start from the definition of St. Thomas, wherein a long tradition of thought is condensed, and will then inspect the opposite opinions; lastly, we will see if it is possible to consider the two traditional positions as two complementary and indispensable aspects of human love, which is a defective participation of Love.

I. ST. THOMAS' THEORY ON THE PHYSICAL FINALITY OF LOVE

Here is how a modern theologian summarizes the Thomistic doctrine of moral dynamism:

Reasonable action must . . . derive its foundation and rule from the principles of universal causality which govern all activities in the universe. Hence the rationality of the moral order must be integrally reduced to the universal finality of the Aristotelian universe. In this finality will be found the metaphysical foundation of moral finality; it will explain the structure of the will, and it is by having recourse to it that we will be able to determine the hierarchy of the ends which constitute the object of moral will. . . . The sequence of final causes will be integrally reproduced in the psychological field, which is that of rational appetite. Man will necessarily seek happiness in all the ends of his action, for his will, just as the other secondary causes and by virtue of the same metaphysical principles, comes under the action of the ultimate final cause. . . . For final causes, the passage to act, the production of their proper effects is identified with the appetite or the desire by which they make for the objects which constitute their proximate and secondary ends. . . . This will be the psychological determinism of the inclination to happiness by virtue of which beatitude will be implicitly and necessarily sought in all particular ends. . . . In this psychology the notion of good, which is the proper object of the will, is thus entirely explained by the metaphysical finality of which it is a function and to which the ultimate subjective end of man is referred. Thus the first function of moral good will be to direct the individual toward his real happiness. On this fundamental orientation will be grafted that of the further moral specifications of the good through the material object of the acts, the relations of justice or charity. The meaning of such values can only be complementary to this first meaning. That is why the first and fundamental moral will will be a *concupiscent* will; the other moral wills of justice or of benevolence may specify it but can never change its interested nature. We have here uncovered the principle of the metaphysical subordination of benevolent love to concupiscent love, which principle has such a depth of meaning in the whole doctrine of St. Thomas.[11]

The preceding lines contain a double affirmation, almost a double reproach to love: it is said to be the expression of a metaphysical finality and to be, by this very fact, reducible to concupiscence. The first affirmation is not especially alarming provided it is understood in a sense wide enough to safeguard that liberty proper to a spiritual being, but the second would seem to involve an accusation of great consequence for the meaning of moral life and particularly of charity. Let us then examine them separately.

I. LOVE AND FINALITY

In the *Summa*, St. Thomas seems to take as the starting point of his description of love, human love under its most exterior and sensible aspect. The first formal study devoted to this subject in his moral treatise of the *Prima Secundæ* is an answer to the question: "Utrum amor sit in concupiscibili?" where he treats of the passions of the soul.

We learn there that love is a passion of the concupiscible power;[12] but it is so fundamental a passion that, if we broaden its meaning sufficiently to apply it to the will[13] and even to God, it will be possible to say of it: ". . . love is naturally the first act of will and appetite; for which reason all the other appetitive movements presuppose love as their root and origin."[14]

First, a word on the physical finality of love. Love can be taken on three different levels: as a passion of the sensible appetite, which is conscious but not free, or as a natural inclination of the intellectual and free appetite which is will, or as an inclination of the unconscious and necessary appetite of irrational beings. On whatever level it is considered, love can always be said to be *the principle of a movement tending to the loved end,* which principle consists in the connaturality of the subject of the appetite with its end, or the harmonious adaptation of the faculty to the good in which it finds pleasure.[15] This very general definition can be extended, *servatis servandis,* to divine,[16] angelic,[17] human,[18] or cosmic love.[19] Because this definition reduces love to the natural finality of all beings, it can be considered as the basis of a physical theory of love.

In this perspective, personal or moral love appears as a species of love: it is connaturality on the level of will, *"coaptatio naturalis secundum voluntatem,"* will being an appetite permeated with reason. Thus Thomism has been reproached for having relegated the liberty of love to the rank of an accidental function, for this liberty will vanish as soon as our will, in the beatific vision, will be in the presence of its necessitating object. Love, even in its spiritual form, would then be reduced to the universal determinism of natural appetites.[20] In the presence of good, its first movement is necessary; if it can choose freely, it is due to the intervention of the intellect, which presents the good as limited and thus as imperfect. But to understand love in this manner, is it not, as Scotus suggested, to reduce man to the rank of a "decent brute,"[21] moved by animal determinism? Reason is determined by its object; will is determined by reason; and there is no place for liberty along the chain.[22]

All this would be true if St. Thomas did not recognize in free being, or more precisely in free action, a proper finality, irreducible to physical necessity. Especially since the interpretation of Sertillanges,[23] it is clear that, for St. Thomas, liberty consists in self-determination of the will. If reason can show that such a good does not necessarily have to be chosen, for it is limited, and if the will accepts this judgment, it is because the will has spontaneously and deliberately admitted this reason; in fact, the will has given itself this motive in order to justify its free decision. Motives do not determine the will, for, after they have been presented, it always decrees that weight should be given to one rather than the other, and this ultimate free determination of the will puts an end to deliberation: "Voluntas movet se concilio." Hence reason and will are in a relation of reciprocal causality; at the root of our activity, whence springs the source of liberty, they are one and the same reality.

Reason only determines choice on condition that it itself be determined to determine choice. There is here an exchange of determinations under different aspects. The unity of the subject permits this, and the profound nature of the spirit requires it. Animated by clear-sightedness as well as by an essential dynamism, the human soul can direct itself and act. The light which is in us, when it becomes ourselves, by being connected with the roots of willing, can have a moving effect; on the other hand, our voluntary dynamism, by becoming reflected reason, becomes capable of directing ourselves. The exercise of this double power, which is, in fact, only one, is properly free will.[24]

Such is liberty here below. It is grafted on a finality—but an authentically moral one.

In a profound and very real sense, the beatific vision itself will not suppress liberty. On the contrary, it leads it to its perfection: it brings it very near to divine liberty, which in intratrinitarian operation is, nevertheless, purely necessary. The act, wherein the will will adhere to its total good, will be the most spontaneously ratified of acts and the freest adhesion possible for a spirit, for the will will be necessitated only according to its nature, which is to be free.[25] But it remains true that the liberty of the blessed and of those still on earth is not a univocal, but an analogical notion. In heaven it will be a *libertas a servitute*, that is, the perfection of an activity conscious of directing itself toward the true good of the subject because it is true good: nothing can be more free than this love. On earth it is, besides, a *libertas a necessitate*, which is not found in the beatific vision. But how would this diminish the genuine spontaneity of our activity?

According to St. Thomas' distinction, we can see the liberty of the elect as a *libertas voluntatis* (will of the end) and not as a *liberum arbitrium* (will choosing the means).[26]

We can maintain, then, that spiritual love, in Thomism, is integrated in a metaphysical finality, but still enjoys its proper finality as a free being, a finality which can be called moral.

This personal love is thus a *velle*. According to Aristotle it is defined: "Velle alicui bonum."[27] This is also the formal definition of good will.[28] But there is here a certain ambiguity which requires further reflexion, for when love is defined in the sense of an act of charity, it necessarily exceeds the notion of good will. "Now this act of the will (that is, good will) differs from actual love, considered not only as being in the sensitive appetite but also as being in the intellective appetite or will."[29] But love which is in the intellective appetite also differs from good will, because it denotes a certain union of affections between the lover and the beloved, inasmuch as the lover deems the beloved as somewhat united to him, or belonging to him, and so tends toward him. On the other hand, good will is a simple act of the will, whereby we wish a person well, even without presupposing the aforesaid union of the affections with him.[30]

In fact, this passage is taken from a question concerning theological charity. But the precision added in the article quoted, because of its generality, applies to all personal love.

Here we see that St. Thomas distinguishes two levels in the activity of the will: a determined explicit exercise of good will and, more deeply, an affective tendency to union with a being with which we are one. "Affective" obviously refers to a spiritual and not to a sensible affection, for here there is question of the love of charity. How is this affection to be understood? It is surely an activity of the will, for it falls under an "*amor qui est in appetitu intellectivo*"; but it is presupposed to the explicit activity of good will and is somewhat passive: "*sic movetur in ipsum.*" Can we not see in it that "root of willing" about which Sertillanges was speaking? In any case this observation of St. Thomas shows that love is too rich to be confined to the simple concept of explicit *velle*. Love is an affective activity of the will tending to the union of complacency, and the act of good will is its manifestation in the field of clear consciousness and moral activity.

2. GOOD WILL AND CONCUPISCENCE

We will now examine the second remark of J. Rohmer. Does the finalistic conception of love imply a reduction of all love to concupiscence? Must we necessarily find an interested desire in this explicit *velle* and this affective tendency to union?

At first sight, St. Thomas seems to give grounds for the objection: Is not the beatitude pursued by the will presented as a possession of the ultimate end?[31]

Moreover, how is disinterested love possible if, by constitution, each person loves himself more than any other, for he is substantially one with himself, whereas any unity he has with another derives from the similarity of their forms?[32] Even in this highest degree of friendship, which is charity, we begin by loving ourselves before other participations of God:

We must hold that, properly speaking, a man is not a friend to himself, but something more than a friend, since friendship implies union . . . whereas a man is one with himself, which is more than being united to another. Hence, just as unity is the principle of union, so the love with which man loves himself is the form and root of friendship. For if we have friendship with others it is because we do unto them as we do unto ourselves, hence we read in *Ethic.* ix. 4. 8, that *the origin of friendly relations lies in our relations to ourselves.**

How deceptive is this egocentric conception wherein love is a mere identification with self! Such a fusion would be easily understood between things, but not between persons, whose intimate depths are irreducible to one another.

---

* *Sum. th.*, 1–2, q. 25, a. 4. "Insofar as he reckons what affects his friend as affecting himself, the lover seems to be in the beloved, as though he were become one with him" (1–2, q. 28, a. 2, cf. a. 1 and 2–2, q. 27, a. 2). "Ex hoc aliquid dicitur amari quod appetitus amantis se habet ad illud sicut ad suum bonum. Ipsa igitur habitudo vel coaptatio appetitus ad aliquid velut ad suum bonum amor vocatur . . . unumquodque amamus in quantum est bonum nostrum" (*In divin. nom.*, c. 4, lect. 9). "Unio pertinet ad amorem in quantum per complacentiam appetitus amans se habet ad id quod amat sicut ad seipsum vel ad aliquid sui. Et sic patet quod amor non est ipsa relatio unionis, sed unio est consequens amorem" *Sum. th.*, 1–2, q. 26, a. 2, ad 2).

These ambiguous appearances force us to delve deeper into the Thomistic meaning of love. The true answer to this difficulty is to be found in the metaphysical order; but we must first undertake a brief psychological analysis.

a) Psychological Aspect of Consciousness. First of all, if love is really an appetite directed toward our end, why immediately conclude that it is self-seeking? The proper effect of the appetitive tendency is to drive us out of ourselves: *appetere = ad-petere*, which means "to go toward" in order to produce union.† St. Thomas says that it causes an ecstasy.³³ All love, even that of concupiscence, does this in some way (*secundum quid*), but the love of friendship does it simply (*simpliciter*).³⁴

In his commentary on the *Sentences*, St. Thomas insists on the unitive force of love and on its ecstatic character.

Love pertains to appetite; now appetite is a passive power. . . . But that which is passive is perfected when it is informed by the corresponding active form; and in this does its movement terminate and rest. . . . When the affective power or the appetite (*affectus vel appetitus*) is wholly penetrated by the form of the good which is its object, it takes pleasure in it and adheres to it as if fixed in it; then is it said to love its object. Thus love is nothing but a certain transformation of the affective power into the loved object. And because everything which

---

† "Quod amatur non solum est in intellectu amantis, sed etiam in voluntate ipsius; aliter tamen et aliter. In intellectu enim est secundum similitudinem suae speciei, in voluntate autem amantis est sicut terminus motus in principio motivo proportionato per convenientiam et proportionem quæ habet ad ipsum" (*Contra gentiles*, 4, c. 19). The possession proper to the will consists in this that it is potentially disposed toward the loved object. Hence, must we not say that the movement of love is not to possess but to be possessed by the loved one and that this is as necessary to happiness as active possession? "In immanent activity, it is the being which is at once subject and term. Hence, two possible forms, depending on whether the principle is put in the subject or in the object, depending on whether the activity emerges from the one or the other: when it is the subject that attracts the object, the intellect is at work; when the object attracts the subject to itself, it is the will that is at work" (P. Scheuer, s.j., *Fragments de métaphysique inédits*, IV, 11).

becomes the form of a being, becomes one with this being; the lover, by love, is one with the beloved which became its form: that is why the Philosopher says (*9 Eth.*, c. 4) that a friend is another self; and the First to the Corinthians (6:17): "He who is joined to the Lord is one spirit with Him." Now all being acts according to the exigency of its form, which is a principle of action and a rule for operation. But the loved good is the end, and the end is a principle in the field of action, just as first principles are in knowledge. . . . The lover, whose affective potency is informed by the good having the value of an end, if not always of an ultimate end, is inclined by love to act according to the exigency of the beloved; and this operation is eminently delightful for the lover, for it suits its form. . . . Because the lover has assumed the beloved as if he were another self, he must put on the person of the beloved in all that concerns the latter. . . . Thus the full meaning of love is conveyed in Dionysius' definition. For in saying that love is a unifying compacting power, he expresses the very union of lover and beloved which is effected by the transformation of the affective power of the lover into the beloved.*

Let us go back to certain points of this analysis. Love is here presented as an intimate, affective—though ontological in tendency—union of the lover with the object loved, a union which would be analogous to that of matter and form. Let us remark above all that love transports the lover toward the beloved: "it is the transformation of the affective power into the loved object." St. Thomas takes up this idea again in the same article: "Love is formally called a unitive force because it is the very union, or the connection, or the transformation by which the lover is changed into the beloved, and, in some way, converted into him."[35]

---

* *In III Sent.*, d. 27, q. 1, a. 1. St. Thomas calls attention to the inclination of love itself to realize what concerns the loved one, whether the latter be a superior, an inferior, or an equal, by quoting Dionysius: "Amor virtus est unitiva, movens superiora ad providentiam minus habentium, coordinata autem rursus ad communicativam alternam habitudinem, subjecta ad meliorum conversionem."

This conversion into the other supposes abandonment of self. This appears even more explicitly in another passage of the same article:

In love there is union of lover and beloved, but here there is a triple division. By the fact that love transforms the lover into the beloved, it makes the lover enter inside the beloved, and conversely, so that there is nothing of the beloved that is not united to the lover, just as the form attains the innermost recesses of that which it informs, and conversely. For this reason, the lover in some way penetrates the beloved so that love is said to be acute: it is the property of that which is acute to tear its way into the intimacy of the thing; in the same way does the beloved penetrate the lover, reaching his innermost parts, and that is why love is said *to wound and to transfix.* . . . But because no single thing can be transformed into another thing without in some way abandoning its own form, for a single thing can have but one form, this separation which comes from penetration into the other is preceded by another separation by which the lover separates from himself in tending toward the object of his love. That is why love is said to produce ecstasy and to be fiery, for that which is fire-hot sighingly exhales and boils out of itself. And because nothing goes out of itself before having unbound that which retains it in itself, just as a natural thing does not lose its form unless the dispositions retaining this form in the matter are dropped, it is necessary that this limitation, which held the lover within his own confines, be suppressed. Hence is love said to melt the heart, for that which is liquid is not held within proper limits.[36]

We can complete these texts with the distinction made by St. Thomas[37] between the union which "is essentially love itself" (the affective union) and the union which "is the effect of love" (the real union). But the first union would not be itself if it did not tend toward the other, directly and simply.[38] Thus we can here consider them together, as conjoined in the movement of love.[39]

The passage from self into the other in order to take on the form of the other, at the price of somehow abandoning its own proper form—such is the audacious Thomistic conception of love. This can only be realized in Christian love, which is an actuation of ourselves by Christ's Love. Hence St. Paul says that we should put off the old man in order to put on Christ, so that it be no longer I who live but Christ who lives in me (Gal. 2:20).

Expressions which a few moments ago seemed egoistic because they reduced the love of friendship to selfish love, can, on the contrary, be interpreted in a sense of generosity:

Love always supposes complacency of the lover in the beloved. Now when someone takes pleasure in another, he transports himself into that other and joins himself to him as far as possible, so that the other becomes his own; that is why love has the property of uniting lover and beloved. . . . If, by impossibility, we were to suppose that they [Father and Son] were not one by essence, it would be necessary to find in them a union of love in order to understand their perfect joy [inasmuch as they are persons loving one another].[40]

Now there is no longer danger of inclining to an excessively egoistic conception but rather of tending to suppress self. This is equally objectionable, for then the irreducible duality of lover and beloved would be fused in identity, thus rendering love just as impossible as it was in the first conception. But St. Thomas only underlines this tendency to union, which is essential to love: the lover joins himself to the other only "as far as possible." There is nothing to cause us to believe that he goes beyond these limits.

Let us here recall Aristotle's definition: *velle alicui bonum*. What is this *bonum?* It can be anything. But this good which I wish for my friend, can it be myself? Nothing prevents us from interpreting St. Thomas in this way. In fact, the development of his thought, as we have just seen, leads us to adopt this interpretation. One of the applications of the definition of love will be then: *velle alteri seipsum.* But it must be understood rightly.

In fact, it is not a complete definition. In the first place, it tends to narrow the notion of love. Love is characterized not only by the person who is its object, but also by the good willed for him; to love a person is to will his complete good, that is, to will for him nothing less than God. It seems then that only God's love for us can be defined as *velle alteri seipsum.* Any created love pretending to be exclusive is vitiated by pride, because it believes itself sufficient for the happiness of the beloved and wishes, in some way, to be his god. Such is the temptation of human love. Love for any creature must be impregnated with humility if it is not to betray the image of divine love hidden in it and not transform it into an idol.

Secondly, the formula *velle alteri seipsum* might lead us to believe that the beloved alone plays the role of *finis cui.* Thus the person of the lover would be reduced to a mere *finis qui intenditur alteri,* to the function of a mere thing, which would be valuable only to the extent that it is advantageous to the other.

This leads us back to the distinction between love of concupiscence and love of friendship which we wanted to examine from the psychological point of view.

At first sight, the preceding considerations on the ecstatic character of love in St. Thomas might have caused us to think that the word "concupiscence" is out of harmony with that of "love."

"Man has love of concupiscence for the good that he wishes to another, and love of friendship for him to whom he wishes good."[41] It is important to note that, for St. Thomas, the antithesis between love of concupiscence and love of friendship does not exactly coincide with that between concupiscence and friendship. He explicitly says so in the article just quoted.[42] He has given to both words the meaning which they have in current language: friendship is essentially altruistic,[43] while concupiscence is essentially egocentric.[44] In current language the word "love" is applied to both the act directed toward the object of friendship and that which possesses the object of concupiscence; this object can be a thing, or a person considered as a thing. Hence the ambiguity of this word.

Love then has two components: one is called love of friendship, for it appears chiefly in friendship; the other is called love of concupiscence because it is found principally in concupiscence. Now how are we to characterize these two meanings? In solving this problem we must not statically divide a movement of the will wherein the two aspects of love are never independent: "The movement of love has a twofold tendency: toward the good which a man wishes to someone—to himself or to another—and toward that to which he wishes some good."[45] On the one hand, our love is directed toward the persons to whom we wish good, and hence we are said to have for them love of friendship; love is here taken in the meaning used in referring to objects of friendship. On the other hand, our love is directed toward the things which we wish for these persons, and hence we are said to have for such things love of concupiscence: love is here taken in the meaning used in referring to the objects of our concupiscence. For St. Thomas there is a love of concupiscence for the good which we wish for another as well as for that we wish for ourselves; conversely, we can have for ourselves love of friendship. But we must also admit that persons can be objects of the love of concupiscence. In this case, they simply become things. It is easy to understand the observation of St. Thomas about friendship based on interest:

When friendship is based on usefulness or pleasure, a man does indeed wish his friend some good, and in this respect the character of friendship is preserved. But since he refers this good further to his own pleasure or use, the result is that friendship of the useful or pleasant, insofar as it is connected with love of concupiscence, loses the character of true friendship.[46]

Where exactly lies the essential difference between these two types of love? In this, that by love of concupiscence the object is attained as a means referred to an ulterior end, while love of friendship attains its object as an end. This latter type of love will be all the more perfect as the end is closer to the ultimate end, and hence less susceptible of playing the role of means. Again, true love of friendship can exist only between spiritual persons, and its supreme perfection is found in the love we have for God. This obviously does not mean that all the love referred to a higher end is a love of concupiscence. When we love ourselves or our neighbor for the sake of God, we do not consider them merely as means to which we would refuse friendship, but we rather see them as participations of the ultimate end, as images of God permitting them to be included in our love for Him. Strictly speaking, only in love for God can there be perfect love of friendship; and only in love for things, or for men lowered to the level of things, love of concupiscence.

In brief, love of concupiscence takes objects as means and subordinates them to its own finality, or to that of some other object of love, while love of friendship subordinates us to its object as to an end. Now which of these is the more genuine type of love? St. Thomas answers this question without hesitation:

The members of this division are related as primary and secondary: since that which is loved with the love of friendship is loved simply and for itself; whereas that which is loved with the love of concupiscence, is loved, not simply and for itself, but for something else. For just as that which has existence, is a being simply, while that which exists in another is a relative being; so, because good is convertible with being, the good, which itself has goodness, is good simply; but that which is another's good, is a relative good. Consequently the love with which a thing is loved, that it may have some good, is love simply; while the love, with which a thing is loved, that it may be another's good, is relative love.[47]

It will be useful to compare this distinction with another where St. Thomas treats of the capacity for ecstasy in both types of love :

As to the appetitive power, a man is said to suffer ecstasy, when that power is borne toward something else, so that it goes forth out from itself, as it were. . . . [This ecstasy] is caused by love directly; by love of friendship, simply; by love of concupiscence, not simply but in a restricted sense. Because in love of concupiscence, the lover is carried out of himself, in a certain sense; insofar, namely, as not being satisfied with enjoying the good that he has, he seeks to enjoy something outside himself. But since he seeks to have this extrinsic good for himself, he does not go out from himself simply, and this movement remains finally within him. On the other hand, in love of friendship, a man's affection goes out from itself simply; because he wishes and does good to his friend, by caring and providing for him, for his sake.[48]

Total love is the normal effect of love of friendship, for, adds St. Thomas,

he who loves, goes out from himself, insofar as he wills the good of his friend and works for it. Yet he does not will the good of his friend more than his own good: and so it does not follow that he loves another more than himself.[49]

This follows from the fact that we can have love of friendship for ourselves.[50] In this case love is a movement toward self, considered as an end (or at least as a participation of the ultimate end), a subordinated end to which we wish good and, finally, the total good of the possession of God.

We will see later the metaphysical foundation for the fact that love for self, in order to avoid egoism, must be referred to its source and end, the love of God. In any case, we do not love ourselves for God in the same way as we love a thing for God.

We have said that both types of love can be either altruistic or egocentric. Henceforth, we shall properly call *concupiscence* the excessively egocentric form of the "love of concupiscence." From egocentric it has now become egoistic. Sensible love, considered formally, is always egocentric,[51] not inasmuch as it is an appetite—for, as such, it bears on the object loved—but because sensibility is a passive power[52] which in being actuated by its object can only be receptive; but it can tend toward its object (ecstatic movement) only in view of assimilating it to itself (egocentric movement). Its effort can carry it no further. True, it began by going forth from self toward the other. But it cannot complete its movement without encountering its limit—an intrinsic indigence which cannot go unheeded. It assimilates the object to which it gives itself. And yet even here we already find an attempt at genuine love. Since Adam's fall this sensible love is no longer merely an egocentric love of concupiscence. It is properly concupiscence in the sense just defined, for it has become disordered by insubordination to the rule of reason.* In our present state

---

* *Sum. th.*, 1–2, q. 83, a. 3; q. 83, a. 4, ad 1. When we call disordered egocentric love "concupiscence," we are fully aware that we are taking into account only one aspect of concupiscence as St. Thomas understands it. At times, he calls concupiscence the passion *appetitus concupiscibilis*, without attaching to it any pejorative sense (cf. *Sum. th.*, 1–2, q. 30, a. 2); and at times, on the contrary, he takes it as disordered sensible love (cf. *Sum. th.*, 1–2, q. 85, a. 3; *In II Sent.*, d. 32, q. 1, a. 1). Moreover, in saying that all sensible love considered formally is, since original sin, disordered, we do not at all mean to say that every act of sensible human love (even if it is purely natural) is disordered. We are simply saying that, because of original sin, our sensibility has an actual "tendency" not to submit itself to the order of reason and grace and that, of itself, it instinctively seeks its own interest regardless of its subordination to the order of reason and the good of the whole. But since this sensi-

of nature, all sensible love, left to itself, is egoistic. The sensitive appetitive faculties seek their own proper good regardless of the good of the whole. However, this sensible love is but one aspect of human love. At its spiritual limit, this love can blossom into friendship or into a well-ordered love of concupiscence, just as it can degenerate into a host of disordered friendships and into a concupiscence of the spirit.

As long as man is a *viator* in perpetual indigence, he will see his most spiritual love mingled with this egocentric love of concupiscence, the desire of absent goods, which, though a secondary aspect, is nevertheless essential to love. In the beatific vision, desire will give way to complacence in beatitude which will delight him because of its correspondence to his attraction for it. Always, even in his purest love of God, will be found these two elements: love of concupiscence and love of friendship. But the first will always have to be subordinated to the second and will draw from it its true meaning, for friendship is the most characteristic movement of love.

We have thus far limited ourselves to a psychological analysis of love in St. Thomas. This analysis has increased our knowledge of the meaning and import of love, even if it has not yet disclosed its metaphysical nature. Already in our experience of consciousness love appears involved in

---

bility, however insubordinate it may be, is not, in itself, corrupted, it remains capable of being subordinated by the will and a fortiori by charity. In the Protestant position, sensibility is profoundly corrupted in its very nature. We simply say that it is, in fact, "not subordinated." In any human act that has moral value, sensibility is never exclusively at work, but is always found together with a spiritual presence which directs its instinctive activity. Thus, when we say that all sensible love, considered formally, is self-seeking, we mean to say that sensibility as such has, in itself, an egocentric preoccupation, and that historically, because of original sin, it conceals an ever-present disordered tendency not to subordinate itself to the spirit and thus to become egocentric. (For St. Thomas, concupiscence, inasmuch as it derives from original sin, is habitual rather than actual; cf. *De malo*, q. 4, a. 2, ad 4.)

a finality. Long before the moderns, St. Thomas was well aware of the movement of ecstatic generosity, of the personal aspect of friendship for another, of the altruism of love, as well as of the movements of self-love. In fact, for him a love of concupiscence is found in all friendship. But it is very important to note that he does not mean by this that concupiscence is the first and proper movement of love. On the contrary, he considers it as *amor secundum quid*, always united in subordination to the true movement of love, which is friendship. Now, we have already seen to what a great extent egocentricity is reduced by the ecstasy of friendship.

Only a metaphysical analysis of love will permit us to overcome the dualism of self and other, of love of concupiscence and of friendship. We can foresee that this reconciliation is to be sought in a communion which would be a tendency toward the conjoint good of self and of the other.

b) *Metaphysical Analysis.* If it is metaphysically true that ontological unity is the principle of love and its ultimate form, must we not say that egocentric love of concupiscence is the exemplar of all possible love? For we can only love others to the extent that we are one with them or that, in some way, they become ourselves.[53]

That which is principal in a genus is the measure of all that is contained under this genus. . . . Now in the genus of human love, self-love is principal; hence, it is on this love that all love for the others must be measured.[54]

But this principle finds its true meaning only if we understand that our unity with God and, through Him, with the universe is more profound than our unity with ourselves as individuals. The following paragraph will gradually establish this statement.

St. Thomas often takes up an argument which, though

not exactly the same, is quite similar and leads to the same consequences. It is the well-known theory of the whole and the part, presented by Father Rousselot as the genuine Thomistic solution of the problem of love.[55] The most suggestive text of St. Thomas is that in which he raises the question whether man can love God above all things, without grace, by his merely natural forces:

Now to love God above all things is natural to man and to every nature, not only rational but irrational, and even inanimate, according to the manner of love which can belong to each creature. The reason for this is that it is natural to all to seek and love things according as they are naturally fit [to be sought and loved]. . . . Now it is manifest that the good of the part is for the good of the whole.[56]

Now it is true* that "each part naturally loves the common good of the whole more than its own particular good."[57]

It follows, then, that

everything, by its natural appetite and love, loves its own proper good because of the common good of the whole universe, which is God. . . . Hence in the state of integral nature, man referred the love of himself and of all other things to the love of God as to its end; and thus he loved God more than himself and above all things. But in the state of corrupted nature, man falls short of this in the appetite of his rational will, which, unless it is cured by God's grace, follows its private good, because of the corruption of nature.[58]

Charity is still higher in dignity than this natural love, for its object is God with whom man is spiritually associated.[59] Hence, "the part does indeed love the good of the whole, as becomes a part, not however so as to refer the good of the

---

* This observation can be a matter of experience. We would prefer to see the argument phrased as follows: the unity of the whole is, in a way, more profound in the part than is the unity of the part itself; "intimior intimo meo."

whole to itself, but rather itself to the good of the whole."[60]
Finally, here is the formal answer to those who accuse St.
Thomas of reducing all love to concupiscence:

That a man wishes to enjoy God pertains to that love of God
which is love of concupiscence. Now we love God with the
love of friendship more than with the love of concupiscence,
because the divine good is greater in itself, than our share of
good in enjoying Him. Hence, out of charity, man simply
loves God more than himself.†

Let us now summarize the argument. We love a thing
to the extent that it is good for us. Now the whole is for
the part a greater good for the part than the part is for
itself. Indeed, the unity of the whole is much more profound and far-reaching than that of the part, and ontological unity is the ultimate principle of love. That which
constitutes the unity of the hand as a hand is its organic
function in the body. "A part has no individuality or unity
that can be reckoned on a par with the individuality or
unity of the whole and, therefore, be opposed to it."[61]

Hence, it is clear that the part loves the whole more
than itself. But God is our whole, and this is why we love
Him more than ourselves. Now God is a greater good for
us than the pleasure we take in Him, hence we love God
more than our possession of God. Thus, ultimately, it is
the love of friendship that triumphs.

† *Sum. th.*, 2-2, q. 26, a. 3, ad 3. The same ideas, about the whole and
the part, recur elsewhere, e.g., 1, q. 60, a. 5; 1-2, q. 109, a. 3; 2-2, q. 58,
a. 9, ad 3; 2-2, q. 65, a. 1.— They are always the fruit of concrete observation. One might use the same reasoning to establish the fact that the
individual is more fundamentally attached to the species than to his own
material individuality; cf. *Contra gentiles*, 3, c. 24, 3. An argument, akin
to the explanation of the part for the whole, seems to explain certain
psychological aspects of love better than the argument we have thus far
presented. It is Father DE BROGLIE's often adopted explanation of the
image and of him whom it represents; cf. "Malice intrinsèque du péché,"
part VIII: "La volonté, faculté de l'amour de Dieu," RSR, 26 (1936),
297-333; see also "Charité, synthèse doctrinale," *Dictionnaire de spiritualité*, vol. 2, 1, coll. 661-691.

Does this last distinction correspond to anything in reality? Can we really love God more than our possession of God? Yes, if it is true that love of concupiscence draws its meaning from friendship and is subordinated to it.[62] In this case, we love the possession of God and refer it to Him. We do not possess in order to derive pleasure; on the contrary, we derive pleasure because we possess, and we possess in order to satisfy our love for God. The movement ends in a going forth from self toward God.

It is now easy to understand that, while preferring her own spiritual good above all other created persons, the soul can love the latter as children of God and not merely as reflections of her own self. Even heavenly beatitude assumes a new character, for, in this perspective, the primary motive of the joy of the elect is not the subjective satisfaction of their desire to know and love, but the contemplation of God's beatitude, which they love infinitely more than their own.

How are we to explain, then, the egocentric appearance of the expressions of St. Thomas quoted in this section? Perhaps because of the fact that common experience is the starting point of his analysis.

When he wants to prove that the natural love of an angel for God is greater than his love for himself, he starts his argumentation from the ordinary fact that the hand can expose itself for the protection of the whole body:

Such a natural inclination is evidenced from things which are moved according to nature. . . . For we observe that the part naturally exposes itself in order to safeguard the whole; as, for instance, the hand is without deliberation exposed to the blow for the whole body's safety. And since reason imitates nature, we find the same imitation among the political virtues.[63]

He goes on to apply the same principle to the angelic order. This is to give much credit to common sense experience.

We are thus tempted to take these expressions in the meaning which they have in common experience, without taking into account the new context in which they are introduced. Just as we observe in daily life that love of self is often more egoistic than egocentric, in the same way we are tempted to see an egoistic conception of love in the pages of the *Summa* where there is only question of ordered egocentrism.

Moreover, the type of love ordinarily met in common experience is very often mingled with sensible love, which, in this world of sin, is always associated with concupiscence. There is always the danger of extending to spiritual love the egoism of sensibility.

3. CRITICAL SUMMARY

This analysis of love according to St. Thomas leads us to the following conclusions.

1. Love is the fundamental movement of all beings; the activity of every creature, and hence of man, is then nothing but a specification of this profound ontological love.

2. Seen as the adaptation of being to its end, love is an appetite and expresses a finality. This is why the Thomistic doctrine of love merits the name of physical and ontological theory. But the finality proper to spiritual love is not a determinism; it leaves the will free, and thus can be said to be a moral finality.

3. Of itself, appetite is not synonymous with egoism; on the contrary, it is ecstasy and reference to the object loved. The ultimate metaphysical foundation of this referential character of created love is the unity which the part forms with the whole.

4. Love is love of concupiscence or of friendship depending on whether it takes its object as a means or as an end. Both forms of love can be egocentric or altruistic. For St. Thomas there is no place in a morally good act of will for an absolute disjunction between love referred to self and love referred to another. The proper effect of love is to associate self with the other. Even the elect prefer their own person to that of the other saints, but this preference is always referred to the love of God as to its source.

5. This is why love, according to St. Thomas, must be conceived as communion between persons, that is, an act by which one affectively associates another with himself and wishes that the resulting unity be perfectly accomplished in a common and identical happiness. This tendency will be realized to the extent that the person wishes for himself and the other the possession of God in heavenly beatitude. According to St. Thomas, the ecstatic character of love must be seen in this context. It is to surpass and at the same time to accomplish oneself. Rather than a mere substitution of love of another for natural self-love, it is a positive interest in self and in others together.

6. If certain expressions of St. Thomas give an egoistic appearance to his conception of love, it is because his starting point and his comparisons are taken from common experience, where egoism often dominates. But this does not weaken the metaphysical bearing of his thought.

7. On this ontological plane, St. Thomas, starting from the principle that the part loves the whole more than itself, subordinates and profoundly unites to the love for God all created loves, and especially self-love. In the same way he subordinates love of concupiscence to love of friendship. Communion between persons most adequately expresses the Thomistic conception of love. Human persons are like so many "images" through which we tend to communion with God, and the deepest bond of this communion consists in enjoying, not our happiness in possessing God, but His own

happiness, which we love more than ourselves. We must reread, in this total context, the lines quoted above:

By the fact that love transforms the lover into the beloved, it makes the lover enter inside the beloved, and conversely, so that there is nothing of the beloved that is not united to the lover, just as the form attains the innermost recesses of that which it informs, and conversely.[64]

Love always supposes a complacency of the lover in the beloved. Now when someone takes pleasure in another, he transports himself into that other and joins himself to him as far as possible, so that the other becomes his own; that is why love has the property of uniting lover and beloved.[65]

Few texts better underline the simultaneous unity and otherness of persons, their union without confusion.[66] Even when transported and transformed into the other, the lover sees the beloved become his own, a fact which proves that he still exists as a person. But henceforward his whole tendency is no longer to have an exclusive self nor to love himself first; he can no longer love himself without loving the other in the same act of Love.

II. THEORY OF MORAL FINALITY OF LOVE

It seems preferable to apply this name, as J. Rohmer[67] suggests, to the theory of love often referred to as the ecstatic theory. In fact, St. Thomas himself considers love as an ecstasy. But we will now turn briefly to Franciscan Augustinianism as represented by Duns Scotus, who inherited this doctrine from Anselm and Bonaventure, and somehow also from Hugh of Saint-Victor and Bernard.

Instead of seeing in human love an expression of the universal metaphysical finality of a being tending to its subjective end, which is beatitude, and in order to remove spiritual love from the rank of a mere function of determined nature, and to avoid reducing Christian liberty to the role of a passing and accidental condition of the morality of our acts here below, the Franciscan school and particularly Scotus recognize in the will, the function of love, a total liberty of indifference and spontaneity which is not geared on the metaphysical finality of other natural causes.[68]

The will is not necessitated even in the presence of its sovereign good in the beatific vision.[69] With greater reason it is not determined by the metaphysical order here below. This order exists and constitutes the hierarchy of all natural causes; human nature itself is submitted to it, and the will, inasmuch as it is a power of desire and concupiscence, is inclined to its own perfection.[70] Scotus admits the whole Thomistic ontological order of beatitude. But precisely because the order of free will and human love is distinct from this metaphysical order, it is moral, and not physical or natural; it does not belong to the level of fundamental tendency. From the very beginning of its apprehension, the will is free and determines itself by nothing other than its own spontaneous choice; in this sense, it is not a natural appetite, that is, determined by nature.[71]

If it is true that the supreme subjective good of beatitude leaves the will radically free and that it is not necessarily sought in particular goods, then we must find some other root for moral activity; it is God, now not as an ultimate, relative, and subjective end of our nature, but as an objective, extrinsic end that we must will freely for His infinite perfection, as an obligatory end. Because God is infinitely perfect in Himself, we can have a moral reason, worthy of our free assent, for loving Him.

Love, which is specifically human and moral, does not consent, even freely, to seek its object in yielding to a natural finality or to the hope of beatitude,[72] but its sole motive for acting is to conform itself to divine order because it is objectively perfect.[73]

Love is characterized by generosity: it does not act for

its own good, but rather seeks the loved object because it is good in itself. We would love it even if we found no enjoyment in it.[74] This moral love essentially constitutes beatitude.

Moral love springs from a "disinterested will in the service of reason."[75] First it directs itself toward God; then, if it wills its own perfection, it is not by mere concupiscence, but in order to conform itself to the divine will, which merits perfect love and service;[76] love, finally turning to others, wills for them the good which consists in being perfect before God.[77]

In brief, Scotus has freed moral love—or rather personal and properly human love—from all determinism and even from all finality which would confine it within the limits of a nature. This is why he can conceive moral love as purified from all concupiscence and so strong that it can, by its own force and even after the fall, attain perfect natural charity. Man is thus able to love God with a wholly disinterested love,[78] so that for Scotists charity is the first of the cardinal virtues.[79]

What an ideal foundation for the doctrine of supernatural charity![80] Beatitude, consisting in an act of perfect charity, is fully free; only by extrinsic grace, and not by intrinsic necessity, is the will of the blessed fixed in the impossibility of sinning.[81]

It is easy to understand why this perspective of the Franciscan school has attracted many a spiritual and ascetical soul, and also why it can be interpreted on many points as opposed to the physical theory of love. The latter starts from and leads back to unity, while the former highlights the duality of lover and beloved, the gratuity of the gift, which supposes two persons. "What is love as a habit, if not liberality, . . . and love as an act, if not the gift? . . . But liberality and the gift cannot take place inside one and the same subject."[82] Hence the first quality of love is disinterestedness.

In the Thomistic theory, even from disinterested love does the lover draw profit, namely, his natural perfection. The "ecstatic doctors," on the contrary, insist on self-denial, victory over self, forgetfulness of self; as it appears in the canticles of St. Francis, love is a form of violence, of suffering, of death.

The physical theory tries to explain love by finality. For the ecstatics, love needs no explanation, for it has within itself its own reason for being:

It suffices to itself, it pleases by its own virtue and for its own sake. It is its own merit, its own recompense. Love has no need of a motive or fruit other than itself. Its fruit is its act. I love because I love; I love for the sake of loving.[83]

Even if love is irrational, it is nevertheless intelligible by itself. It is the ultimate end; possession by love is the essence of eternal beatitude.

This "ecstatic theory" explains more conspicuously than the other that character of love which is the gift. It better emphasizes the movement of the will, which is a going forth from self, the subject's attraction toward the object, including a certain renouncement of self. It fosters a better understanding of Christian love, which imitates Christ in His humiliations, self-abasement, and sufferings. It compensates for what seems too rational or natural in the "physical" theory. Apparently it safeguards better the absolute value of person and spirit by conceiving love as justified without being referred to a finality of a determined nature.

However, we think that the chief positive tenets of the ecstatic school—particularly the Franciscan—cannot be opposed to the doctrine of St. Thomas. The latter, as we have seen, is himself an ecstatic: he recognizes that the spontaneity and liberty of moral love are irreducible to the purely physical finality of determined natures; he affirms that even in beatitude love remains free, though necessary. It is clear, then, that, for him as well as for Scotus, there exists a specific moral order organically integrated into the metaphysical. Moreover, St. Thomas maintains that love for God above self is essential to charity; in so doing, he preserves the suprarational and disinterested character of charity and thus is closer to Scotus than is often thought.

But the truths so clearly highlighted by the Scotists are, in fact, less emphasized by St. Thomas. And it is understandable that Suárez could mistake his thought and affirm that the charity of the saints for God, if taken in the Thomistic sense as determined and necessary, cannot be called a moral act.[84]

The Franciscan theology of love, instead of being opposed to the doctrine of St. Thomas on these points, has happily developed them to explicitness. In fact, it has recast and broadened Aristotelianism in a perspective more consistent with the Christian revelation of liberty and love.[85]

On the other hand, in spite of its unquestionable advantages, this doctrine seems to forget that the moral order itself is metaphysical, and must be conceived according to metaphysical laws, that is, according to a finality. Is there not also here a regrettable tendency to disincarnate human spiritual love? If it has no part with nature and its metaphysical finality, there is danger of separating it from love of concupiscence. Is the unity of man not compromised by seeing in him, on the one hand, a being submitted to the animal determinism of appetites centered on beatitude (love of concupiscence), and, on the other hand, a will radically free from all ontological finality and enjoying its own specific moral finality (love of liberality)? Here we are simply following the interpretation of Rohmer himself: "The distinction between natural and moral finality is so emphasized that it creates a sharp gap between the plane of universal, metaphysical causality and that of moral action."[86]

It seems to us more desirable to integrate the richness of Scotistic analysis into Thomistic finality than to insist on their opposition. Without denying the proper movement of both types of love, we must recognize that they are two complementary aspects of a single act.

III. THE SYNTHESIS: LOVE

If we tried to integrate the psychological and moral exigencies of Scotism in a Thomistic metaphysical context, would we not reach an understanding of love which would retain the richness of both traditions?[87]

The mystery of love can be reduced to the mystery of being and unity. St. Thomas teaches that love is the fundamental activity of being. In us, love is nothing but our spiritual being insofar as it is active; there is continuity between being and action just as between first and second act. Love is nothing but the exercise of our being, of our form of being. And so in love we will find the same degrees of analogy that we distinguish in being and action. And since the fundamental activity of any being is to realize the unity proper to it, all love must be an active tendency toward unity, more or less intense, according to its degree of being. In perfect being, love will be the act of unity itself, under the form of a total identification with self.

In the degree of created spirits which is our own, this activity prompts us to more and more intimate union, not only with ourselves, but also with others and with God. In fact, this union with ourselves must be understood as a unity *in fieri* rather than *in esse*, since our form, that of a created human being, is submitted to change and is only capable of imperfect unity. Love, seen as an identification with ourselves, can never be fully realized here below.

Secondly, this need for unity inclines us to union with God. Our being subsists only by virtue of a never ceasing creative influx which sustains it in existence. Its *esse* is *ab alio:* it is intrinsically constituted by a relation of dependence on God, its creator. If it is true that love is but the active aspect of our being, then it is, just like our being, intimately constituted by an actual relation to God. It is the active union of a being whose unity cannot achieve in itself the full circle of its perfection and hence remains essentially open to the divine; actual reference to God is an absolute condition of its existence. There can be no authentic self-love which is not, in the first place, love for God. There is no way of escaping the fact that the ontological cohesion of any being is possible only through actual participation in Being. Our love for God is a more intimate constituent of ourselves than love for our own selves! In other words, the love we have for ourselves is but a participation of the love we have for God's being. And conversely, since our being also participates in God's being, our love is a participation in the love which God has for us.

Finally, there is a third element inscribed in the very nature of love: our human love is necessarily also a tendency to union with other men. In us, the spirit is closely limited and confined to a carnal individuality incapable of developing, or even supporting all the virtualities of our spiritual form; but it retains, nevertheless, a transcendental relation to the totality of this spiritual form, to its richness that cannot be exhausted in the individuals that we are. This ontological richness both requires and explains the multiplicity of human individuals in space and time: it is unthinkable that the human species contain only one man. If such is the exigency of our being, it must also be found in our love. It is inconceivable for human love not to have an essential relation to all beings which participate in the form of humanity. The agent of our union and unity with ourselves and with God, love is also the principle of our communion with others. In his active love-relation with God, man somehow perceives his association with all other beings who share with him and, like him, deficiently realize the same spirit. And since his being maintains a relation to the spirit, as such, and to its material indetermination, his love also retains an active inclination to associate with other human loves, which all ascend unanimously toward God, as so many voices in one harmonious choir.

Starting from this Thomistic ontological base, it seems that we can account for all the characteristics of love already encountered, but only on two conditions: first, that we grasp the meaning of the unity, or better, of the unities which love strives to realize through its essential effort toward communion; and second, that we throw on this ontology the light of revelation, which has disclosed the secret of love and made it the center of the Christian message. In this light, the *velle bonum*, love of concupiscence and of liberality, generosity and Scotist disinterestedness in love—all take on their full meaning.

We will first examine love in its divine Exemplar. We will then pass on to man and study his love for others, for himself, and for God.

I. LOVE IN GOD

Since we are involved here in a process of deduction and not in the dialectics of invention, it seems preferable first to contemplate love at its source, and then go on to consider its deficient participations. The latter will be more easily understood when seen in their ontological origin.

We characterize love at its supreme degree as an act of active identification of a being with itself; this is the highest form of that unity which love ever promotes as the fundamental activity of being. Natural reason presents God as a being who loves His own plenitude and rests in it (*vult bonum sibi*). In Him, love of concupiscence for the divine good which He wishes for Himself coincides identically with the love of liberality which He has for His unique divine reality, for in Him the unity remains absolutely unloosened by any distinction whatsoever. Here love of concupiscence is in no way a desire, since it does not—and, in fact, does not have to—seek an increase of its being. It does not even suppose a reflection of God on Himself, nor any return of love on itself, for this is possible and necessary only in a composite being which is not perfectly identical with itself. If we must reflect in order to be conscious of ourselves, it is because our being is not identical with luminous consciousness; and if we need some kind of reflection in order to love ourselves, it is because our love is not identical with our being and is ever running up against the latter's limits. Just as knowledge, love, in God, is simple and direct, forward-reaching in one continuous stream that knows no bounds. Even the expression "to go out from oneself" cannot be strictly applied to God, for it supposes limits to be crossed. It is impossible to go out of infinity. Natural reason discovers divine love neither as a going out from nor a turning back on self, but as simple and serene diffusion from an infinitely luminous and generous source.

When He creates *liberrimo consilio*, it is still in virtue of love, for love is the active aspect of being, and creation is the only divine activity which reason can detect in the finite world. When He creates, God manifests absolutely gratuitous love which pre-exists its object and even produces its lovability without any possible enrichment on the part of the Creator. He creates images of Himself capable in their own way of being sources of conscious love, and in this consists His glory, the only possible end of creation.

This rational view might insinuate a sort of egoism in divine Being, seen in its solitude, but this is only an appearance. There can be no question of disorder in the self-love of a necessary Being who cannot but love Himself infinitely.

But Jesus Christ came to reveal something entirely new concerning love in God. Not only does God have love, but He is *agapè* (1 Jn. 4:8), which St. Thomas interprets in saying: "Ipsa essentia divina caritas est."[88] Jesus explains and shows by His whole life and death the meaning of divine charity (Jn. 15:13). In fact, they were the natural sequence to what He revealed about the nature of love. In reality, there is no solitude in God. Divine life is a society of persons. Absolute Being subsists eternally in an exchange of love. The Father generates the Word as the perfect image of Himself, thus communicating to Him the totality of the divine nature, and only in this act of paternity is He distinguished from the Son. Since They possess in common a love which is the substance of Their lives, Their whole activity consists in allowing personified Love to proceed from Them as an ecstasy.*

Absolute love, the type of all created loves, is, therefore, revealed to our faith as a will achieving communion between persons, a will wishing the same good to the other as to itself in such a way that none of the persons wishes to keep for himself alone the divine good. To say that the Father loves and glorifies Himself (Jn. 12:28), evidently

---

* G. SALET, S.J., "Le mystère de la charité divine," RSR, 28 (1938), 22; cf. T. L. PENIDO, "Gloses sur la procession d'amour dans la Trinité," ETL, 14 (1937), 33–68. We do not wish thereby to suggest that the processions of the Son and of the Holy Spirit are both processions of love. In God, intellect and will are neither distinct from each other, nor from the divine substance. God acts by His very substance. To say that the Word proceeds by way of intellection does not imply that love is absent from His generation, even if it be not its formal element (cf. Jn. 5:20), nor that the luminous quality of intellection is absent from the procession of the Spirit of Truth (cf. Jn. 14:17). If the intellect in God generates, is it not because it is one with love? Our own intellect can only understand its knowledge of real being because it is dynamic, that is, because it lives on our fundamental tendency of love.

excluding any reflexive love—has no meaning if we do not understand at the same time that He loves and glorifies the Son and the Spirit in the same act of love by which He loves Himself, since His goodness is numerically one with that of the other divine persons. Generation and active spiration, which are operations of giving, are the only intratrinitarian activities revealed to us. Passive spiration is love considered in its fruit rather than in its source; the Holy Spirit, which is the mutual gift of the spirating persons, does not withdraw within Himself, for, as a person, He is not distinct from the love of the Father and of the Son. He is the subsistent love of the Father and of the Son united in a single activity. He is then a subsistent activity of communion. Thus that alone is proper to each person which makes Him relative to the two others: paternity, filiation, and spiration. All that is not relation is common to the three and strictly identical in them.

This double communication, this mutual intratrinitarian gift, is absolutely gratuitous, since one operation engenders, and the other causes to proceed, a person in such a way that the person is not logically prior to the operation itself, even though they are equally eternal. Hence this operation is not attracted by the lovability of its term; love in the Trinity is totally gratuitous, even though absolutely necessary.

The depths of the nature of love revealed in the mystery of the Trinity as a communion between persons in the strict unity of a nature has caused Blondel to exclaim:

To love oneself in sincerely loving another; to give oneself and duplicate self in this gift; to see oneself as another in one's own self and to see oneself in another; not to be solitary and yet to be alone; to be united and embraced in distinction; to have all in common without any confusion and to remain two in order to ceaselessly fuse both as in a single whole and a single being . . . such is the natural cry of the heart.[89]

The most perfect and generous longings of our human hearts are, in fact, realized in a manner we cannot even imagine, so far does it surpass the possibilities of human conception and realization! Here unity is perfect, for the substance is numerically one; and yet the persons remain really distinct, so that unity is in no way equivalent to confusion. It is impossible to conceive a more profound communion—or even a more total one, for here all that is absolute in each person He communicates to the others; only the relative element which is the real foundation of this personal community is proper to each person. Love is entirely gratuitous, egoism impossible, because the object is loved infinitely without any turning back on self; any form of duplicity is unthinkable where simplicity is perfect. And yet this total gift of all He possesses absolutely in no way deprives the person of what He gives, for obviously He cannot part with His own substance. But this substance is common to the Three Persons and undivided. In the Trinity, all that richness found in us under the form of distinct faculties of intellect and will is common to the Three Persons to such a degree that no one Person can have a thought or an affection that is not shared with the Others. *Velle alicui bonum* is here identical with *velle se alteri* and *velle sibi alterum;* in both cases, that which is willed is the totally beatifying good. Human intelligence could never have contrived such a doctrine of love. And even after revelation, the proper mode of the Trinity and of the love of God remains a strict mystery.*

---

* G. DE BROGLIE, S.J., "Du caractère mystérieux de notre élévation surnaturelle," NRT, 64 (1937), 337–376. It is significant that during recent years several works have appeared, consecrated to the study of the mystery of the Trinity under its aspect of mystery of love; for example: A. GRAHAM, O.S.B., *The Love of God*, London, 1939; R. JOHANN, S.J., *The Meaning of Love*, Westminster, Md., 1955; M. C. D'ARCY, S.J., *The Mind and Heart of Love*, New York, 1945; C. V. HÉRIS, O.P., *Le mystère de Dieu*, Paris, 1946; and J. H. NICOLAS, O.P., *Connaître Dieu*, Paris, 1947, not to mention the numberless articles on charity that have appeared since

2. LOVE IN MAN

Even if revelation alone gives us this new insight into the trinitarian being of God, nevertheless, every being, because it is a participation of this Being, must bear in itself traces of the Trinity. This does not mean that we can understand or even discover the mystery of God by starting from creatures, for the proper mode of the divine Being totally escapes us; only after revelation are we authorized to transfer analogically into God the intimate structure of human being. But now, taking revelation as a starting point and always keeping an existential outlook on reality, we can draw from what is revealed to us its logical consequence, namely, the trinitarian constitution of being. We can say that in his very nature man participates in trinitarian being so that "etiam homo totius Trinitatis sit imago."[90] The proof: intelligence and will in the unity of a spiritual person. Such is the so-called "Augustianian explanation" of the Trinity.

It is not difficult to find in every degree of being and even at the material extreme of the universe traces of a participation in the love of the Trinity. Is it not a ternary rhythm that seems to be the basic movement founding the cohesion of the material universe: a going forth from self always led back to unity? All the rhythms of our world— that of the sun, that of the days and seasons, of lives growing and declining, that of ebb and flow, that of respiratory beings, that of all types of waves and their harmonies, even the alternations of illumination and dryness in the mystical soul, the balance between spiritual expansion and recollection, all these are submitted to one fundamental rhythm which tends to the giving, or so to say, the unfolding of self into two, followed by the coming back to self in unity;

---

the war. They surely fill a providential need and offer the only hope of salvation for our industrial age by attempting to restore to love its true, all-embracing role in our lives.

such is the fundamental melody of the material universe trying in its own way to take up the theme of love reflected from the Trinity.[91]

But we will not insist on the possible occurrences of this trinitarian structure in the material extremity of the world, so little penetrated by our intelligence. It suffices to recall the words of St. Thomas: "Omnia appetunt assimilari Deo."[92] And Bergson affirms that "nothing prevents the philosopher from pushing to its limit the idea, suggested to him by mysticism, of a universe which would be nothing but the visible and tangible aspect of love and of the need for loving."[93] And again, "The fundamental note of the universe is a note of generosity."[94]

When it reaches man, the participation of love attempts to reproduce an image of the trinitarian society in a society of incarnate spirits. Thus manifestations of human love, until now contradictory, become intelligible: between lovers there is a tendency to unity which, nevertheless, respects the irreducible duality of their spiritual personalities.*

a) *Love of man for man.* There is an infinite distance separating the divine Exemplar and His participations in man. Instead of a strict unity of nature and substance result-

---

* "The relation between God's charity for us and fraternal charity is more strongly emphasized [in St. John] than in the theology of St. Paul. The movement or river of charity flows from the eternity of God and terminates in the fraternal charity of Christians who are thus identified with the divine unity. The exercise of fraternal charity is, therefore, the blossoming of this divine movement of charity: still more clearly than in Pauline theology, charity appears as an element belonging at once to this world and to eternity. Charity is the completion par excellence of celestial realities, for charity is God (for God is love) present and realizing His presence. It is in this sense that the charity of God reaches its full stature (*teteleiôtai*) in those who keep true to the word of Christ (1 Jn. 2:5), when they love one another (1 Jn. 4:12 and 17), and when they are made perfectly one with Him (Jn. 17:23)" (L. Cerfaux, "La charité fraternelle et le retour du Christ," ETL, 24 [1948], 329–330).

ing not only in the possession of a common good but also
in the numerical unity of their being, here we find only the
generic unity of humanity scattered among distinct individuals which are further separated by matter. What is
more, each human person is not completely unified in himself. Even his essence suffers from being extended in space
and time. At any given moment, we can only be fully
present to one part or phase of ourselves. And if we are
not fully present even to ourselves, how can we be totally
present to another spirit, especially if this spirit is incarnate
and thus suffers the same dispersion? While the gift of God
is total, in us it can only be partial. The good which we
will to the other, our contribution to mutual communion, is
very far from being the total good; it is even very far from
being the good which is our total person.†

Again, the distance between divine and human love
becomes more striking when we consider their mode of
communication. In the Trinity, each person communicates
to the others all that is absolute in Him, keeping as His own
only the relation which constitutes Him as giving or given,
for the person as such is a pure relation, and everything in
Him that is not relative is common in the three; at the same
time He loses nothing in this communication, since the
good communicated remains rigorously common.

But human substances are separated from one another,
and even in the most intimate moments of friendship what
remains proper to us is more than a pure relation which
would distinguish self from friend as giving from given.
Besides, there is the fact that incarnate persons never

---

† Rightly, we should here study at length the "reciprocity of conscience" or of personal subjects, in order to discover the ontological root
of our relations with others and thus go beyond the individual and social
point of view. But for the moment we have not the time required for
such a study. We refer the reader to the works of M. NÉDONCELLE; see
especially *La réciprocité des consciences*, Paris, 1942, and *Vers une philosophie de l'amour*, Paris, 1946.

become fully transparent to the eyes of the spirit if this spirit be not God Himself; because of their sensible constitution, something in them always remains egocentric; at least they always oppose to another their spatial exteriority, for perfect fusion would mean alienation of self and hence death. "Bodies are in a strange state of solitude; all that has been said about the union is nothing in comparison with the separation which they cause."[95] This remark applies to love between human persons, but not to our love for God, for God is more intimate to us than ourselves. We will come back to this point later.

We have already pointed out that in God love is entirely gratuitous and that the persons do not seek personal enrichment in the procession of another person from themselves. For this reason more than any other, no egoism is possible in God. But for human loves, on the contrary, rooted as they are in indigence, the object loved is necessarily sought in view of personal enrichment. There is nothing wrong in this, for sincere love sees in this enrichment a first communication of God or of the beloved, a prelude to communion. Love even finds in it a way of unifying its natural dispersion and of thus becoming able to contribute to this communion a sufficiently concentrated and rich ego. But love becomes egoistic when it ceases to see this enrichment as a phase of communion and refers it to the ego as an absolute. We know very well that our love finds all too many connivances in our sensibility and concupiscence favoring this type of self-idolatry. Another type of idolatry consists in giving to a human being an unlimited love due only to God.

These remarks indicate the distance between our love and that of the divine Exemplar. But our love is a real participation of love as it is in God, and this singular resemblance gives any value they have to our human affections, for however imperfect it may be, our love remains an

authentic communion. The conditions of relative solitude
in which it is realized account for that characteristic pain
which is almost constitutive of all human love. In fact,
there is a very beautiful proof for the existence of God to
be found in man's longing for total communion possible
only in divine unity. This pain becomes even sharper when
man discovers in himself the egoism of concupiscence,
which is so opposed to the gratuity of true love. Because of
these limits, all profound love is flavored with humility.
Since there is in love a trace of divine gratuity causing it to
overlook the limitations of the beloved while being keenly
conscious of its own poverty, humility is here always
nuanced with admiration and gratitude to the other, who
gives himself and is transfigured by our love.[96] We have
here an image of the Father's admiration for His Word,
splendor Patris; image also of the perfect gratitude of the
Son for the Father's diffusive plenitude;[97] image, finally, of
the Spirit, the ecstasy of love.

True communion realized in human love consists in
taking full consciousness—direct rather than reflex—of the
pre-existing unity by which we communicate in being with
our fellow men. We will see later how this unity is further
strengthened through fraternity in Christ. Such a unity is
not founded merely on knowledge, but on an affective and
volitive tendency which becomes present to us through
knowledge. In the affective and cognitive whole of our
spiritual consciousness, love creates, in place of the consciousness of the self, the consciousness of "us" wherein the
"I" and the "you" are intimately joined.

Ontologically speaking, the "I" will not have to suppress itself or to renounce its spiritual destiny, for it also
is spirit and there would no longer be communion if it
ceased to be present. Hence it is established that the "I"
does not disappear in communion. But how can we account
for the other-centeredness, the ecstasy, the generosity, the

tendency toward the gift of self, which are, undoubtedly, essential to the psychology of love even when it is realized in men? This, we recall, was delicately pointed out by St. Thomas. Here again ontology comes to our aid. We have already recognized that our spiritual being, limited as it is in carnal individuality, retains a transcendental relation to all other individuals which realize the multiple virtualities of the total spirit, which our "I" can only partly express. It is normal that the "I," in becoming conscious of self, becomes no less conscious of this personal insufficiency which puts him in connection with all others of his kind and even causes the voices of these others to echo in him much like cries of persons in need. Self-consciousness, if it is at all profound, includes, at least implicitly, consciousness of others. Here we understand consciousness in the wide sense adopted earlier.

Love of the neighbor, inasmuch as it is communion, causes us to prefer, in this consciousness, attention to the other; it causes us to prefer, in this total conscious tendency which constitutes our being, the aspect of tendency to the other. Not that it involves renouncement of all conscious adhesion to self, for this is only too intensely present to our intellect and will and too exclusively emphasized by our concupiscence. This is why, in practice, communion appears in consciousness principally as a going forth from what is exclusive, egoistic, and falsely absolute in self; it inevitably, as it were, involves the giving of self, the abandonment of excessive egocenteredness which is connatural in us since Adam's sin. Love is truly an ecstasy which causes us to go forth from carnal self, with which we are easily tempted to identify ourselves because our sensibility is so infected by egoism. This is why love normally appears as an abnegation, a sacrificing of our temporal interests, and hence as gratuitous and disinterested—an attempt to attain, in its own way, the perfect gratuity of divine love. This is even more obvious when we consider that the mutual exteriority of lover and beloved, the limitation of their individualities requires that once a perfection has been brought to one by love it be somehow lacking to the other.[98]

These observations permit us to understand and to easily adopt the more appealing aspects of Scotus' doctrine, namely—the ecstasy, the moral finality, and the gratuity of love, without being forced to accept his defective metaphysics and certain other negative characteristics of his philosophy. They further permit us to highlight the necessity of insisting on the generosity of love, for man spontaneously prefers himself to any other. Here there is no risk of forcing our ontology, for it is not self, but the excess of self that is suppressed. In this perspective we also become aware, in a more metaphysical and, as we shall see, in a more Christian manner, of the fact that our being is relative to that of others and even more so to that of God.

To love is to abandon this self instinctively locked in isolation, in order to rediscover the genuine ontological self, which is necessarily the center of a whole network of relations. Under its psychological aspect, love is then the gaining or regaining of consciousness of our being. Union or communion with others exists in our being in first act before we are conscious of it. Love, being above all an act of the will, even more than it is a content of consciousness, leads this pre-existing potency into second act. Hence love contributes something real to our ontological unification itself; it fastens a new link and so achieves a further deepening of self, for our being is that of a free person and realizes itself through free and conscious activity. What reaches the consciousness of the lover is not merely the pre-existing ontological datum, but the latter appears already modified and enriched by the act of love, which thus participates in the creative power of God, for it is a completion of being.

It is not surprising that conjugal love, the privileged form of human love, terminates in the generation of a new being wherein father and mother discover, in the unity of one personal being, their mutual gift. But this personal unity, fruit of their love, is not, as in God, their love itself personified; it is a loved person, for human love cannot be so intense as to become subsistent.[99] In the same way, all spiritual loves create a new spiritual unity wherein we are transported into one another; the thoughts and ideals of the one become the thoughts and ideals of the other, for the spirit has this property of being permeable to another spirit and of being limited in this intimacy only by its carnal condition. Again, to transport oneself means to establish a new ontological link which will be finally fastened by free will; or, in other words, it is to make the effort which will permit us to coincide with the spiritual interiority of another, with his thoughts and affections.

This ontological approach throws light on the classical distinction between love of concupiscence and love of friendship. We have seen that in God these two forms differ only by a distinction of reason, for the good which the divine Persons will for one another is identified with Their proper Person as well as with the Person of the other. Because of their substantial multiplicity and irresistible tendency to consider themselves as individual unities, human lovers, when they give their attention and affection to the other, consider their own self as a possession which they bring to the beloved and, conversely, they consider the beloved as an object to be possessed. The lack of unity between beings accentuates both psychologically and ontologically the distinction between these two forms of love. But it is obvious that love of friendship formally realizes communion, which is so characteristic of love, since the type of possession proper to love of concupiscence is only a means of realizing this communion. Though it is a necessary and even an essential means, love of concupiscence nevertheless remains a love *secundum quid*, as St. Thomas puts it.

b) *Love of man for himself.* Until now we have directed our attention to human love for the other, with whom it achieves communion. We will now see that genuine love for self also has an aspect of true communion.

We can only love ourselves according to the degree of our being. But we subsist essentially by virtue of a relation to God, who creates us at each moment, and we are inserted into a complex network of relations binding us to the world of spirits and bodies. This ontological situation does not permit complete exclusiveness in our self-love. We can only have for ourselves a relative love which is essentially open to the love of God and of other men; our self-love can be absolute only to the extent that it meets an absolute in us, that is, the creative presence of God who constitutes us in being. When we take up the subject of charity, we will see that the divine presence is amazingly close to us and that we can have for God, our neighbor, and ourselves the same theological love.

In this relative and open self-love there is no egoism; egocentricity remains, but is ordered to communion. Communion with ourselves seems to involve an improper use of an expression reserved to union with another. It is identity with self, adhesion to self, but on condition that self be such that we can be present to it and at the same time be present to God and others. Self-love becomes egoistic the moment that it forgets this relation. Since original sin, our sensibility forgets it automatically and so is said to be the seat of concupiscence. Our spiritual love, in the measure that it imitates superficial common experience, is instinctively tempted to make self an absolute, an individuality with a separated reality. In this measure, it depends almost exclusively on sensibility. If we abstracted from the power of supernatural charity, we would all live in this more or less conscious idolatry of self. In the world (as opposed to the new creation), this egoism is practically universal, for this world obeys its instincts.* Charity appears there as a miracle. Just as genuine love is the fabric of all moral life, in like manner, egoism is the fundamental constituent of all sin.[100] Every sin is some form of egoism. Because of its specific attitude, it is the only obstacle to communion; it is opaqueness and isolation introduced into the luminous exchange of love which is the very stuff of the created universe.

If these considerations are true, ordered self-love forbids us to love ourselves without, at the same time, loving some other. To love ourselves as humble participations of God is to love God more than ourselves in the very act in which we love ourselves. And in loving ourselves as bound to others by a necessary relation, we implicitly allow them to participate in the love which we have for ourselves. It is impossible to take ourselves as exclusive objects of love without parting from the universal order, precisely because we participate in trinitarian love wherein a person cannot love himself without loving the others.

We must also love our neighbor as ourselves in this metaphysical sense. This means that love of neighbor is a condition of ordered self-love. This is very important when applied to our concrete state as sinners. If it is true that we must struggle against the egoism of uncontrolled self-love, and that only by going forth from self toward others and toward God are we liberated from this egoism, then we

* E. DE GREEFF, *Notre destinée et nos instincts* (Paris, 1945), describes well what our instincts can lead us to when they are left to themselves. But our spiritual tendencies and especially our supernatural gifts permit us to be less pessimistic; thanks to these gifts, Christian personality is able to influence human destinies.

must admit that love for others is the most practical form of love for ourselves.

c) *Love of man for God.* When the "other" is God, our love takes on a very particular significance from the onto-logical point of view. Here trinitarian love is more perfectly imitated than in the love of one man for another. Here our carnal individuality no longer prevents the penetration of the divine spirit, for He is more intimately present in things than their very being. Communion can become more perfect. We can subsist ontologically only by virtue of this communion; morally and psychologically it becomes effi-cacious in the measure that we make it more intensely present in us. Our attention and adhesion to it can only take place during the "present moments" which ceaselessly succeed one another. But these moments can be so concen-trated that they seem to escape time and bring into con-sciousness our spiritual depths, retaining, as it were, some scraps of the past. Besides, is it not true that the present contains our whole accumulated past?

Whether we like it or not, there is no communion so indispensable for us as that with God. It pre-exists onto-logically, but becomes truly human only if we freely ratify it, and if, by acts of love, we fulfill it in the measure that God has left it open to our cooperation. Here again we participate in a creative power.

Still more than our love for men, our love for God ap-pears as a going forth from self, as a gift and an ecstasy, for God's role in our being and action is so preponderant and constitutive, so continuous and intimate that we never quite succeed in giving Him His true place in our love. We always find a dose of self-idolatry in our love when we weigh it before God.

Love for God is also more enriching than love for men. The act of giving ourselves consists in freely ratifying our ontological bond with God; it is an act wherein we deliberately disfavor self in making God the center of our consciousness and tendencies. This act is an invasion of self by God, perfectly fulfilling our fundamental needs, for it puts us in contact with the source of our being, or better, it is an opening of self to total being. To give or to refer ourselves to our Creator is to live consciously and deliberately the act of receiving ourselves from His hands.

When we give what we have, we seem to lose what we give, and, in fact, we do lose it to the extent that we must part from it; but when we give spiritually what we are, the gift is as much an irruption of the other into an interiority hitherto closed in on itself, as a presence of the "I" in the other. This act is most characteristic of the spirit, inasmuch as the latter means openness, unlimitedness, and the property of being a center of consciousness and tendency able to coincide with other like centers. Communion is the least inadequate expression to convey this effort toward coincidence in knowledge and affection.[101] Coincidence does not imply simple identification, for otherwise it would suppress love or reduce it to an adhesion of some new being, born of this fusion, to self. The "we" resulting from communion does not suppose so much an actual unity as the very act of unifying beings which remain irreducibly distinct. But what love seeks is not to distinguish, but to transform each of these beings into a relation to the other, and this relation is intended to be as pure and voluntary as possible. Thus created love imitates its exemplar, the *agapè* which takes place between persons who are subsistent relations. In a genuine psychology of love, the "we" cannot consider the interests of the one separately from the interests of the other; it stigmatizes as egoistic any exclusive turning back on self. The one cannot help seeing in himself an image of the other, and he cannot direct his attention toward the other without seeing himself there as in a mirror. It is in this movement of communion that the lover most fully realizes his spiritual and interior nature. For only then does the person escape the limits set up by ego-centered self and the opaqueness of separated individuality, which so resembles the material beings of the universe, scattered as they are and opaque to one another. When one is essentially relative, he possesses himself only by communicating with others.

This is singularly true in love wherein God is involved. Love which directs us toward Him at the same time directs us toward what is most interior and profound in us: our very being as it springs from its source. If we love God at all, we can only see ourselves as images of Him; we no longer want to see ourselves otherwise than in God, without whom we are not truly intelligible. In other words, our whole desire is to see and love only God and thereby realize the only self-love which can correspond to our spiritual nature and fulfill it.

But why are we comparing love for God with love for the neighbor? Is it not because love for others is as it were the form of love for God proportioned to our carnal being? "For how can he who does not love his brother, whom he sees, love God, whom he does not see?" (1 Jn. 4:20) The going forth from a closed self, required for communion with images of God, is really the first step toward an opening of self to divine communion. This is fully realized in Jesus Christ, since He is God inserted into humanity; now we can really love God when we love man in Christ. The second commandment is like to the first and even occupies more place than it in the New Testament.[102] Christians love their neighbor and God with the same theological love. The true measure of our love for God is our love for our neighbor, for the latter requires concrete acts which rid us of our egoistic self, whereas love for God separated from love for others can very easily be content with words or sentiments and leave egoistic self comfortably sunk in its illusions.

Can we say that love considered under its ontological aspect still realizes the definition *velle alicui bonum?* It seems rather that this definition is cast in a broader context and expresses the determined moral and psychological aspect of this profound communion. In communion I wish the good of the common "we" rather than the good of the "I" and "you" separately. It cannot be said that I wish to refer the "you" (or any other good) to the "I" as a means in view of my happiness. And, properly speaking, it cannot be said either that I wish to refer the "I" (or some other good) to the "You" as a pure means for the latter's happiness. No doubt the one is a good for the other, and conversely. But communion is more than a *velle bonum* wherein it looks as if a thing were wished for the other or for oneself, for love pertains to the order of personal relations. In love we are less interested in bringing to the other a good to be possessed than in wishing that he be in a relation of communion with us and with God. It can be said that the expression *velle alicui bonum* is the translation, in terms of objects, of this reality experienced above all as a state of relations between persons, who cannot be possessed as mere things but can, and, in fact, do spiritually communicate. The enjoyment of union, the *bonum* in the definition, is not so much a constitutive element of communion as it is its atmosphere or its necessary effect.*

* Our statement would no longer be true if one were to understand the enjoyment of union in the sense of "beatitude," where it would not be distinct from obtaining our end (cf. *Sum. th.*, 1–2, q. 3, aa. 1 and 4). This is evidently a sense it can have. But here we understand it rather as an element distinct from the obtaining of our end, as the enjoyment or delight that accompanies or follows the possession of our end and can be the object of a distinct concupiscent desire (cf. *Sum. th.*, 1–2, q. 3, a. 4; q. 4, a. 1; q. 4, a. 2, corpus and ad 3).

We did not have to broach the technical problem of what formally constitutes beatitude. But the question does arise in a Thomistic, eudaemonistic moral theology, whether charity, which holds the primacy in moral life here below, is not to yield this primacy to beatitude in heaven. In our perspective, it seems that the answer should be formulated as follows.

Communion with God is the end toward which we tend. Here below it comprises, under its ontological aspect, principally grace which "divinizes" our substance and which is ever active through the theological virtues: charity permits us already actively and immediately to realize communion with God, while hope causes us to count on God Himself to attain it. The light of faith permits our intellect, once it has been "affectively moved," to enter also, however obscurely, into contact with God.

Ultimately, grace becomes glory; but charity remains (1 Cor. 13:8); faith gives way to the light of glory. This definitive communion fully realizes the conditions of beatitude, for its essence is the *consecutio finis ultimi* (*Sum. th.*, 1–2, q. 3, a. 4). What is specifically new in beatitude is the vision of God through the light of glory which divinizes the intellect. And this is why beatitude is formally specified by the vision which is an act of the intellect (*ibid.*), causing us consciously to possess the ultimate end. But the "total possession," or total beatitude, is much more extensive and profound than this "intellectual" act of vision. This vision is rather its conscious, luminous aspect, which totalizes our ontological communion with God through love. The latter thus plays a preponderant role.

Acceptance of the Thomistic position does not seem to imply that charity must yield its primacy to beatitude.

Moreover, the very act by which the intellect possesses God is not an act "adequately distinct" from the act of the will. In fact, as Father MARÉCHAL notes, in every act of knowledge—and we would say in every act of explicit love—the intellect and the will mutually penetrate one another. "Voluntas et intellectus mutuo se includunt," says St. Thomas (*Sum. th.*, 1, q. 16, a. 4, ad 1; q. 87, a. 4; cf. J. MARÉCHAL, *Le point de départ de la métaphysique,* cahier V, 1st ed., pp. 298–304, and n. 2; 2nd ed., pp. 403–410, 416, n. 1.

In this reciprocal causality of our two functions, a faculty such as will or intellect is not an *id quod* but an *id quo;* the will is the dynamism of a form and the intellect is the form of a dynamism. This form, it is true, has its own proper act, the luminous act of "consciousness," an act which is transparent to itself, an act, in brief, irreducible to appetite. But consciousness itself or its quality of luminosity coincides with the possession of the object; and this possession, which is the essence of beatitude, is the work of the intellect subtended by the tendency of the will, or of the form subtended by the appetite; it results from the reciprocal causality of intellect and will.

Ontologically, therefore, beatitude is the communion which we have been discussing in this chapter, but it is so, formally, as fully possessing its object by taking consciousness of itself and of its object by means of the light of glory; communion and the light of glory are mutually interdependent.

Cf. Th. DEMAN, O.P., "Eudémonisme et charité en théologie morale,"

Happiness, thus considered as enjoyment, is not love; it is not even the end of true love, for this end is communion, which suffices to itself. But he who loves is necessarily happy. In our present state as *viatores*, it is normal that we are led to communion-love by the desire for the pleasure which it promises. Sensible love, because it is concupiscent, is obviously attracted by the happiness corresponding to it. But it cannot arrive at communion by its own power. Spiritual love, unless it is very purified as among mystics and saints, often needs to be attracted by some elevated and well-ordered happiness if it is to effectively struggle against spiritual and sensible egoism. Happiness, in the sense just defined, is not an ultimate end and thus lends itself to play the role of a means to attain a more perfect love. When we take this true happiness as the object of our will, we are driven beyond this object by its very movement, without egoistically stopping at it. In fact, this happiness directs our attention toward the personal communion which creates it.

Is this not to say that love considered as personal communion lies beyond the distinction between love of concupiscence and love of friendship? Are these not merely two aspects of one complex reality distinguished by an intelligence which needs many concepts to exhaust such a rich object?[103]

Once communion is put at the base of moral life, it must necessarily personalize the latter to a degree which can be attained only through love. In spiritual love are found at once the spontaneity of liberty answering to an individual vocation, and the irreducible depth of consciousness which is nothing but the presence of the substance to itself while

---

ETL, 29 (1953), 41–57. Father DEMAN, in a context quite different from our own, studies this problem of conciliating the primacy of charity with that of beatitude in the moral theology of St. Thomas. He refers to A. MANSION, "L'eudémonisme aristotélicien et la morale thomiste," *Xenia philosophica* (Rome, 1925), pp. 429–449.

still being a presence through communion to the other. Are not these necessary to the integral constitution of the person? And is it not in this way that the truest image of the divine persons, foundation of our human personalities, is traced in us? In its trinitarian exemplar the spiritual person is infinite, free from any determination; it is conscious communion in its purest possible form. In us, personality is limited by individuality. But these limits are not obstacles, provided they are surpassed by an ever-renewed option.

Moral doctrine should present each action as an inchoate personal relation with men and with God, as an answer to a call addressed to me alone. This is to replace the hard mask of law with a living face. How many men, still not humble enough to comply with the demands of a legislator, would joyfully accept the most austere abnegation in order to answer the call of a friend!

§III. In the Christian This Love Is Charity

In the preceding pages, we have not explicitly distinguished between the natural and the supernatural in speaking of human love. We will now take a last step and explain that in the just this profound love is transformed into charity. It is the supernatural presence of God's own love in the natural principle of love, so that the just man cannot love without his love being divinized by charity.

1. THE PRIMACY OF CHARITY

Theology establishes that nothing in the just escapes the elevation of his being to participation in divine life. Just as the soul is divinized in its substance by sanctifying grace, so too is it divinized in its faculties by the theological virtues, in the will by charity and hope, in the intelligence by faith.[104] Together with these virtues and habitual grace, a whole spiritual organism is infused in the soul.[105]

Thus charity is the intrinsic elevation of our principle of action. Sanctifying grace is not a substance added to our substance, but a completion and deepening of our being which renders this substance capable of being divinized while remaining integrally itself. Grace "is ourselves, but ourselves inasmuch as we are divinized";[106] so too charity is our principle of action inasmuch as it is divinized. It is indeed we who act, but also God acting with us.

What is this active principle that is elevated by charity? The common doctrine holds that it is the will,[107] the rational appetite whose first movement is love: "Primus . . . motus voluntatis et cujuslibet appetitivæ virtutis est amor."[108] Taking into account another text, where St. Thomas sees in love an act of the will which "presupposes an affective union,"[109] we are inclined not to limit the principle of action—or of love, which amounts to the same —to this determined faculty which decides only under the light of clear reason and is usually referred to as explicit will. We would rather consider as our principle of action the whole ensemble which the explicit will forms with its deep-reaching roots.

Even if we cannot say that our being acts by its very essence, even if our being is so little identified with itself that it needs a principle distinct from its essence in order to act,[110] nevertheless we must recognize that the profound dynamism of which we are speaking is already the principle of our action, perhaps precisely at the point where it springs from our essence, although at this point it has not yet attained the clear light of reflex consciousness. In fact, our very substance tends to complete itself by its faculties, just as these faculties tend to their perfection through acts. Hence charity extends its divinizing influence even unto the depths whence it springs from sanctifying grace; no part of our spiritual organism escapes this contact with God to which our total being is elevated.

On the supernatural plane, charity plays the role of the will understood in this wider sense or, better, it is this will insofar as it is divinized.[111] Just as the will, in moral activity, commands all the active powers,[112] so charity commands the powers now that they are divinized.[113] This Thomistic perspective is decidedly ontological: the activity of charity in moral life does not depend on an intention extrinsically added.[114] For the Christian in the state of grace, all good voluntary activity is necessarily elicited by a divinized will, that is to say, by charity-love.

II. FURTHER DEPTHS OF CHARITY

We have tried at some length, in the preceding section, to grasp the meaning of love: its mysterious roots have led us to communion with God, and its extension to communion with men and the universe. Love intensifies our relations with Creator and creatures. Now how can supernatural charity delve deeper in this abyss?

Does supernatural life mean anything else than a more intense communication of the living God Himself? We must be what we are in some infinite manner and yet remain ourselves—for we have been divinized.[115]

Instead of giving us merely to be ourselves, as He does in creation, God gives us to be, in some way, Himself. "Since God is being itself, He grants man to be more fully, infinitely more fully; in other words, since to be means to be self and to be in oneself, God gives us the possibility of being more fully, more totally ourselves and in ourselves."[116]

That which sanctifying grace produces in our substance, charity produces in our will; it permits us to love, that is, to enter into communion with God and with others, not in our own limited way, but with God's love itself. Over and above the relations which creatures can realize in imitation of the Trinity, charity realizes between us bonds which the divine Persons Themselves establish in us when They love through our own love. Charity somehow transfers trinitarian love into us, or rather transfers us into it. And when we love someone with charity, we enter with him into a communication like to that of the Father with the Son, or of the Father and the Son with the Spirit. Just as the common possession of the divine nature and beatitude fundamentally constitutes the unity of the Trinity, so charity consists in willing the union of ourselves with others and with God according to the mode of beatific vision which is a participation in life and happiness proper to God. Already here below, charity establishes a contact of love which will continue in heaven, when faith will give way to vision face to face. Such unimaginable interiority pertains not to the psychological, but to the ontological order. Such is the range of our love of charity, which is "super-love."

It is obvious that this divine love bestowed on us becomes our own in some real manner, and so incurs a limitation, although at the same time retaining its infinity. It is useless to try to inclose in our concepts this love whose one pole is so closely in contact with God that it is God Himself, while its other pole is identified with our love; for it is a created charity whose whole novelty consists in changing and adapting us to the divine. We can never represent to ourselves more than its created aspect. This does not prevent us from conceiving it as a relation between two terms actually united, in terms not of their distinction but of their active union; in brief, it must be conceived as "a being of union."[117]

Our human love, insofar as it is elevated by charity, is precisely this created aspect of divine charity. Here more than ever, divinized human love must be presented as a mediation of divine charity. For example, we witness an outflow of divine charity whenever we see a Christian mother devoting herself to her sick child or a Christian father forgiving his ungrateful son. From the very beginning, the activity of the just has translated trinitarian love in visible form, not only by a mere imitation, but also by an actual manifestation wherein the Trinity is at work. Just as, in addressing a man, it is not chiefly his body that we contact but the whole man who is soul as well as matter, so here, in a similar manner, we do not perceive merely men who love, but just men, divinized men; we attain God through the transparency of the actual term of His action, just as in perceiving light-pervaded air it is not only the air which we see but also the actual light of the sun. A sunny atmosphere is the best image of human love penetrated by God. And this explains how our lives can be living witnesses of the Gospel.

Furthermore, charity is not only a mediation of divine love because it is an extension of trinitarian love, but also and especially because its proper end is to associate us in God's life. It is a mediation of the end as well as of the source.[118]

In the concrete historical order wherein God's plan finds realization, it is essential to charity that it be Christian. Up until now we have spoken of charity without explicitly relating it to Christ, in order to avoid overloading our exposition.

However, only by connecting it with Christ can we throw some light on the mystery of charity. How can we explain that our charity, though created and finite, can enable us to act divinely and permit God to act in us, if not because we can say that in Jesus Christ, created man and God are one and the same person and that His charity enables His humanity to be the humanity of the Word? Charity and sanctifying grace in us can only be explained as participations in the charity and grace of a God-man. They are a created effect, a modification of the humanity of Christ and of His members, and nevertheless this created effect is the result of the actual union of the divine with this humanity. These two aspects, finite and infinite, human and divine, can only be conceived in terms of their unity, which is characteristic of the supernatural order, and not in terms of their distinction in the purely natural order. Grace and charity, in Christ and His members, "are beings of union."[119]

Charity causes us first of all to participate in the humanity and the human activity of Christ. While it is true that the humanity of Christ has the power of influencing all men by virtue of its unity with the divinity of the Word, nevertheless it is by humanity that Jesus Christ is Head.

Finally, what we have said of human love and of its sense as communion must also be said of charity, provided we make it approach what we already know of trinitarian love. This means that human love will lose some of its limitations, for the ontological union between God and us and between ourselves as sons of the same Father has now become more intimate. Charity intensifies our need of getting rid of our closed self by giving ourselves to God and to others. It gives us the strength to reach heroic generosity in this struggle against egoism and to reach total communion through perfect abnegation. The desire for beatitude will always be present in this life, but as the necessary accompaniment of a longing for communion stronger than this desire for beatitude. In the supernatural vision of heaven we will find more satisfaction in communion with God than in our happiness in contemplating Him.

Such is the perfection of charity. But it would be neither Christian nor human to despise the imperfect realizations of charity which uses our desires by directing them toward the most desirable of goods;[120] yet it remains true that this imperfect love derives its ultimate meaning from pure charity which tends toward communion.

CONCLUSION

The interior experience of our dynamism, which we undertook to analyze in this chapter, has now revealed its name and meaning: in fact it is love, and, in the Christian, it is contact with divine *agapè:* charity which participates in the charity of Christ Himself.

CHAPTER III

The Virtuous Act, a Mediation
of Charity

INTRODUCTION

Since we have shown, in the first chapter of this section, that the moral act is a mediation of our profound spiritual tendency, and in the second chapter that this fundamental dynamism is nothing but charity-love, it would seem that we can conclude our syllogism right now and say: Therefore, the moral act is a mediation of charity. Why then bring up the virtuous element of the moral act, which we have not employed in the course of the two preceding chapters?

Is it merely in order to mark the continuity of these chapters with the first section, where charity appeared exclusively in the context of the virtues? Of course the present chapter will permit us to compare our conclusions with those drawn from the analysis of the texts of St. Thomas. But the question of virtue does not suddenly crop up here merely for the sake of symmetrical development. The reality of virtue springs from moral action itself, for this action does not appear as scattered in a multiplicity of individual acts with no other link between them than the subject that elicits them. It is rooted in our faculties, and the traces which it leaves there, in their turn, perfect the faculty and its further activity. It was only to simplify the exposition that we did not introduce earlier the notion of virtue.

Assuming what has already been said about the opinion of St. Thomas, we will now see that the concrete nature of virtue is to be a mediating function. We will then determine the respective roles of charity and the virtues. In so doing we will first study the objective aspect of the mediation of virtues and show that the proper objects of the virtues are able to be explicitly referred to the terrestrial as well as the supernatural ends of charity. Secondly, the implicit role of charity in the virtues, which is the subjective aspect of their mediation, will be studied.

§I. Virtue as a Mediating Function

I. ACQUIRED VIRTUE

Just as we did in the case of love, we will take as our starting point an element proportioned to our natural knowledge: natural virtue; but we are conscious here of making a methodical abstraction.

Just as our being, so too our activity is magnetized by two poles: spirit, with the complexity of its proper ends, and matter. If our person were identified with one or the other, we would have no need of natural virtues. Pure spirits such as angels do not have them.[1] In God they only exist in an eminent[2] or metaphorical manner.[3] At the opposite extreme, an irrational being, in which the precision of instinct leaves no room for liberty, does not know virtue.

But because in us both spirit and matter are joined, we have neither the perfect self-actuation of pure spirit nor the perfect determinism of instinct. Our spirit has a fringe of indeterminate passivity springing from its contamination by matter which robs it of perfect adaptation to its *actus primus proximus*; and our sensibility, because it is con-

taminated by spiritual liberty, has not the rigidity of autom-
ations which removes the possibility of choice.

There coexist in us a potentiality—that is, a privation of
and a need for act[4]—and a capacity of freely determining
ourselves to this act.[5] We need certain instruments of selec-
tion which will orient our liberty among the innumerable
possibilities of choice found in material combinations. This
is precisely the role of virtue; it is an operative habit, a
durable trace left in the power by repeated action, just as a
piece of cloth becomes wrinkled by frequent pressure and
as each drop of water thickens the stalactite.

Contrary to what these images can suggest, virtue does
not derive its stability so much from material, subjective
repetition of acts as from the spiritual, objective character
of these actuations. Virtue is not a habit in the ordinary
sense of the word. For example, it is not primarily by the
automatic repetition of just acts that we develop the virtue
of justice, but rather because in each of these acts our spirit
contributes an objective spiritual rule, a principle of practical reason concerning justice which impregnates the will
and becomes its intrinsic possession. This spiritual rule
elevates the will, stabilizes it—just as an accident modifies
the substance—and finally forms together with it one single
stable principle of activity.[6]

Our action proceeds wholly from the principal cause
which is the active power and wholly from the instrumental
cause which is the virtue; virtuous activity is nothing but
moral activity seen under a special causal aspect. The active
faculty specializes in the practice of good, so that every
action that follows finds it less undetermined in its choice,
more capable of acting easily and perfectly in the same line.[7]
Virtue inscribes in the faculty a presumption favorable to
certain choices.

Even if virtue is an ontological reality, we must be care-

ful not to conceive it as a thing. The active power which it perfects is not itself a substance, but only a function. Virtue is a functional reality, a dynamism specified by an object. How then is it related to our fundamental dynamism, which is love?

We have already pointed out that this profound tendency of our will is opposed to determinations and that it manifests itself through the mediation of moral acts. Virtue, except in the very first acts that create it, is the normal intermediary between these two poles, between the fundamental indetermination and the concrete acts. Hence, in order to be a mediation, all moral activity must pass through virtue. Virtue is the creative reaction of spiritual love coming into contact with dispersion and wishing to overcome it. Virtue is a first and habitual determination of first act before it passes into second act; being *actus primus proximus*, it is midway between act and potency.[8] It springs from love and spirit; but because the spirit here below is in contact with multiplicity, virtue is, as it were, spiritual interiority emerging into multiplicity. Thus we can recognize in habitual virtue a mediation of our profound tendency, a mediation more profound than our acts, though in fact manifested only through them. Virtue is, so to say, a habitual activity.[9]

Because the being of virtue depends on the profound tendency of love, so also will its activity. Since this tendency is concentrated in the will, we can say that every exercise of virtue will actually depend on the will.

II. INFUSED VIRTUE

It is a common opinion among theologians that together with charity and the theological virtues a whole organism of supernatural moral virtues is infused in us.[10] Even if charity divinizes our love and directs it toward the ultimate

end, there remains in us a complex structure which has already been strengthened by acquired natural virtues, but must now be proportioned to the supernatural end in all its detail.

It is sometimes said that the infused virtues differ from the acquired virtues in that they do not confer primarily the *facile posse*, but the *supernaturale posse simpliciter*.[11] But St. Thomas explicitly says, "To the extent that he is moved by charity and the other virtues, the penitent practices virtue with pleasure and without difficulty."[12] What is clear is that the infused virtues do not make up for what is lacking in the acquired virtues, and they leave untouched any difficulties or resistance arising therefrom. But these difficulties are merely an extrinsic impediment. If such an impediment is not found, it is because the repetition of acts has so implanted acquired virtue in us that the contrary dispositions had to disappear.[13] In fact, it would be surprising if the infused virtues which give a capacity for supernatural action, that is, an elevation caused by the actual and active presence of God in our faculties, did not also give the faculty ease as well as possibility for action.

Thus infused virtue plays the same intermediary role as acquired virtue, but now between our fundamental tendency, supernaturalized by charity, and its supernatural acts. Just as the acquired virtues depend on the will in their being and exercise, so too the infused virtues depend on the will elevated and divinized by charity.

We must now examine the mode of this dependence. It manifests itself under the objective aspect of the subordination of the ends of the virtues to the higher and more general ends of charity, as well as under the subjective aspect, where the actuation of the virtues appears springing from charity as their efficient cause.

§II. The Respective Roles of Charity and the Virtues

1. THE OBJECTIVE AND EXPLICIT ASPECT OF THE SUBORDINATION OF ENDS

Imperfect beings that we are, ever tending to a still unattained perfection, action would be impossible for us were it not aiming at an ideal. It is the presence of this ideal in our faculties that drives them to act. In the supernatural order in which we live, charity gives finality to the will, orienting it toward that supernatural communion which we have found in love. Properly speaking, it is through our divinized will that we tend to our end. It is necessary that the end be presented to the human will, at least implicitly, as an object or in an object. That is why we can reduce this aspect of the problem to a study of the objective ends of charity.

Charity tends to realize this communion on two different levels. First there is the higher level, that of our communion with God, and with everything in God, under the form of the beatific vision, to which we have access not as isolated individuals, but as members of the community of the elect. This supernatural communion is substantially begun here on earth, for our life of grace and charity already puts us in direct contact with God in Himself and in our neighbor. Even while on earth, grace and charity divinize us not as isolated individuals but as members of the Mystical Body to which we belong and by means of which alone we participate in the grace and charity of our head, Christ. Such is the first level on which we realize communion with God and with men in God.

However, because we are incarnate spirits, we must seek this ultimate end by certain means; we must tend toward the spiritual world through certain sensible symbols. We sincerely aspire to celestial beatitude and communion only if we simultaneously aspire to terrestrial communion with men; and this second communion is to be realized not only by the spiritual means which prepare our final beatitude, but also by a certain collective, terrestrial beatitude which is an image of the celestial society. This is why charity, as such, fixes on numerous terrestrial objects through which it aspires to its own celestial objects. This is the second level on which ultimate communion begins to be realized.

We must try to realize this twofold ideal of charity by means of our complex being with its multiple faculties of action, which translate, in the diversity of the sensible, the richness and the varied exigencies of our spiritual love. This means that our charity will need the help of a certain number of virtues; charity will elevate and give finality to our will, while the virtues will orient the diversity of our active powers. Just as charity is attracted by the total ideal of the ultimate end, so each virtue will be put into action by a particular ideal, a specific end deriving its attractiveness from the general end of charity, which it adapts to this or that virtue. From this point of view, the specific ends of the virtues are thus all subordinated to the ultimate end of charity. In the explicit exercise of the virtues, these ends are presented to consciousness through the intermediary of the formal object proper to each virtue. These formal objects, being those of infused virtues, are obviously supernatural.

We will now briefly examine how the object of each virtue is an objective mediation of the supreme ends of charity on both the celestial and the terrestrial levels.

1. VIRTUES AS OBJECTIVE MEDIATIONS OF THE TERRESTRIAL ENDS OF CHARITY

Charity tends to realize on earth a human community finding its happiness in communion among persons, and

thus is patterned on the society of the elect. Such a community seeks the particular good of each person not as an
isolated individual, but as a member of the human family in
Christ. Terrestrial ends do not here mean material ends. On
the contrary, even on earth charity tends to a communion
among spirits, to a real, that is, to a supernatural communion. But because our spirits are incarnate, charity, in
seeking its terrestrial ends, must extend its activity into the
properly temporal order. We need only recall the persistent
effort of the Church, which for centuries has patiently
labored at introducing the sweetness of love into moral and
physical suffering, into poverty and painful toil; and all
because Christ has said, "You gave me food . . . you
visited me in prison."

It is a necessary consequence of what we have already
said on our fundamental tendency and on the nature of
love that our terrestrial end consist in forming as happy a
community as possible among persons united by love. If it
is true that our intimate being is a tendency of love and
that the very nature of this love is to reproduce on earth
an image of the trinitarian society, then it follows that our
whole human activity, as a mediation of this love, will be
ordered to the establishment of a state of communion
among persons. This finality is deeply inscribed in our
being and action. It is no less necessary to insist on the fact
that, on earth, this inclination toward communion, if it is
to be sincere and total, must be translated into visible
manifestations, at once spiritual and material. The infinitely
varied specifications of our moral activity will be so many
different ways of saying, not in words but in acts, "I
love." To admit this completely, one must believe that the
sensible and the psychological have, over and above their
particular ontological reality, the role of symbolizing the
spiritual reality of love. One must even believe that this
particular ontological reality is above all a concrete mani-

festation of the creative love of God and of human love completing creation.

It is not difficult, then, to understand that the particular end of moral virtues is to direct the diversity of our acts toward realizations of love. And since the concrete order in which we live is supernatural, all the infused virtues help our activities to attain charitable ends. And so it is necessary that the objects of these virtues be capable of being referred to the ends of charity. We cannot here make a complete inventory of the virtues, showing for each one of them how its object is related to the intention of charity which commands the virtuous act. In the last section of this book we will do it for the more important virtues. Suffice it to recall here the general principle of St. Thomas that charity can command or move all the virtues because it is itself the faculty of the end, whereas the other virtues are merely faculties of the means or of intermediary ends which are participations of the ultimate end. One and the same act of the will, which can pursue several ends at the same time, can still more easily pursue two ends of which one is a participation of the other.

To carry out an act under the inspiration of the virtue of prudence in no way excludes the possibility of our performing it at the same time out of love. Prudence guarantees that the act is performed in conformity with reason and faith. Not only is there nothing in this end which prevents it from being willed in order to seek more intimate communion with God and men, but the intrinsic necessity of this end and its adaptation to universal communion are evident. For example, if out of prudence we refuse some immediate service, this refusal must appear as the condition of some yet farther-reaching act of charity. Again, we may be anxious to pay some debt in order to fulfill justice, but it is also possible that by this act of justice we manifest our affection for the creditor. And the same is true for all virtues which have a terrestrial end.

In brief, since every partial end is eminently contained in the ultimate and general end of charity, it is easy to turn objects of virtue into objects of love. Our entire terrestrial community life can be made charitable.

But the terrestrial ends of love are, as we have said, symbols of supernatural ends.

2. VIRTUES AS OBJECTIVE MEDIATIONS OF THE CELESTIAL ENDS OF CHARITY

Celestial ends are obviously opposed to terrestrial, but they are both supernatural, for they concern the divine aspect of our terrestrial activity.

It is quite clear that we can objectively refer all possible activities of particular virtues to the love of God and to its blossoming in grace and glory. For example, the immediate end of the virtue of religion is to attract us to render to God the worship owed Him by a creature. This end is quite obviously the partial realization of the more general ideal of charity, which is to enter into communion with God. The virtue of religion realizes the initial condition of communion in duties of worship, moving us to accomplish them with ease, so that acts of worship become so many manifestations of love. Hence there is no difficulty in performing an act of worship out of charity; on the contrary, the very nature of worship invites us to do so.

The same is true of our supernatural communion with men. When we tend a sick person, we can also, out of love, tend in him a suffering member of Christ, and thus transform our corporal act of mercy into an authentic act of theological charity. And so for all other virtues. Suffice it to recall the principle of St. Thomas according to which one and the same act is at once an act of charity and an act of a particular virtue. But we will not insist further on this point, since the perspective of supernatural ends has been underlying most of our considerations.

II. THE SUBJECTIVE AND IMPLICIT ASPECT OF THE SUBORDINATION OF THE VIRTUES TO CHARITY, THEIR EFFICIENT CAUSE

We will now take up the following question: how is the subjective activity of the virtues ontologically subordinated to the efficient causality of charity, not only when charity is explicitly at work, but especially when it is not the object of an expressed intention.

1. EFFICIENT AND FINAL CAUSALITY

Here, once again, we meet the position of St. Thomas, who sees efficient and final causality in the influence of charity on the virtues. In fact, charity is the fundamental dynamism, which, at the very roots of our power for action, order us to our divine end; it puts our activity, taken at its source—at the point where it is most free and least dependent on material determinations—in contact with trinitarian life. Since we are not pure spirits, this spiritual dynamism constitutes one total principle of activity with active powers which are closer to concrete sensible determinations. As we have said, the moral virtues—and we are thinking primarily of infused virtues—organize our powers on this level. Hence, these virtues and powers are but ramifications of the fundamental tendency in the dispersion of the sensible.

Charity is the efficient dynamism *in actu primo*, still profound and simple, which takes on various forms when it penetrates into an activity parceled out by the determinations of various objects. When charity appears to us, it no longer has the indetermination of first act. It is imbedded in specifications—it is at once charity in second act and particular virtues—which diffract it, just as natural light spreads out through the prism into a colored spectrum, or just as electric current appears as light in the lamp, as movement in the motor, as attraction in the magnet, and as heat in the furnace. No more than solar light is the mere addition of the spectral rays, nor electricity the mere sum of all forms of energy, is charity the sum total of the virtues.

Thus the virtues have some really specific element. When charity *in actu primo* appears under the form of the virtue of religion in second act and then under the form of an act of patience, these are two specifically different apparitions of charity. These two acts of virtue are not two fragments of charity or even two species under the same genus, but two different participations of charity. Participation seems to be the best way to express the ontological relation between charity and the other virtues.[14] Participation expresses actual dependence, total similarity, and, at the same time, total dissimilarity: similarity, inasmuch as the virtues are partial dynamisms actually deriving their functional activity from the fundamental dynamism, just as the spiritual creature draws from God his personal liberty, a spark from divine creative power; dissimilarity, inasmuch as the virtues have introduced into charity particular objective determinations which affect it intrinsically and specify it, thus adapting the exigencies of the total and ultimate end to various fields of action. And so the end of each virtue retains in itself something of the attractive power of the total end.

In fact, what do we mean when we say that charity on entering the soul bestows on it the infused moral virtues? We mean that as soon as our being is put into contact with God by sanctifying grace, it is wholly elevated: its substance by grace, its will by charity, and its sensible powers by the virtues. On the other hand, we have already shown that our active powers are powers of love, for, in fact, the very fabric of our action and being is love, image of the Supreme Being who is charity. Hence, supernatural elevation takes place in the line of love and charity, and that which divinizes us in any degree is a form of the presence of divine charity, which is specified according to the functions elevated and the objects of these functions. St. Augustine translated this in his definition of virtue: "Ordo est amoris,"[15] and again: "Virtus est caritas qua id quod diligendum est diligitur."[16] He affirms that "virtue is absolutely nothing else than the sovereign love of God," and he sees in the cardinal virtues four "movements of love."[17]

We have said that charity influences the virtues and their acts as a total dynamism acting on partial dynamisms whose activity depends on it. That is to say that charity exercises on the virtues an efficient causality, for the particular functions are by definition merely functional, and, therefore, can be put into movement only by the general function of action, the will elevated by charity on which all decision depends. This efficient causality of love, whose movement is essentially generous, obeys an internal moral finality which urges it to communion with God and men. In fact, the efficient causality is provoked by this finality transmitted to all the particular functions by the charity-animated will. The latter would not put all the virtues in motion were it not attracted toward God, directed toward Him by its very constitution, which is vivified by a divine activity.

This influence of charity is most interior to the virtues, for it is participated as a life which animates them, as an ever efficacious presence.

How can it happen that two spiritual movements, of which one evokes the other, are in a relation of mutual interiority? By their compenetration in a functional unity, resulting in an organism animated by one and the same undivided spiritual life. In mechanical movements it is always possible to isolate that which is proper to the efficient cause and that which it transmits to its instrument. But in spiritual causality, exteriority is unthinkable, for it is a sign of materiality, and so here any conceptual distinction corresponds to successive partial views of the same complex living being. To wish to be temperate is an act proceeding at once entirely from the will, entirely from the virtue of temperance and the sensible appetite, and entirely from self, for *non voluntas vult, sed homo per voluntatem.* Beyond all distinctions there is the spiritual unity of the person who is acting.

2. SOME CONSEQUENCES

a) Specific nature of the virtues. It is now easy to solve the objection which claims that the present doctrine suppresses the diversity of virtues to the profit of charity alone. But we have just seen that participations retain their own specific nature; for example, by participating in God men do not become God.[18]

On the contrary, the virtues recount, each after its own fashion, the inexhaustible potentialities of charity; in the course of a single life, love must take on the nuances of patience, of purity, of obedience, of piety, of fidelity, as demanded by the different complex situations with which we meet. And this array of spiritual colors reveals the richness of our profound love; charity is eminently every one of them, just as sunlight is eminently red and violet.

But we meet here with a still more serious objection: if virtues are merely participations of charity, must we not say that, in any apparent conflict between the exigencies of charity and those of some other virtue, charity must always win out to the detriment of its opponent? To accept this position would be to suppress objective morality and approve the saying that the end justifies the means. For example, why can we not lie if by so doing we can save a soul incapable of bearing some necessary truth? Why is suicide forbidden even when it is the only means of not betraying friends who are in grave danger? Why not permit birth control where it is the only means of maintaining or restoring love in a home? Are we not, in fact, witnessing here the triumph of charity over the virtues of truthfulness, justice, and chastity?

No, charity does not triumph here, for when one consciously acts against a duty specified by a virtue, even if one does so with the most genuine desire of sincerity, one nevertheless objectively destroys true charity, since particular virtues are participations of charity in the various fields of our activity. They express the exigencies of charity corresponding to each of these fields. Truthfulness expresses the exigencies of charity in the communication of truth; chastity adapts the exigencies of charity to sexual love. To contradict truthfulness or chastity is to contradict charity in the fields of social truth and sexual love.

As a matter of fact, the proper ends of the virtues are nothing but expressions of the absolute end adapted to the particular fields which they specify, and refer to this absolute end insofar as they are informed by charity. Hence the proper end of each virtue participates, in its own field, in the absolute character of the end of charity. To contradict this absolute, wherever it is met, is an absolute evil and thus destructive of the ordering to an end and of charity which leads to it.

We are not denying that virtuous duties—or virtuous ends—are subordinated to duties of charity; it can happen that the act of some virtue may have to be omitted to perform an act of charity. But in the present objection there is no question of omission or substitution, but of acts positively opposed to particular virtues in grave matter and which one would pretend to perform in view of the proper ends of charity.

To recognize in the virtues participations of charity is thus in no way to deny that our being and action are really structured, and that, because of this structure and its corresponding organism of virtues, there may be acts contradictory in themselves, objectively and intrinsically evil; in fact, they would be evil precisely because they would contradict our human structure and consequently the virtues which correspond to it. For example, an act of onanism, even when apparently performed out of love, still contradicts the physiological, psychological, and moral structure of sexual love and of the virtue of chastity which rules this field. Such an act cannot be more opposed to our finality; it cannot be referred to our end and hence cannot be assumed by charity. To think that by such an act we can safeguard and even increase charity, is to believe that it is possible to tend to our end through an act which actually estranges us from it.[19]

The same conclusion holds for suicide apparently motivated by charity. In fact, the final result of this act would be to suppress ourselves as principles of charity in the community. Let us take the case of a prisoner of war who clearly foresees that under the influence of drugs he will inevitably denounce his friends, even though involuntarily and unconsciously. Can he commit suicide to save these lives? The denunciation would be involuntary and hence nonmoral; this means that a merely material evil, though grave in its consequences, is avoided, but at the price of a formal evil, which is a violation of a fundamental law of being; to be capable of moral action or of charity here on earth, one must first of all accept living on earth. Suicide fundamentally contradicts the finality of our being, for it involves using life to destroy life itself. It affects not only the structure of one active power, but the very root of our terrestrial activity.[20]

Besides, one must not give to this question of the specific nature of virtue a significance which it does not have. The diversification required by traditional Catholic doctrine affects, first of all, the psychological and ascetical level; it does not bear directly on the ontology of the virtues. The reason for a doctrine of specific virtues is to be found in the human necessity of performing multiple virtuous acts corresponding to multiple psychological activities and moral situations. There is nothing in Catholic doctrine which prevents charity from being alone the ultimate root of this diversity, as Augustine formally teaches,[21] for charity not only supports diversity but even explains it and requires it, just as the soul at once explains and supposes the body.

Here is also the answer to the following difficulty. If the virtues are merely partial realizations of charity, would it not suffice, in order to be perfect, to perform as frequent and as pure acts of charity as possible, leaving aside the practice of particular virtues? We will come back later on to the ascetical aspect of this objection.[22] But it is immediately apparent that leaving aside the virtues implies the complete neglect of our human condition as incarnate beings. Yes, acts of charity must be repeated as intensely as possible, but this does not justify the abandonment of virtues. Do we stop feeding our body simply because we have discovered the superiority of our soul? On the contrary, the fact that we are spiritual obliges us to feed our body. Since our being as incarnate spirits is complex, our activity must reflect some of this complexity. Interior acts of love reflect the spiritual aspect of our being, but this does not exempt that part of us which is engaged in the sensible from reacting in the multiple and complex fashion of incarnate spirits. This part must also be virtuous, and thus will be charitable in its own way. Light does not lose its identity by diffraction through a prism. In fact, moral life becomes progressively more simple as it becomes more interior: the virtues of a mystic are not exactly those of a beginner. But this is not to indulge in the illuminism of the Beghards, which teaches that only the imperfect need practice the virtues: the perfect can do without them.[23]

We will add here two reasons from the psychological order to prove that virtuous acts must be named after the virtue which immediately elicits them, even though, fundamentally, they are acts of charity.

First, we must denominate our activities after their object and their most exterior and most particular specification (*species infima*), which is also the most immediately known. This is true even when the intention of charity is explicit. For example, acts of mortification or of adoration performed with the explicit intention of loving God are still called acts of penance or of religion, even though they are still more acts of charity. Charity is the fabric of all these acts, and hence their specific determination comes from the virtues.

Secondly, acts of virtue wherein charity plays only an implicit role are named after their most conscious and explicit motive. If we perform an act with the intention of fulfilling a contractual obligation without explicitly thinking of doing an act of charity, we will then be conscious of performing an act of justice, even though the profound implicit movement which guides this act springs from a charity-powered will.

b) Charity, the "sense" of virtues. The intimate connection of virtues with charity brings into better light their relative character. St. Thomas recognizes that a virtue is not authentic, *simpliciter vera*, if it is not informed by charity,[24] for in that case it would not be ordered to the ultimate and

total good. This conclusion becomes all the more evident
if the virtues are conceived as participations of charity.
What would a participation be without a direct relation to
what is participated if not an interior anticipation awaiting
fulfillment?

If the virtues are merely different specific forms which
charity takes on when in contact with diverse faculties and
objects, it is impossible to understand the virtue of justice,
for example, without realizing the exigencies of charity-
love in the specific field of strict "mine-thine relations"
which is proper to justice. This follows from the fact that
justice is merely the substitute for love on the level of
commutative and distributive equality. The same is true
for all the other virtues. Their fundamental dependence on
charity must enter into their definition if it is to be concrete, that is, truly moral and Christian. For it alone gives
them their true "sense." In fact, charity determines their
sense even more than it perfects their definition. Of course,
it is possible to define a virtue abstractly without taking
into account its concrete sense and to say, for example:
justice is "the habit which causes one to render each man
his due."[25] This is an extremely poor sketch, a first approximation of justice which tells us nothing about the range of
this virtue, the context in which it is included, and its Christian sense. Why render to each man his due? Is it in view
of consecrating this opposition between "mine" and "thine"
and the division of persons which results from it, or in view
of uniting them? The above definition gives me no indica-
tion. If we build a treatise of justice on it, we run the risk
of overlooking the very life which justice must regulate
and of not seeing the supernatural deepening of human
relations created by the infused virtue of justice. This is
why it is not surprising that the current theology of justice
differs so little from the treatise of civil law on the same
matter. On the contrary, if we were aware that the func-

tion of justice is to realize, in the field of goods which can become objects of possession and of rights, a climate of human and Christian communion among persons, then our treatise of justice would be profoundly transformed. It would have a Christian "sense."

And the same applies to all other treatises. In this perspective, the virtues would be grouped according to specifically Christian values; the Pauline virtues of humility, kindness, tender compassion, gentleness, and patience* would then have and would follow an order of priority quite different from that found in Aristotle's *Ethics*. Practical applications will be suggested on this matter in the third part of this study.

Obviously it is the infused virtues that fall under this informing by charity. But something analogous must be said of the natural virtues which are in the service of natural love. We have already pointed out that all of our activity springs from love. But the proper objects of this natural love are themselves embodied in and surpassed by the supreme object of infused charity.

c) Interrelation of the virtues. Since charity plays a substantial role in the virtues, it is easy to understand how these are related to one another. On entering a soul, charity creates, in a certain fashion, the organism of the infused virtues. But when sin drives charity out of a soul,[26] the infused virtues are also uprooted, even though "uninformed" faith and hope remain behind.

This connection between the virtues is so intimate that one virtue calls for another; for example, piety must always be obedient. In fact, it is impossible to understand any particular virtue without taking into account the whole

---

* Cf. Col. 3:12; Eph. 4:2. This grouping, which is more in harmony with the gospel, is recognized as both legitimate and useful even by those who consider the "speculative" classification of the *Secunda Secundae* as definitive; see M. LABOURDETTE, o.p., in RT, 47 (1947), 566–569.

complex reality in which it is included, for it is not at all easy to separate the different manifestations of one indivisible love. St. Thomas was keenly aware of this and defended the theory of the interrelation of the acquired virtues as well as that of the infused virtues, which had been admitted since the time of Godfrey of Poitiers.[27] He was also aware of the compenetration of the cardinal virtues,[28] seeing in them the general conditions of any virtuous act.[29] For him, prudence has priority over all the moral virtues[30] as their necessary condition;[31] and, conversely, the moral virtues are indispensable to the exercise of prudence.[32] Justice, as a general virtue, "orders the acts of all the other virtues to the common good."[33] We would only have to draw up a schema of the virtues as found in the *Summa* in order to see how they are mutually interrelated.

d) *Merit and intention.* What we said of the unity in participation[34] and of the living complex[35] formed by charity with the other virtues simplifies the doctrine of merit and answers the objection brought against some scholastics,[36] that they attribute all merit to charity and none to the virtues.

In accordance with the common doctrine, we recognize that merit comes from charity and, at the same time, that real merit *de condigno* must be attributed to the works of particular virtues, for we consider these insofar as they form a real unity with charity, and not insofar as they are distinct from it. The moral act is at once the exercise of the virtue of charity and the exercise of particular virtues whose ends it consciously pursues. Thus we can say, with the Council of Trent, that eternal life is the wages of "good works,"[37] and we understand better that the beatific vision will have for each of us a special nuance, for it will crown a life consecrated to some specific work and to some particular virtue. The degree of glory will depend on the degree of charity, but the latter will be intrinsically influenced by the virtues which form with it one living whole.

Virtuous acts are intrinsically proportioned to attaining the ultimate end, for what is proper to them remains under the dependence of charity. They really attain the ultimate end, not precisely by virtue of themselves, as if they were nothing but themselves, but by virtue of their intimate unity with charity.[38] Here again we find the doctrine of the Salmanticenses[39]—its real content, if not its abstract technical formulation. The participation which we are considering here is vital and existential. That is why Christian morality is really uplifting while remaining perfectly humble. It is man who creates himself, who redeems himself, who gives himself, for his activity is one with the efficaciousness of charity. And yet these results are achieved, not precisely by virtue of his own activity, but because God acts in him by charity: *"Sine me nihil. . . ."* The mystery of the Incarnation consists in this—that God and man form one person and that grace in us is a "being of union."

It is now easy to solve the complex problem of intention. The elements to be reconciled are the following: charity must exercise a real influence on the moral act in order to make it meritorious, but, on the other hand, it is psychologically impossible to renew the actual intention for each action or even to prolong throughout our daily activity the virtual influence in the strict sense. And yet a purely habitual intention is not sufficient. By way of compromise, some authors have suggested a virtual intention in the wider sense, which would be sufficient to order the acts, but not to cause them. But when faced with the two objections examined earlier,[40] this doctrine, which supposes at least a previous explicit act of charity, does not fully maintain the universality of the following principle: "In him

who has charity, every act is either meritorious or it is a
sin: no act is indifferent."[41]

With St. Thomas we see no difficulty in admitting that
charity has an actual and really effective influence on all
acts of virtue. We maintain that charity really passes into
second act; it does not simply remain as a habit ontologically present in first act, which evidently would not be
sufficient for merit.[42] But, on the other hand, we do not
think that an explicit psychological intention of charity is
required for this. Our ontological and supernatural constitution prevents us from exercising voluntary activity without
at the same time exercising charity-love. Hence the efficaciousness of the supernatural in us does not necessarily
depend on our explicit and reflex consciousness:[43] merit is,
above all, the creation in us of a supernatural ontological
capacity. That does not mean that this ontological capacity
is in no way reflected on the psychological and moral level,
for moral qualification is indispensable to merit. In the
consciousness of the just performing a good action, there
must be something distinguishing it from the consciousness
of the sinner performing the same material action. Such
consciousness may be only direct and in exercise, without
passing to the state of explicit reflex knowledge. To aim at
the end of a particular virtue implies an intention directed
toward the end of charity, for the ends of virtues are participations of this ultimate end.[44] Moreover, persevering in
the state of charity and acting according to this state requires a vital attitude, at least half conscious, which orients
the whole acting person toward his divine end. The just
and the sinner, in giving alms, do not see the poor man in
exactly the same light, even supposing that in both the
explicit intention bears only on helping a man in need. The
fundamental orientation of our life must necessarily find
an echo in consciousness.

This also sheds light on the relationship between natural

and infused virtues. The ideal of action proper to the infused virtue includes and surpasses that of the corresponding acquired virtue, for supernatural finality does not suppress natural finality, but rather deepens it and leads it into contact with God.* In wanting to give our neighbor what belongs to him, we can do so from the point of view of the natural community existing between him and us. But if we want to do so in a Christian manner, that is, as members of the community uniting men in Christ, and willingly meet its minimum requirement which is justice, then this higher intention obviously includes the friendship already contained in the natural intention, but takes as its ideal a supernatural union, that of members of Christ.

Can the exercise of infused virtue be explicitly conscious as that of acquired virtue? We have already pointed out that the representative elements of the concept pertain to the natural order, while the judgment bearing on the concept, in the present hypothesis, is engaged in a supernatural finality, and of this we can be directly conscious.[45] In the same way we can have vital consciousness of the exercise of infused virtue. Of course, we can be explicitly conscious of the characteristic motive of a given infused virtue when, for example, we mortify ourselves in union with our Redeemer. In explicit consciousness there will also be elements of representation which will appear under a natural form. But through them we become conscious of an infused activity.

But the question may well be raised whether, in practice and from a pastoral point of view, this position would not become dangerous, for in rendering the supernatural intention useless, it would distract the attention from the supernatural and from charity. Such a result would surely be unexpected, since our whole effort has been to restore not

---

* We are not denying that infused virtues can exist without the corresponding acquired virtues.

only the preponderance but even the universal and total presence of charity in moral life. The very method of mediation, which reveals by transparency the presence of charity in all acts, supposes that the attention is always more and more fascinated by this presence. We find here an invitation to harmonize our psychology with our profound ontology. A man always ends up by thinking according to what he is and especially according to what he loves.

But there is a more direct and pastoral reply. It is certain that as long as charity is present in us, an explicit intention bearing on charity or a supernatural motive is not required to effectively apply charity to each of our virtuous acts and thus render them meritorious. But it is equally certain that an explicit intention is frequently required to maintain in us the living presence of charity.

Moreover, the supreme purpose of our formulation of morality is to make explicit this implicit reality which constitutes our deeper life and to point out the numerous obstacles which oppose such a making explicit in our action. When we consider moral acts as mediations, we better perceive how instinctively we tend to render these mediations opaque by resting in them,[46] for their own sake or for the pleasure we find in them, thus hindering the influence and growth of charity.

Our egoism automatically refers most of our actions to self, at least by a secondary intention, and we take this tendency as a natural intention. It is, in fact, a deficient intention caused by deep-seated concupiscence, which has its source in sin. The act loses its merit to the extent that by stopping at self-love it is prevented from being actually referred to charity. This is why, in practice, the psychological supernatural intention must be frequently renewed. The child, engaged as he is in the sensible, often acts in a typically egoistic fashion; maturity consists in freeing oneself from this egoism, and this requires a persevering effort.[47]

The method here proposed reminds us that in order to simply live in the state of grace we must react against numerous obstacles and ceaselessly restore *transparency* in our actions by constantly rectifying our intention of charity. And so we are led to require frequent explicit intentions, not as a theoretic condition of merit and of the efficaciousness of charity, but as a practical condition of the presence of charity in us.

The following difficulty is thus easily solved: if all acts of virtue implicitly contain an act of charity, how is it that the sanctification of Christians progresses so slowly, since it should be increased by each good action? If the facts do not more openly reveal the presence of charity in what we call the good actions of Christians, is it not because its flame is dormant under the ashes of natural and even positively egoistic intentions? Charity, of itself, is incapable of decreasing, but our egoism can neutralize the radiation of its heat and light. In the activity of many Christians, the charity of Christ is far from shining forth in all its splendor, but rather appears as filtered light whose heat has already cooled off. The fire continues to burn, but our act, which should have been aflame with it, serves rather as an insulating screen, for its motives are connected with other sources.

Thus the task of Christian morality and of asceticism, which is intimately linked to it, is to render the intention and exercise of charity in us always more and more explicit.[48] As we have said, acts of charity are the most meritorious among human acts; this means that they increase, in the present life, our capacity for God and that they are Christian acts par excellence.[49] An ideal Christian life should consist in making each day an uninterrupted series of acts of charity.*

* Here we leave aside the questions whether our acts which are *"remissi"* are also meritorious, and whether the increase in charity takes place in a discontinuous manner. Cf. *Sum. th.*, 2-2, q. 24, a. 6; F. de Lanversin,

Father de Guibert, in his *Leçons de théologie spirituelle*, asks which is more important for perfection, actual or habitual charity. Where there is question of acquired perfection, it is habitual charity that matters. But when perfection is in the making, an act is meritorious in proportion to the degree of habitual charity and according to the intensity and frequency of the acts of the active charity which elicits this habitual charity. Besides, if charity is considered as eternal life inchoate, it is acts inspired by love, more than the infused habit from which they proceed, that give more glory to God.[50]

s.j., "Accroissement—Accroissement des vertus d'après Suarez," DSAM, vol. I, col. 156–166.

Conclusion of the Second Part

We have recalled all the elements necessary to understand that virtuous acts are mediations of charity and to draw the consequences from this truth.

Christian moral life, with its multitude of humble as well as significant acts, is a creation springing from the gushing sources of charity. In the heart of the commonplace realities scattered along the course of our days, it is possible to perceive God's activity passing through us. Our moral life, the result of liberty creating our spiritual person, appears at last in its naked reality: it is a work of love springing at once from God's heart and from ours. The measure of this love depends on us and our limits, be they necessary or effected by our free will.

But charity is not only the source and efficient cause; it is also the very "sense" of our moral activity. It acts through all particular virtues and these, in turn, have no other purpose than to lead on to love and to increase charity. Hence the role of moral theology will be to discover in each virtue in what way it can contribute to the orientation of the soul toward charity.

That is why it was so important to determine the real sense of love. It is communion between men and with God; it constitutes society among spiritual persons and so is an image of the Trinity among finite beings.

We have called "mediation" rather than "participation" the mode of transparency of charity in virtuous acts, in order to underline the functional and active role of this

relation between the surface and the spiritual depths of our
being.*

It seems to us that this manner of considering moral acts
under their relational aspect, which emphasizes so well the

* We find these two complementary exigencies of interiority and
exteriority, of the static and the dynamic, in BERGSON, under a slightly
different aspect, however. For him they derive from the "two sources"
of morality: the one exterior, the social pressure at the origin of determinations of the law; the other interior, the inspiration and attraction of
the presence of love and of God in the soul. Should these two sources
really be considered as parallel? Morality seems to have only one genuine source—this tendency of love, that we have been discussing, which
can be called an "inspiration," especially if we consider in it our infused
contact with God in charity. Social pressure does not seem to us to have
been a source of morality, if not in a merely secondary sense, when considered as a *de facto* limit and an element of determination. It has always
played an important role in enabling man to progressively become conscious of various moral determinations and to formulate them. Nevertheless, it is not their criterion but merely a field of experience which
permits our profound tendency to reflect on itself and to progressively
improve its knowledge of its own interior exigencies. At most it is a
criterion in the measure that the conscience of the elite, of the "wise
men," which gradually impregnates the collective conscience, can serve
as an example and a norm for individual consciences which compose the
mass. But this second, imperfect source of morality is to be found in
personal consciences and not in a social pressure; it can, in fact, be reduced to the first source of which it is no more than an echo. It is, as
we have said, merely the correlative and subordinated limit-aspect of the
profound source. Those who consider morality primarily as the experimental science of human facts base themselves chiefly on this exterior,
visible element, that is, on the pressure or convention of man's social
nature, or the advantage of life in society. Now that we have distinguished our points of view, we can with profit search out points of
contact and complementary aspects in BERGSON's doctrine which can enrich our own study. Bergson underlines the twofold level of morality:
a static level centered on justice and a dynamic level centered on charity;
the one infraintellectual, the other supraintellectual, but both projecting
themselves into the compass of the intellect which discerns their rational obligation (see, for example, *The Two Sources of Morality and
Religion*, chapter 1). In spite of this apparent meeting on the rational
plane which might suggest mediation, BERGSON seems to insist on the
rupture which separates the two moralities more than on their continuity
and union; having once separated the two domains, he observes them
with great delicacy. While taking full profit from this treasure of observations, we can fasten our attention rather on the link that unites these
two domains and constitutes our "meditation." But here again we must
remember that this mediation is not at all static, for it participates in
our profound dynamism.

aspiration of love to "communion," answers the methodological question raised in the beginning of this second section.[1] There is no difficulty in giving to charity the role of
a soul present in the whole of moral life; in fact, this position is traditional.[2] And there is no difficulty in formulating this presence in a technical manner.[3]

The method we have adopted prevents us from considering the immediate object of any particular moral
treatise as an autonomous reality, an absolute object in
which it would be possible to rest. We see in it, above all,
a mediation, that is, a manifestation of something other than
this object; the latter cannot be taken independently of the
source from which it springs and the end to which it tends.
In other words, we are unwilling to cut off the moral
concept from its intrinsic relation to the ultimate end and
from the new light thrown on its very notion by charity-
love. The definition of a moral object will lose none of its
particular elements, but these will all be oriented in line
with supernatural moral consciousness. The iron filings do
not cease to be iron in being ordered by the magnetic field;
however, each of them is polarized and intrinsically penetrated by a current without which they would remain void
of any "virtue" and direction. In the same way, the moral
objects would lose their highest meaning if they were not
intrinsically carried and oriented by the current of charity-
love, since this current, unlike the above example, mediately
produces the moral objects.

In the first part of our study, we have shown that this
result on the level of methodology is not attained by
abandoning the scholastic tradition, but rather by developing one of its most intimate tendencies. Our second part, in
which we have used the notion of mediation brought into
better light by modern thought, shows the permanent value
of the *theologia perennis*, and, at the same time, gives us

hope of reconciling modern tendencies with Thomism without any detriment to the latter.[4]

In fact, the whole of morality should be seen as a transparency of love, and this not from a sentimental but from a doctrinal point of view. Such a personalizing[5] perspective confers on morality an attraction which it does not always have, for its abstract formulation, badly understood, too often cloaks it with the cold apparel of a negative law rather than in living traits appealing to generosity.[6]

The method of mediation is existential as well as essential. Instead of considering the various moral activities isolated from their ontological relations, it will always take up the whole context along with each particular operation, in order to find therein the real "sense" of the given moral action.[7] Hence moral theology comes much closer to dogma; it appears as the prolongation and application of dogmatic theology in the concrete field of human activity. Its internal exigencies situate it in Christ and in the Church. That is why one might be surprised that St. Thomas did not write the *Secunda Pars* after the *Tertia*. But one must take into account the very different intellectual atmosphere in which the medieval mind used analysis as a didactic method; this atmosphere was, in fact, predominantly synthetic. Even so, one might well regret that the Angelic Doctor was so exclusively preoccupied with the formal aspect and the particular laws of the virtues that he did not sufficiently emphasize the ends implicitly pursued by the subject, taken as a member of Christ, in the concrete context of the Christian universe centered on the Incarnation.

And so the whole of moral life reveals its theological value as a blossoming forth of charity. Since the relations arising from this virtue constitute our intimate bonds with God, it follows that morality is inseparable from religion[8] and truly merits the name of theology.

The conclusions grouped here may well answer the

following practical difficulty: How can moral theology be concretely formulated according to the primacy of charity-love? Will we merely repeat the word charity, at every line? How would this change the visage of moral theology? No, one must understand that charity-love is a "sense," an orientation. Everything is changed when immobility is replaced by movement and this movement oriented according to its true "sense." The Gospel, even though it does not always talk of the love of the Father, is, nevertheless, impregnated by it. And this does not prevent the Gospel from vigorously formulating precepts and prohibitions, from demanding obedience and from solving many particular cases of conscience. Charity-love will order the general pattern as well as each treatise of moral theology, just as the soul orders all human attitudes by its active presence and without any need of being named. In the following section, we will try to outline some of the effects of this presence.

THIRD PART

Outline of a Charity-Centered Moral Theology
(*Practical Part*)

INTRODUCTION

The value of a method is perhaps best judged by the quality of its results. Having established a method in its generality, we must now verify it by applying it to various objects of moral theology. A complete demonstration would involve taking up in turn each treatise found in standard textbooks and would thus mean rewriting the whole of moral theology. But the scope of the present study permits us to outline only the more important methodological applications.

Our method is above all an instrument of spiritual vision which permits us to see moral realities transparently as so many mediations of divine charity. Our whole task, then, is to recognize in each reality how it derives from this love, and, consequently, how it leads back to it, for love acts only in view of a more intimate communion. It is the very soul and sense of our moral activities that we want to bring into better light. We want to grasp these activities as participations of charity; this involves going beyond their purely abstract definition and immediate context.

Moral activity appeared to us as the determined, exterior aspect and, so to say, the limit of our more profound charity, somewhat like the concept may be said to be the limit of the intuition and the body the limit of the soul. That is why this exterior aspect will be for us a sign refer- ring us to something beyond itself. But this sign is indis- pensable, for, though its value is wholly relative and subordinated to what it signifies, it remains specific, and yet by its nature of mediation it participates in the absolute dignity of charity, being one with the latter.

From this double viewpoint of mediation and determi- nation we will, in this third part, proceed by way of the following steps. Since we must find everywhere the authentic presence of charity, we will first determine the fundamental moral attitudes which derive from the fact that our Christian activity springs from, and is a mediation of, charity. These fundamental attitudes are already a con- crete application of our method, but they are so broad that we will find them again in all the particular applications; in fact, they are the primary conditions which any moral activity must realize in order to be Christian (Chapter I).

We will then go on to point out a few applications in General (Chapter II) and Special Moral Theology (Chap- ter III).

CHAPTER 1

Fundamental Attitudes of Charity-Centered Moral Theology

These attitudes constitute the Christian spirit, the soul which animates our daily activities and the ideal model which they tend to reproduce. These attitudes are the prolongation in moral activity of a basic ontological structure according to which all our acts are manifestations of charity. They constitute the "charitable temperament" of our actions. They are not yet particular moral realizations, but rather real vital wishes to which moral activity must conform in order to be perfectly what it ought to be.

§I. Generous Communion with Others

What we have already said on the nature of love and of charity leads us to the most important of these fundamental attitudes. Love is a force driving us to communion with others; it tends to constitute, on the model of the Trinity, a spiritual society; this invitation to love has been infinitely broadened, since charity opens our love to the ineffable intimacy of God's own life, and this not merely by participation, but by direct communication.

If such is the fabric of our profound activity, it must in some way appear in our moral realizations. The most intimate characteristic of each moral act is to be an effort toward communion with God and with men. And even

if, because of the limitation of our love, it still retains a
need for self-enrichment and possession, nevertheless this
indigence cannot compromise its principal movement,
which is generous and self-giving. Communion puts the
"we" before the "I."

This is why the first commandment, to which all the
others are reduced, is: "Thou shalt love thy God . . . and
thy neighbor as thyself" (Mk. 12:28–31). It is impossible
to love oneself fully and correctly without in the same
movement being carried to love others, for we participate
in the love of the Trinity wherein a person cannot love
himself without at the same time loving the others.

This is of primordial importance for the orientation of
Christian moral theology. Compared to non-Christian
ethics, be they Epicurean, utilitarian, sentimental, or volun-
taristic,[1] Christian morality has, as a specific element,
generosity, a charity which favors spiritual union with God
and other persons.

If we delve deeply enough into each moral act, we will
find in it an attitude opening us to a giving of self or, at
least, in the case of imperfect love found in desire, an
attitude preparing us indirectly for a better giving of self,
for it makes us richer, so that we can give ourselves more
fully. In any case this attitude prevents us from ever losing
sight of this generous intention.*

§ II. Christ-Centeredness

We said earlier[2] that charity in us is a participation in

* One could easily tie in a development on the social aspect of morality with our Section VII on community life and obedience (cf. *infra*,
pp. 233 f.) and our considerations on love (pp. 138–146). This aspect is of
prime importance; if we have not developed it at length in this study,
it is not because we underestimate its importance. In fact it is necessarily
implied in the very constitution of charity. We hope one day to devote
a separate work to its study.

the charity of Christ and that it relates us first of all to the humanity of Christ and to His human activities. Hence it impresses in us an exigency for resembling the humanity of Christ in that which elevates and adapts us to His divinity. Grace confers on us divine ways of acting and is wholly conditioned by the human attitudes of Christ. However, we must not forget that these human attitudes are those of a God-man and are transmitted to us by grace and charity. They are supernatural human attitudes and cannot abstract from the actual presence of the divine, and are even required by this presence.

It follows that a moral theology founded on charity is, by its most intimate exigency, an imitation of Christ. He inspires us interiorly to express in our virtuous activity His own attitudes adapted to the circumstances in which we live; at the same time He teaches us and shows us exteriorly, in the gospel-revelation, the living doctrinal rule of Christian morality.

To organize moral theology on the basic principle of charity-love does not, therefore, in any way contradict its being an imitation of Christ, but rather founds it as such. And yet it is the principle of charity which immediately and intrinsically organizes the science of Christian morals; for our moral theology is the science of free and conscious Christian action which the member of the Mystical Body accomplishes according to the law of Christ. Moral theology is concerned with consciousness* and conscience, wherein one perceives and judges the good together with its motives and lovableness, in view of the ultimate end. Now the immediate principle which elicits or commands

* We understand "conscience" in all its human and supernatural mystery, in all its existential context (Cf. R. CARPENTIER, s.j., "Conscience," DSAM, vol. II, coll. 1555–1561), but this does not prevent us from considering that the task of moral theology is to show what the Christian must consciously do, that is, follow the precepts and counsels, to have everlasting life.

our moral action is, in the member as well as the Head,
charity. By studying the dynamism, the laws, and the
exigencies of this charity as they are revealed in the Person
of Christ, it is possible to determine the laws and structure
of a theology of Christian moral action. Hence it will be
an imitation of Jesus Christ, a morality patterned on the
teachings of the Gospel, and, by this very fact, it will be
impregnated by charity, which reveals itself as the soul of
Christian life in Christ's actions as incarnate Son, in our
actions as adopted sons. In such a morality the reference to
Jesus Christ is implicitly or explicitly, but always vitally,
present.†

I. CHRIST HAS NO HUMAN "SELF"

Christ has but a single personality, that of the Word.
He has no human personality (hypostasis). When He
speaks in His own name and says "I" or "myself," the
ultimate subject of attribution is not the man, the human
will or intelligence, but the divine Self of the Son. But this
divine Self wills with a truly human will and, at the same
time, with a will which He has in common with the Father
and the Spirit; in the same way, He understands with a
human intelligence and His human interior life finds expression in a human consciousness capable of all the
nuances of joy, anguish, and compassion found in any
perfectly constituted man. But considered in Christ's total
Self, this consciousness has no human limit and, so to say,
does not reach the level of a human self, for it is the human
consciousness of the Word.

This is why the human love of Christ has a nuance and
movement which are particular to it. It is the love of a man
whose only Self is divine. The Christ-man is incapable of
any egoism, for He cannot grasp some last limit of Himself

---

† Cf. R. CARPENTIER, s.j., "Vers une morale de la charité," Greg, 34
(1953), 53–55: "Obviously the primacy of charity and the imitation of
Christ are mutually interdependent."

which would not be immediately referred to the divine Self
which is the sole subject of love, a love entirely directed
toward the Father in recognition of a gift which constitutes
Him Son, and toward the Spirit which proceeds from Him.
For the man-Jesus a turning back on self would be a turning back on God. His self-love is a love of God; it is a
human love of God selflessly detached from the created
world, which cannot appear to Him as presenting a possibility of enrichment for His true personality.

Traces of the human disinterestedness of Christ are to
be found on every page of the Gospel, for He could have
said of each of His actions: "Of myself I can do nothing.
As I hear, I judge; and my judgment is just because I seek
not my own will, but the will of him who sent me" (Jn.
5:30). And again, "For I have come down from heaven,
not to do my own will, but the will of him who sent me"
(Jn. 6:38). His human will is an instrument in the service
of the divine Self, and the latter has but one will with the
Father, for He proceeds wholly from the Father. In God
there is only one will which is common to the three
Persons, and that is why Jesus could say: "He who sees me
sees also the Father. . . . Dost thou not believe that I am
in the Father and the Father in me? The words that I
speak to you I speak not on my own authority. But the
Father dwelling in me, it is he who does the works" (Jn.
14:9–10).

Everywhere, Jesus appears as a man free of human
touchiness. To the Jews accusing Him of being possessed
by the devil, He calmly replies: "I have not a devil, but I
honor my Father, and you dishonor me. Yet I do not seek
my own glory; there is one who seeks and who judges"
(Jn. 8:49–50). If Jesus is indignant, it is against those who
violate the house of the Father (Mk. 11:15), against bad
faith deceiving simple souls (Lk. 11:42–52), but never
against those who harm only His own humanity: He prays

that His accusers and executioners be forgiven (Lk. 23:34);
He finds an excuse for Pilate (Jn. 19:11); as for Himself,
He suffers without complaint (Acts 8:32), and even finds
in His heart words of consolation for the daughters of
Jerusalem (Lk. 23:28) and for the good thief (Lk. 23:43).
The story of the passion is remarkable from this point of
view: the Good Shepherd forgets Himself to save His sheep
(Jn. 10:11); He does not do His will but that of His Father
(Jn. 6:38). To the end, Jesus has nowhere to lay His head
(Lk. 9:58); He thinks of souls before thinking of His
own sustenance (Jn. 4:32); and He never performed a
miracle for His own human advantage (Lk. 4:1–13). No
man had ever spoken and acted as this man (Jn. 7:46);
indeed, this is not surprising, since all other men have a
human self to which they necessarily refer all their natural
acts. Jesus Christ alone has no human self; He alone is free
to lay down His life and free to take it up again (Jn.
10:18), for this human life is not possessed by a human self;
no other man is master of his own life.

We find the same idea in the moral aspect of St. Paul's
Christology, where the first Adam (Rom. 5:14; I Cor.
15:45; Eph. 4:22), the prototype of egoism, is opposed to
the new Adam, characterized by the surrender of self to
God in perfect obedience (Rom. 5:19; Phil. 2:8).

It is evident that Christ could not help desiring His final
glorification (Jn. 12:23) as the necessary issue of His Incarnation. But even then, because His love ever tends to communion, He considers His own glory as one with the
glorification of the Father in Him (Jn. 13:31; 17:1–4;
12:28) and with the glorious life which He will confer on
His own (Jn. 17:10; 17:22–26; 12:26) in the everlasting
communion of the Trinity.

II. APPLICATION TO THE CHRISTIAN

Just as men were astonished and almost scandalized by
the disinterestedness of the historical Christ, so now are we

troubled when He invades our lives with the same requirements of detachment (Mt. 10:34) and mortification (Mt.
10:38).

"If anyone wishes to come after me, let him deny himself, and take up his cross, and follow me" (Mt. 16:24;
Lk. 14:33). Following Christ implies death to self (Mt.
16:25). In fact, as members of Christ, we participate in His
humanity, which is void of all human egoism and wholly
centered on God. The penetration of Christianity in individual lives and in the whole world means progress in disinterestedness in what concerns purely temporal self. There
is question here of giving to men, who have human selves,
nothing less than the attitude of Christ, who does not have
this human self. We will never go as far as losing our
human personality; nor will we have to renounce our desire
for salvation and our genuine spiritual interests, for this
desire includes no egoism, but is rather founded on the
desire which Christ had for His own glorification in union
with the Father. In fact, our Lord urges us to take care of
our own spiritual interests, but by taking on the attitudes
of Christ so that in thinking and loving we behave exactly
as Christ. Our analysis has shown that human loves are
wholly relative to God, but that they always leave us with
a temporal self which vindicates its legitimate share of
interests and attachments. But the present consideration
invites us to a disinterestedness in terrestrial life which is
unthinkable without Christ. Herein lies the whole morality
of St. Paul: to abandon the egoism of the old man and to
open oneself to God, to no longer search for *"quæ nostra
sunt"* (1 Cor. 13:5), but *"quæ sursum sunt"* (Col. 3:1), to
die with Christ in order to rise and live *"in Christo,"*[3] in
charity and without any trace of egoism.

This attitude of disinterestedness in our human activity
derives from its participation in the charity of Christ, since
it is by charity that we act as members of Christ. Now,

taken formally as members, we are more Christ than we are ourselves. Hence the fundamental sense of Christian action is radically different from the sense of a pagan life, insofar as the latter is not influenced by Christ. The attitude of charity in Christian life is understandable only in Christ; outside of Him, it is impossible to explain why our adhesion to God's will can be wholly, so to say, "theoverted," an adhesion which goes so far in the mystic as to create the impression of his having totally lost his human self in God;[4] indeed he sometimes conveys this impression in rather immoderate words.

It is metaphysically impossible for us to lose our human self; but the Christian being, involving as it does the status of member of Christ, can take such a place in the psychology of the contemplative that the human self, in its temporal and sensible manifestations, loses all interest for him and gradually ceases to preoccupy his attention in proportion as he takes on the attitude of Christ. In the mystic, the man has given place, insofar as it is possible in this life, to the Christian as such, that is, to real participation in Christ.

Even if every Christian does not attain this perfection, he nevertheless lives on this same reality and his being has the same sense. That is why the fundamental tendency of our lives as members of Christ is a total surrender to God, a will to destroy in us all personal desire which would not be in conformity with His, and even the will to act in positive dependence on His will, that is, in virtue of His and not our own movement. In brief, the fundamental tendency and sense of our charity, inasmuch as it conforms to the human attitudes of Christ, consist in the love of God disinterested in all that is not He, a love of communion by virtue of which we find more pleasure in Him and in His interests than in ourselves and our own interests. This is properly theological charity toward God.

III. CONSEQUENCES IN MORAL THEOLOGY

1. Our human actions, because they are actions of Christians in the state of grace, necessarily call for a tightening of our bonds with the divine Person of Christ. Moral life is a personal commitment to Jesus Christ, for it is a mediation of the created charity of Christ which adapts His humanity, and hence ours also, to the Person of the Word. A secular morality is in no way modeled on reality: it is an abstraction.

2. We also see here in what sense Christian morality favors humanism. It does not directly aim at developing our human personality, but, on the contrary, to shift the center of interest from our autonomous human self to that of our self as a member of Christ, docile to the inspirations of our Head. It follows that a Christian humanism can only exist on condition that it surpasses itself by becoming Christ-centered and accepting the necessary sacrifices that this implies; but under these conditions it favors a most unexpected development of the human person, less on the purely human level than on the divine, since it enables man to live as "man-God" and to reproduce the divine manners in human form with their demands for purity, truth, generosity, detachment, and love which a purely natural humanism could never have dreamt of. The supernatural causes a man to be what he is, but infinitely more profoundly than could be expected from his nature: it shatters the limitations which men regard as highest among human values. We do not deny here the personalizing power of charity; on the contrary, it attains its maximum development through conscious communion with another presence —that of Christ. It can be questioned whether the name of humanism can still be applied to such an unbelievable surpassing of human possibilities, for this word, inherited from the Renaissance, was meant to designate self-sufficient human plenitude, which did not surpass itself by dying to natural instincts to put on Christ and to take up His cross. Personally, we regret neither the word nor the thing itself, for we know that only the *new* man, the son of God, has the promise of life and resurrection, and that the *old* man has already been sold out to death.*

3. The whole of Christian morality can be summarized in the imitation of Jesus Christ, who is its concrete and perfect exemplar, as F. Tillmann has shown so well in his moral theology entitled *Die Nachfolge Christi.* It supposes frequent recourse to the sources of tradition. The norm of morality is a person rather than a law. It is a loving imitation of a God-man who Himself continues to act interiorly by grace and the sacraments. Such a rule of life is incomparably more complete, more human, and more powerful than any theoretical morality.†

4. This disinterestedness toward human self in view of a life of higher charity is a Christian value which cannot be understood or practiced to such a degree were we not intimately bound to Christ. The virtue of abnegation is closely and necessarily connected with charity. Moral acts

* A. GAUTHIER, O.P., studies one aspect of Christian humanism in his work entitled *Magnanimité*, Paris, 1951 (for a review, see NRT, 75 [1953], 937–950). It seems difficult, however, to admit with the author (in spite of the corrections he has added to his thesis) that if theologians had recognized a "natural magnanimity," it would be possible today to constitute a spirituality proper to the laity—the more so since, for him, this recognition dates from St. Thomas and would have contrasted with the "monastic" ideal of the Middle Ages. The chief quality, or even the very essence of a Christian spirituality is to be evangelical, to be informed by the supernatural love of the Father. It is understood, however, that the gospel being an aspiration, all do not realize it in the same manner even though all are stirred by it.

† On the question whether it would be better to center the technical formulation of moral theology on the Person of Christ rather than on theological charity, see R. CARPENTIER, S.J., "Vers une morale de la charité," Greg, 34 (1953), 32–55; cf. J. FUCHS, S.J., "Die Liebe als Aufbauprinzip der Moraltheologie," Schol, 29 (1954), 79–87.

detach us from ourselves; they cause us to surpass our human self and are the concrete means of our divinization. That is why the early Christians were right in seeing martyrdom as the typical realization of Christian perfection.[5]

§III. Devotedness to Others

1. christ's humanity is wholly in view of men

The Incarnation of Christ gives to His human love and to His charity still another fundamental nuance. The humanity assumed by the Son brings Him no advantage whatsoever; the Word had no need of any enrichment; and if He takes on a human nature; it is in view of enriching it. By its very constitution, therefore, the humanity of Christ is the prototype of a creature who is created "for" others. For the moment, we are not insisting on the fact that Christ's humanity is entirely referred to the divine Person of the Son, but on the fact that in the divine economy it exists wholly for the advantage of other persons, since it can in no way enrich the Person who possesses it. This does not in any way prevent it from being created for the glory of God, for it is evidently a manifestation of His goodness. For this new reason, then, the humanity of Christ is a gift, and its most intimate law is a kind of altruism which cannot be found in any other creature. All individual persons, as spirits, have an individual end and, in some way, an absolute finality, inasmuch as they are destined to partake in the absolute Life, even though this individual destination is not separable from the destination of the whole Church as a community. When we considered the humanity of Christ as lacking a human personality, we were led to discover that it was entirely opened on God; but our present reflection leads us rather to its fundamental inclination toward men. A creature existing only for the advantage of others, and in no way in the interests of the person to whom it is united, has, necessarily, a fundamental tendency corresponding to this ontological finality. This same tendency, which projects the thought and heart of Christ toward God, also projects them toward humanity, and this movement in Christ is as spontaneous as the natural movement which carries us toward our proper self. When He thought of Himself, He could not help seeing Himself wholly oriented toward others; and reflection upon Himself always implied thinking of all other men. Love for others was just as innate in Him as love for God.

But does this fundamental, ontological altruism of Christ's humanity concern His charity, in which our charity participates? There can be no doubt about this. By its very constitution, the Person of Jesus implies a grace of union, and the human activity of this Person is modeled on its being; it follows that all the human love of Christ is essentially a love united to the divinity and is, therefore, charity.

The New Testament abounds in manifestations of this attitude of Jesus toward men. He came *propter nos homines*; He went about doing good (Acts 10:38); He loved us to the very end, delivering Himself (Gal. 2:20) up to death (Phil. 2:8) and even to the Eucharist (Jn. 13:1);[6] solicitous lest He lose any of those entrusted to Him by His Father (Jn. 17:12–19) and wishing them to be with Him close to the Father (Jn. 17:24), He identified Himself with them as the vine with the branches (Jn. 15:5). Just as He thought of others during His life, being moved by human suffering (Lk. 7:11–13) even to tears (Jn. 11:35), He does not forget us when He is about to leave us: He recommends us to the goodness of the Father (Jn. 17:11), He promises not to leave us orphans (Jn. 14:18) but to send us another to befriend us (Jn. 14:16). And on the cross, before dying, He gives us His own mother (Jn. 19:26–27).

His work on earth is entirely a solicitude for men: He comes to heal and not to judge (Jn. 12:47); He does not condemn repentant sinners and watches for the first word of sorrow (Lk. 23:43), for He wishes that all men be saved (1 Tim. 2:4).

His new and proper commandment is to love one's neighbor (Jn. 13:34, 15:12).

II. APPLICATION TO THE CHRISTIAN

Christian charity causes us to participate in this attitude of Christ toward men, for grace in us is a participation in the fullness of the "grace of the Head." "Caput et membra sunt quasi una persona mystica."[7]

Now it is not only as members of the human race that we must love other men; our union in Christ binds us to all other men in a unity infinitely more intimate than that which is founded on our nature. No doubt, the latter does cause us to participate in a certain unity: "Omnes homines sunt unus homo in natura communi."[8] In fact, philosophy has not yet discovered the full meaning of this natural unity, which is so profound that each man can be considered as a synthesis of humanity.[9] But human nature is dispersed in a multitude of individuals engaged in matter, which isolates being and makes it exterior to itself. In Christ this unity becomes still more profound, for here men do not participate merely in human nature, but also in divine nature. And this brings us closer to the Trinity, the ideal of love and unity, wherein the Persons possess one and the same nature without multiplying it. A Christian separated from Christ is a sheer ontological monstrosity and even more inconceivable than an individual man who would not include humanity. Too often our way of thinking of man somewhat resembles the picking of a flower. We are too attracted by what is exterior and visible in it. To see a flower ontologically is to see the sap in it sucked by the roots and ascending in the trunk and branches; it is to know that the flower breathes and lives by its leaves. Otherwise it has no meaning: a picked flower is no more a flower than a corpse is a body. A man, and especially a Christian, cannot be thought of as an isolated individual, for he actually includes all Christians, his brothers; his Head which is Christ; and the Trinity wherein his super- natural life is rooted.

United as we are to all men in the Head, we must adopt toward all the attitude which the Head shows toward men. If it is true that grace in us is but participation in the grace of the Head, the fundamental components of this capital grace must be found in some way in its members.

As we have seen, the fundamental attitude of Christ toward men can be expressed in the following manner: He is created "for" them.

To hear Jesus Christ say "Love one another as I have loved you" cannot remain without some consequences. We know that He loved us *in finem*, that is, far more than His own earthly life. Hence, there is in the Christian a force which causes him to prefer others to his own temporal self. And this is not contradicted when Jesus says elsewhere, "Thou shalt love thy neighbor as thyself" (Mt. 22:39; Mk. 12:31). In this last formula, Jesus summarizes the Old Law in answer to a doctor who had asked, "Which is the greatest commandment of the Law?" (Mt. 22:36). But it is only at the end of His life when, after a long formation, the apostles have become capable of bearing it, that Jesus gives them "a new commandment" (Jn. 13:34) which is also His own commandment: "This is my commandment, that you should love one another as I have loved you" (Jn. 15:12). And His immediate comment is, "Greater love than this

no man has, that one lay down his life for his friends"
(Jn. 15:13).

It even seems that the Gospels and the Epistles insist
more on love for one's neighbor than on love for God. We
find in St. John the reason for this: "If anyone says, 'I love
God,' and hates his brother, he is a liar. For how can he
who does not love his brother, whom he sees, love God,
whom he does not see" (1 Jn. 4:20).

Love for our neighbor is, in some way, the visible sign
of our love for God; it is its incarnate form, the proof of
its genuineness. Coming back to the formulation which we
have already worked out in our Second Part,[10] we can say
that the realizations of our love for men are a mediation of
our love for God. Because love for men demands to be
embodied in visible works and, though fundamentally theological, involves a sentiment which quite easily becomes
conscious, it can be formulated in terms of morality and
thus become the tangible and incarnated apparition of our
love for God. Besides, God has become in Jesus Christ our
human neighbor. Now men are really one with Jesus Christ,
so that what we do to a Christian we do to Jesus Christ,
not in a metaphorical, but in a most real way (Acts 9:5).
Again, he who sees Jesus sees the Father (Jn. 14:9). Charity
that is directly addressed to God can no doubt give rise to
other conscious moral manifestations, such as prayer, liturgical cult, the giving of self; but in its profound reality
it is the ineffable contact and giving of the soul to God; it
does not consist only in words or exterior acts, but is the
ontological giving of our whole being. Because it is such a
radical gift, it requires manifestations to prove its sincerity;
for if it is the gift of all that we are, it must also be the gift
of conscious realizations of ourselves, which we more easily
control. That is why Jesus said that the best proof of love
is the observance of His commandments—and His all-

embracing commandment is that we love our neighbor (cf.
Jn. 15:10–12).

In this perspective, the concrete love of our neighbor in
its turn gains in theological depth: the most incarnate of
our moral duties attain, through men, Christ Himself and
are all reduced to love.

We find here a theological application of the theory of
mediation which we have already described from the philosophical viewpoint. Our duties toward the members of
Christ are a mediation of our charity toward God, since it
is the same theological charity that attains man and God.
We are not insinuating that it is impossible that charity be
directly oriented toward God. In fact, even if we are
incarnate and social, it remains true that we are spirits and
persons; this is why, besides mediation, there must be an
"immediation" which is the direct contact of theological
charity with its object.

III. CONSEQUENCES IN MORAL THEOLOGY

Christian love, as such, is then wholly inclined toward
others. Of itself it is not a new inclination toward our
isolated terrestrial self; our natural love suffices for this role;
besides, charity divinizes it and gives it a nuance of communion. Indeed it requires all the power of Christ's charity
to draw us out of ourselves.

While the first movement of natural love for our neighbor is to give ourselves to him "reasonably," that is, by
still maintaining the legitimate preference for our temporal
self, the spontaneous movement of the Christian is to give
himself without counting the cost. We are familiar with the
"folly" of the saints as opposed to human "wisdom." Ordinarily the two loves complete one another, but if they com-
pete, it is clear which must be the victor. In this case,
Christian love does not cease to be reasonable; it can never
go contrary to reason, if we mean by this word "Christian"

reason enlightened and transformed by faith, thus admitting a total giving of self.

It is normal for a saintly Christian to sacrifice his own interests for the souls of others. We do not mean that he will sacrifice his spiritual interests, which are those of his self as a member of Christ and are the expression of God's will for him,[11] but his temporal interests, on which his human self fixes as on its possessions. It is normal to give one's own life to save the soul and even the life of another; one can even go further if it is clear that his gift is a genuine manifestation of the charity of Christ.[12] What appears in the natural man as folly can be in harmony with the supreme wisdom of charity, for the fact of becoming a member of Christ gives to the Christian a new ontology.

It can be said that the whole of Christian moral conduct is perfectly defined as "acting as members of Christ."[13] This explains the solicitude of the Christian for all men: the numberless services provided by Christian charity, especially toward the most abandoned, who are precisely the least attractive from a natural viewpoint;[14] the Christian apostolic spirit which must act in each member so that the body may continually expand; the martyrs of charity who have died in the service of the plague-stricken or lepers; and, in general, all those who daily offer their lives for their brothers.

So in its very structure, Christian morality is a drastic anti-individualism which in no way contradicts its personalizing value.

§IV. Filial Sanctity

I. FILII IN FILIO

We have recalled two characteristic aspects of our morality which derive from the fact that it is a mediation of a charity participating in the charity of Christ: it is altruistic and Christ-centered. This charity of Christ puts us in contact first with His humanity, since it is in this total humanity that we have a part. But we cannot forget that Christ includes us in His Mystical Body in order to put us in contact with His divinity. Thus the mystery becomes all the more meaningful for us.

What is the formal effect of our incorporation in Christ by charity? Is it only to put us in contact with God as He is one in nature, or rather with the Trinity as such? Father Mersch replies:

When the Incarnation took place, the Son as Son, God as revealed in the mystery of the Trinity, was given to a creature before God as considered in His nature was thus given; this priority is manifestly logical and not chronological. In other words, the God of the Incarnation is God as attained by faith alone, rather than God as known analogically by our unaided intellect. Therefore the Incarnation is a communication of the Godhead as Trinity rather than as simple Godhead, and the Christian as Christian knows God because he knows the Trinity, not vice versa; he knows God through the Son in the Father and the Spirit.[15]

Of course, the works *ad extra*, even the humanity of Christ, are works of the whole Trinity, if we consider them *in fieri;* but considered *in facto esse,* as the term of divine activity, the humanity of the Word, His grace, and His charity subsist in the Person of the Son and in it alone. This grace and this charity are no longer merely works *ad extra,* but adaptations permitting a humanity to be hypostatically united to the Word and hence to subsist *ad intra Trinitatis.* The humanity of Christ is adapted to the divinity and is divinized only by being first adapted to the Son. It is this essential relation to the Son that we emphasize when we call the grace of Christ a *filial* grace and His charity a *filial* charity.

Since the Mystical Body of Jesus prolongs His physical humanity, it is by this filial grace and charity that the being and action of all Christians participate in Christ and, through Him, in the Trinity and in the intratrinitarian activity of the Word.

The consequences of this doctrine in the field of our charitable activity are considerable. They would even seem too daring if the total self-giving of Christ had not revealed to us the incredible generosity of God and the intimacy to which He invites us.

The God-man is, with the Father, the principle of the Holy Spirit. Of course it is not as man that He is spirating with the Father, but Jesus the man, insofar as He is personally the Word, is spirator. The whole being of the Son consists in possessing the divine nature as received from the Father; but his whole action as Son is to spirate the Holy Ghost with the Father, that is, to love, since the Holy Spirit proceeds by way of love. The Son, and hence Christ, "is love, as the Holy Spirit is love, but in His own way, in the relationship of principle to term."[16] Therefore the theological charity of Christ enables His human activity to be the activity of the spirator, and His human love to be the love of the spirator. Theological charity is the human-divine principle by which the human love of Jesus takes part in the love of the Word, which is the active spiration of the Holy Spirit. We must come to the striking conclusion that all the human activity of Christ proceeds finally from charity:[17] His most humble doings as well as His miracles, His joys and sufferings, and even the situations He had to undergo, which were always voluntarily assumed by Him—all were referred to the same love whence eternally proceeds the Holy Spirit, but on the level of His divinized humanity.

Now charity in the Christian participates in the charity of the Head, the "spirating" charity of the God-man.

Though created and finite, inasmuch as it is ours, our supernatural love cannot be separated from the spirating love of the Word: it includes an intrinsic and ontological participation in the operation whence the Holy Spirit proceeds. Of course it cannot be said that the Holy Spirit proceeds from our love as members, but our love breaks in on the intratrinitarian life where the Holy Spirit is spirated; in its existential structure, our love necessarily involves a relation to the Holy Spirit and to this spiration. Christ as cospirator possesses the Holy Spirit and gives Him to whom He wills: "But if I go, I will send him to you. . . . He will glorify me, because he will receive of what is mine and declare it to you" (cf. Jn. 16:7, 14–15).[18] This is why the Church, the body of Christ, acts with the same astonishing authority as her Head, as if she herself could dispose of the Holy Spirit and give Him. And, in fact, she can, in union with Christ. The apostles gathered together in council at Jerusalem write with calm assurance, "The Holy Spirit and we have decided . . ." (Acts 15:28). In each Christian, the following words of St. Paul find their full meaning: "And because you are the sons, God has sent the spirit of his Son into our hearts, crying 'Abba, Father' " (Gal. 4:6; cf. Rom. 8:15–16). The Holy Spirit is in us, in the sense that He proceeds from the Christ of whom we are members by grace.

Since Jesus Christ was possible only through the co-operation of the Virgin, His grace and His charity in which we participate have necessarily a Marian aspect; and this is why a Christian life, and hence a Christian morality, must contain in their ontology and their psychology a confident, filial quality corresponding to this maternal presence in the economy of our action. "Because of Mary, Christianity has a unique spirit of hope, joy and human truth," and for sinners especially "Christianity would lack some of its goodness if the Blessed Virgin, the Mother, were not there."* This should not be forgotten in pastoral theology, where moralists must determine not only principles, but attitudes to be adopted toward sinners.

II. CONSEQUENCES IN MORAL THEOLOGY

I. FILIAL SOUL

Once he has entered the divine family, the Christian sees in moral law, much more than mere legislation, the expression of paternal love. Obviously the latter is more exacting than the former, but the spirit of their demands differs by all the distance there is between the attraction of love and the constraint of law. We will come back to this distinction later, when we discuss the obligation of love.[19] The filial quality of our charity impresses on our being and, to a certain degree, on our consciousness and activity, a disposition causing us to accept confidently our life as coming from a God who is also our Father; for the whole reality and "psychology" of the Son is, so to say, a total reception of self from the Father. Hence there is nothing "tragic" in the Christian soul; on the contrary, she has the tranquil certitude that everything that happens is a messenger from a personally attentive love. The invitation to become once again a child (Mt. 18:3) is a pedagogical way of leading us to become conscious of our condition of sons. This receptive attitude toward God also reveals a characteristic trait of the intimate Christian attitude, a certain passivity which makes us accept that God be, with us, and, we might say, even more than we, the principle of our own actions, and

* MERSCH, *The Theology of the Mystical Body*, p. 192. The whole chapter consecrated to Mary, the mother of Jesus, forms one of the most beautiful passages written on our Lady. See the author's thought more fully developed in his article, "Sainte Marie, mère de Dieu," NRT, 67 (1940), 129–152.

that we be nothing but the thoroughfare of God's love, ever conscious that this divine activity is also really ours through the mystery of our participation in Christ. Moral action is not primarily man's conquest, but the collaboration of a son in the work of his Father. That is why the first particular moral virtue after charity is man's humility in confronting God's advances.† Perhaps it is not useless to recall this fundamental attitude of Christian action at a time when many think that the essence of their life is a nauseating absurdity, and others are still not cured of easy and seductive activism.[20]

2. CALL TO SANCTITY

Our action is drawn into the Trinitarian activity and takes part in the most excellent operation of sanctity: that whence proceeds the Spirit of sanctity—the interior Gift, Love, and Life of the Trinity. From our activity also proceeds saintly love and true divine life, for each act, insofar as it is one with charity, increases charity and sanctifying grace,[21] which means at the same time an increase of divine life and of personal sanctity. In Christian morality there is no longer question of merely producing perfect men, but rather of enabling men to live as God Himself and to live by His own life. Merely human morality knows nothing of this call to sanctity, for sanctity is conformity with the supreme goodness of God.

3. RELIGIOUS MORALITY

If morality puts us in intimate contact with the divine Persons, it must necessarily be religious. This affirmation is surely astonishing to those accustomed to an autonomous secular morality conceived in a Kantian manner.

† A plan for a course in moral theology would have to take into account the order of the Christian virtues.

Of course we must distinguish religion in the strict sense, which governs divine worship as such, and religion in the wider sense, which comprises all activities putting us in relation to God.[22] The first meaning refers to the moral virtue of religion; we will treat later of the animation of this virtue by charity.[23] When we say that morality is essentially religious, we refer to the second meaning just defined. The principle of union between morality and religion is essential to Christian revelation.*

In fact, it is impossible for charity, which institutes personal relations between God and man, not to be the very essence of the religious attitude. It is not surprising to find a treatise on pastoral theology in which, in the section dealing with the duties of man toward God, the theological virtues come under a chapter entitled "The Duties of Interior Divine Worship," while the moral virtue of religion comes under the title of "The Duties of Exterior Divine Worship" (*Die Pflichten der äusseren Gottesverehrung* as opposed to *Pflichten der inneren Gottesverehrung*).[24]

4. THEOLOGICAL MORALITY

From all we have said, the most important conclusion we can draw is that our morality must be above all a theology. The moral agent, whom we consider, is in the state of grace. Hence the center of interest of morality is shifted to a higher level. Can such a morality be accused of depreciating properly human and natural values? Surely not human values, since the supernatural remains properly

---

* Cf. M.-J. LAGRANGE, O.P., *La morale de l'Évangile* (3rd ed.; Paris, 1932), pp. 204–207. Pope Pius XI, in his encyclical *Mit brennender Sorge*, wrote: "On faith in God, guarded intact and spotless, rests the morality of humanity. Every attempt to remove morality and the moral order from this solid rock foundation of faith, in order to establish them on the quicksands of human rules, sooner or later leads to the moral ruin of both individuals and societies" (AAS, 29 [1937], 158).

human while being also divine; nor the natural values, since we take them as mediations, that is, as being existentially one with our whole being: we have already pointed out that a mediation cannot be used and then left aside as a mere instrument.[25] But, on the other hand, if the mediation remains in actual and intrinsic relation with the true value, it appears nevertheless as limited and exterior. And so the "natural" is not replaced and may well occupy in our treatises a space proportioned to its exteriority and dispersion; but the emphasis is not to be placed on it. It must be studied in a higher qualitative perspective, where the human agent no longer pursues human perfection, but divine life.

III. COROLLARY: NATURAL AND SUPERNATURAL MORALITY

Do the determinations of natural morality remain unchanged in this new perspective? We have described earlier, from a psychological viewpoint, the relations between nature and supernature.[26] In its ontological and existential aspect, the problem can be summarized in the following theses:

1. There are two degrees of gratuity in God's gifts to man, that of creation and that of "divinization." The latter is entirely gratuitous in relation to the former, and no strict requirement can be found for it in created nature: it is absolutely supernatural.* Such is the traditional teaching of the Church,[27] formally embodied in the Vatican Council.[28]

In fact, reason teaches us that when God takes the

---

* "As for the other gifts, we receive them only by having them. . . . But the divine gifts are constitutive and even though they always come from without, what they give is the 'inside' itself. The first of these gifts is the divine communication of creation: by it God gives man to be man, to be himself. . . . The second of these gifts is the second creation, that communication of God which divinizes. What it gives is again being, but divinized being, which permits man in some way to be God. . . . Since God is being itself, He grants man to be more fully, infinitely more fully, and since to be is to be oneself and in oneself, to be more fully is to be more totally oneself and in oneself" (É. MERSCH, S.J., *Morale et Corps Mystique,* II, 29).

initiative in creating a being to whom He can communicate His own life, it is necessary that this being be other than He. This would be impossible if the creature were already defined by this supernatural communication, for such a communication is precisely the gift that God makes of Himself as God, the gift of His own life, of that which is incommunicable in Him, or better, of that which He cannot communicate without also giving His divine intimacy. God could not directly create purely supernatural being.

2. Hence the natural and the supernatural must be strictly distinct. But, in the concrete, how are we to delimit their respective fields? Natural man never existed. In the concrete man, nature and supernature form one complex being.

Perhaps it is easier to begin with the notion of the supernatural. Its most current meaning is "that which exceeds the powers and requirements of nature." Without forgetting this characteristic of the supernatural, theologians give it a further concrete meaning. "Supernatural" qualifies, above all, the ultimate end of "elevated" man, whom God calls to the beatific vision. As of now God gives to man the preparation and beginning of the beatific vision, which is grace, a supernatural gratuitous gift. All that pertains to the order of the vision and of grace will be called supernatural.[29] We add, with Father Mersch, that the supernatural cannot be understood unless it is related to our inclusion in Christ, who introduces it into humanity and is, by this very fact, its center of intelligibility.[30] But in the concrete, what is the extension of the field of realities related to the beatific vision? After all, do not miracles, the preternatural, and grace suppose that we know the limits of the natural?

Starting from the other extreme, the notion of the natural, it is clear that its field was first determined from experience; natural first meant "inborn," that which we have by birth, by generation.[31] That will be natural which we can be, have, or do by virtue of an inborn principle which is our "nature," our essence, and all that is proportioned to it.

However, in the concrete, this experimental notion of the natural has certain inconveniences, for the beings which we meet with are from their birth and from the birth of the universe, ordered to the supernatural. Who would say that a Buddhist or a Confucianist is a purely natural man? Have there not been, from the very beginning, preparations for Christianity outside the Church?

3. In fact, if not by strict necessity, the natural coincides with what we can be or do by our faculties of action without the aid of positive revelation or of extrinsic help. In the moral order, it coincides with that which every man can understand and perform in virtue of the mere possession of his spiritual faculties; in brief, it can be reduced to that which is reasonable and more precisely to what can be expressed in concepts—however imperfect these may be—without the help of revelation. A natural morality is a "reasonable" morality. Now, does it contain only that which is naturally ontological in man? Does it not contain certain elements which we believe to be simply proportioned to our own powers, but which are actually gratuitous though generalized gifts of God? In fact, who can adequately describe the *homo naturalis*?

In any case, we can recognize that there is no heterogeneity between natural and total morality. We could even say that, for us Christians, the former is a section artificially cut out from real, complete morality, a rational systematization of that which man can and must do, considering what seems common and proportioned to all men. It comprises all that synderesis alone can by itself discover and command in the moral order. On reading the current textbooks, one gathers the impression at times that the "natural" occupies the most important place in Christian morality.

But this is true only in appearance, for the implicit, qualitative aspect is actually quite different. Since these determinations have been elaborated over the centuries by men who were, consciously or unconsciously, under the influence of a supernatural finality, it is not surprising that they are fundamentally in accord with revealed morality and can be assumed by it.[32]

4. But even though striking in resemblance, Christian and natural morality are radically different, much more than a fugue of Bach played on a grand organ is different from the same fugue played on a piano or transposed in a different key. Because the being of the Christian is entirely new, his end, his consciousness, his action, his liberty are new; consequently the spirit of his morality is absolutely specific and its determinations have another "sense."[33] But why do these determinations seem to simply be taken from natural ethics? First of all, the minimum demands remain unchanged when the whole life is called to a higher perfection. Ordinarily current textbooks are chiefly concerned with strict obligations, so that a formulation in terms of natural morality can appear quite sufficient to them. Besides, the natural law is really exacting, and it is far from being a superfluous task to insist on its fulfillment, even among Christians. Secondly, the supernatural value of moral life arises from its impregnation by charity. Now it suffices that charity be present, even if it is not formally conscious. That is why in describing minimal duties, many authors do not think it necessary to express the animation by charity on the level of the virtues. They think it is sufficient to affirm in the chapter on charity the obligation of repeated acts of charity in order to maintain the state of grace. But in reality we have not only direct consciousness of our supernatural activity, motivations, and intentions, but the supernatural appears also in reflex consciousness under the form of conceptual representations; in their conceptual expression, the specific ends of the infused virtues are clearly distinct from the corresponding ends of the natural virtues. The demands of the natural law are not only reinforced; they are also changed, in the sense that they are transported onto a higher plane; for example, Christian justice, which governs the relations among rights on the plane of supernatural brotherhood, has requirements quite different from those of justice on the purely human plane, for there the intimacy of relations is radically different;[34] the chastity of a member of Christ has motives and requirements quite other than those of natural chastity,[35] and so too for all the other virtues. Each new degree of being postulates a new law, new forces proportioned to it, and a type of knowledge proper to it. The Christian is no exception to this rule.

And so if natural morality becomes a constituent of Christian morality, it does not do so without receiving a new "sense" and without acquiring many new specifications. The theological and infused virtues find their normal complement in the sacraments and the commandments of the Church. In any case, the so-called "natural" morality is itself influenced by the Christian or supernatural context in which it was elaborated.

5. The fact that natural morality is, so to say, a rational systematization cut out from concrete and ontological moral reality explains the rather abstract character of the formulation found in our textbooks. On the contrary, the morality found in the gospel, as revealed in the Person of the incarnate Word, eternal Son of an eternal Father, is wholly concrete and vital. In Him become visible the filial duties binding us to our Father and the brotherly duties binding us to the other children of God. However, this does not suppress the necessity of a systematic formulation of morality, apparently separated from the revelation of the good in Jesus. But must we conclude that when a Christian

thinks he is following mere natural law, his action does not in fact reach beyond this natural plane? Definitely not. When it is necessary to judge whether a given action performed in the state of grace, but having all the appearances of being purely natural, is meritorious, the true, existential, supernatural finality is to be considered, not the natural finality which, in the Christian, is an abstraction. This consideration justifies what we said earlier, namely, that the explicit intention is not necessary for supernatural merit.[36] Since the whole being and activity of a Christian living in charity are plunged in the supernatural current, there can be no purely natural action in him unless he excludes the finality of grace.* Hence, in the order of concrete acts performed by the just, there is a presumption and priority favoring the supernatural; the purely natural must reveal its identity in order to be recognized as such. An act of courage, for example, can appear to us as having a purely natural goodness without any explicit supernatural content; but does this mean that it is, in fact, an act of natural courage? No, for it is drawn forth by a finality which centers it on the living God and is performed by a faculty elevated by grace. This is why we have been able to affirm that the supernatural finality is, in a certain manner, really represented, at least in the direct and vital consciousness we have of our supernatural intention. Hence, action has a supernatural moral aspect which Christian morality can and must try to express with some degree of precision. Even if we are content to consider in the rich complexity of this act of a son of God only that which is proportioned to the natural forces of human intelligence, it is, nevertheless, obvious

* It is true that a more or less egoistic and sinful intention often at least partially prevents this finality of grace from fully producing its effect and merit; and the same is true of the absence of a truly human act due to human imperfection, by which men often act according to their instincts (even if these be good) without even an implicit reference to morality.

"that any motive of moral virtue suffices to relate my present action to the ultimate end. For I can only conceive moral virtue as defined by a relation of essential conformity between certain categories of acts and the movement directed toward my ultimate end. Therefore, to act immediately in view of this conformity is to act mediately in view of the ultimate end itself."†

All this follows from the fact that our morality is, above all, a theology and that our moral life is a participation in the very life of the Trinity in the charity of the Son.

§V. A Mortified Life

We come now to an essential aspect of the charity of Christ, namely, redemption through suffering, which we meet with everywhere in daily life. We will show that in Christ the greatest act of charity is His redemptive death, which has given a particular nuance to His whole activity. We will then examine in what way our own moral action and morality inherit this nuance.

I. IN CHRIST

The humanity of Christ of whose grace and charity we partake had to meet with corporal death. Because it was voluntarily undergone in expiation for our sins, His death was the object of a moral act of supreme value, in fact, of the greatest moral act of His life.

For all men, death is not only the final event of earthly life, but also its apex; and through a fully voluntary acceptance, that should be prepared and offered long in advance, it should become the occasion of the moral act par excellence.

† M. DE LA TAILLE, s.j., "Le péché véniel dans la théologie de saint Thomas," Greg, 7 (1926), 33. However, the author does not come to the conclusions we suggest here, for he studies the matter in a different context.

To explain how this is possible, we must have recourse to a philosophy of death based on the profound interdependence between body and soul even in the most spiritual activities in life. Such a philosophy does not see in the "act of dying" a distinct human act, but the culmination of the whole series of previous acts, which in spite of their gradually failing vigor nevertheless remain true to themselves. A man who really "thinks" his life, sees it disintegrating daily. Apart from ever-rebelling pride and lust for pleasure, he accepts this law. If he loves God, this submission can increase, can become more concrete, more experimental with the physical harbingers of death. It can even be transformed into a desire, an aspiration of a really spiritual and redemptive nature, in union with the dying Christ. Such is the supreme duty of Christian morality.

Father Mersch goes further and proposes a metaphysics of death. For him, this passage of soul, consciousness, and liberty into another state must be a conscious and free act.

This "change that occurs in the soul itself, in its very consciousness and liberty, has to be an act of the soul, a conscious and free act. It consists in spontaneously willing, as spirit, what an unescapable necessity forces on man as body . . . , in willing this event as such, with its unescapable necessity. This shows how starkly in opposition with the human act of dying is the attitude of soul which suicide supposes. Acceptance is what makes bodily death a human event. . . . Therefore death is an act; but . . . is a very special act. It is a unique act and has no more than an analogy with the acts of which we have daily experience." [37]

While all the preceding acts are partial and limited in time, this act, ultimate in the series, is temporal only insofar as it frees itself from the temporal. If the preceding actions were conscious and free, the act which consummates the series and frees the soul from the material limitations which it had while informing the body, thus permitting it now to subsist as a pure spirit, is all the more conscious and free, though its liberty is, in fact, influenced by previous training. It does not matter whether death is undergone as an event resulting from physical laws, for the soul can be active and free in accepting a necessary law. The soul is free especially in the act wherein it concentrates itself as a spirit. If the preceding acts have been moral by their conformity to particular precepts of moral law, then death will be the moral act par excellence, for it does not merely conform the soul in a partial and passing manner to one aspect of the law, but it causes it to coincide with this moral ideal to which it surrenders; death is the act which totalizes the soul by uniting it to the plenitude of the law. That is why death, which for the body implies the ultimate failure, is for the soul the supreme act of life. The only "total" human act which the soul can perform while still united with the body is precisely the act by which it accepts separation from that body which disperses it in space and time.*

* No more than Father MERSCH, are we thinking of a theory of illumination of the soul at the moment of death, as is suggested or defended by L. GETINO, O.P., *Del gran numero de los que se salvan* (Madrid), 1934, nor even as A.-D. SERTILLANGES, O.P., *Catéchisme des incroyants* (Paris, 1930), II, 165–166, or P. GLORIEUX, "Endurcissement final et grâces dernières," NRT, 59 (1932), 865 ff.

Cf. MERSCH, *The Theology of the Mystical Body*, p. 263, n. 41. The author here considers the free act at the very moment of the separation of soul and body: it is "an act of the present life and of union with the body, but so far as that life and union cease. . . . It is . . . the passage from here to there, but regarded from the standpoint of here. . . . It is the passage of a free being to the definite stage which its liberty has prepared" (*ibid.*, p. 265). This is why other acts "preserve their undiminished importance, including their importance as the commencement of the last act. At all periods human life is formidable in its seriousness. . . . For the wicked, the last act is terribly hazardous; but for the good it is, so to speak, prefashioned in good" (*ibid.*, p. 268).

It seems to us that this act can only be improperly called "the act of dying"; taken as such, the physical separation, the "fact" of dying, is not a free act of the soul: only the body dies; the soul merely suffers a passive change. But "the change that occurs in the soul itself, in its very consciousness and liberty, has to be (we should say "necessarily implies")

Whatever the validity of this hypothesis, we must admit that death is the summit of our life as *viatores*. If our life is a tendency toward God and a love expressed in multiple acts of love, the acceptance of death is the supreme gift of love totalizing all the others, which were merely its progressive preparation. This would already be true in a natural order. From the point of view of charity, the moral acts which were its partial mediations give way to a total mediation of charity, whether death itself implies this act, according to Father Mersch's hypothesis, or whether it is the culminating point of a life passed or at least finished in charity.

The whole purpose of our life is to succeed in making this last act an act of perfect charity.

Hence in Christ, as in all men, charity was oriented toward this final total gift in full acceptance of death. This perspective places Christ's death in striking relief. Not only is His whole life directed toward and summarized in this great act of love, but the whole universe and the whole of history converge toward this privileged moment; the death of Jesus is the center of the world and of time.* Condren has said:

The masterpiece of God is Jesus Christ, and the masterpiece of Jesus Christ is His Church and His religion. But what is the most high, most holy, most august in Jesus Christ, in the Church and in the Christian religion is the priesthood and the sacrifice of Jesus Christ.[38]

But Jesus Christ became incarnate in order to redeem

---

an act of the soul, a conscious and free act. It consists in spontaneously willing, as spirit, what an unescapable necessity forces on man as body" (*ibid.*, p. 264). This act is thus an acceptance necessarily required by, and in, the very fact of dying. Formally, however, it seems to be distinct from this fact. Christian prudence requires that we discuss this theory only with those who are capable of not abusing it.

* Since the Mass is the continuance of this offering, it is the actual center of the world. Cf. *infra*, pp. 231 ff.

us, *proper nostram salutem.* This fact is essential to Christ; it determines His whole charitable behavior and especially His attitude toward suffering and death.

In consenting to become man in order to save us, the Son accepted a destiny to suffering and a painful death, for He became bound up with a humanity turned away from God (Jn. 12:27; 2 Cor. 5:21). Once the divinity came in contact with human weakness, it had to provoke in assumed humanity a purifying tension, an internal need for destroying the evil with which this humanity was in solidarity. "But I have a baptism to be baptized with; and how distressed I am until it is accomplished" (Lk. 12:50). Since contact took place in our Lord between the divine sanctity and corrupted humanity, it was really in Him that the wound met with the red poker. The life of Christ was intrinsically destined to suffering: "Did not the Christ have to suffer these things before entering into his glory?" (Lk. 24:26) Hence it is voluntarily that Christ laid down His life (Jn. 10:18); He came precisely for that, and the events which led to His death are less a determining cause than the visible parallel of His interior drama. The passion, which is the hour of darkness (Lk. 22:53), is at the same time His hour (Jn. 13:1; 12:23). The suffering and death of Jesus give us the final explanation of God and of love, for God is love (1 Jn. 4:8), and Jesus shows us that the perfection of love (Jn. 13:1) consists in laying down one's life for one's friends (Jn. 15:13).

The cross is the true revelation of the charity of Jesus Christ. We have said that this charity is wholly turned toward God and men; the cross expresses this truth better than any reasoning. Toward God: "That the world may know that I love the Father. . . . Arise, let us go from here" (Jn. 14:31). Toward men: "And I, if I be lifted up from the earth, will draw all things to myself" (Jn. 12:32). "Jesus, knowing that the hour had come for him to pass out of this world to the Father, having loved his own who were in the world, loved them to the end" (Jn. 13:1).[39] And it could not be otherwise, since the offering of His death was the supreme act of His life, and charity was at the root of all His activity.

Charity in Christ is, therefore, intrinsically impregnated with an inclination toward suffering and death, toward the sacrifice of His temporal life in order to save men who could be saved by no other. To our strict need of Jesus Christ and of His sacrifice corresponds in Him and in His charity an interior ordering to the giving of Himself to expiate even at the price of His corporal life. Christ and His charity are directed toward the goal of the acceptance of a redemptive death. Not only does Jesus accept the common law of death, but He chooses to be killed by the enemies of God in order to seal with His blood the testimony of His whole life to offer God supreme homage to compensate for our failings, and to give us back to the Father in the measure that we die with Him.

II. IN THE MEMBERS

Our charity participates in the charity of the Redeemer and appears in us already endowed with the interior dispositions of Jesus Christ. Hence the Christian living in charity has in himself an interior exigency and power to welcome suffering and death otherwise than a non-Christian. In his eyes, suffering is the victory of good over evil; it is the purifying burning of the wound by the red poker, the contact of divine goodness with our misery; it prepares the total liberation of death and is, above all, the proof of love given by Jesus. "The Cross" is the Christian name for suffering. Inasmuch as it continues the passion of Christ (Col. 1:24) and is attached to His suffering, it has a redemptive value by the simple fact that it is not refused by His members.[40]

Since charity has driven Christ to freely choose this suffering, there is in our charity an acceptance and even a preference for the suffering-aspect of our life and death. St. Teresa says of her sufferings: "And it seems to me that there is nothing worth living for but this, and suffering is what I most heartily pray to God for. I say to Him sometimes with my whole heart: 'O Lord, either to die or to suffer! I ask of Thee nothing else for myself.' "[41]

The saints have a refined Christian sense; they simply realize to perfection the invitations included in charity. The true Christian adds to his inevitable sufferings voluntary mortifications, in order to affirm his desire to resemble the Crucified. This is in the very logic of love.

Just as Christ's charity expresses itself in love for suffering and is wholly directed toward redeeming all men, so too our charity compels us to accept painful trials, not only for our own salvation, but in view of repairing that which other men have destroyed. This new solidarity reinforces that which we have already discovered;[42] it adds a generous inclination not only to the giving of self, but also to the sacrificing of self even in suffering, in view of reparation and satisfaction. Love for enemies is an indispensable characteristic of Christian charity, since it is precisely this love that led Jesus to the cross. Otherwise we would love as pagans, not as members of the Crucified (Mt. 5:43–47). This heroic charity causes us to participate in the perfection of divine love (Mt. 5:48).

III. CONSEQUENCES IN MORAL THEOLOGY

In this perspective, it is easier to understand the choice of virtues enumerated by St. Paul and the other apostles: mercy, mildness, and abnegation dominate and are grouped around charity.[43] Self-renouncement, together with charity and humility, constitutes the background of the Christian soul (Lk. 14:33). And charity itself is rather mercy: it is not discouraged when it finds no response, for, far from being attracted by the good in others, it is wholly gratuitous and rather creates the lovableness of those whom it attains.

In fact, all the virtues must feel the effect of being mediations of charity. Our virtuous activity must have a special overtone if it is but the prolongation of an attitude of offering. Christian "strength" is virtually the strength of a martyr; Christian justice is virtually the justice of a savior capable of dying in order to forgive. As Christians, it is not only men who act and love in us; it is members of the Crucified loving other crucified members.

Christian morality also has specific positions in face of hedonism, amusement, euthanasia, etc. Nevertheless, it remains a morality based on true happiness and joy, precisely because it accepts suffering, integrates it, and gives it its true value.[44]

Christian morality is realistic as well as optimistic, for it can transform suffering into happiness and can give value even to the consequence of sin. It does not deny the reality of evil in man, and because of this does not find itself unarmed against it; stronger than sin, it can draw good from it.

It discovers the positive aspect in all things, namely, the possibility of loving which lies hidden behind every trial and obstacle.

§VI. SACRAMENTAL ATTITUDE

I. THE EUCHARIST, THE CENTER OF THE SACRAMENTAL LIFE

According to St. Thomas, a Christian cannot belong to the mystical body of Christ by charity without having, at least implicitly *in voto*, a reference to the Eucharist,[45] the *sacramentum caritatis*.[46] Our charity is necessarily con-

nected with the Eucharist and implants in us an ontological
need for the sacramental help essential to any normal moral
life. The Eucharist is the actual prolongation of the Incarnation of Jesus Christ in time, so that His present humanity
cannot be complete without this sacramental aspect. It is
no longer possible to reach Christ otherwise than through
the Eucharist. That is why this sacrament is necessary to
salvation,[47] not only by a necessity of precept, but of
means, provided these terms are correctly understood. Invisible membership in the visible Church saves men only
because divine mercy has promised salvation to the visible
Church; perfect contrition does not justify without being
related to the sacrament of penance, for the promise of forgiveness is included in the sacrament even for those who
are ignorant of its existence; in the same way, charity is
possible only because the Eucharist, *sacramentum caritatis*,
exists in the Church.

If we saw our actions, mediations of charity, in their
ontological reality, they would appear as so many elements
of the eucharistic sacrifice which is perpetually offered on
earth since Calvary; our daily works, joys, and sufferings
would always be seen as preparing or prolonging the Mass.
The profound meaning of each life is progressively to
realize the "Mass" which will be totally offered when our
death will identify us with Christ dying on Calvary and
which will be at once our ultimate offering, consecration,
and communion. It is our way of being present, in time, at
the sacrifice of Calvary, which is the center where the
whole universe converges, is offered to God, and is saved in
a single Mass.[48]

We must add that the Eucharist is the center and explanation of all the other sacraments. Among the latter,
some prepare it: baptism, penance, confirmation, and orders
enable us to offer the sacrifice or to participate in it; extreme unction permits us to unite our ultimate personal

sacrifice to Christ's sacrifice; marriage sanctifies conjugal life by putting it in the service of Redemption.

II. CONSEQUENCES IN MORAL THEOLOGY

Our acts are not fully moral if they escape the influence of the sacraments. Of course they are connected with the sacraments by their very being, but this must be translated on the psychological and practical level where it will become a principle of action. Moral life wilts when it strays from the sacraments, especially from the Eucharist. The "Mass" which is our life can be effectively offered only in union with the sacramental Mass. Moral life is endangered when we do not take seriously these words of our Lord: "Unless you eat the flesh of the Son of Man and drink his blood, you shall not have life in you" (Jn. 6:53).

In the use of the sacraments, the Church imposes a strict minimum. Here as elsewhere, the role of the moralist should be not merely to comment on the minimum necessary to avoid sin, but to insist on the positive aspects of this duty.

The treatise on the sacraments is intimately related to moral theology, not only as an extrinsic means to live a Christian life, but as a constitutive element of Christian morality. Besides, moral action, considered as a mediation of charity, resembles the sacramental act, which is, in the fuller sense, the visible and efficacious apparition of the interior reality of grace and charity. The sacrament is an efficacious mediation *ex opere operato*.

It is highly desirable that the liturgical practice be re-adapted to this fullness of sacramental life so that Christians may become conscious of the vital necessity of sacraments in their moral life.

§VII. COMMUNITY LIFE AND OBEDIENCE

The Mystical Body, the society of charity, is made up of men, not of pure spirits. Its social nature is required by

the very nature of man. And so our moral life, the exterior
aspect of our charity, must be influenced by this social
nature. If it is true that charity is a bond of unity and communion, then the exterior diversity of men must tend, not to
juxtaposition, but to an organic unity intrinsically required
by the elements which are to be unified. In other words,
our life must be a community life, and the communities
must correspond to our various needs for unity: family,
trade, state, and especially Church.

Christian morality must receive from the Church and
from the authority which God has conferred on it, the
"tradition" of the doctrine of Christ and directives for
action. The fact that our morality is based on authority
derives from the very demands of our being.[49] Obedience
is a Christian virtue of the first order.[50] It is the visible
answer to the interior invitation of the Spirit leading each
man by the inspiration of charity.[51]

§VIII. THE SURPASSING OF SELF

To say that moral life is a mediation of charity is to
recognize that it contains an active leaven which impels it
to a constant surpassing of self. Every act springing from
charity causes it to become more and more demanding. It
is in the nature of a fire never to be satisfied. This demand
first penetrates the strict minimum of moral obligations and
expresses itself in an increasing fidelity and obedience which
shuns all mortal sin, then all deliberate venial sin, and finally
all voluntary imperfections; concomitantly, there is a positive resolution to tend steadily to perfection. The demands
of love spread from the field of strict obligation to that of
the counsels and works of supererogation. The obligation
remains unchanged, and the counsel does not become law;
but the urgent demands of love are even stronger than the

obligation under pain of sin. We will take up this delicate point later.[52] We are content here to underline this increasing refinement of our moral knowledge and tendency: through the influence of charity our consciousness becomes more and more transparent.

The aim and limit of this progress is the ideal charity of the elect. From this point of view, moral life is the inchoation of our supreme and final act of charity. "Cupio dissolvi et esse cum Christo," said the Apostle (Phil. 1:23).

Now because moral acts are mediations, we must not stop at their determinations as though they were absolutes. We would fail to understand the interior invitation of the spirit of charity if we rested in acquired virtue without trying to go beyond it to attain a still more interior and more generous way of loving. Virtue is only a mediation, not an end in itself. All resolutions must be revised, readapted to the ever-increasing demands of charity; the rigid limits of overdetailed programs may become obstacles to further progress. The fundamental attitude of our life must spring from the insatiable spirit of the Beatitudes, which is diametrically opposed to the spirit of self-satisfaction and satiety, for man here below cannot escape the law of growth.

The sense of this maturation is an interiorization. It is a returning into ourselves starting from an exterior pole, that of childhood immersed in sensibility; we progressively and painfully leave it behind and reach the attitude of generosity in which we finally give ourselves to God and to others. Our life consists in quitting an alien country to direct our steps toward the intimacy of communion with God and others. It is at once a simplifying and a unifying process.*

---

* When taken in this context of mediation, there is no danger that this doctrine of a continual progressive spiritualization will ever develop into a sort of "angelic" spirituality. We have insisted on the necessity of always considering the "body" and "soul" of moral life together. It must

CONCLUSION: ATTITUDE OF CONSECRATION TO THE HEART
OF CHRIST

A morality exclusively based on representative determinations would insist much less than we have on the attitudes arising in each moral act from its connection with
charity.

On the contrary, if we want to respect the existential
aspect of morality, that is, if we consider the act as an
actual mediation of charity, we must in our analysis take
into account the ontological reality involved in each of our
actions, the vital subjective atmosphere forming the context
wherein action is rooted, for the "sense" and finality of
action are just as important as its determined representation. Now the real "sense" of an act is conditioned by its
ontological implications, just as the growth of a plant is a

---

not be denied that in the course of these last centuries we have witnessed
in Protestantism and modernism a sort of overly abstract spiritualization
which postulated a disincarnated spirit; and at the other extreme, matter,
thus misunderstood and abandoned, has emerged as an absolute, and has
given rise to soulless materialism; both complementary heresies fundamentally deny the Incarnation. Mediation does just the contrary. Should
not this progressive characteristic found in individual life be expressed
also, due allowance being made, to the total body of humanity? This
humanity, which must be the apparition and instrument of charity, also
spiritualizes itself, at least in its elite who form its advance guard. It is
easy to be deceived into believing that humanity also suffers backward
movements. This is due to the fact that evil also progresses, "spiritualizes" itself, by profiting from the discoveries of the spirit. This does not
prove that humanity ceases to pursue its spiritualization, but that it risks
pursuing it along a dangerous route. It risks no longer seeing in progress
a mediation of love. There is an urgent need to lead man and his marvelous progress back into contact with his profound source where he
may rediscover the course that carries him along to God. Nothing positive need be suppressed; but there is a profound discovery to be made—
that of the soul and sense of man and of things. This is why it is so
urgent to show that the whole of morality and all of human progress,
even technical progress, are but a gradual unfolding of charity and that
the genuine human attitude is openness in the gift to God and to men,
not a turning back on self nor a selfish pride in one's works. Cf. J. Mou-
ROUX, *The Meaning of Man*, trans. by A. H. G. DOWNES, New York,
1948.

function of the soil. As we have seen, this soil is love oriented toward the giving of self, the sacrificing of self in suffering and death in connection with the cross and the Mass; it is consecrated to God and to men and thus achieves the communion of all the members of Christ in the life of the Trinity.

If such is the fundamental attitude and soul of Christian moral life, we must underline the very intimate relation which unites it to the demands of consecration to the Heart of Christ. This is not a chance coincidence. Pope Pius XI in his encyclical *Miserentissimus Redemptor* said that this "devotion contains the summary of the whole of religion and thus of perfection." And, in the words of Pope Pius XII, it "must be held to be the most excellent profession of the Christian religion."[53] Provided it is not considered as one devotion among others, but as the very attitude of Christian self-devotedness, consecration to the Heart of the God-man must also be called the soul of Christian moral life. Does its essence not consist in the return of love, with a special insistence on reparation and the acceptance of redemptive suffering? Is it not perfect disinterestedness confiding to God all our own interests in order to take only His to heart?* Both from the point of view of etymology and reality, this consecration is a sacrifice: it means coming as close as possible to divine sanctity and being transformed into it. It is obviously akin to the cross and the Mass and just as obviously identified with charity, which is our holiness and transformation into God. It is also evident, as the encyclicals quoted suggest, that our moral life, our religious life, and our life of perfection are substantially identical. Hence we would be fully justified in calling charity "the heart of our moral life" as well as its soul.†

* Such is the sense of the rich booklet by Father ALCANIZ, s.j., *Personal Consecration to the Sacred Heart*, Bombay.

† "In Holy Writ the heart often signifies all the interior sentiments of

Having described the attitudes which give a common nuance to all our activities, we must now suggest how the mediation of charity can impregnate and animate the various treatises of moral theology.

man in contradistinction to his exterior acts. . . . The heart of Jesus, therefore, symbolizes not only love, but all the inward sentiments of His soul. . . . For Father Olier, the Interior Life and the Heart of Jesus were but one and the same thing, that is, *the center of all the dispositions of Christ's holy soul and of his virtues,* the sanctuary of love and of worship, where God is glorified and whither fervent souls love to withdraw" (A. Tanquerey, s.s., *The Spiritual Life,* nn. 1257–1258). Love is the interiority and center of the virtues (note the words we have underlined); it is that which we can attribute as well to the heart as to charity.

Practical Applications
in General Moral Theology

INTRODUCTION

Now that we have progressively elaborated the theme of a charity-animated moral theology, we will outline some of its possible variations. The fundamental theme is the transparency of charity in all moral activity, which is its mediation and to which it gives soul and sense.

In suggesting here a few applications, we will follow, particularly for special moral theology, an order akin to that followed by Mausbach, Schilling, and Tillmann in their textbooks. It would take us too far outside the scope of this study to elaborate the detailed plan of a course in moral theology wholly centered on charity. For the moment it will suffice to take the following principle of classification, which will permit us to develop a few practical applications in their reference to charity.

For general moral theology (chapter II), we will closely follow the traditional order of the treatises. First we will examine, in the perspective of a charity-centered morality, relations between moral theology and spiritual and pastoral theology (Sections 1 and 2); the textbooks ordinarily discuss this matter in their introductions. We will then consider obligation and law in face of charity (Section 3), relating this question to the treatise *De legibus;*

the relation of charity with the moral virtues in general (Section 4), a problem pertaining to the treatise *De virtutibus*; and finally, the opposition of sin to charity (Section 5), found in the treatise *De peccatis in genere*.

For special moral theology (Chapter III), we prefer to follow an order closer to that of the German textbooks referred to above, for they divide the matter according to the objects of charity, that is, first the duties toward God as expressed in the theological virtues and the virtue of religion, and then the duties toward self and neighbor,[1] in the field of spiritual goods, corporal life, the transmission of life, material goods, etc. In fact, we will simply emphasize the following points: the relation of the virtue of religion to the fundamental attitude of charity (Section 1); fraternal charity toward others (Section 2), with special insistence on theological love for the neighbor and the possible conflict between love for self and love for others; Christian respect for the body in the perspective of charity, with a special note on suffering (Section 3); charity in its relation to the transmission of corporal life, that is, charity and chastity (Section 4); and finally, the role of charity in justice, which corresponds in the plan suggested above to the treatise on material goods (Section 5).

Ours will not be an exhaustive treatment even on the subjects we have chosen to discuss, since the present work is not a textbook nor a complete treatise on moral theology. We rather aim at highlighting one aspect of these often complex problems, namely, the influence of charity on them.

§I. Relation of Moral Theology to Spiritual Theology

1. THE TEXTBOOKS

The textbooks study this question in their introductions.

On this matter, our method forces us to take a position which, in fact, tends to become more and more common.

Some time ago many authors held that moral theology should content itself with studying what is strictly necessary to observe the precepts and to avoid sin, leaving to ascetical theology the field of perfection. It must be recognized that for practical teaching reasons some textbooks have accredited this conception.[2] Father Vermeersch, among other moralists, reacted strongly against this "minimalism" and claimed for moral theology the right and duty to concern itself with the counsels and perfection as well as with the precepts. Lehmkuhl,[3] Mausbach,[4] Vittrant,[5] J. de Guibert,[6] and others are of the same opinion.

They are led to this conclusion by the very definition of moral theology, for if the object of this science is the human act in its relation with the ultimate end, there is no reason why the best among human acts, though not strictly obligatory, should escape the scope of moral theology; and since human life is a tendency to possess God more and more fully, it is by essence a progressive march toward perfection. To content oneself with examining only the starting point of human life would lead to a mutilated morality, the more so since all Christians without exception are obliged to tend to evangelical perfection.[7]

This conclusion becomes even more urgent if the soul of human life is charity and if human acts find their value only in it. We have recognized that, since we participate by the charity of Christ in the sanctity of God and the spiration of the Spirit of sanctity, a morality based on charity must count among its fundamental attitudes a tendency to sanctity.[8] Besides, is it not essential to love never to be content with minimum obligations, but always to endeavor to surpass them? This attitude inspires our whole moral life and not only our mystical or religious activity, for the moral act by its very nature is a mediation of this charity. Now a mediation always remains in actual contact with its source and, by its very nature of sign and "transparency," calls for a continual surpassing of itself toward that which lies beyond.

Finally, it should suffice to remark that the essence of Christian perfection is charity[9] and that the substance of moral life is the same charity, in order to be convinced that moral theology and spiritual theology can no more be separated than moral life and perfection. The latter is, in fact, an integral part of the former. The fact that spiritual theology is chiefly concerned with perfection does not prevent moral theology from being concerned with it also.

Authors of textbooks have been led to separate morality from perfection because of the opposition between the two poles of our being: the pole of exteriority characterized by the strictly determined minimum, and the pole of spiritual interiority which eludes the grasp of determination. Minds too exclusively prone to static representations encounter these two aspects as distinct and by applying their method irremediably separate what was merely distinct. If it is true that in our knowledge there is necessarily an actual relation of the representative static content to the dynamic intuition[10] and that our moral activity has meaning only if taken in its tension between the particular determinations and our profound tendency,[11] then we cannot separate minimal morality from spiritual theology any more than we can drop either exteriority or interiority in the analysis of our knowledge and action. Such a "relational" and existential approach to problems insoluble on a purely static plane causes many a difficulty to disappear.

In our perspective, spiritual theology should devote itself to a technical study of the means of perfection, whose principles and profound meaning are furnished by moral theology; it should also endeavor to move affectively the will toward perfection.[12]

2. ASCETICISM AND MYSTICISM

The method of mediation, besides obliging us to outline with greater precision the relations between moral and spiritual theology, offers the latter a threefold advantage. It brings into better light the organic connection between asceticism and mysticism;[13] it emphasizes the mystical element of Christian life without exposing it to false mysticism; finally, it guards us against exaggerated asceticism by determining the role of human effort in our complex supernatural activity.

The organic unity between asceticism and mysticism follows naturally if we admit that moral or ascetical activity is the determined mediation or exteriorization of a theological activity of charity. The latter is mystical in nature, since it rather causes our activity to be a docile and hence a somewhat passive collaboration with the mysterious, ever-present action of God. Ascetical theology will study the human moral aspect, and mystical theology the divine aspect of this complex reality; but right from the beginning of Christian life, both elements—divine influence and human cooperation—are present and intimately interdependent. Here again we can grasp the spiritual life only under the complementary aspects seen together in their actual and necessary relation; this is impossible in a purely static perspective.

The same method leads us to enlarge the field of the mystical element in Christian life, since this element was born in us with the divine life. It gives to Christian asceticism a nuance of docility to grace and the Holy Spirit which counterbalances voluntarism.[14] At the same time, this mystical element is controlled by generosity and the practice of virtue; for, in our life as incarnate spirits, the theological "soul" of our action is inseparable from its "body" of determinations which necessarily manifest the former on the moral level and thus prove its authenticity. There is no place here for "the pure love" of false mysticism.

Nor is there any danger of exaggerated asceticism. Asceticism finds here its normal role, but always remains related to the divine action in us, since it is a mediation of the theological activity of charity. Hence the practice of virtue will always be seen as an increase of charity and not as an absolute value to be cultivated for itself.

3. THE "THREE WAYS" AND CHARITY

The fact of considering asceticism and charity as necessarily interdependent corrects what may well seem as excessive in the classical division of the three ways: the purgative, the illuminative, and the unitive. On the one hand, it explains perfectly the progressive interiorization of love, an interiorization starting from the sensible pole of our being, from which we are detached through a giving of and a going out of self (purgative way); thus our profound tendency becomes more and more intimately present to itself under its luminous aspect of consciousness through the equilibrium of the virtues (illuminative way), and under its aspect of communion in love (unitive way). But, on the other hand, the method of mediation reminds us that, even at the highest degree of union, charity always remains the incarnate soul of moral life; this means that it will always need its body of virtues and that from the very beginning of its purification it already possessed a real though slight degree of light and union. That is why these three degrees can never be separated into three sealed-off compartments of our spiritual life; at each moment, the interiorization of love is a progress in light and union, for tendency and consciousness are two correlative aspects of our fundamental love; and, at the same time, it is a progress in detachment.[15]

4. CHARITY AND THE MYSTICAL LIFE

Charity remains the substance of our Christian life even in the mystical state. Contemplation, which is ordinarily identified with mystical life, is currently attributed to "illuminated" faith; nevertheless, it consists only in becoming aware, through intelligence and "illuminated" faith, of a union pertaining to the order of love[16] and of the term of this union. We have several times recognized, in the course of this study, that consciousness is inseparable from the tendency and hence from love, of which it is only the transparent aspect. In fact, for St. John of the Cross, "it is through love that spiritual goods are communicated,"[17] and the summit of contemplative life is love in the spiritual marriage; its ascension terminates in the "living flame of love."

The substantial element of the mystical life is, therefore, union in charity, which can become conscious in infused contemplation; but it seems that we should not limit the mystical life to properly "contemplative" realization of this union. Souls can be authentically mystical, in a life of extraordinary self-devotedness, which always supposes a special activity of God, and still not enjoy consciousness of this divine activity in formal "contemplation."[18]

The method of mediation, which emphasizes the fact that exteriority and determination are wholly relative to the profound life of charity, is here in harmony with the ascetical and mystical teaching of St. John of the Cross. We mention this confirmation because it is perhaps this application in spiritual theology which best illustrates what we have said above[19] on the sense of our life as a progressive return from "determination" to "soul," from the pole of exteriority to the unification of the spirit.

Why is there so much insistence in the *Ascent of Mount Carmel* on detachment or rather on going beyond all that is sensible and even conceptual, in brief, beyond all determined objects of the intelligence and will of him who is called to contemplation? It is not because determined things and thoughts are evil, for St. John counsels beginners to meditate and to use creatures in order to rise to God. But determined realities can be nothing but mediations; and so the spiritual man must go beyond them to their interiority, and finally to God Himself, who is the "indeterminate" and perfectly saturating object. On the ladder of creatures, once a step has been passed, it no longer helps us to mount, but only to descend if we come back to it.[20]

That clear conceptual knowledge and sensible affection attached to determined objects distrust mysticism is all too easily understood. They present our knowledge and affections as possessions and so prevent man from being a pure starting point, a pure relation to God. On the contrary, Christian charity tends to the forgetting of self in communion.

§II. RELATION OF MORAL THEOLOGY TO PASTORAL THEOLOGY

The inclusion of pastoral theology in moral theology is less questioned, for the former is the adaptation of moral theology to the apostolate. Pastoral doctrine is included in morality inasmuch as the apostolate is a fundamental moral attitude of the Christian.[21]

We will briefly outline the contribution of the method of mediation to this part of moral theology. As elsewhere, above all, it provides a "soul" and "sense" for "apostolic mediations."

I. THE APOSTOLATE

What does it mean to be an apostle?* In our perspective, it consists in yielding to the pressure of love and transmitting the message which our life of charity bears in itself, thus offering to other men the possibility of discovering the love of Christ and of giving themselves to Him in an act of charity. "I will make you fishers of men" (Mk. 1:17), said Jesus.

The starting point of such a gift can be, in the other, the egoism of a sinner or the tepid charity of a weak soul. The essential task consists in arousing or in intensifying charity. All the rest is mediation, and hence has sense and value only in relation to this task of helping a man to put aside his self-love in order to love God. The apostolic "method"—if one may speak of method for what is love and life—will consist in discovering how one can be detached from self and how love can be roused, or more simply, how one can be led to that love of true generosity, for detachment from self is but the reverse side of attachment to Christ.

Now in this work the apostle—that is, he who is sent—plays the role of Christ. It is Jesus Christ who works through my activity of charity in order to lead the man whom He wants to love to this act of love. Love can be aroused only by love. The ideal of the apostle is to *be* a witness of the love of Christ for this man. We say it is an ideal because the apostle must always tend to this fullness of his vocation, even though short of this it is already possible to bear witness to the love of Christ by teaching the accomplishments of this love in Christ Himself, His Church,

---

* We have just pointed out the "structural" requirements of the apostolate inscribed in our being as members of Christ: each cell of a growing organism must work, in its own manner and place, at the extension of the whole body. And, therefore, the Christian must extend the body of Christ.

and His saints. That would be a very narrow conception of the apostolate which would make the subjective sanctity of the apostle the essential element of the transmission of the message. But it is obvious that the sense and soul of the apostolate must be charity, so that the spoken word may have its full value of sign and its full ontological and psychological efficacy. But our human words express only a part of what is conveyed by our total attitude. In the apostolate, what we have to express is a doctrine of life and an invitation to the love of Christ, which can be truly expressed only in love-impregnated behavior. The efficacy of apostolic activities will depend on the intensity of this love of which they are so many mediations. The apostle must be, in a certain way, a prophet speaking under the inspiration of charity, rather than a functionary who administers or a professor who teaches.

2. CONSEQUENCES IN THE SUBJECTIVE ATTITUDE OF THE APOSTLE

First of all, the apostle must make or allow himself to be loved only as a witness of Christ and not permit himself to be the focusing object of this love. He is merely a mediation, and hence must avoid becoming an opaque obstacle. "He who listens to you listens to me," and so "he who loves you loves me."

Secondly, men must be respected as persons, that is, as subjects of charity: love admits only personal relations. There is no question of amassing apostolic spoils, but of carrying Christ to a spiritual person. Others must never be treated as objects nor the apostolate as a business. In other words, our apostolate must aim at loving out of charity and at giving ourselves sincerely out of a genuine need of our love, which must ever expand, for the Christian order of things requires that men give themselves and give Christ to those who do not have Him in the same degree. Before being a conquest in view of the "interest" of the Church, it is the offering of salvation and happiness. It is a conquest because the kingdom of love must spread over the whole earth; it is salvation that is sought after the example of Paul and Francis Xavier, and not domination in the manner of conquistadores. It is not constraint; it is Good News.

Thirdly, the apostle makes use of means in the measure that he sees them as mediations of charity for this particular soul and at this given moment; with much tact and sympathy he must meet each soul on her own level. For example, sermons, even though absolutely necessary, are not the only nor the most important mediation; the word that we preach must be accredited by the word that we are and that we live. There are men who are incapable of listening to sermons on love as long as their children lack bread. The first sermon they will understand will be preached by the apostle who gives them work. There is many a city district where the teaching of the Church is done solely by the Little Sisters of the Poor, for they really express something with their hands and with their heart. In the same way, missionaries first establish dispensaries and only then do they preach in sermons what they have already expressed in their actions. "Cœpit facere et docere," is said of our Lord. Even if the apostolate is no longer accompanied by miracles as in the early days of the Church (Mk. 16:17–18), the authentic miracle of charity always remains as a sufficient sign of credibility.

Therefore, it is possible that the level where charity meets men may have to be that of physical suffering; however, it can also be that of intellectual culture, art, or professional interests.

It is also possible that the mediation of charity in the sacraments be inaccessible to certain categories of men estranged from the Church. That is why some methods of regaining the masses include a transitional period of progressive Christian practice[22] quite akin to the catechumenate found in mission lands. These remarks obviously apply also to the missionary methods properly so called, which deal with much more delicate problems of adaptation. The missionary must choose among mediations those best adapted to the mentality and culture of the natives.

In spiritual direction, these general remarks should simply be applied to individual cases. The art of the director consists in discovering for each soul the mediation of charity which she needs at this particular moment and the exigencies of divine love which she can bear today.

The same applies to education, for it consists in leading to generosity a child who begins by being wholly immersed in instinctive egoism. It is a work of love. A personality can be awakened only by being treated as a "you" through personal relations of respect and charity.[23]

Finally, we must absolutely avoid all that could be an obstacle or an occasion of scandal rather than a mediation. For example, the real or apparent richness of the clergy or of religious can become a dangerous handicap. This handicap can be surmounted by genuine pastoral love.

We have outlined here only a first approximation of possible applications of mediation to the subjective attitude of the apostle.

3. CONSEQUENCES IN THE OBJECTIVE PRESENTATION OF THE MESSAGE

We will only mention a few consequences which, in fact, pertain to dogma and to its doctrinal presentation. The Christian message itself must also appear as the loving gesture of a God who saves. Conversion, of course, consists in leading a man to charity, but he first must be led to its preparation, which is faith. The message becomes demanding and obligatory only by the love it bears in itself. The Incarnation causes man to return from his most exterior limit to divine interiority. The visible human life of Christ is the mediation of God in the exteriority of the sensible world. Such is also the meaning of the sacraments.

There are souls who must be led back to God from the lowest human states. Until now we have considered only souls possessing a certain nobleness and who understand the meaning of love and of self-devotedness. But for the more egoistic, the mediation of charity must be chosen on the level first of servile fear and then of self-interest. And it is important to show that such mediations which become necessary at certain times are still mediations of charity and not mere instruments of human constraint. Here we meet with an application of the principle of St. Ignatius according to which the apostle must enter by their door in order to come out by that of Christ.

As we have seen, fear, interest, suffering, even past temptations and sins—anything can be a mediation of charity, provided its actual relation to love is transparent, for love can always straighten out our lives and direct them toward the spirit, no matter how far they have strayed.

4. OBJECTION: INTERIORITY AND ACTION

Perhaps someone will object that the method of mediation, since it fosters increasing interiorization and union with God in charity, is quite opposed to the apostolic attitude, which is directed toward exterior action. This objection results from a misunderstanding of interior life and action arising from a naturalistic mentality too preoccupied by a multiplicity of exterior works. Exterior works are only determinations and acquire apostolic value in the measure that they manifest the soul of which they are the body. Every work strengthened through organization runs the risk of sclerosis when its interior spirit weakens. It follows that true activity is measured by interiority. When the spoken word is in vital contact with the inner spirit, it is not mere *æs sonans*, but enters into essential conversation with the soul, thus answering its deepest longings. To reach the center beyond the surface is to enter into relation with all the points of the sphere; the process of interiorization consists in leaving self as a limited individual in order to find self anew as a spiritual person, that is, as a relation to God and to others in Christ. Interior solitude is communion.[24] Charles de Foucauld was an apostle in the desert. True action is spiritual and lives on charity, and its "works" must be an incarnation of that gift of self. A multitude of works which requires but a slight giving of self is an immense body inhabited by a tiny soul. They change nothing, not even our egoism. And yet a soul cannot live in a state of disincarnation: interiority, if it is sincere, must translate itself into apostolic works. As Bergson reminds us, activity overflowing from the contemplative life is a genuine mark of true mystics participating in divine action.[25]

We have first brought up these points which concern method, for the present work is mainly methodological in scope. Rather than in an introduction, they should be presented as consequences of fundamental moral attitudes: the tendency to sanctity and the apostolate.

As for the relation between moral theology and canon law, it will be discussed in the following section.*

---

* Normally, a "Treatise on Conscience" should be developed here. We are happy to refer our readers to Father R. Carpentier's excellent article on conscience in the DSAM, II, coll. 1548-1575. He shows here, better than we ourselves could have done, how a morality of charity can lend greater depth to a study of the Christian conscience, which is at the heart of moral as well as of spiritual life, without in any way compromising the primacy of charity since conscience is, as it were, the voice of the great law of love. He also shows how a morality of charity can solve the apparent antinomies of law and liberty, obligation and counsel, and others which we will soon encounter, and how charity confers on probabilism its profound sense, thus placing it in its true perspective of a morality of perfection rather than in its habitual role of a casuistry of minimum obligations. This rich, timely article also integrates the acquisi-

§III. Obligation, Law, and Love

Turning to the treatise on law, which determines a fundamental Christian attitude, we will now examine how our method can explain the relation between obligation and charity, obligation and perfection, obligation and law, legalism and the dynamism of life.

In fact, who has not, on the level of theory or of practice, met with these painful and irritating antinomies? A mother who loves her child needs no law to command her self-devotion; in the same way why should we have to be commanded to love God? "Dilige et quod vis, fac," said Augustine. And St. John tells us that "there is no fear in love; but perfect love casts out fear, because fear brings punishment. And he who fears is not perfected in love" (1 Jn. 4:18). What then does law have to do with love? Is he who loves not liberated from the law? And yet our Lord says that love is the greatest *commandment* (Jn. 15:13; Mk. 12:28–31).

It is useless and even ridiculous to tell a passionate lover that he is obliged to love the cherished object of his love, for he surely goes far beyond his strict obligations. Does love then suppress obligation or render it useless?

We are called to perfection, and our Lord addresses His counsels to us. It is a matter of generosity. But in what measure are we obliged to choose this perfection which is concretely offered to us?

Of course, it would not be easy to harmonize all these antinomies if we were to force them into narrow, closed concepts. But let us try to grasp, rather than the terms

---

tions of characterology into the treatise on conscience. But its chief merit is that it recognizes in the Christian conscience the exigent concrete voice of a law of love inscribed by God in our very being which dictates our attitudes toward a Person who is always present and reminds us that our principal duty is to love ever more purely and freely.

themselves, the relation which is always in the making between these terms.

<h3 style="text-align:center">1. OBLIGATION AND LOVE</h3>

In the preceding pages we have been continually confronted with this opposition which reveals the fact that our life is in a state of tension between two poles. But opposition between two aspects of the same reality often means that they are mutually complementary.

Ours is an incarnate spirit; being a spirit, it is invited to surpass the limitation of its carnal condition; our being is "bent" toward fuller being, toward infinity. It is urgently invited and even absolutely impelled to surpass its own being and, since being is love and communion, to communicate always more fully with God and with others without ever stopping at any particular determination. But insofar as it is incarnated, this same spirit is "bent" toward fixing its spiritual movement in determinations and stable norms.

Therefore, this fundamental drive is exercised at the same time on two levels or under two aspects—expanding interiority and limiting exteriority—but in the unity of one and the same total activity. We recognize at once in this ontological drive which is at work in our being the root of obligation. It is first, in its more general meaning, a duty-to-be before being channeled on the level of determined activities into a properly moral duty-to-do.[26]

We can reserve the name of "moral" obligation in the strict sense to this apparition of "the duty-to-be" in our clear and reflex consciousness,[27] where it imposes a "duty-to-do" which has the rigidity of the conceptual determined order in which it is expressed, provided we recognize in it a limit-obligation, a mediation of a broader and more profound obligation which is nothing but the absolute instancy of spiritual love. And thus we find again, in obligation, the limit and the mediation which characterize moral reality in its relation to fundamental love. It follows that the most authentic obligation is love, that nothing is more fundamentally obligatory than love, and that all moral obligation derives its absolute character from what we might call our built-in necessity for loving, which God constantly impresses in our being. Through this necessity for loving, we participate in God's power of creating and of creating ourselves by answering the vocation implied in our very being.

Our particular obligations transcribe, in the diversity of action, the implicit demands of love which God transforms into demands of charity. Our acts yield to these norms just as iron filings arrange themselves along the lines of force of the magnetic field. The magnetic force is much vaster and more mysterious than this manifestation of itself in one of its sensible effects. In the case of moral obligation, the interior necessity acts and obliges only when it is perceived by a conscience and finds an echo in a free will; it is an objective moral necessity. It is the dignity of the spiritual being to fully engage himself by ratifying what he sees he must do and by accepting the objective necessity, which is absolute, since it arises out of the nature of things as the actual term of divine creative thought.

The obligation thus considered in its determined, fixed demands is the exterior or inferior limit of the total obligation. This is why obligation is ordinarily understood as the minimum under which one cannot rest without sinning. And this is also why obligation is often defined by that which must be done under pain of sin, and thus one scarcely conceives of an obligation concerning duties which can be omitted without committing any qualified fault. It is in this sense that St. Thomas defines obligation negatively by the evil to be avoided: "Hoc est obligare, scilicet astringere voluntatem ut non possit sine deformitatis nocumento in aliud tendere."[28]

In this same sense, obligation is made dependent on law —it is even its first effect—in the measure that law determines a duty perceived by "clear" consciousness. Then we must say that law, understood in this sense, also has the character of exteriority and limit in what concerns human activity.[29]

Must we then restrict obligation to this strict sense and make it a guardrail bordering the abyss of sin? Certainly not, if it is only the mediation of a more profound positive obligation which is the seductive or constraining aspect of love itself. This obligation of love will not have the determination and rigidity of obligation taken in the strict sense, since it is a spiritual and interior reality which is limited and determined by the latter; it will not inspire the fear ordinarily aroused by the presence of forbidding limits. On the contrary, it will be wholly attracting, since it is merely the expansive power and energy of love. But we must always remember that these two aspects are intimately united in our consciousness. Now can we not recognize in this love-obligation, without in any way excluding the other aspect, the obligation to perfection, which ordinarily gives rise to certain false problems when conceived in an excessively static manner?

Perfection, like the love-obligation, concerns the interior pole of our being, whereas the limit-obligation concerns the exterior pole. Perfection, as we have seen, consists in the total giving of self out of charity; here then there is question of a love-obligation extending to the perfect gift, that is, not primarily a duty to carry out determined obligations, but to liberate the total force of charity and to yield to the full spirit of charity.

At this interior pole of our being, we are not compelled by the fear of sinning, but are driven on by the compelling attraction of love. At this spiritual level, perfection engages our whole liberty; it is the masterpiece of our most personal initiative.

But we are also present at the opposite pole of our being. At the interior pole, this obligation reveals itself as attracting and urgent, while at the exterior pole it becomes a strict obligation imposing determined duties. At this second level, fear will appear with the command forbidding us to fall below a certain minimum; and it will become necessary to use this mediation of love which is the lower limit of our moral being, and to ever surpass it following the orientation of charity. These different prescriptions constitute also, in their own way, a fundamental tendency to perfection, namely, to ceaselessly go beyond self toward love and interiorization. And so they transpose the theme of charity in the mode of "the strictly obligatory," proportioned to this inferior level; but the fundamental theme is exactly the same as that which echoes in the most personal depths of our being, where it urges us on to perfection by the attraction of love. When the duty of perfection appears on the level of moral obligation, it requires that it be sought through the observance of precepts and by a surpassing of the imposed minimum. It is clear that here the duty of perfection has a less elevated sense than at the other pole, though the surpassing of the minimum supposes the positive will to progress continually.[30]

Because of the intimate unity joining these two levels of our interior life, it is the same being who perceives both the spiritual urging and the obligation to go beyond the minimum, in such a way that the personal invitation to perfection is tainted with the rigor of moral obligation and strict obligation partakes of the attractiveness of love. This permits us to explain the psychology of the obligation to perfection.*

* Compare this with the double aspect—gift and concupiscence—of

It will be useful to insist here on this vocabulary, in which the limit-obligation is contained in the love-obligation, which far surpasses it. Even if it is not familiar to a morality preoccupied mainly with the determination of sins and of obligations imposed under pain of sin, the distinction between these two degrees of obligation is nevertheless required if we want to formulate morality in a positive manner. Here love is the chief precept. Unlimited in itself, it must always be incarnated: "If you love me, *keep* my commandments." But it can be incarnated only in works which are essentially limited. In any case, it is certain that we are not bound to translate unlimited love into works proportioned to it, for this would be to make obligatory what is most perfect and to fall into pure rigorism. And so we are forced to recognize an indefinite appeal of love, containing first indistinctly what will later be distinguished into counsels and strict precepts. This is why we speak of love-obligation and limit-obligation; the first is an obligation in the broader sense, containing the counsels in the unlimited precept of loving, while the second refers to the practices of love which are absolutely necessary in order not to lose this love. For example, there is the unlimited virtue of religion, which obliges us to praise, to adore God and to offer Him the Holy Sacrifice, and there are also limit-practices such as the minimal obligation of Sunday Mass. Positive morality insists, therefore, on the total obligation and develops the aspiration to practice it with generosity. But at the same time it must insist also on what remains free in such a practice, for even when we do not perform that which is concretely *counseled*, we do not necessarily cease to love God and to accomplish some other good which can also be chosen by our free will. We think that herein lies the outline of the proof by virtue of which

---

human love; on that level also there is question of a positive tendency and its limit; cf. *supra*, pp. 129–133.

it can be established that a charity-centered morality admits the existence of "positive imperfections."

If the obligation under pain of sin is only the limit-aspect of the total obligation, then there is a whole area of the field covered by obligation wherein it is possible to fail without sinning, provided one remains faithful to the limit-obligation and retains a sufficient disposition to act according to the norm of good. In other words, the duty-to-be or the duty-to-love, which seems to constitute the basis of obligation, confers its imperative character on the duty-to-do when it becomes determined. But this imperative character is not so tightly bound to all particular determinations that many of them cannot be interchangeable, especially those, such as counsels, that are not indispensable for attaining the goal of love. By interchanging the determinations, one will reach the goal more or less quickly, more or less generously, but will always remain substantially faithful to charity. In this whole area where limit-obligations are embodied in and reigned over by a genuine though indeterminate love-obligation, "failings" are deficiencies, not morally qualified faults: they are, in fact, the much-discussed "positive imperfections."* For example, religious rules which do not oblige under pain of sin become monstrosities when they are compared to purely penal civil

* VERMEERSCH, *Theologia moralis*, I, n. 405; Bibliography, p. 405, nn. 2 and 3. We readily recognize that our explanation only finds sense on condition that one accepts this tension, which binds together the two poles of our being and action, and hence the analogical meaning of obligations derived from it. It would be hardly intelligible in a static context where the two aspects of our activity would be separated from one another. Just as in our spiritual-material being, there is a tension between the "infinite" needs of the spirit (revealed in the limitless capacity of the intellectual dynamism and in the natural desire for the beatific vision) on the one hand, and on the other, our spatio-temporal limitations—a tension which translates the transcendence of the spirit over all material limitation—so too, in our tendency and activity, precise determined realizations of strict moral obligation never adequately coincide with our "spiritual duty of loving" which transcends all realizations in time and aspires to surpass every limitation whatsoever.

laws.† In fact, they really do oblige; otherwise why would they be called rules or laws? But beyond the level marked by the inferior limits extends the realm of the counsels and generosity; and, on the other hand, the higher a soul rises in this realm, the more her deficiencies provoke her regrets, which are regrets of love.

Concerning religious rules, let us remark that limit-obligations vary according to the personal or public commitments of each person. If failure to observe the rule also detracts from the special commitment of generosity contained in the religious profession, then it will also be a fault. The religious, in choosing the state of perfection, has, so to say, raised the minimal practice of charity starting from which the tendency to surpass self must constantly be exercised. He has formally accepted as his duty of state to not renounce tending to perfection according to the specific obligations of the three vows. Beyond these three determined duties and because of their repercussions on his whole life, the religious is bound to the spirit of gratuitous love which flows from them, for he has made the counsels his law. The spirit of gratuitous love becomes henceforward the characteristic element of his new state, of his specific way of tending to perfection. If by violating a particular rule he falls below this new minimum level of charity, if he comes back to calculating and renounces the desire of always tending to what is better, then he will commit a moral fault, which will actually be slight insofar as this falling back only touches on a detail. In spite of this, it remains true that the rule does not of itself oblige under pain of sin; it expresses a counsel, however urgent, personal, and concrete it may be.

Now we are rid of the antinomy that existed between

† They are better named "laws of the purely exterior forum" and are imperfect by their very nature, whereas the religious rule aims at being more "interior" and at facilitating obedience of love for the religious.

the obligation for all to follow the spirit of the evangelical counsels and the liberty left to each one to realize these counsels in his personal life in order to answer the divine invitation. On the one hand, we recognize a love-obligation which truly obliges us to a spirit, to fidelity to the spiritual pole of our being without the exterior determinations involved in it. On the other hand, when this obligation to the spirit of the counsels reaches our exterior limit dispersed in determinations, it cannot oblige us with the strictness of a limit-obligation to choose such and such a "better means," among which are the concrete realizations of the counsels; but it only obliges us to take the "necessary means" in order not to refuse the general tendency to perfection in what is indispensable to it—the general desire of progress— nor certain surpassings of the minimum-limit.

Our distinction between love-obligation and limit-obligation also resolves the apparent contradiction in "obligations of friendship" which we mentioned at the beginning of this section. A friend realizes that by not being sufficiently attentive to his friend he has failed in an "obligation" of friendship, but he cannot accuse himself of a fault against any formulated law; a mother feels that she has omitted an obligation of love when she has neglected some act of devotedness toward her child which her heart spontaneously dictated, but in the light of cold reason one cannot reproach her with any fault. In our relations with God, we feel that when we are refusing a concrete invitation to be more perfect and choosing an alternative which is, nevertheless, good, we are forgoing a duty-to-be or a duty-to-love, an increase in charity corresponding to the fundamental tendency of our being, which does not oblige under pain of sin but proposes to us a commitment of self out of love. Again we see without difficulty that this love-obligation, even after the pressure of fear has been removed, is more profoundly perceived as obligatory by a soul apt to understand it, and even more so than the limit obligation is perceived by a soul cut off from any higher love. The love-obligation binds us to the most intimate depths of our being. The limit-obligation is more easily felt as a more exterior though more imperative constraint. When Augustine said: "Dilige et quod vis, fac," he was thinking of the interior bond which is stronger than "law." To this extent love has no longer need for law, for it accomplishes *eminently* what the latter commands. And so love is called the interior law of charity: *interna lex caritatis*.

2. LAW AND LOVE

We no longer have any reason to oppose law and love except as two complementary and indispensable aspects of our being.

If we were to take law here in the metaphysical sense, that is, as an internal principle of order which drives forth and directs activity,[31] we would recognize in it the two aspects of our profound tendency: dynamism and consciousness.

Reason has its power of moving from the will. . . . But in order that the volition of what is commanded may have the nature of law, it needs to be in accord with some rule of reason. And in this sense is to be understood the saying that the will of the sovereign has the force of law.[32]

It is a conscious tendency, for law is not really distinct from our active tendency itself, but is merely a way of seeing our conscious love, just as "law" in God is nothing other than His being which is love.[33] But in this very consideration, law and love are formally distinguished, even if they are materially identified. Law is but one aspect of this complex reality, the regulating rather than the motive aspect; law is of itself *"aliquid pertinens ad rationem."*[34]

Hence derives its specific character and its formal

rigidity. This is also why it calls for a complementary dynamic aspect, the will-aspect, which permits it not to remain an abstraction and to find its "obligatory" character. St. Thomas expresses this mutual relationship in two successive concepts, rather than in terms of a relation: "The command is an act of the reason, but presupposes an act of the will."[35] Thus conceived, law, even metaphysical law, is akin to determination; but it is the determination of love.

We say, "thus conceived," for the kinship of law with concept and determination reveals the exteriority of formulated law in relation to activity. In a way, it plays the role of the concept in relation to the intuition. And so it is closer to the moral determination of acts than to the roots they find in the profound tendency.[36] But just as the moral act, law retains a relation to this tendency which is its soul. The same exteriority explains also that law often takes the aspect of a limit, just as the determined activity is the limit of the total activity.[37] This is why law represents the minimum that must be respected if one is not to fall into moral fault; this is also why its expression is often negative.* It follows from this that the observance of law has its true meaning only when referred to its positive complement, the interior dynamism of love and charity which is at the heart of Christian liberty.

By thus bringing together properly "moral"[38] activity

---

* "By its very definition a law is composed of a number of precepts the observance of which must be within the power of all who are subjects of the law. It is of the nature of a law to command, not to offer advice. . . . [Jesus] wished men to act from a motive that is higher than mere obligation, the motive, that is to say, of charity; and it is of the nature of charity that it is capable of always greater perfection. From laying down rules demanding the minimum of good conduct, He gives counsels of perfection that are bounded by no limits. The paradoxical form in which some of His directions are expressed is clearly intended to show that in this way of the counsels charity can always surpass itself" (M.-J. LAGRANGE, O.P., *The Gospel of Jesus Christ* [Westminster, Md., 1943], I, 159 f.). It now seems clear, after our development of the last few pages, that obligation and charity are not to be opposed to one another.

and law, we render intelligible the classical identification between the morality of an act and its conformity to an ultimate norm which is law, either in itself (objective, material morality) or as it is perceived in consciousness (subjective, formal morality).† It is important to note that this identification does not yet transform morality into legalism. We will reserve the term legalism to what concerns positive human (civil, ecclesiastical) law, the field of the jurists. Moral doctrine does not coincide with positive law; the extension of the former is broader than that of the latter, and the juridical order contains elements which are not directly moral.[39]

Nevertheless, by considering morality almost exclusively under its aspect of conformity to law, we would risk having our attention too exclusively fastened on its exterior elements, to the detriment of its interior richness, and interpreting it in a merely juridical manner; thus we would fail to strongly emphasize, as it should be, the fact that law itself necessarily refers us to charity-love, which is its life, sense, and inspiration. A purely legal morality has no soul; it is a "legalism" wherein charity for the person yields its primacy to obedience to principle. The dangerous consequences of this conception have been pointed out: if morality is only conformity to a rigid and general law, does it not favor a certain equivalence between moral value and exterior conformity to law? Does it not tend to a justice founded on an ever-more-minute observance independent of the intention of love? Pharisaism is the extreme form of legalism.[40] Excessive objectivism tends to ignore interiority and to reify juridical norms.[41] We will point out presently how strongly love itself calls for a positive juridical norm.

† GENICOT-SALSMANS, *Institutiones theologiæ moralis*, I, n. 31. In fact, St. Thomas describes conscience as coinciding with law itself: "Nihil aliud est lex quam dictamen practicæ rationis" (*Sum. th.*, 1–2, q. 91, a. 1). Conscience, the "dictamen rationis ad actum" (*Sum. th.*, 1–2, q. 19, a. 5), is our particular law, for it is adapted to concrete action.

Positive human law and love. But we will first direct our attention to the relation between positive human law and love.

Positive human law often expresses or specifies our interior law,[42] but it also considerably accentuates the exteriority which already characterizes law as such. It is fixed in a general formula, while natural law is adapted to each individual case, provided the virtue of prudence intervenes. Positive human law is abstract and cannot take into account particular personal situations.

Moreover, positive law is the product of limited human reason; it is primarily designed to attain the temporal common good proportioned to the degree of development of a given society. This is why it has certain limitations which increase its relative imperfection. As St. Thomas points out, many human laws establish mainly a *"disciplina cogens"*; thus peace and order are assured against those who challenge them and for whom paternal discipline does not suffice.[43]

But still more generally, its juridical domain is restricted to the external forum, because its purpose is to organize the relations between individuals and the community or between individuals in view of the common good.

And what is more, the theologian must be aware of the fact that, because of sin, terrestrial human society—that is civil society—can no longer fully coincide with the society of love. Here we refer to a *de facto* possibility, which corresponds to the social reality such as moral disorder has shaped it. They who govern neither want to nor are able to apply the order of charity; and, for the most part, they who are governed neither want to nor are able to observe this order. Powerless as it is to fulfill its true role as a mediation of the community of charity, civil society must often content itself with legislating, without taking morality into account. It is obvious that it can do so only insofar as it cannot do better or insofar as the common good requires it, but never in view of establishing laws which would be objectively immoral, such as the granting of permission to remarry after divorce. For example, it declares that prescription is acquired after thirty years even without good faith, although the latter is always required in conscience for the validity of such prescription. Civil law often doubles the amount of indirect taxes, for it is presumed that many will escape paying half of them; hence it accepts the illegality, makes it part of its system, and imposes it on all. Can such laws be considered as simply invalid because they are unjust? They would be unjust if advantage were taken of them to dispense from good faith; but it is not unjust to establish such laws in order to prevent legal action being taken when such action has become too difficult through the presumed fault of the negligent proprietor. Such laws derive from the fact that the legislator has to establish laws and is unable to do any better in a society which has lost the sense of love, and will only rediscover it once Redemption has been fully achieved.

Moreover, because of the presence of a divinely instituted Church, civil society is limited to the terrestrial order; hence it is necessarily subservient to the superior value of the persons which compose it, and it can restrict their free evolution only in the measure required by the common good with which civil society is concerned; consequently it cannot bind consciences unless this is required by the nature of its object.

These last two considerations invite us to admit the existence of a purely external forum, that is, one which of itself extends to no reality pertaining to conscience; for it does not of itself govern the tendency toward the ultimate end. Such a purely external forum will safeguard the order of revealed charity, which is not a mere order of terrestrial equilibrium. Here find their place laws traditionally called "purely penal." We will come back presently to this expression and its content. But let us note right now that the Church escapes the imperfections which frequently harass civil legislation. In any case, the Church never consents to legislate against divine law and, by its spiritual nature, is already the pure mediation of the celestial community.

The preceding remarks underline the imperfections proper to human law and make us aware of a danger which can be avoided by our method of mediation. Human law, limited as it is to the external forum, seems to create a domain for itself, the juridical domain, so that the legislative or juridical system can appear as self-subsistent; for example, we talk of juridical responsibility or fault and even of juridical persons. These are fictions, no doubt, but they have a foundation. It is worth noting also the "constructual" character of the juridical order,[44] its strict definitions, its tendency to simplify reality, to consider quantity more than quality, and to remain on a superficial level.[45] Only acts at least partially exterior fall under the juridical order,[46] and as facts must be capable of proof, the use of legal presumptions is introduced.[47]

Here we meet with the problem of how this order is related to the moral order. Certain jurists tend to separate these two orders as far as possible, with the result that the moralist might be tempted to consider the juridical order, at least in civil society, as of itself foreign to morality, unless it is proven that the common good does actually require that it bind in conscience. In this conception, civil laws, except those which govern commutative justice, would be ordinarily considered as purely penal, except in particular circumstances, as in time of war, when by an accidental necessity they would bind in conscience.

Our method of mediation, while leaving intact the specific value of the juridical order, will permit us to correct this conception, which seems to go against a fundamental Christian principle preached by St. Paul, the respect and obedience due to the rulers of this world, even to pagans and tyrants, as long as they restrict themselves to their own field of authority.

The juridical order is the "objectified exteriority" of the moral order in its social aspect; so it is then a mediation of the moral order which, in turn, is a mediation of charity. It is, so to say, mediation in the second degree. It has the existence of "objectified exteriority," that is, a relative existence like the concept, or rather like the "word" in its relation to the intuition, the letter in relation to the spirit. The juridical order finds its sense only in the total complex ensemble wherein it is the rigid body which love must assume and penetrate in the diversity of social reality. It is the carapace which protects the interiority of charity, a carapace all the harder as society is closer to the biological level and farther removed from the spirit; martial law and the state of siege are the hardening of the law required by a society which has replaced love by force. But even then law is a mediation of charity: in order to avoid the sheer brutality of the actual situation which would be governed by the law of the jungle, martial law brutally sanctions elementary human rights. On the contrary, the more a society practices charity, the more law approaches interiority and even spirituality. In any case, such are the laws of the Church. In his book on the Church of Christ, Father Lippert has paid her canon law the following tribute:

The juridical life of the Church springs ceaselessly from her most profound sources: her religious life, . . . her faith and her charity, her ever vigilant and active sense of responsibility. . . . In brief, even what is apparently wholly exterior in canon law still pulsates with an immediate experience of life.[48]

It is thus impossible to separate law from morality, for the mediation would be cut off from its source and would lose all its meaning. This is why a positive law which fulfills all the conditions required for validity[49] has all that it needs to bind in conscience. If, as we have seen, certain laws, more or less numerous according to the moral value of different legislations and societies, must be limited to the purely external forum, nevertheless there always remains an indirect obligation in conscience not to trouble the public order implied in such laws, to respect the superior who supervises their observance, to comply eventually with their sanction, in brief, to recognize society even here as a mediation of the community of charity. Hence these laws are also part of the juridical order and, in their own way, enable it to fulfill its role as a social mediation of the moral order.

Our age has lost the sense of the obligation of laws insofar as it can no longer understand charity-love which is its soul. It is urgent to restore this sense of obligation. If the human legislator cannot judge conscience nor legally bind it to purely interior acts, he can bind it when he commands actions necessary for the common good. Even then it is love that obliges, for love is so deeply rooted in our being as members that a law can oblige an individual, in an individual case, even if the observance of the law does not profit him individually, because, in the present hypothesis, the observance of such a law is required by social necessity, and therefore an exception cannot be tolerated. This hypothesis is realized in the case of laws founded on the presumption of common danger. This follows from the fact that the member loves the whole more than himself "as a member." In this sense, the obligation derives from the common good, or rather from the love one must necessarily have for the common good.

On the other hand, the fact that human law is a rigid, general, abstract mediation explains the possibility of excuse, dispensation, or epikeia, and the necessity of jurisprudence. A rigid formulation does not perfectly match particular cases in their concrete reality. Many human laws must be successively readapted if they are not to become foreign to concrete life, which always pushes forward and at times causes the too rigid elements in human law to crumble. Some have wanted to remedy the generality of law by individualizing the penalties. But law, by its very nature of social mediation, requires a certain inflexibility, which must not however be exaggerated through excessive exteriority with regard to the moral order. But some rigidity always remains necessary, for otherwise we would tend to arbitrariness, in the disincarnation of love, and, in fact, in a partiality which would easily creep in under cover of charity.*

Though the juridical order and charity are complementary, the former can nevertheless retain a certain number of laws which do not directly concern the orientation to the ultimate end, but are related to it in the sense that in the purely external forum the member must respect the society of which he is a part and the legitimate superiors who govern it. We will now consider these laws, which the virtuous legislator can diminish in number, without ever succeeding in totally suppressing them. We will give more precision to their notion; we will then justify the particular kind of obligation binding us to comply with their sanction; finally, we will examine whether the name given them is justified.†

---

* Le Senne, *Traité de morale générale*, p. 550. In fact, jurists are divided on this problem into two opposed tendencies; some rather defend the integrity of law and thus allow less latitude to the interpretations of jurisprudence; others tend to give more initiative to the judge in view of adapting the law to the individual cases. M. Dabin represents the first tendency.

† For a contrary opinion, see M. Herron, t.o.r., *The Binding Force of Civil Laws*, North Miami, Fla., 1952; and G. Kelly, s.j., "Current Theology," TS, 14 (1953), 34 ff. In fact, we do not place our own development on either side of the controversy concerning "merely penal laws." Our perspective of the primacy of charity seems to completely modify

We have already discussed certain laws which, though
inevitable for the human legislator, would contradict the
moral order if they were imposed in the forum of conscience. It would be contradictory to make of them direct
mediations of the moral order and hence of charity. Apart
from the indirect juridical obligation created by these laws,
they do not, of themselves, bind or unbind conscience. The
citizen who has been despoiled by a legal but certainly unjust prescription cannot have recourse to revolt, but to
occult compensation. As for the conscious beneficiary of
this prescription, he has no right to believe that he is in
order with the rules of honesty: he must make restitution.

There are other cases where juridical obligation covers
practical determinations which are of themselves morally
indifferent. Such are, for instance, certain very material
prescriptions, as the obligation to carry our identity card,
to secure a fishing permit, to obey traffic laws or customs
regulations, etc. The same must be equally true for the
secondary prescriptions of many of our present laws, which
are extremely complicated and able to be understood only
by specialists. Are not then such laws, at least in their
detailed applications, addressed directly to specialists, to

---

the traditional discussion. In spite of certain similarities in detail and of
the fact that we also follow the conception of St. Thomas, our argu-
ments are quite different from those ordinarily advanced. The moralist
who explores each section of moral theology independently, as, for example, that of the obligation of human laws, is left to his own lights and
can reject "merely penal" laws for various social and philosophical motives; or again he can admit them because practically he depreciates
human organizations, at least where they concern the personal conscience.
We are far from generally depreciating human laws, but nevertheless,
the primacy of charity-love intimately links all the various sections of
moral theology to the fundamental revelations concerning the original
fall and divine adoption. In this light, it appears impossible, as we explain
in the text, that an organization of "wounded" humanity can ever identify itself with the order of conscience proper to the children of adoption, with the order of charity. It will more or less resemble it. Redeemed
nature aspires to coincide with divine supernatural law; but a gap will
always remain, thus determining a "purely external forum."

the judges, for example? We are thinking here of fiscal legislation, of which the taxpayer can often know only the main prescriptions; and even these prescriptions are modified and again complicated by numerous instructions and particular decrees of application of which the layman can normally know nothing.

These prescriptions can be considered as devices which efficaciously, though in a rather exterior and mechanical manner, assure the functioning of certain elements of the practical order which, of themselves and in virtue of their abstract object, have nothing to do with our moral and spiritual destiny. Public authority has the duty to obtain uniform behavior in this material domain.* But by the very nature of things, it ordinarily suffices that public authority seek merely the material fulfillment of the law without the help of a "sin-limit." Therefore, these measures will of themselves ordinarily remain on a level foreign to our moral destiny; for example, the latter is simply not involved in the fact that I shot a hare without a permit on my own unfenced property.

These laws can, therefore, be considered as inframoral in their object, which could be specified otherwise, since it is indifferent in itself, and in their mode of efficacy, which sufficiently orders the activity from the outside somewhat in the manner of a psychological guardrail. Their inframoral character will often appear in the fact that in order to act in a concrete case it will be necessary to transgress them and to deliberately incur their legal penalty. A doctor in answering an urgent call must choose between the risk of breaking the legal speed limit and his natural duty to arrive at the scene of the accident as soon as possible, without, of course, endangering the lives of others. Here not only does the general and exterior formulation not

* Cf. Vittrant, *Théologie morale*, p. 38, n. 60, speaks of "indirect laws."

foresee the particular cases, but their object, being too material, is incapable of a spiritual formulation or of a moral orientation, and so in no case does it, of itself, involve eternal destiny. This is why we said above that the juridical order does not perfectly coincide with the moral order.

Can a transgression in this juridical field, taken in the wider sense, be subject to a morally obliging penalty? We have said that civil authority has duties in what concerns these measures. It must take these measures, render them efficacious, and see to their execution. For example, once legal prescription has been realized, the beneficiary will obtain the public protection of "his" property. Any infraction will incur the sanction of law, and the sanction will be such as to obtain the effect intended by the legislator. Under pain of rendering the measure ineffective, the legislator must see that the sanctions are applied and, even at the risk of acting unjustly, he must apply them impartially. It is possible that the sanction be not a moral nor even a properly juridical punishment. But it remains true that if our infraction is juridically imputable and if we refuse to accept its sanction, we exteriorly disobey an authority who acts legitimately and carries out his "moral" duty by applying the sanction, for he has no other means of urging what this sanction must obtain. Our conscience, then, requires submission to the authority which commands some legitimate act in the purely external forum.

It can be questioned whether the name "purely penal" is correctly applied to these laws, for this expression seems to suggest that such laws involve no moral obligation and yet imply a morally binding punishment. It also happens that the name only very imperfectly describes the thing. As we have seen, these laws, by requiring that respect which is appropriate to the merely external forum to which they are restricted, indirectly introduce obligations imposed by love for society and respect for the legitimate superior.

Before they reach application, these so-called "merely penal" laws do not permit open defiance of authority, but suppose that it is possible, while observing the general laws of Christian conscience, to act without becoming involved in the external forum. If, in spite of this hope, we do not succeed in keeping clear of the external forum, then the law is imposed by the direct authority of the superior, though of itself it would always remain what it is, "a law of the purely external forum." Is this not then the appropriate name for such laws?

These explanations were necessary to show that it is possible to consider law as an objective mediation of morality and hence of charity-love without thereby falling into rigid legalism, for the social imperfection of man cannot support such absolute rigidity, any more than it can render possible here on earth government based solely on morality and charity. In fact, the transparency of charity throws new light on the deficiencies of our present humanity and thus reveals the feebleness of certain sections of human law, but it also solidly founds the direct moral value of the juridical order as soon as the natural order of the common good appears in human law, whether the common good had to be specified by it in order to impose itself socially, or whether, in fact, the common good requires that the law oblige in conscience in order to save the endangered society.

Certain moralists will find it easier and more "reasonable" to treat these so-called "merely penal" laws as ordinary laws binding in conscience; but, at the same time, they will declare that the moral indifference of their object, taken in itself, and their much too material formulation render them imperfect and that consequently they easily give occasion to an excuse, even that of using our personal liberty when the common good does not demand us to renounce it. It would thus be easy to establish absolute equivalence between the juridical and the moral orders. But would this not place us in an abstract, purely philosophical order which considers some ideal type of humanity? And can the theologian, taking into account the historical fact of sin and its consequences, limit himself to such an order? Besides, in this perspective, how can a legitimately excused transgression result in a morally obligatory punishment or sanction? And would we not be obliged to come back to the theory of obligation in the purely external forum which these moralists have tried to eliminate in order to simplify— but in vain—the real order? Finally, would we not run the risk of abandoning to subjective appreciation too many cases of obedience to the law?

In any case, both opinions have the same practical effect. The purely penal laws—as well as probabilism, which we will take up in a moment—have been accused of harming morality, the former by seriously weakening positive law, the latter by endangering fidelity to natural law itself. The mediation of charity, even when it is a mediation in the second degree, helps us to determine the "indirect moral" nature and the limited number of these laws. Moreover, it shows that when one is liberated from an imperfect and material law he passes from an exterior to a more intimate mediation, where the invitations and orders are more directly connected with love. Thus conscience does not fall into anarchy, but rather is more firmly bound by love to the common good.[50] If we speak of laws "of the purely external forum," we should do so in a spirit of sincerity and obedience to the common good in view, not of diminishing, but of deepening the respect due to it.*

* Besides, the aim of the conscientious moralist and legislator must be to create the circumstances which permit the law to be less imperfect, thereby raising the level of public morality and thus eliminating as far as possible these imperfect laws "of the purely external forum." We have already insisted on this same need a few pages earlier, cf. p. 270.

Probabilism. This same principle justifies the use of probabilism in the presence of any law, even natural, whose
formulation leaves a doubt as to its application here and
now by moral conscience. If law is the objectified exteriority of the moral order, it takes on its character of precise
obligation only when it can be grasped by the intelligence
as a *necessitas objectiva,* a moral necessity seen as deriving
from the object and susceptible of being freely accepted.
The objective order, being that of "determinations," has to
be determined and certain; more or less probability does
not make a determination certain. When we have, in the
same objective order, a solid reason preventing us from
recognizing an objective certitude in a given law and for
a concrete case, we escape the determination of this objective law and obey the more interior and personal obligation
of our charity-love, for the objective field of law is neither
the sole nor even the principal source of obligation. Only
the specifications of obligations find their source there; the
obligation itself, as we have seen, derives from love. Probabilism does not free us from any obligation; it merely
replaces a particularized obligation, not sufficiently specified for my own concrete case, by a higher, more intimate,
and more universal obligation, which I myself concretely
specify by reasonably presuming that the legislator wants
it so. In this case, conscience plays more perfectly its role
of being "my particular law." Probabilism does not compromise the equilibrium between the objectivity of law and
the subjectivity of conscience in favor of the latter; it safeguards the exigencies of the spiritual person in the face of
those of objective law.

The necessity of law. We have often pointed out that the
juridical order is the limit-aspect of moral activity. In so
saying, we have no intention of diminishing its importance;
we rather want to insist on the rights of the positive and

interior aspect of moral activity, which derives its value
not from determination, but from love. But we also wanted
to safeguard the necessity of law in its proper role of
determination. Just as human knowledge is in a state of
tension between the intuition and the concept, and human
activity in a state of tension between the fundamental tendency and the moral determination, so also is obligation
simultaneously polarized by creative love and rigid impersonal law.

Just as love, law too is indispensable to morality, but as
a complementary element. Since we live in a community of
incarnate spirits, mutual communication, at the level of our
carnal limit, must maintain a certain zone wherein our
spiritual interiority can be defended against the indiscretion
of other spiritual interiorities. In this sense the imperson-
ality of law is perfectly adapted to the impersonal extremity of our being by which social and material contacts
are established. It is a fact that a society where law is suppressed and is replaced by a would-be love ends up in
tyranny. Love is the most demanding and insatiable of
forces; it wills to the maximum the good of the loved one.
But, in man, love is at the same time a spiritual act and a
passion. What dangerous anarchy prevails when love,
especially love as a passion, recognizes no other law than its
own impetuosity! In such a situation, love itself replaces
law, and the worst results can be expected from this confusion of two poles which should exist only in a state of
balanced tension.

But when order reigns, law serves love as a condition of
equilibrium created by love in the carnal and social zone of
our being. At this level, exchanges between persons retain
an objective, extrinsic character; it is rights and things that
are exchanged. But these means of communication avoid
indiscretions and assure a minimum of social contacts,

which can later freely develop into a more intimate union of charity. Daily social and juridical relations cannot be understood unless they are seen as the possible beginnings of personal relations of charity. In this perspective, charity gives meaning to the apparently impersonal details of our daily life. Without charity, no matter how much we would respect rights, we would never reach a truly Christian, or even a truly human, life. For example, there is a Christian way of taking down the details of a legal offense and of placing an order for supplies. Charity appears when, over and above legal dealings between functionaries, one sees relations between persons among whom a bond of charity must ever prevail.[51]

Thus law has a negative aspect inasmuch as it defends society from anarchy, and a positive aspect inasmuch as it is the point where the order of charity is inserted into social and biological reality. Such a twofold function is characteristic of a limit-determination and of a mediation.

The prevalence of love over law. Finally, we must point out that the Christian way of considering law as the exteriority of love and of the moral order shows that the substance of moral life is not obedience to law, but charity toward persons, the human superior, and God; obedience, however indispensable, is second to love. This is why St. Paul exalts the liberty of the sons of God and their liberation from the yoke of a law devoid of soul. But Christians are not free from all law, for they receive "the law of Christ" (Gal. 6:2). However, this "law of grace" (Rom. 6:15) is no longer a heavy yoke imposed from the outside; it is required by charity as its necessary determination. Jesus Christ came primarily not to give us a new law but a gospel whose interior law is "the sweet yoke and light burden" of loving. It is this commandment of love which résumés the whole law. Was there any better way of making us understand that law is only relative to love?*

§IV. CHARITY AND SIN

Christian life is defined much more profoundly by fidelity to charity-love than by the observance of law. Moral obedience to law is rather the exterior aspect, the necessary mediation of our profound life which is love, so that moral life can be defined only by reference to charity. It consists in ever preparing an act of perfect charity.

As an immoral act, sin is a transgression of the law,[52] but this transgression is only the moral and exterior aspect of an actual disorder in our power of loving. St. Thomas says that all sin is *appetitio deordinata*.[53] We can say that actual sin is an act of love, but of an unnatural love. Just as law is the regulating and determined aspect of moral activity, whose obligatory aspect derives from love, so, in the case of sin, the transgression of law formally specifies the sin, but its malice properly derives from its infidelity to charity. Moreover, all sin is defined by its opposition to charity. Mortal sin is *the* sin against charity (*contra caritatem*), while venial sin is an act imperfectly subordinated to charity (*præter caritatem*). Charity is the bond which relates us to our supernatural Ultimate End.

Only that which goes against charity can break this bond: all impiety, sacrilege, blasphemy, perjury, etc.; any attempt on our neighbor's life, on his physical or moral, temporal or spiritual goods; every attack on the interests of the human race by turning to the advantage of egoistic ends what the transmission of life requires to pursue its own higher end in the providential

---

* LACROIX, *op. cit.*, p. 59. In their stimulative little book, *Suisse, nation européenne*, Brussels and Paris, 1949, R. CARPENTIER and J. LANNOYE show that an inspiration of charity has its place in the "political institutions" themselves and can by these institutions educate a people and create a social atmosphere of respect and love for the person.

plan of conjugal and domestic society. Outside these faults which directly or indirectly wound charity, there is no place for mortal sin; however, there remains a vast field open to venial sins, which neither destroy nor cut into charity, since they do not attack it; but they withdraw from its influence more or less considerable portions of an activity which should be entirely ruled by it.[54]

Such is the opinion of Father de la Taille. But it seems that even venial sin must, to a certain extent, be called a sin against charity,[55] for even if it does not despise the object of charity, it despises its actual exercise. An indelicacy on the part of a friend may not dissolve the friendship, but it is not for this reason simply *præter amicitiam;* it is really opposed to friendship, but in a matter that does not damage its substance; the minimum requirements without which friendship is no longer possible are safeguarded. Besides, the friend, in so acting, knows that friendship will be preserved. The same psychological attitude is found in venial sin and substantially distinguishes it from mortal sin.

Thus sin is replaced on the level of personal relations, which is its normal context, since it violates love between persons:

A man making void the Law of Moses dies without any mercy; . . . how much worse punishments do you think he deserves who has trodden under foot the Son of God, and has regarded as unclean the blood of the covenant through which he was sanctified, and has insulted the Spirit of grace? . . . It is a fearful thing to fall into the hands of the living God.—Heb. 10:28–31.

In this perspective, many of the elements of sin are easily explained.

Habitual sin. The state of habitual sin is particularly serious and dangerous; we are not speaking here of the habit of committing any particular sin, which may be the cause or simply the manifestation of the state of sin which we call "habitual sin."[56] The latter fixes man in a fundamental attitude of refusing love. In this context the particular act of sinning assumes its full malice.

Sin and egoism. All sin stems from egoism. When we fall into sin, our profound tendency, which is made to be wholly oriented toward the giving of self in communion with God and men, takes as its end a good which we choose, not to give ourselves to it nor to possess it in an orderly manner, but to possess it without subordinating it to God or to give ourselves to it simply because we have chosen it, knowing that it is inordinate.[57] "The very fact that anyone chooses something that is contrary to divine charity proves that he prefers it to the love of God, and, consequently, that he loves it more that he loves God."[58] In both cases the final end is self revolting against God. In fact, this love for self is evil, not because it is love for self, but because it is not subordinated to the love of God. This insubordination derives finally from the objects toward which love tends. Hence, love is at the root of all sin: "Two cities were built by two loves: the terrestrial city, by self-love going as far as to despise God, the celestial city, by the love of God going as far as to despise self."[59]

If pride is defined as "disordered love (*appetitus*) for one's own superiority," we must recognize that it is "the general sin"[60] just as charity is "the general virtue"; it is "*initium omnis peccati*"[61] just as love is the root of all moral activity.[62] Hence all sin is fundamentally pride. Our fundamental tendency, even when it is corrupted, retains its two poles: there is pride of the spirit and pride of the flesh, which is impurity. The former brings disorder even into spiritual interiority of love, the latter into its carnal exteriority. This is why the former is more profoundly disordered than the latter.[63]

The more sin is interior, the graver it becomes. These prides depend on one another as body and soul; a disobedience of the spirit endangers the subordination of the senses, just as impurity enslaves the will and causes it to lose its subordination. Impurity is not necessarily the gravest of sins, but because it is found at the pole opposed to spiritual pride, it is the sin which most deprives man of his interiority, his dignity, his personality. St. Thomas says that it is the most shameful of sins. Modesty instinctively protects our interiority against it. In this sense, impurity is, after spiritual pride in all its various forms, the most serious obstacle to spiritual progress.[64]

Charity tends to communion in unity and thus reveals the true sense of being. Sin has a sense opposed to being and thus to unity, since it puts our force of love completely out of focus. This is why the sinner is abandoned to a dispersion of his being in a multitude of different loves.[65]

Original sin. The dependence of sin on love better takes into account the consequences of original sin. If the latter was the refusal of the gratuitous gift of God inviting human love to surpass itself in supernatural charity, it is easy to understand that its moral fruit is concupiscence. This concupiscence consists in turning back on self this force of love which is destined to find its end in the presence of God's love. In Adam, man lost that polarization toward the higher level by which he could have escaped his own limits, so that each power, now deprived of this interior rectification, falls back heavily on its particular good with all the force that natural inclination has, to work for itself alone. This is true even of his natural power of spiritual love. It should not be forgotten that man's very being is love and that every act leaves behind an ontological trace; the fundamental refusal of his vocation to love necessarily leaves a trace in his being. Moreover, the very nature

of love contributes to the explanation of original sin: that
love becomes strangely blighted which has refused the
gratuitous invitation to communion with its Creator.

These considerations are primarily true of the author
of original sin. Nevertheless, they are also true for his
descendants, who have not personally committed it, in the
sense that they have inherited a being, and thus a love,
deprived of the interior rectification which would be assured by its being directed toward God supernaturally
present. This privation of communion does not involve
personal responsibility in them, but *in causa, voluntate
principii naturæ.*[66] Here we are in face of the mystery of
original sin. But it is possible to think that we inherit from
Adam a blighted love, a love coined with ontological infidelity because of our solidarity through human nature in
what concerns the refusal of God's gift.

Temptation. When sin is considered in the perspective of
love, the psychology of temptation comes into better light.
In our being, love, as the giving of self, inevitably meets its
intrinsic limit, which is concupiscence. We bear our ad-
versary within ourselves, an ever-present, ever-active tendency which, to say the least, does not lead us to the giving
of self. True, by union with Christ this tendency becomes
an occasion of victories for charity-love; but this limit-
mediation can be an obstacle if it is cut off from its relation to charity. We have seen that, by nature, our sensible
limit contains the root of egoism. The process of temptation is simple: to fall into it, it suffices to indulge in natural
tendencies which are no longer under the control of charity-love. This seems to be the meaning of the meditation
on the Two Standards, a very fine piece of psychology
which St. Ignatius places in the middle of the *Spiritual Exercises.* There it is the tactics of Satan rather than the
weakness of our nature that is studied. But it amounts to

the same, for Satan stakes precisely on our weak points, and our weakest point is found in our natural tendency which precipitates us into egoism as soon as it ceases to be a mediation of charity.*

Therapy for temptation and sin. Since temptation and sin tend to egoism and to the turning back on self on every level of our being, the chief remedy against them is the disinterestedness of charity translated into specific virtues, which will introduce it into the various sectors menaced by temptation. To give a tempted soul an occasion for self-devotedness is the best way to neutralize the venom of egoism. He who loves a person will not readily offend him (1 Jn. 3:9). Once a sinner opens his heart to generosity, he is already on the way that leads to the Father. This basic treatment will have to be adapted to each particular case. Prayer and the sacraments are obviously indispensable, for it is charity that must be recovered or preserved.

§V. Charity and the Moral Virtues

We have sufficiently studied the relations between charity and the virtues[67] to content ourselves here with one brief practical remark.

The virtues, as we have often repeated, are mediations of love: they find their sense only through their soul, which is charity. When they are considered or practiced independently of charity, they tend to lose their quality of virtue and can even become dangerous, for they could lead to a negative, exterior morality which would insist on the avoidance of evil rather than on the practice of good.

What would become, for example, of the virtue of

---

* L. Bouyer, "The Problem of Evil in Early Christianity," *Blackfriars*, 30 (1949), 6–16; 53–59. The author shows how Scripture denounces the Evil One and his activity hidden behind the events of this world, thus also hidden behind the deficiencies of our psychology.

fortitude if it were cut off from love? Would it not verge on cold, stoic apathy or aggressive, pitiless hardness? There is a vast distance between a Marcus Aurelius and a St. Ignatius of Antioch. Force does not of itself lead to union, but to resistance or victory. In scholastic teaching, it is said to moderate the irascible power and to give it vigor in face of obstacles; this is why it may be exposed to violence. In the same hypothesis, prudence, an intellectual virtue, easily becomes overly cautious and fails to understand the audacity and even the risks of charity, which gives without counting the cost; or else, since it is a function of reason, it can easily fall into mean calculations. Once outside the perspective of charity, temperance and chastity would soon reveal their limits, for they would have no other role than that of restraining the concupiscible power. Poverty without love finds itself in want and misery; obedience, in constraint and tyranny. And what a fearful hegemony justice would exercise if it were exalted to the level of an end! "Noli esse justus nimis" is the advice of Scripture, knowing that the natural effect of justice is to render to each his pitilessly strict part. Religion itself, the moral virtue which orders our duties of adoration and cult toward God, would emphasize the distance that separates us from Him and could easily neglect the communion of charity, which is the true purpose of revealed religion. If religion is made to depend on justice, its function would be to render to God what is due to Him, not as the fruit of personal love, but as a strict obligation to the other, thus projecting on our Father the exteriority which separates and opposes human persons on the material level. In fact, it seems that all the virtues just named and especially the cardinal virtues would quite normally assume the exteriority of justice as soon as they were separated from charity. The rigidity of fortitude, the calculations of prudence, the constraint of obedience, the moderating effect of temperance, the fear of religion—

all these refer of themselves to precise restrictions imposed from the outside, rather than to communion with God, author and end of all moral goodness.

When these virtues are given a soul and are intimately impregnated with charity-love, what a change takes place in their visage, for they are now Christian virtues! St. Augustine saw all of them as apparitions of love:

If it is true that virtue leads us to beatific life, I dare say that virtue is absolutely nothing other than the sovereign love of God. For when it is said that virtue is fourfold, as I understand it, it is said of the various movements of love itself. Hence, as for these famous four virtues (the cardinal virtues), I will not hesitate to define them as follows: temperance is love giving itself to what it loves; fortitude is love easily supporting all things for the sake of that which it loves; justice is love serving exclusively what it loves and therefore ruling with rectitude; prudence is love shrewdly separating what is useful from what is harmful to it. This love, as we have said, is not any kind of love, but the love of God, that is, of sovereign good, of sovereign wisdom, of sovereign harmony. This is why virtues may also be defined as follows: temperance is love preserving itself integral and uncorrupted for God; fortitude is love easily supporting all things for God; justice is love serving none other than God and, therefore, ruling rightly all things submitted to man; prudence is love lucidly discerning that which helps man from that which prevents him from going to God.[68]

We will later come back to the influence of love on justice and chastity. As for the act of obedience, it would be easy to show how strong, intelligent, and personalizing it becomes once its whole ambition consists in fulfilling the desire of the loved one. There is an abyss between the execution of an order by a slave and by a lover.[69] Poverty, for a loving heart, is a real liberation; it cost the Poverello nothing, for it was his Lady. All forms of abnegation and temperance are easily supported by a soul possessed of

love. "Ubi amatur non laboratur aut labor ipse amatur."
What strength springs from this love that is stronger than
death!

Once virtues are taken over by love, they lose their
tendency to resemble the rigidity and exteriority of justice.
They also cease to be foreign to one another and take on
the smile of sweetness that pervades the gospel, thus revealing their Christian kinship. Though multiple in origin, they
are all magnetized by a common center. Such is the true
sense and role of charity: while each particular virtue
works at a partial ordering of our being, engaged in multiplicity, charity directly attains our ultimate End and brings
about a total ordering of the whole. St. Thomas recognizes
that charity is "the virtue of the end" and that as such it
has power over the particular virtues, which are only
"means in view of the end."

Thus we can say that charity gives its sense to the
whole of moral life, just as the soul gives its sense to the
body and the sentence gives its sense to the word. Hence
derives the rule for using virtues and also their necessity.
They should not be cherished and practiced for themselves,
for they are not ends, but paths leading to charity. There
are many ways of entering on these paths, according to the
degree of intimacy one has attained in love. The practice
of virtue in the novice is different from what it is in a soul
purified, humble, and already impregnated with the perfume of divine union. Just as education must pass from the
drilling stage to a higher phase of personal contacts, it can
be said that the practice of virtue must pass from a rather
rigid asceticism to a more simplified and peaceful phase of
maturation.

But we should always beware of the illusion that virtues
can ever be dispensed with. That would not be an authentic
mystical life which would pretend to have passed beyond
the stage of the practice of virtue. The pure love of

quietists is no less to be rejected than moralism or rigid asceticism taken in their pejorative meaning. The method we have devised guards us equally from both excesses, for it forces us to say that virtue cannot be genuine without love, and that charity, without the practice of virtue, is sheer illusion. Until our death, and even after it, we always remain incarnate spirits.

But our perspective invites us to recognize a progress and an interiorization of virtues, and, at the same time, a profound change of sense in their relations with charity. In him who begins and progresses in the spiritual life, the practice of virtue takes the form of a courageous conquest of love: a hard, progressive ordering of one's life which day after day brings the soul nearer to spiritual unity. On the contrary, in him who has reached the fullness of love, virtues appear as an overflowing of this love attesting the genuineness of its union with God. The purified soul has passed from one pole of her being to the other, and, nevertheless, at both poles she has met with virtue and charity, body and soul, exteriority and interiority.

❖ CHAPTER III ❖

Practical Applications in Special Moral Theology*

§I. RELIGION AND CHARITY

The word "religion" may be taken in a more or less technical sense. For many it indicates the religious attitude in its totality and thus includes all our relations with God. Taken in this wider sense, religion is very closely related to the theological virtues; we can even say that the latter are not wholly distinct from it, since their function consists above all in putting us in contact with God. It is obvious, then, that the theological virtues, and chiefly charity, have a supreme religious value.

The virtue of religion, taken in the more restricted sense, has a determined role in moral life. It is a habit inclining us to render to God the respect which all creatures must have for their Creator.[1] As a moral virtue, it facilitates acts which put us in relation with God; as an

---

* We consider here only a restricted number of practical applications. Obviously, as we have already pointed out (p. 196 n.), many of them should be social applications of the mediation of charity. Even though they are implied in the doctrine and are perhaps more easily deduced, still we would consider the distribution of matter in the present chapter as unbalanced if we were willingly accepting this omission in a would-be complete treatise. The social aspect is not secondary but essential in a catholic moral theology (cf. p. 233). Likewise, if our study aimed at being exhaustive, an important place would have to be reserved to the virtue of prudence.

infused virtue, it elevates our faculty of action, thus rendering these acts supernatural. St. Thomas says clearly that the object of this virtue is not, as in the case of the theological virtues, God Himself, but acts by which we recognize the excellency of God, that is, acts of interior and exterior cult.[2] Hence its object is not the end itself, but the means in view of this end.

Are we to dismiss the matter as the product of mere scholastic subtlety on the ground that acts of love, which are means, are also the object of charity, or that religion also directly attains God in the respect it renders to Him? Such an attitude supposes faulty understanding of our interior activity and of our relation to God. Our direct contact with God is ontologically based on grace, which is our being as divinized; actively, it is founded on our divinized faculty of action, that is, our will elevated by charity, whose proper act is love. This can be said only if it is admitted that our very being, as a participation of divine being, is already fundamentally love. But "respect" as such is not such a substantial element of our action; it is rather a quality of our fundamental love. It is the active attitude which love assumes in a creature faced with Him on whom it wholly depends for its existence. Created love is necessarily respectful. Respect, as a fundamental attitude, is "respectful love." But in the stricter sense it is a specific activity consisting in giving signs of respect, that is, in performing determined acts of interior and exterior cult. It is a moral activity "by means of which" one manifests his respectful love. Hence the virtue, which regulates and supernaturalizes acts of cult, orders certain "means" in view of the end; it is not itself the virtue of the end. In this sense, religion is not a theological virtue, "although it can take the acts of theological virtues as matter for homage."[3] Religion is "a virtue of cult by which we endeavor to prove to God our faith, hope and love, by setting about ordering

some human matter to Him; and so the virtue of religion
in some way arises directly out of the theological virtues."[4]
It can offer to God an intellectual act of faith and thus
transform it into an act of religion; it can turn a cry of
hope into an authentic prayer.[5]

We wish now to insist on its union with charity, the
most fundamental, most real, and most interior element of
our activity directed toward God. Charity, we have said,
is "respectful"; it will, then, arouse in the soul and in
exterior behavior certain attitudes of respect. This profound demand of charity will be translated into specific
acts by our complex psychological organism. First, the
body will bow in an exterior attitude of reverence by
genuflecting, performing liturgical rites, reciting vocal
prayers, etc. The virtue of religion will then incline the
soul in a spiritual "gesture" of adoration, the fundamental
religious attitude by which we recognize our subordination
on the level of being itself.[6] Adoration develops into a
prayer expressing the creature's sentiment of absolute dependence on his Creator. Adoration especially expresses
itself in the offering of sacrifice, the sign of total surrender
to God. Sacrifice is that interior act by which every being
must consecrate itself wholly to God;[7] since Christ's death,
by a necessity of means, this act must be united to the
sacrifice of the cross. The soul can eventually express her
adoration in a more stable, and even definitive, manner by
way of a vow, that is, a promise made to God;[8] in this case,
God wholly reserves to Himself what has been consecrated
to Him. These various acts all translate the same requirement of respectful love. Supernatural love is the soul of all
religious activity giving it its true finality and sense.*

* O. LOTTIN, O.S.B., thinks that there is no infused virtue of religion,
but that "all the reality implied in the concept of the infused moral
virtue of religion, that is, the habitual supernaturalization of acts of religion, is sufficiently explained by the influence of faith and charity penetrating into the acts of the natural virtue of religion" (in ETL, 24 [1948],

And yet it seems that the proper movement of the religious attitude, we might almost say of the religious instinct, is oriented in a direction opposite to that of love; this is at least what its *tremendum* aspect seems to indicate. However, the object of religion also appears as fascinating, and under this aspect it attracts the soul and draws her nearer to God.[9] In fact, love fosters communion, while respect maintains a certain distance.

The transcendence of God fosters the idea of the nothingness of the creature in face of the Almighty and emphasizes the infinite distance that separates one from the Other. Such a consideration, were it alone to occupy the whole of consciousness, would raise an insurmountable barrier between God and His creature. Religious instinct, left to itself, easily falls into excesses and deviations; from sheer terror when confronted with invisible forces, it devises magical practices in an attempt to conciliate or to submit these forces to its own power. Human religious sentiment, especially in a Christian, may manage to avoid such gross excesses, but is nevertheless inclined to see God as the fearsome Almighty rather than as a loving Father. The virtue of religion, of itself, refers us to the unity of the divine nature rather than to the Trinity of persons. It recognizes in God the Creator to whom we must submit rather than the Father who invites us to partake of His own life.

Hence the very necessary role of the *Christian virtue of religion.* It is the revealed rule and the infused force per-

---

352). For Dom Lottin, the natural virtue of religion is itself a moral virtue which is related not to "the means in view of the end," but to the ultimate end itself (*ibid.*, pp. 345–351). It corresponds to charity in the natural order. In this solution, which certainly permits a satisfactory classification of the virtues (*ibid.*, p. 350), one readily sees the intimate connection of religion with charity. But is there not a place, or even is there not necessarily a place, for the infused virtue of religion, if there exists, as we shall later point out, a whole field of religion and of religious instinct which must be governed and "elevated"?

mitting charity to penetrate into the domain of human religious instinct. Religion as a father-and-son relationship could be fully revealed only by and in Jesus Christ. The infused virtue of religion is a mediation of charity which confers on the human religious instinct a disposition of communion capable of transforming this attitude of holy terror into an attitude of adoration and loving self-abasement. It perfectly harmonizes two contrary movements, love's tendency to union and fear's instinctive retreat. Love becomes respectful and respect assumes a certain quality of tenderness. According to St. Thomas, this union of two opposite tendencies is most perfectly realized in the act of devotion, which consists in willing to consecrate oneself wholeheartedly to all the demands of the divine service.[10] This act of serving God with generosity is an act of religion.[11] And St. Thomas adds that the immediate cause of devotion is *dilectio*.[12]

Now it is clear that charity in man needs to assume a religious attitude, that is, a "devout" attitude of adoration and prayer, for however intimate may be our participation by charity in the life of the Trinity, we always remain creatures. Conversely, human religion cannot find its ultimate meaning if it is not rooted in charity. At their deepest level, our religious attitudes are love-attitudes. Among Christians, a "religious soul" is one that lives the theological virtues as well as, and even more than, the virtue of religion. On the other hand, he who merely observes exterior religious practices without living the great commandment of charity is not a "good Christian"; his religion is mere *exteriority*, a body without a soul, since it has lost its true sense.

This aspect of exteriority brings into better light the kinship between the virtue of religion and justice.[13] As one theologian has put it, religion points at the debt-aspect of our love as creatures.[14] It commands respect for God's "right" to our homage. Christians concerned only with exterior practices observe at least these minimum requirements of the respect due to God, but they do so in a juridical manner, as if they were paying a debt. This same exterior, minimum aspect, and hence this kinship with justice, exists in another "obligation" of religion, that of the religious vows. The scope and spirit of religious life is to tend to perfect charity by starting with the observance of certain minimum obligations due to God in justice. To content oneself with fulfilling these strict obligations is to omit the most important and meaningful element of religious life, that is, its value as a mediation of charity. This would be to reduce to mere juridical observance a life which, in view of assuring more perfect self-devotedness, covers the inner fire of love with a protecting mantle of rules. To transform religious life into a mere "observance" due in strict justice would be to mistake the protecting mantle for the inner fire; rules having thus lost their animating fire would no longer protect the fervor of charity. But the sincerity of love would be illusory if it led us to despise rules—that necessary juridical, objective minimum—on the pretext of Augustine's "ama et quod vis, fac." In fact, this formula is true only when charity is perfect and profoundly respectful.

Because it is a mediation of charity, the Christian virtue of religion necessarily reveals in its exigency for respect a tendency to communion. A respectful soul will find in the gospel all that she needs to progress in this virtue of religion that tends inevitably to communion. There God appears as the Father loving His creatures even to the giving of His own Son. The Son Himself comes to His creatures by taking flesh. The gospel reveals God's mercy much more than His almighty power. This is why the Christian religious attitude contains a definite preponderance of charity over the specific element of religion, in other words, a preponderance of interior life over exterior cult. The latter exists only in view of the former. But there is no question of transforming this hierarchy of values into an exclusion of one by the other, for this would be a fault against charity itself as well as a misunderstanding of the incarnate nature of man. The Christian virtue of religion must deepen our natural respect for God; it must always remind us sons of God that we are creatures and that the amazing condescendence of the Father calls for all the delicate nuances that adoration can assume by being impregnated with tenderness.

§II. FRATERNAL CHARITY

I. PSYCHOLOGICAL FOUNDATION OF FRATERNAL LOVE

Up until now, moral life has appeared to us as a preparation for an act of total charity, a wholly gratuitous giving of self to God. We have also often said that the Christian, because he is grafted on Christ, is in intimate communion with his Christian brethren, and even with all men, for they are all "potentially" Christian. On the other hand, the individual man must, through progressive interiorization, center his life on God alone. But is not this ideal opposed, at least psychologically, to an explicit love of our neighbor?

We think that to consider the very being of man as love, in the sense explained above, is to take into account the plurality of men and to lay the foundation for communion among them. In God, "love-being" reveals itself to us as a society of Persons. In the same way, the being which we participate from Him ontologically implies a society; but this society is dispersed in time and space. Individual being, because it is love, is also fundamentally a relation to others. We even think, with G. Madinier, that personal life is awakened in man through a progressive conscious realization of the relations which bind him to other men.[15]

We have already seen that, because men are spiritual beings restricted by material limits, they must be many; this is an exigency of their condition as incarnated spirits. If it is true that one *loves* according to what one *is* and that our being belongs to the order of love, then it follows that our very condition inscribes in us a love essentially oriented to communion. And there must be in human psychology some manifestation of this real community. In fact, man is a social being by need. Charity elevates and divinizes this natural disposition of the soul so that others are no longer seen as merely "fellow men," but as members of the same Body of Christ.

The apparent conflict between the individual's vocation and fraternal charity can now be resolved. The action of charity consists in interiorizing and centering him on God; but it does not pursue this aim without involving, in its very movement, love for other men. The love which is to be interiorized is, in fact, a "community-love"; the movement of charity directs toward God a love which is already directed toward men, seen as images of God, sons of God.

Of course, there is no question of denying the individuality of man. Because of the exterior pole of their being, men are separated from one another and incommunicable. Because we are material, we occupy a space which cannot be occupied by any other, and no one else can live and experience our particular duration. Others are exterior to us. As spirits, on the contrary, we are "open" to one another; we communicate in the being of others and are able to coincide with them through knowledge and love. This is what being a person means. But we also are distinct from one another by the most interior aspect of our being: our spirit alone is responsible for the depth of our consciousness, which we possess so inalienably that it makes each of us a unique being, capable of becoming a "you" worthy of love. On the other hand, their material limit requires that men be many, that they tend to union and collaboration; this exigency is just as legitimate as the former and should therefore not be denied. But it is a fact that matter separates men more than it unites them; or rather, of itself and taken at its limit, it is an element which tends to separate. Matter becomes an agent of unification only when it is a mediation of the spirit, that is, when it is taken not according to its proper sense, but with relation to the spirit.

It follows from this analysis that love emphasizes primarily the personal aspect of our being and relegates to the background the limitation of its "individuality." It does not deny the latter, but replaces it in its true perspective. That is why the Christian, animated by charity, tends to think in terms of community-interests wherein his own interests as well as those of others merge. For example, a lawyer confronted with a case may simply say, "I will do my best to get you out of this mess as quickly as possible." If he is genuinely Christian, he will endeavor to think in profound accord with his client and say, "This is our case and we will do all we can to win it." In the same way, the Christian doctor may tell his patient, "Ours is a painful case, but we will pool our hopes and our efforts and will win out." Is he not thereby much more Christian than the practitioner who casually declares, "Your case is really interesting; I will gladly take it"? When one has discovered that disinterestedness proper to charity and is able to apply it to fraternal charity, he can think of other men in no other way than as a father and a mother who always think of *their* child and *their* love. Charity transforms human psychology and, consequently, calls for a complete reform of human activity.

II. THEOLOGICAL FOUNDATION OF FRATERNAL CHARITY

But how are we to perfectly unite our love for our neighbor, which we might say is "horizontal," with our love for God, which is decidedly "vertical"? The theological answer to this problem leaves no doubt: we must love God and our neighbor with the same theological love; in both cases, the formal object is the same. In our perspective it is easy to justify and explain this traditional doctrine. Just as the body is a mediation of the soul, the whole man is a mediation of God and, in a more special manner, of Jesus Christ. At its most profound level, our interiority is not closed in on our own spirit, but reaches even unto Christ. He is intimately present in the depth of our being and transforms us there in such a way that our whole life and action become a "mystery," a manifestation not only of ourselves, but also of Christ Himself. To love our neighbor for Christ's sake is to really attain Christ in His mediation. And so it is quite clear that love which goes no further than man, allows for no progress in surpassing self. When love is content to stop at creatures, it is literally, though unconsciously, idolatry, for it transforms an image into a thing or, we would say, a mediation into an absolute. If the nature of mediation is well understood, there is no point in objecting that a love that loves man for God's sake is not truly a love for man. A mediation is never a means that can be left aside once it has been used to attain the end. It is the intermediary, the actual "visibility" ever necessary to attain God through the community of men. It is necessary not like a step that is tread on momentarily and then left behind; for if it is true that the brother we love is somehow intrinsically one with Christ, then our very love for him constitutes an act of charity for God. Paradoxically enough, it can be said that man must be loved for himself "as an image," as a mediation. This formula, while affirming that our love must be directed toward the whole man, recalls that this love will always remain essentially related to God.

III. LOVE FOR NEIGHBOR AND LOVE FOR SELF

Textbooks of moral theology, when treating of charity toward others, often repeat the formula "Caritas non obligat cum nimio incommodo,"* which, at first hearing, sounds like an open affront to the gospel. Without the slightest doubt, this saying can be found nowhere in the gospel. Its origin is probably to be found among the practical "juridical rules"; but we have seen that the juridical order is the "exteriority" of charity. The formula assumes that the question of the priority between love for self and love for others has already been solved. The same is true of this other saying which can easily favor egoism: "Well-ordered love starts with oneself" or more popularly, "Charity begins at home."

There is certainly such a thing as Christian self-love. Each of us is for himself the closest of neighbors. But is he entitled to a type of love specifically different from that which he must have for others? Here we must distinguish between the "I" and the "me," between the source and the object of love. The "I" is responsible for my eternal vocation and hence plays a unique role in my life of love, for the most urgent of duties is to intensify my charity; I accomplish this duty by loving others and myself in an orderly manner. The "I" therefore never comes into conflict with others, since it is itself a source of love and, being spiritual, tends to communion. The gift of a spirit knows no limit. But the reflex-self, the "me," appears to be in conflict with the neighbor as soon as there are "goods" to be assigned.

Under this more objective aspect, we can wish "goods" of two kinds for ourselves and for other men: spiritual

---

* The historical and critical investigation of Fr. van Kol, s.j., on the origin and sense of the saying "Caritas non urget cum tanto incommodo," *Bijdragen*, 14 (1953), 388–408, shows that it dates only from the nineteenth century; as it easily lends itself to false interpretations, it is desirable that it disappear from manuals.

goods related to and preparing celestial beatitude, including all that facilitates the practice of virtue, and terrestrial goods, insofar as these are an image of celestial happiness.

Now charity toward our neighbor leads us to wish him the latter as well as the former. But, specifically Christian charity causes us to wish spiritual goods even more intensely for ourselves than for our neighbor, for we are "nearer to ourselves" than he is; and, on the other hand, this same charity detaches us from terrestrial goods through mortification.[16]

Rivalry between these two forms of charity is always possible, for by our carnal aspect we are always exterior to one another. We are even forced to defend a certain indispensable degree of exteriority: under pain of death, we must eat, seek shelter, etc.; in a word, we must possess certain things that cannot be possessed by others at the same time. The zone of conflict, which is also that of rights and law, lies at the exterior pole of our being. It is here that legal-minded theologians compare and carefully weigh what is "mine" and what is "thine," thus gradually introducing the scales of justice into the domain of charity itself. In a shipwreck, for example, one may decide to sacrifice his own life and leave to others the floating plank; but must he do so? When needs are equal, do all men not have the right of loving themselves more than their neighbor? For, as one moralist has put it, "proximi dilectio similis, non æqualis esse debet dilectioni erga seipsum."[17] This reasoning can be very useful in solving a case in confession, but it does not teach us in what spirit such cases should be solved. In fact, the conflict can arise from our ontological limit, which makes it impossible at the same time to adequately look after our own interests and those of our neighbor; but it can also arise from our egoism, which opposes the interests of others by complying with the exigencies of the "me" and not of the "I." Both our ontological and psy-

chological limits are closely akin to egoism, and it is easy
to pass off one for the other. In any case, our conscience
always tells us whether there is question of impossibility or
simply of egoism. But this requires some explanation.

Let us first suppose that in a given case it is impossible
for us to prefer the interests of others because of an absolute impediment and not merely on account of a disorderly
movement of self-love; and just as any limit imposed on the
diffusion of love, it causes us to suffer. This suffering shows
that love is present, for love always tends to surpass limits.
This is an ideal disposition which forbids us to measure our
neighbor's needs in degrees and to thus calculate his necessity according to the categories of *extrema, quasi-extrema,
gravis,* or *ordinaria.* Since, by hypothesis, love is present and
since impossibility alone can arrest the movement of love,
the rule will be to do all that can be done over and above
the strict minimum imposed by justice. Here we can call
to mind a St. Vincent de Paul, a Don Bosco, so many other
confessors and missionaries, mothers who forget themselves for their children, nuns and Brothers who consecrate
their whole life to others' children and to the abandoned;
and above all, we should see Christ acting and loving in all
these devoted Christians. They are, so to say, a multiple
and catholic Christ who goes on repeating and proving that
there is no greater mark of love than to lay down one's life
for one's friend; such is the normal tendency of love. And
one can sacrifice his life little by little, day after day, just as
well as by shedding his blood once and for all. One can
prefer the interests or life of one's neighbor to one's own,
unless the future of other persons depending on him prevent him from doing so; and even in this case he would
prefer others to himself. It is always legitimate to prefer our
neighbor to our own temporal "self."

Pure charity stops only, and in fact reluctantly, at its
own natural limits. But most of the time we are far from

this ideal, for we very soon meet with the shortcomings of our generosity, the "limit" of our moral forces. This limit may well be due to a lack of prayer or to the relative absence of the Eucharist in our lives; but it can also be caused by the weakness of human psychology. Here we only consider the limit arising from our egoism, or at least from our refusal to go as far as charity would lead us; this refusal prevents us from realizing our true vocation of saints. Now, when we are confronted with the duty of fraternal charity, what can we say of this egoism that struggles against love in us? We must oppose it with some definite rules, and thus are led back to the ways of justice, to a careful weighing of obligations. But we do so humbly in that attitude we must always adopt before the minimum of strict obligation. This attitude is quite akin to that "suffering" we have already described which bears witness to the presence of love. Because of our ever-present egoism, we must then have recourse to the norms laid down by moralists, which assure at least a certain indispensable equilibrium; in case of extreme necessity, a neighbor must be helped *etiam cum gravi periculo vitæ;* if he is in grave spiritual necessity and I have not the courage to expose my life or my belongings to grave danger in order to rescue him, I am not thereby cut off from the life of grace, unless my station in life obliges me to save him. I must take into account my own moral force, the inspiration of the Spirit, and my actual degree of charity. Here is a positive answer to the question arising from the conflict between self-love and love for others. It is undoubtedly preferable to other solutions which fasten attention on the minimum limits of love, for example, "In gravi necessitate spirituali versanti, non est succurrendum cum gravi periculo vitæ, famæ vel bonorum, nisi ab iis qui ex officio in salutem animarum incumbunt, ut parochi."[18] The same holds true for the duty of fraternal correction, of alms, of love for our enemies, etc.

We have already explained that conflicts of charity arise

mainly from the carnal pole of our being, which causes our mutual exteriority. But these conflicts do not always center on material, external goods; they are at times much more subtle. For example, must one expose himself to occasions of sin in order to assist a certain category of souls? If one must prefer one's neighbor to one's own temporal self, must one also prefer him to one's own spiritual self? Under this latter form, the question can easily be solved: charity can never command or permit an act that would suppress in us the source of charity or the possibility of a still greater love. Sin limits or destroys our love; in spite of appearances to the contrary, it can in no way be useful to our neighbor. The same answer holds for the question of whether one should expose oneself to an immediate occasion of sin; if this occasion is necessary, one should at least make it as remote as possible. If the occasion is decidedly remote, Christian prudence, sincerity, prayer, and the advice of a wise director will help to determine whether it is good, supernaturally speaking, to run this risk. Thus the problem falls into the field of pastoral practice.

In conclusion, let us examine whether the formula, "Love thy neighbor as thyself," is the most perfect expression of Christian love. Our Lord Himself says that it sums up the whole Law of the Old Testament. But when He gives us His own commandment, He expresses it in the following manner, "Love one another as I have loved you" (Jn. 15:12). Now "Greater love than this no one has, that one lay down his life for his friends" (Jn. 15:13); and in this manner did Jesus love men. The true tendency of perfect Christian love for one's neighbor is to love him as our own spiritual self, and more than our own carnal self.

IV. THE ORDER OF CHARITY TOWARD THE NEIGHBOR

The following question may now be raised: does charity cause us to love more those who are nearer to God, or those who are nearer to ourselves? As a supernatural force leading to communion, it unites us interiorly and more profoundly to those who participate more intensely in divine charity; it gives us greater joy in their perfection and causes us affectively to wish them the greater good. But effectively we are more obliged toward those who are nearer to us.[19] This is easily understood. We have seen that our being has an interior, spiritual pole and an exterior, carnal pole. Our love for our neighbor is patterned on this structure. By our spirit we are nearer to God and to those akin to Him. Spiritually, we love others with a spiritual, interior, supernatural love of complacency which of itself is measured by the degree of grace in each Christian. This love heeds not the diversity of human kinships, of races, or of sensible friendships. It is, properly speaking, a "catholic" love. At its opposite pole, our being is exteriorized and dispersed and thus gives way to a terrestrial diversity of loves. At this level, the interior unity of love manifests itself in a great variety of specifications. Since our acts of effective benevolence and kindness take place in space and time, the intensity of our effective love will be proportioned to the local, temporal, or carnal "proximity" of our neighbor. Formally speaking, conjugal, familial, and patriotic love, because they imply some carnal bond, are less profound in us than the spiritual love of charity. We love our mother more profoundly as a Christian than as a mother. That is why our Lord considered His disciples, who were to receive the life of grace, as His true family: "Behold my mother and my brethren" (Mk. 3:34). Hence spiritual Christian love eminently contains all terrestrial loves, even the most natural. In this perspective we also understand our Lord's counsel to leave behind father, mother, and all things whatsoever, in order to live wholly for the kingdom of charity wherein supernatural love alone will remain (cf. Lk. 14:26).

Our psychology is in conformity, in its own way, with what is revealed in the gospel. The love we have for our parents is more sensible and more acutely felt than the love we have for other men "in Christ." But sensible love is much less profound than spiritual love, and this is precisely why it can be perceived on the level of clear consciousness and of sensibility. Nor is it surprising that sensible love and friendship are so frail. They become deeper and more stable when they are interiorized, that is, when they become spiritual and Christian. Natural love for our parents, however legitimate and obligatory it may be, does not find in itself its full sense. It is a mediation of spiritual love, and its sensible attraction is only there to entice further interiorization.

On entering religious life, the young man soon hears the voice of Christian ascetical tradition telling him how he should renounce the parents he has left behind in the world: "Let everyone . . . account that he is to leave father, mother, brothers, sisters and whatsoever he had in the world. Moreover, let him consider as addressed to himself these words, 'He that hates not father and mother, yea and his own life also, cannot be my disciple.' "[20] On hearing such words, he should not have the impression that he is commanded to betray his filial love; on the contrary, he is invited to give it its true supernatural sense and to make it a mediation of charity: "And so he must make it his duty to put off all carnal affection toward his kindred and convert the same into spiritual, loving them with that only love which well-ordered charity requires, as one who, being dead to the world and to self-love, lives only to Christ our Lord and has Him in place of parents, brothers and all things whatsover."[21] Spiritual union is possible only through abnegation of the sensible limit-aspect of our being, which, in our sinful nature, too easily becomes an obstacle to progress. But how strong and affectionate is this purified love when it comes back to those persons who are dear to us, seeing them now as manifestations of Christ's goodness! Here we can understand the intimate union between St. Benedict and his sister St. Scholastica, and the delicate filial sentiments of St. Thérèse of Lisieux for her father and sisters. "The heart of saints is liquid," said the Curé d'Ars; and how true it is, for in him all the hardness and all the egoism of sensibility had, as it were, dissolved. Nothing now hinders the spontaneous flow of self-giving in perfect disinterestedness.

Since we must judge the manifestations of effective love in reference to what is more exterior in us, must we not recognize that our obligations of charity—which pertain, as all "limit-obligations," to our exterior pole—are to be measured according to the degree of carnal or natural union which binds us to our parents, leaving the degree of spiritual union to be measured by other norms? But we should not forget that carnal bonds are mediations of a spiritual bond, so that one is inseparable from the other. All carnal love is apt to become Christian by deepening in charity; and charity assumes various nuances according to the different degrees of natural proximity among men. It seems that the hierarchy of natural bonds presents the following pattern: first comes the bond between husband and wife, and then that which unites parents to their children, children to their parents, children of the same family, members of the same family taken in the wider sense, members of the same country, of the same society; and inside this latter category of social bonds, first in importance is the bond of friendship. For husband and wife, carnal proximity is, so to say, an actual and permanent mediation of their spiritual love; besides the free choice that unites them, the very constitution of their sexes implies a physical complementarity, which founds a more exclusive attraction between them, whereas there is only a bond of origin between parents and children, a bond of origin, however, not only of life, but of numberless gifts. Again, the love of parents for their children seems to come before the love of children for their parents; love is said to "descend," for parents love their children as part of themselves even before they are born, whereas children become truly capable of love only when the carnal bonds are already loosened; in fact, these bonds go on loosening and make room in the growing man for a more personal and spiritual love. Spiritual parenthood, a bond which father and mother acquire in educating the souls of their children, is much more profound than carnal parenthood and is apt to found spiritual love. Children of the same family have a common origin and also a certain attitude of mutual sympathy, which however differs from spiritual love, just as the two poles of our being differ from each other; sympathy between brothers and sisters is founded on their mutual likeness.[22]

Patriotic love is familial love broadened to the dimensions of public life. Its first element is a certain filial love for a permanent collectivity which plays a maternal role toward each of us; to this element is added a certain fraternal sympathy between citizens. There is, therefore, quite a difference between love for the fatherland, which is, in some way, an extension of the family, and love for the nation: the former is founded on a filial love for the ancestors and is somehow akin to the familial bond, while the latter stems from fraternal sympathy; in the first case love is, so to say, vertical and, in the second case, it is horizontal. "National order is social order par excellence. . . . The nation is a social reality composed of social entities: it is made up of groups more than of individuals."[23] That is why we have said there is ample room for friendships inside patriotic and social love. We might note in passing that the order of charity we have followed in our analysis is the classical order usually adopted by moralists.[24]

The necessary collective good must always be preferred to the private good.[25] In our perspective, this is absolutely normal, for charity naturally develops devotedness to others; besides, society is a more perfect mediation of Christ than is the individual. But it remains true that the person is somehow an absolute and must be respected as such. The rights of the community are not wronged by this respect for persons; in fact, the most characteristic trait of a person is his power to enter into communion with others.

There should also be a certain hierarchy among the various goods we wish for others as well as among the persons for whom they are intended. Once we have understood that being and love are polarized and have a definite "sense," it is easy to accept the classical hierarchy among the goods that love can pursue: first come the supernatural, then the natural goods of the soul, the intrinsic goods of the body, and finally all external goods. External and corporal goods are fully ordained to the spirit, which is immersed in the supernatural presence of Christ. In considering external love as a mediation of charity, we safeguard its relativity, its necessity, and its participation in the absolute value of love: it is only the body of spiritual love, but an indispensable body.

Love for the neighbor is part of the first commandment. This is quite normal if the neighbor is considered as a mediation of Christ and of God. When St. John says that it is hypocrisy to claim that we love God who is invisible, if we do not love our neighbor who is clearly visible, does he not suggest that our neighbor is, in a certain way, a "visibility" of God? And we should not forget that for St. Paul and St. John the word *caritas* refers primarily and above all to love of one's neighbor.[26]

V. THE MANNER OF LOVING

The doctrine of mediation also sheds some light on the manner in which we are to love, on the manner in which we are to manifest our charity. It warns us at once against an overly material manner of realizing our charity as well as against a type of disincarnated love. When speaking of apostolate, we said that in order to reach certain souls, we must often start by exterior, and even material manifestations of charity. Without at all denying what we have already said, we will now point out that this material charity is not an end, nor even a means, but a mediation. When visiting the poor, we must relieve their misery, and continue to do so as long as it lasts; but alms are void of any value if they are nothing but alms, and not a manifestation of love. Alms given reluctantly or with disdain can even have evil effects on the poor, for then the gesture of charity is reduced to its material content. There is a saying that "the manner in which one gives has more value than what one gives." This is true, for the manner reveals the giving of one's own self, and to give one's self is much more valuable than to give a mere thing. Material gifts should be so many occasions for personal relations with others. In a way, it is very distressing to see hospitals taken out of the hands of nuns and entrusted to the state with its ways of justice. It is a pity to have to witness charitable organizations transformed into mechanical administrations.

But if charity cannot be content with its material aspect, neither can it be disincarnated. A would-be spiritual charity which would limit itself to preaching and would pay no attention to the concrete needs of men, risks reaching neither the soul nor the body, for man is both material and spiritual, and his body is the normal way to his spirit. "Supernaturalism" is always an illusion.

Charity must be personal. In other words, it must reach unto the depth of being, and this is possible only through love. How many of the poor need a friendly smile more than a crust of bread, for they are utterly alone despite the fact that by their very human constitution they need to have a "relation" to others. The supreme manifestation of charity might very well be the acceptance of this role which consists in being the term of a personal relation, in being for lonely men that "other" of whom they have need.

§III. THE BODY, SUFFERING, AND CHARITY

In all moral treatises, there is a chapter on charity toward the members of Christ in what concerns their corporal life. This chapter should first accurately determine the "sense" of corporal life in a perspective of charity. For the moment, we will limit ourselves to a discussion of what should be our attitude toward our body and the satisfaction of its needs. But the following observations will call for some further precisions and nuances which we will add when we treat of our duties toward the corporal good of others.[27]

I. PRINCIPLES

Just as elsewhere,[28] so here in considering the body, Christian thought encounters a sharp antinomy. On the one hand, Catholic doctrine clearly condemns the Manichæan tendency to see the body as an evil creature[29] and often manifests its great respect for it as the temple of the Holy Spirit which the Church honors even after death; on the other hand, there is a tradition dating from the apostles, according to which the body must be submitted to strict asceticism; among authentic saints, this latter trend develops into open and often fierce struggle against the body.

First of all, the word "body" is itself ambiguous, for the body, as such, does not exist. It is not a "thing" informed by the soul. It is only one aspect of an incarnated spirit. That is why the Church asserts and maintains the essential unity of man wherein the soul is the substantial form of the body.[30] The body considered as a "thing" may well define a corpse, but certainly not the living body, which is only the "exteriority" of the soul. The body is, so to say, the function by which the person is inserted into and becomes effective in the sensible universe and in the field of moral activity, the latter being understood in the sense already explained.[31] If it has life only by its union with the soul, the body has no "sense" outside of this union. It exists only for the spirit. Its bipolarity explains the antinomies we have just encountered. If it plays its role of a mediation leading to the soul, then the body is a positive element of our salvation and the Church defends it against all Manichæism; in this case, it becomes a mediation of charity, for our being elevated to the supernatural order is a participation of charity-love. If, on the contrary, we take the body as an end and thus cut it off from its onto-logical relation with the soul, it becomes an idol and, morally speaking, a corpse. It is this idolatry that Christian ascetical tradition has so fiercely fought. The body is a mediation, not an absolute: a good servant but a bad master. When the body is made an absolute, it is treacherous for several reasons. First, it is situated at the exterior, material limit of our being; and at this limit, love tends sharply toward concupiscence.[32] Secondly, it is a very tangible reality, directly accessible to our sensible consciousness; its demands can easily express themselves more loudly than the discreet requests of the spirit. Thirdly, since original sin the body has a preponderant tendency to encroach on the domain of the spirit, and so the normal balance can be maintained only by constantly reacting against this tend-ency.[33] As soon as our vigilance fails, we are easily dragged down toward our inferior limit.

It is true that at certain periods, and especially at the

time of Jansenism, this necessary reaction was so violent that it tended to separate the spirit from the flesh. As a result, the body was left to its "brute" nature and the spirit suffered by being deprived of its necessary mediation; hence a "return to reality," in the sense of a reincarnation, became very urgent. Some have judged Gustave Thibon's plea for such a reincarnation as too "carnal," this word being understood in the sense given it by Péguy; but it is at least a forceful testimony of the divorce between the angel and the beast in man. Our age is rediscovering the positive value of the body, but at a certain risk. This rediscovery is taking place in a materialistic atmosphere which fosters not only legitimate "culture" of the body, but also a certain "cult" for the idol it can easily become. Christians must give to physical "culture" and corporal values their just measure of importance by emphasizing their spiritual sense; the importance many now attach to them is not necessarily a sign of health, but rather of a spiritual emptiness that satisfies its cravings with a substitute.

II. MORAL CONSEQUENCES

Physical culture is a useful and, to a certain extent, a necessary complement of spiritual culture. It must provide the spirit with a balanced "organon," docile to the soul so that she may use it artfully for her spiritual and material tasks. On the other hand, physical culture cannot be separated from total human culture, for the body has of itself no "sense."[34]

Because our sensibility is prone to egoism and because original sin has put it in a state of disequilibrium, it must ever be controlled by the spirit. We can never "abandon" ourselves to it. The cardinal virtue of temperance or detachment* has precisely this role of putting order into our

* We are thinking of a more elaborate system of the virtues, which we can not insert here.

sensibility by means of mortification, abnegation, sobriety, abstinence, and chastity.

Christian temperance differs from natural temperance by the fact that it is a mediation of divine charity in the field of "fallen" sensibility. It begins therefore by a painful straightening which compensates for this disequilibrium; that is why it is always accompanied by the virtue of penance, which inspires regret and repairs the moral deformities, and by the virtue of vigilance, which prevents a return to these evils. This ordering puts our sensible appetite in harmony with the requirements of charity toward God and our neighbor. Because its task is to see that the opacity of sensible consciousness no longer remains an obstacle to supernatural communion, the Christian virtue of temperance is much more demanding than natural temperance. As a mediation of charity, it impregnates our carnal affections with spirituality; it renders sensible tendencies transparent, revealing in them an attraction and a finality which are far more interior and more important than their egoistic, exterior counterpart. Through temperance, sensible appetite becomes transparent to charity,[35] so that the Christian definition of this virtue can be formulated in the following manner: temperance is that virtue which corrects the concupiscence of the sensible appetite by ordering it toward the spiritual communion of charity with God and the neighbor.

The body is, therefore, a mediation and normally it must be surpassed (2 Cor. 5:2–3, 6–8) if we are to reach a richer spiritual maturity. It is only worthy of that interest which a mediation merits. In fact, it can easily become an obstacle. For example, physical suffering often appears more as an obstacle than as a positive value. As a disorder introduced into the most exterior part of our being, it tends to concentrate all our attention and energies on this inferior pole. This is true only insofar as suffering is considered independently of its true sense, the more so because it is never the body alone that is sick; the body does not exist as a separate entity. It is the whole man who is in a state of physical disorder. Hence suffering, just as the body itself, appears as a limit; that is to say, it has value only in the measure that we pass beyond it and refer it to something else. Of itself, it is a burden, an obstacle to be cleared in the ascent toward the spirit. Thus it can become a precious mediation and a very efficacious means of spiritualization. It can be the occasion of a greater love and even, at times, of a desperate effort toward charity: in certain lives suffering cannot be accepted without at the same time accepting sanctity. In our analysis of the double nature of love, as at once a gift and a desire, we have already found that suffering is always intimately connected with a generous effort toward spiritual love, even the mere surpassing of our limit.[36] Such is our plight since sin destroyed our original equilibrium. But a Christian can never forget that his body is a participation of the crucified body of the Saviour and that this assimilation is strengthened by every communion. In this perspective, suffering has a redemptive value and meaning; by the mere fact that it is supported without revolt, it retains its meaning as a participation in the cross of Christ and hence becomes expiatory.[37] But how much greater is its redemptive value when we "will" it in a spirit of charity! From a Christian point of view, physical suffering is positively good, for it is the occasion of a victory of the divine good over the evil in us. "The misfortune of the present moment is surely great. . . . That is why I offer my body in labor in place of crumbling Christianity. How powerful is suffering when it is as voluntary as sin!"[38] To impose suffering on self is genuinely Christian, provided this suffering be moderated by prudence and does not turn into a morbid and selfish desire to prove to oneself that one is generous.

What has been said of physical suffering must also be applied to spiritual and to moral suffering. Here the obstacle is more profound, the surpassing of self is more deep reaching, and thus requires a more generous display of charity. That is why the "mystical night" brings the soul very near to divine union by purifying her most intimate recesses and thus converting her wholly to God.

III. DEATH

Considered from the point of view of the body, death consists in the fact that the soul abandons the function whereby it was inserted into the world. It cannot be said that at the moment of death the soul leaves aside a "thing" which she possessed, for man does not "have," but "is" a body. This is why man has no right of ownership over his body; this is also why it is absolutely forbidden to take one's own life or to mutilate one's own body, for in doing so one attacks one's own person. To commit suicide is not to set aside the body, as a mere piece of clothing, but to renounce one's insertion in the world, to render oneself inapt for further "moral" activity;[39] in thus mutilating himself as a spiritual person, one transports himself to his term before maturity and hence refuses spiritual growth. By such an act, a man renounces being insofar as he has the power to do so, for he really deprives himself of a possible increase in spiritual existence and love. But our fundamental obligation, as we have seen, is to keep ever increasing in being[40] in order to keep ever increasing in communion.[41] No moral duty can permit us to voluntarily suppress ourselves as moral subjects, for such an act is intrinsically immoral. We are essentially, and not accidentally, "incarnated spirits."

IV. THE VOCATION OF CHARITY TOWARD THE BODY

In a Christian perspective, the doctor can be said to be the apostle of charity toward the corporal mediation of the person. And this is true of all those who nurse the body. In order to realize their vocation, they must attend patients as persons[42] and as members of a family; they should endeavor to grasp the "sense" of "corporal reality" and its relations with the psychological and moral orders. Sickness concerns the whole man; it is at times rooted in moral deficiencies; in any case, its healing always requires the collaboration of the will and of the whole soul, so that the medical cure and the moral cure are often intimately related. It would be contradictory to use an immoral means to save the body; in so doing the doctor would lose the absolute in saving the mediation. The vocation of the medical apostolate supposes, therefore, over and above scientific knowledge, the generosity of charity which attains through bodies and persons, the very members of Christ.

The medical vocation clearly indicates what must be the attitude of the Christian toward the corporal needs of others. He must be "detached" from his own body and accept whatever suffering comes to it, without neglecting the duty of sustaining and nursing it reasonably well, for divine Providence always sends us sickness together with the duty of curing it. But he must have toward others' physical needs, and especially toward their suffering, an attitude which fully corresponds to the movement of Christian charity. Now charity prefers the terrestrial goods of one's neighbor to one's own. History testifies that the Christian soul is inexhaustible in her heroic self-devotedness toward the suffering bodies of members of Christ; she is ever provident for the social and human welfare of the downtrodden and ever watches with maternal care over the birth of each new baby. Charity sees other men as mediations and thus reaches their soul and, finally, Christ; this is why all men are in the eyes of charity occasions of self-devotedness. And charity is also aware of how much asceticism and abnegation are required to assure that our self-love does not become an egoistic search for self.

§IV. CHASTITY AND CHARITY

Christian chastity is a virtuous disposition created by charity to put order into the field of sexual instinct and love so that this instinctive love may no longer be opposed to communion with God and men, but rather be elevated and directed toward it.

I. HUMAN LOVE AND SEXUAL LOVE

Sexual instinct is found in man not by reason of his spiritual nature but of his corporal exteriority and in view of a very specific end, the propagation of the human species on the earth.

It is clear, then, that sexuality is not an exigency of spiritual love as such, but is rather related to the carnal limit of the human spirit. No doubt the spirit receives in its incarnate state certain nuances which vary according to the sexes;* and, conversely, instinct is elevated when it is informed by the spirit. But the sexual remains wholly relative and subordinated to the spiritual; it does not, of itself, enrich the spirit, but rather limits and disperses it. This limitation does not suppress the spirituality of human love, but, because of its material aspect, imposes on it a very definite tonality. Conjugal union directly enriches and complements the sensible being of both husband and wife; only indirectly does it really complement their spiritual being, inasmuch as it is one with the sensible.

Moreover, the differences between man and wife in the physical organisms, in their psychology, and in their charity

---

* We would call this nuance of love "sexual *in actu primo*," and reserve the qualification "sexual *in actu secundo*" for the sexual life exercised in marriage.

itself are finally rooted in the divine plan that has thus arranged for the propagation of the human race on earth. This is why there is no question of "exercised" sexual love among the elect in heaven, despite the fact that the soul forever retains the particular nuances it has acquired through union with the body.†

Sexuality is, therefore, a necessary aspect of love among those whom God has chosen as His cooperators in the creation of new lives.‡ Because of this function and in the measure that each one performs it, their love requires the presence of another love, if it is to be complete according to the plan of God; in this perspective, man and wife can only attain unto perfection together.

Total community life makes it possible for them to perfect their love even on the sensible level; and, in the measure that this love is spiritualized, it should foster union of souls in spiritual communion, which in its turn gradually appears as a profound mediation of divine love. But even then it remains a limited mediation, since it takes place only between two persons; and we must recall at once that because man is by historical status a sinner, it is always difficult for him to suppress the natural egoism of the flesh which tends to obscure the "sense" of this restricted and, under a certain aspect, "privileged" mediation.[43]

But we must add that sexuality *in actu secundo* is only one aspect of human love; even between husband and wife, friendship and charity have other nuances than this primarily "functional" aspect. Their love should normally become more and more interior and gradually set aside or elevate to its own spiritual level the sexual aspect[44] which will finally no longer correspond to a definite need.

I can see husband and wife at an age when the burden of years

† Cf. Mt. 22:30. We speak of sexual love as it exists historically in redeemed humanity.

‡ We will point out immediately how this procreative finality is united to a finality of mutual development of husband and wife.

becomes heavier. . . . Their communion has grown so profound that little by little they have lost the need of carnal exaltation to raise them to the highest plenitude of love. Their mutual total gift is no longer realized in the flash of a passing ecstasy; from now on they belong to each other by the center of their being. Because they love each other in God, the human aspect of their affection has been sublimated.[45]

Such a union in charity is no longer rooted in sexuality, except for certain nuances that pertain to the very being of man and wife: the delicate, intuitive nature of a woman's love will ever be different from the stronger, more intellectual love of a man.[46] Moreover, their mutual sexual love in no way prevents them from loving other persons with a love that has no specifically sexual component.

Some persons, by virtue of a special grace, do not have the vocation of propagating corporal life; their love does not need to be complemented by another love, for it is not ordered to the function of procreation. And so they renounce certain nuances of human love; but these nuances are not essential, nor useful to love as such, however useful and necessary they be for those who are called upon to propagate life. We are here speaking of those nuances which are derived from "exercised" sexual life (*in actu secundo*), not of those which pertain to the very sex of persons and differentiate feminine from masculine affectivity. He who is not called to marriage also renounces the profound though special mediation of divine love found in the personal union of man and wife. But the mediation he finds through this renunciation is, in the present supernatural order, much more profound than the former and permits a still more real and intimate union in charity with God and all men. We will come back on this point later.

In brief, the sexual aspect *in actu secundo* is an important but accidental component of "spiritual" human love; this component is enriching and necessary only in view of a specific function; it does not pertain to the spiritual pole of our being, but to its carnal limit. It is possible, therefore, to discover a type of perfect supernatural love void of any nuance of "mutual" sexuality.

II. INSTINCT AND EXTERIORITY. PERFECT CHASTITY AND CONJUGAL CHASTITY

In order to understand the necessity and sense of chastity in the field of sexuality, we must point out here, as we will later for justice and the vindictive instinct, that instinct is egocentric; moreover, since original sin it is sharply prone to egoism. It has been said that sexual instinct, left to itself, leads to indifference for what concerns the personality of the "partner"[47] and to a kind of psychological isolation that can beget fierce strife; the higher human tendencies will even degenerate, following the degradation of love itself.[48] This is not surprising, since the instincts are situated at the inferior, exterior pole of our being; they have "sense" only when they are referred to spiritual and supernatural love. Instinctive carnal love derives its human value not from itself, but from its informing by love and, on the supernatural plane, by charity; left to itself, it will disintegrate, but charity can put it in line with our profound tendency to communion. It is indispensable, therefore, that charity penetrate the field of instinct. But the specific function by which charity penetrates sexuality is precisely the Christian virtue of chastity.

Chastity will foster respect for the power of generation and for the form of love peculiar to it. It can put order into this field of activity in two ways: by regulating the use of instinct according to the specific end of procreation or, in the case of celibacy, by assuring the spirit total domination over this instinct. In both cases it produces a real liberation: it frees the soul either from the tyrannical excesses or from the instinctive attraction of sexuality when this has become purposeless. Conjugal chastity corresponds to the first function and perfect chastity to the second. In both cases, the role of chastity is to foster a union in charity between spiritual but incarnate persons; it does so by assuring, on the level of sensibility, an equilibrium such that spiritual love will never be endangered by the weightiness of the flesh. It may be asked whether this virtue is more necessary to moderate the use of a tyrannical instinct or to totally renounce this instinct. In reality, both victories have their particular difficulties.

In the present economy of salvation, perfect chastity leads human love nearer to total charity, for the latter tends to spiritual communion among persons themselves and with God, whereas the normal movement of instinct since original sin is to isolate persons in their carnal egoism. Perfect chastity tends to liberate us totally from egoism and to enable our love to establish spiritual relations without the risk of being dragged down by the weight of the flesh, and so without the risk of dividing and "particularizing" itself. Supernatural charity has created interior bonds with God and other members of Christ which are more ontological and profound than sensible or sexual bonds can ever be. These direct relations with God and other men in Christ are, in fact, our really important and irrevocable bonds; compared to these, merely human bonds play the role of means, or rather of mediations. Because of special grace, those who are called to practice the counsels of the Gospel do not have to use this mediation, but are put in direct contact with divine charity and universal fraternal charity. Here there is a positive gain and only an apparent loss, even if certain natural qualities are left undeveloped. When a man is called to follow this way, perfect chastity is of itself more perfect than conjugal chastity. It provides the possibility of devoting oneself without limit to God and all men, and this possibility is an effect and a sign of the liberation that perfect chastity can afford to the exercise of charity. This superiority was, in fact, revealed by our Lord Himself (Mt. 19:12).

Obviously perfect chastity does not produce what Freudianism would label "repression of instinct." Instinct, as we have just said, has its own proper direction, but it derives its total and ultimate "sense" only by being oriented toward personal love and charity. If virtue is an ontological, psychological, and moral dynamism assuring the equilibrium of human energies whose center of attraction is the superior pole of our affective being, then we must recognize that the energy, which instinct would have used in its normal exercise, now finds in total love for God and men an occasion for its fullest development: charity does not repress but rather absorbs and transforms the energy of instinct.*

By its very nature, perfect chastity is the ideal of conjugal chastity. True, it is somewhat of a transcendent ideal, and this is why it is apt to inspire and maintain the proper ideal of conjugal chastity at a very high level; it aims at reproducing in its own way the union of Christ with His Church. And since the Church is united to Christ in the measure that she dies to the world, conjugal chastity is also somehow involved in the mystery of Redemption.

---

* Cf. Yves de Monticheuil, s.j., "Formes de la vie religieuse," *Formes, vie et pensée*, published by the Groupe Lyonnais d'études médicales, philosophiques et biologiques (Lyons, 1934), pp. 398–399. Moreover, Providence and the Church herself, realizing the enrichment which man finds in feminine psychology, have given to all men, even in their religious life, the heart of Mary with all its motherly delicacy.

The weightiness and relativity of the carnal aspect is perhaps not recognized with sufficient realism by A. Christian in his book, *Ce sacrement est grand* which we have already quoted. This work appears to present as "normal" certain spiritual realizations which are, in fact, possible by a great fidelity to grace in very advanced souls.

Yet another common source of error is the illusion of a more or less sensual pseudo-mysticism—an illusion which young couples yield to all too easily today. Cf. H. Mogenet, s.j., "Mariage et virginité," *Études*, 251 (1946), 322–332; Th. Camelot, o.p., *Virgines Christi* (Paris, 1944).

We can never insist too much on the requirements of conjugal chastity as a mediation of the charity of Christ. It requires the crucifixion of daily abnegation, for the task of chastity in regulating instinct is not an easy one. Of course the spirit and grace of Christ gradually penetrate instinct and effectively fight its egoism, but instinct has a violence proportioned to the difficulties involved in procreation. The least concession to instinct increases its attraction, which, since original sin, can easily become immoderate. The gradual spiritualization of instinct is the normal result of the special grace attached to the sacrament of marriage, provided it is seconded by generosity, constant prayer, and communion with the body of Christ which sanctifies the human body. And even if the practice of chastity remains difficult, it will also be the occasion of an ever more perfect surpassing of self.

We have said earlier[49] that the community of married life was a somehow privileged, though limited, mediation. But as we have said in speaking of suffering,† the very use of instinct introduces a certain heaviness into moral life; it often consumes much spiritual energy and to some extent prevents the soul from giving herself totally in charity. It can easily divide our love between the spirit and the senses and thus restrict it to a limited number of persons and bind it to material tasks which diminish direct contact with souls and with God. On the other hand, these very tasks can be the occasion of an authentically generous charity.

As all members of Christ, the Christian husband and wife feel a secret nostalgia for progressive purification. For them, this purification is contained in the very dynamism of the virtue of chastity. Chastity invites them to seek more interior and spiritual union, to penetrate into the soul of

---

† "Although sensible goods can legitimize certain pleasures when man uses them to go to God, this fruit is nevertheless hazardous and experience teaches us that ordinarily more damage than profit results therefrom" (St. John of the Cross, *Sayings and Spiritual Counsels*, n. 305).

one another and to gradually come to see the carnal elements of conjugal love, apart from their creative function, as the imperfect beginnings of a love of benevolence. When maturity has been reached, the role of instinct can gradually begin to disappear; two souls are then united in communion without being distracted by the sensible. Carnal union and sensible love cannot, therefore, be considered as the absolute end of marriage, but as a mediation that must be gradually surpassed, and as an introduction to a still more perfect union. When the Church recognizes that the sacrament of marriage has as its secondary end to be a *remedium concupiscentiæ*,[50] she does not mean that this remedy is to be found in a free exercise of the sexual instinct, but rather in its natural use ordered by the virtue of chastity and the sacramental grace, thus in a spiritualization of this instinct. In Christian doctrine, marriage reproduces symbolically the union of Christ with His Church and is, therefore, a union in charity. Pope Pius XI said that

this love is not based on the passing lust of the moment, nor does it consist in pleasing words only, but in the deep attachment of the heart which is expressed in action, since love is proved by deeds. This outward expression of love in the home demands not only mutual help, but must go further; it must have as its primary purpose that man and wife help each other day by day in forming and perfecting themselves in the interior life, so that through their partnership in life they may advance ever more and more in virtue, and above all that they may grow in true love toward God and their neighbor, on which indeed "dependeth the whole Law and the Prophets."[51]

III. THE ENDS OF MARRIAGE

The encyclical *Casti Connubii* recognizes that it is possible to see this mutual interior formation of husband and wife as "the chief reason and purpose of matrimony, provided matrimony be looked at not in the restricted sense as instituted for the proper conception and education of the child, but more widely as the blending of life as a whole and the mutual interchange and sharing thereof."[52] This does not contradict the fact, stated in canon law,[53] that the primary end of marriage is the procreation and education of children; in this latter context, marriage is considered as an institution. Now it is certain, first, that the primary end of the institution of marriage, considered in general, is the procreation and education of children: sexual instinct finds here its only reason for existence; second, that the primary end of the conjugal act is procreation; third, that the immediate end that inclines a man and a woman to life in common is the good which they wish for each other, their desire as spiritual and incarnate persons for mutual communion and help.

It does not follow from the fact that carnal union is a means to attain the primary end of procreation that spiritual union among persons is also merely a means. Personal union is more than a means, just as their spiritual community life is more than an institution to assure conservation of the species.

If it were possible in married love to separate the carnal from the spiritual pole, then it could be said that, insofar as it is spiritual, this love is not a means, for it attains charity, and that, insofar as it is carnal and sexual, it is a means whose end is procreation. But such a division is illegitimate, for these two poles are merely complementary aspects of one and the same love. Conjugal love considered as a whole surpasses the mere "institution"; but, because of its carnal aspect, it intrinsically depends on and must be submitted to the creative finality of the institution which alone legitimizes the nonspiritual elements of conjugal love.

Fecundity is a divine property of charity; this is why the union of husband and wife as persons will finally blossom in the birth of a child. St. Bonaventure says that in God the fruit of union is Love, that is, the Holy Spirit; among men, who are carnal beings, the fruit of union is a loved one. Nevertheless, the child is the bond which best realizes the ideal unity of love, for he is a real reciprocal gift in which each can always recognize something of himself and of the other, intimately fused in the unity of a living person. Moreover, it is on the spiritual plane that the child becomes the fruit of his parents' souls, for education consists in "building" a spiritual soul, and in so doing the parents really undertake the "creation" of a person. In this perspective, procreation is the end of marriage which best realizes and sustains the spiritual union of persons; there is between procreation and personal union a reciprocal causality and finality which is the sign of a reciprocal need for unity inscribed in our nature by God Himself. This is why the Church formally disapproved of certain writings[54] wherein the child, the primary end of marriage, passed to the second plane and was considered rather as an effect, an extrinsic end, while primary importance was given to the mutual perfection of husband and wife, which seemed to be considered as the immediate, intrinsic end of marriage;[55] and in this mutual perfection special emphasis was put on carnal union. The latter seemed to be taken as an end, instead of as a mediation which would find its meaning by being oriented toward the function of generation and spiritual union in charity.

IV. THE DISORDER OF IMPURITY

Since the carnal, sexual pole of love is oriented toward generation, it is easy to understand how grave is the disorder caused by impurity (*luxuria*), and especially by solitary impurity. It perverts a function conferred on man and woman only in view of the objective good of the whole human society; this objective good is essentially superior to the good of the individual and reveals not only a particular aspect of God's transcendence over the individual, but also an exigency of "community" life. It is an injury to the rights of God as author of the human family and also an injury to the rights of the community—an injury which has its origin in selfishness.

Man needs mediations in order to reach God. It is normal, then, that his spiritual subordination to God be reflected in a specific duty by which his sensible instincts and his sensible individual self is submitted to the "collective human being." Impurity is the *non serviam* of the flesh as such. It despises human community which is for us the living image of God; it is essentially the "pride of the flesh."

The gravity of impurity comes also from the fact that it puts disorder into that carnal love which actually pertains to our fundamental love-tendency. Sexuality is an all-pervading, though accidental aspect of love; it penetrates our whole being, body and soul; and though an accident, it is one with our substance and modifies it profoundly. Once disorder finds its way into love even on this sensible level, the entire order of love suffers. Impurity is egoism taking possession of love on this exterior level; from this point of view also, it is well named the "pride of the flesh." Since our being constitutes an undivided whole, impurity is an effective attempt to materialize love, to neutralize its tendency toward spirituality and charity. In fact, when this sin becomes a habit, it gradually smothers a man's interest in the spirit and interior life and drags him down to the level of the beasts. Little by little it draws him toward his material exteriority. It is a degradation for the spirit to be thus submerged among bestial instincts: this is why impurity is called a "shameful" sin.

V. A NOTE ON FREUDIANISM*

Did Freud not mistake the true sense of our profound

---

* We are not competent to attempt even a slightly comprehensive study of Freudianism. We will confine ourselves, therefore, to a few remarks suggested by our point of view.

being when he assigned sexual instinct as the fundamental tendency of our whole psychic life and thus gave a materialistic interpretation to man? The following remarks apply to Freudianism taken in this strict sense. We have seen that there is at the source of all moral life a love ultimately oriented toward the giving of self in spiritual love elevated by charity. How was it possible for Freud to see nothing there but sexual love craving for egoistic pleasure which he called *eros?* This is quite easily understood once we consider his method. Not only does he concentrate on the analysis of morbid cases, wherein psychical egoism manifests itself more obviously, but he is further content with examining the spontaneous instinctive and imaginative manifestations of the psyche in dreams and in the association of phantasms. In other words, his analysis bears on facts directly related to sensibility, that is, on the exterior, inferior limit of the person. It is not at all surprising then that egoism rules over this domain, and that sexuality, that most powerful of instincts, often appears in the leading role; besides, when the interior, spiritual pole no longer controls the instincts, it is easy to interpret their first reactions in a very materialistic sense. The lower level of our being has "sense" only when referred to spiritual, voluntary activity. And it is clear that the spirit cannot be discovered if it is excluded by the very nature of the method of investigation employed. Freudianism does not analyze the soul, but only that limit where spiritual being is engaged in matter and instinct.*

If sexuality were not deliberately cut off from its spiritual sense, it would still be possible to discover in it a mediation of the spirit and of love. But as soon as this mediation

---

* R. DALBIEZ concludes his monumental work as follows: "Freud's work is the most profound analysis that history has ever known of the less human elements in human nature" (*Psychoanalytical Method and the Doctrine of Freud*, trans. by T. F. LINDSAY [New York, 1941], II, 327).

is transformed into an absolute, nothing but instinct will be found in it. Freud considers our instinctive limit as our *profound* tendency because it is subconscious and hidden, at least from clear consciousness. But we have already seen[56] that there are two levels in the depth of our being: a supraconceptual level, which is intuitive and spiritual, and an infraconceptual level, which corresponds to sensibility; the former is our true interiority, whereas the latter ever remains obscure because of its exteriority and dispersion. Besides, our conscience tells us that our true self is not that "self" which finds expression in dreams or "free associations," but that "self" we want to be through our own spiritual effort. Our true self is more in the future than in the past. It builds itself and we build it with the help of God, because our being is spirit and love, and because love essentially consists in giving and surpassing self, rather than in a turning back on self in a sterile evaluation of the past.[57]

On the other hand, the delicate analysis of Etienne Borne has shown how Freudianism unconsciously confirms the authenticity of certain Christian values, such as the importance of the interior life, the value of the least of our thoughts, which all remain inscribed in our psyche. Even omitted acts have a moral meaning. The Freudian "censor" bears witness to the spiritual presence and activity of a moral conscience that reaches even into the field of instinct. Psychosis may at times be like the agonizing sanction of a past life—be it individual or collective—utterly void of true love on the level of the profound tendency. Thus Freudianism affirms the reality of original sin and of inherited egoism and testifies in favor of the liberation that a sincere confession can produce.[58] It recalls that, aside from clear consciousness, there exists in us a more profound level which is the scene of strikingly intensive activity; but Freudianism does not discover the true sense of this activity, because it remains on the easily accessible surface of our true depth which is ever glistening with day- or night-dreams.[59]

Freudianism, thus understood, is pessimistic and dangerous because it abstracts from man's fundamental love and only considers in him the instinctive beast given over to autonomous forces. But man is one, and it is impossible to first submit him to a Freudian instinct-analysis and only then to a spiritual cure. The instinct-analysis is itself false and harmful, for human instincts are impregnated with spirituality. Even as a psychic cure, independently of its doctrinal context, psychoanalysis can easily be unreal,[60] incomplete, and even harmful, unless it is handled by profoundly spiritual and Christian men. Total liberation cannot come from the simple fact that one takes consciousness of his "fault," nor from a certain "sublimation" of instinct understood in the Freudian sense, for such "sublimation" consists merely in providing this purely instinctive tendency with a harmless object. True liberation consists in assuming this tendency or deficiency into that profound flow of human life which is the giving of self, now ontologically and psychologically transformed by charity into a flow of divine life and force.*

§V. Charity and Justice

At first sight, justice and charity seem to be opposed to one another as two contrary movements. If charity is the force leading to communion and unity, justice is the virtue of "otherness."

* We do not wish to insinuate that psychoanalytic research has not shed valuable light on human psychology, especially on experimental psychology. As a method, within its own well-defined limits, it can even obtain felicitous spiritual results, but, we believe, only if it is not sublimated, but assumed into a spiritual behavior; for, in this case, it again becomes a mediation and rediscovers its own human value by readopting its own proper place.

Justice is *ad alterum*. And so justice is possible between two beings in the measure that they are other. In the measure that they are one, there is no place for justice. . . . Justice, as such, governs the relations between strangers, in the measure that they are strangers.[61]

Superficially, one might say that justice divides and that love unites.

It is of the utmost importance to dissipate the ambiguity of this saying, for it can have grave consequences. Human and Christian life can, we said, be considered as the blossoming of charity-love which tends to realize through all our moral activity a communion among spiritual persons who are destined to become interiorly united with one another without, however, losing their own proper personality. And we have also seen that every virtue is a mediation of this tendency to communion. Is the very important virtue of justice to be an exception? Cannot it too be a mediation of charity?

I. INSTINCT AND JUSTICE

Several times already we have been led to recognize that the apparent opposition between two aspects of moral life was in fact a sign of their complementarity and of the bi-polar tension of our spiritual-carnal being, rather than a sign of their irreducible duality. Even if, at the spiritual pole of our being, our interpersonal relations are a communion of love, we still remain individuals engaged in sensible and social multiplicity, and this pole of our being still remains impenetrable. On this level the distinction between persons is translated by the somewhat exclusive and localized "otherness" of "mine" and "thine." Two men cannot occupy the same place. On the animal level, where sympathy adjoins brutality, this "otherness" is governed by the instinctive equilibrium of biological forces. In us, the biological level is not that of pure animality; our instincts are penetrated by the spirit with its exigencies for communion. In fact, is not justice itself this tendency of spiritual communion penetrating the exteriority of our instincts, which, left to themselves, incline us toward outside material good? Indeed, St. Thomas fixes as the matter of the virtue of justice *"exteriores actiones et res."*[62] And in what concerns the exteriority of instinct, a psychologist who has studied the instinct-element in justice writes: "When considered closely, the notion of [instinctive] justice corresponds to the conscious representation of the unconscious resistance with which man opposes the exterior world and the principle of reality."[63] And again: "The 'resentful man' is a product of the sentiment of justice which is often experienced under the form of the sentiment of suffering injustice."[64] We should not be surprised at this. When studying the sense of love, we recognized that, on the sensible level, even love is egocentric;[65] instinctive love always tends to be egoistic. We should not be surprised, then, that the instinctive function called "justice" is "an essentially egocentric function,"[66] and that its movement bears on the claims and defense of self by putting others on the same level as self[67] and by seeking revenge. This vindictiveness is the more dangerous because it is often taken for authentic justice.[68] All too often the virtue of justice is identified with these spontaneous reactions, which are neither objective nor virtuous, but, on the contrary, render virtue necessary, just as disorder calls for order. Virtue, as we have seen,[69] is a stable mediation which introduces the order of the spirit into the multiplicity of sensibility.

II. THE VIRTUE OF JUSTICE

By its function of mediation, the virtue of justice governs the relation between the vindictive instincts and self-defense and the fundamental tendency to communion.

It derives from love and becomes the specific form of love that must rectify the instinct of self-defense and of the opposition of self to others and its prolongation in exterior possessions. This seems to explain the particular characteristics of the virtue of justice and also its apparent antinomy. Indeed, justice, considered as a mediation of charity on the level of opposition between individuals, will be related to the two poles between which it is stretched, between exteriority and interiority.

I. EXTERIORITY

Justice governs that level on which men are separated as incarnate individuals bound to exterior goods and hence as opposed to one another. These goods situate them locally and root them in "things," whether these things be their own bodies or possessions which they have appropriated to their "individual selves" by previous acts. They are material things which they have "occupied," or even spiritual realities, such as reputation, inventions, etc., which are, however, bound to visible manifestations and imitate more or less the occupation of exterior goods.

On this level, where possessions are in some way materially or locally divisible, a norm of distribution must be found—an equilibrium not merely of forces, such as that suggested by instinct with its need for breathing space, but of rights, such as is demanded by love enlightened by the intelligence, or rather by charity illuminated by faith. This equilibrium will take on forms more or less rigid and obligatory according as owners are more or less separated from one another; it would by degrees lose its justification and be transformed into a common possession, in the measure that owners become united by love. It is by reason of its lower level then that justice tends toward the division of "mine" and "thine," toward strict equality between what is owed and what is paid, toward objectification, distinctness of situations, the determination of a minimum threshold below which one cannot fall without provoking the reaction of self-defense, that is, the claims of the other that immediately rupture the bonds of charity-love. Here there is question of mortal sin *ex genere suo*, for there is a rupture of the relations of charity. At its lower limit, justice is rather negative, in the sense that it obliges us to respect the other's good, to simply give it back to him rather than to promote his possession of it positively.

Here we see why "justice obliges more than charity," with a limited and strict obligation. It does so not because it is more perfect than charity, but, on the contrary, because it assures the minimum of charitable relations necessary to safeguard further progress in love.*

The exteriority and objectifying tendency of justice explain why it has rights as its object. Rights are the objective exteriority of the moral order inasmuch as they determine relations between persons in what concerns exterior goods. Rights make a balance between "mine" and "thine" a matter of strict obligation. Here morality finds its maximum degree of exteriority, for justice does not derive from our personal dispersion as incarnate beings, but from the social dispersion of humanity in separated individuals. As such, we are, to a degree, necessarily opposed to one another, for we must submit to our terrestrial condition; justice is born of the fact that we are inescapably "others."

---

* This consideration re-echoes these words of Pius XI where he determines the respective roles of charity and justice in the establishment of peace: "But in effecting all these social reforms, the law of charity, 'which is the bond of perfection' (Col. 3:14), must always take a leading role. . . . Admittedly, no vicarious charity can substitute for justice which is due as an obligation and would be wrongfully denied. Yet even supposing that everyone should finally receive all that is due him, the widest field for charity will always remain open. For justice alone can, if faithfully observed, remove the causes of social conflicts, but can never bring about union of minds and hearts" ("Quadragesimo Anno," NCWC trans.; cf. AAS, 23 [1931], 223).

We respect rights in the other. The subject and object of justice are as such opposed to one another.

Because of their utmost exteriority, rights become the preferred matter of human law, especially of civil law. Law translates in written form the objective exteriority of the moral order envisaged under its social aspect.[70] Justice is directly related to this positive law.

[Justice] is in a way the natural matter of the juridical system, and that by several titles. First, because the accomplishment of the moral duty of justice is wholly indispensable to the public good. . . . A second reason derives from its particular structure. Justice is, in fact, characterized by its objectivity, exteriority and distinctness, qualities which render it eminently suitable for the juridical imperative.[71]

There are cases where justice must abstract from the intentions of the accused person and judge him simply on the presumptions of the law. Perhaps that is why justice is often represented as blindfolded; this is not only the symbol of an intrinsic perfection, but also of an inevitable limit found in the objective order. From a certain partial point of view, by considering social life as the field of exterior objective relations, one might say that justice is the social virtue par excellence and that the law which governs this society is the spatio-temporal incarnation of justice,[72] or "an attempt to realize justice."[73] We have already seen that this attempt can never wholly succeed,[74] for the juridical order can never perfectly coincide with the moral order. For us, the substance of Christian social relations cannot be justice alone, but mediately charity, the supreme social virtue.[75]

a) The various degrees of exteriority. The exteriority of justice varies with the different modes of exteriority found in its objects, the rights to be rendered in relation to the subjects who must render them. Its exteriority is sharpest where it separates individuals as such. The object of particular justice is individual rights that must be rendered by other individuals. This is commutative justice, the justice of an individual-subject toward an individual-object, the strictest of justices, since it governs the most total exteriority. But we can also distinguish another type of particular justice, that of a group-subject toward an individual-object. This is distributive justice; it loses in rigor what the exteriority between the group as such and the individual loses in distinctness. In commutative justice, which is found between two individuals who are equal precisely as individuals, the debt is measured in strict arithmetical equality between two things, between obligation and right; since there is question of an immediate right, either the obligation must be fulfilled or restitution must be made.[76] In distributive justice, which is found between the group and certain of its members considered as particular members, the debt is measured according to the value of the relations which these determined members have toward the group; it is the merit or need of each and also the merit and need of the others that is decisive. In reality, the "otherness" that exists between the group and its members is not adequate. And so what is due is measured not by arithmetical equality, but by proportional equality which takes into consideration not only the persons, but also their particular relation with the group and only through this particular relation to each, the "proportion" of the things distributed.[77] Here restitution urges only if commutative or strict justice is also involved, for, of itself, "distributive injustice" violates only a mediate right.[*]

The virtue of general or legal justice,[†] whose subject

---

[*] VERMEERSCH, *op. cit.*, II, n. 316. The individual has a right to the distributed good only because he is a member of the group (mediate) to which this good immediately belongs; and so he has to this good a particular relation of merit or need.

[†] Also called today social justice. PESCH, NELL-BREUNING, HORVATH

is the individual, has as its object the common good inasmuch as it is the right of the group as such. For this reason general justice subordinates all human activities to itself in the degree that the common good requires this.[78] Here too there is an inadequate distinction between the group and the individuals who compose it; nor is this form of justice "strict," like commutative justice. What it exacts is not capable of a precise determination imposed by the things themselves. It is in general justice that so-called "social" obligations are established which, for example, recognize in any factory worker the rights he has in common with all other men in the nation. In reality, "What is owed to the citizen as such (as equal to every other) is owed to the 'city' in him."[79]

We see, therefore, that the more exterior the field governed by justice, the stricter the latter becomes. It is the inferior form of justice, that is, commutative justice, that obliges the most, with a limit-obligation under pain of the most disordered sin, for it is this justice that safeguards morality on the lowest level. The other forms of justice temper this obligation more and more with love in proportion as they rise above this minimum.

b) *Christian justice.* If justice is possible between two persons in the measure that they are "other" and loses its reason of being in the measure that they are one, then *Christian* justice has a nuance which is completely foreign to pagan or natural justice, for the unity between Christians has been made infinitely more intimate in Christ. Now its limit-obligation takes on a deeper sense of charity-love, which makes it quite clear that this objective minimum is

---

SCHILLING (quoted by MAUSBACH, *Katholische Moraltheologie*, III, 193) would call it social justice to the extent that it obeys not only positive but also unwritten laws. For MESSNER (quoted by MAUSBACH) social justice designates justice in the measure that it is charged with resolving the modern "social question."

made only to be surpassed by the personal giving of self. What is more, Christian unity gives to the limit-obligation itself a greater intensity; under the impulse of charity, of which it is the mediation, it takes a larger vision of the rights of others, who now are loved as brothers in Christ. And charity facilitates any step in this direction by its inspirations of self-forgetfulness. Finally, no longer content with respecting the rights of others, Christian justice positively tends to promote them, for they are the rights of fellow members of Christ.

2. INTERIORITY OF JUSTICE

Justice intervenes in the field of biological exteriority only to create there a milieu where love can penetrate and take up its abode. Justice only finds a "sense" in making love possible. Cut off from its root of charity, it leads to division and ceases to be mediation. *Summum jus, summa injuria*, so the saying goes. No greater injustice can be done a man than to consider justice as the highest relation one can have with him. It is to refuse to enter into a personal communion of love, to limit oneself to mere objective communication with him; it is to consider him as an alien "thing." The Christian virtue of justice respects goods, but in view of relations with the person who possesses them. It is personalist.

The movement proper to Christian justice, as a mediation of charity-love, is concern for the rights of others, thus entailing a victory over the vindicative instinct which leads us all too often to claim in an egoistic manner what we think to be our own rights. This must be so, if justice is to prepare a milieu open to charity. In fact, natural justice, as a mediation of love, already carries out this function, but much more feebly. This is of the utmost importance, for it is precisely on this point that Christian justice is most radically opposed to egoism, the principle of disunity.

It might be useful to compare the two following attitudes of soul. An industrialist, remarking the insufficiency of his workers' wages and the social risks they run in his factory, spontaneously raises their wages and insures them against these risks, because his conscience tells him that in justice he must respect the rights of these men who are bound to him by personal ties and, therefore, have a special title to his love in charity. Such a Christian attitude—in the ideal hypothesis that it were to become general—would permit and even compel the workers to adopt a similar disposition. A second attitude is that of workers and employers alike vindicating their rights by every means in their power, especially by the economic constraint of lockouts and strikes. Such is the attitude of instinctive justice, which is in no way dictated by the virtue of justice; on the contrary, it opposes two groups who are thinking primarily of themselves. The former attitude tends to union, the latter to division and strife. In the first, "other-centered" attitude, each party says, "I render you your right because it is yours." In the second, "self-centered" attitude, each party says, "I claim my right because it is mine." We do not say that this second attitude is always illegitimate, but it is only justified as a makeshift, when the former attitude is absent. A society wherein neither charity nor the virtue of justice reigns is soon reduced to the equilibrium of biological forces. We must add, however, that the necessary demands of the weak are often at least partly inspired by genuine charity for those whom they have a duty to defend, their family and their less fortunate companions. We are not here reproaching the necessary vindication of rights, but merely regretting the absence of the virtue of justice in our social milieu, especially on the part of the powerful property owners. Vindictive justice is so widespread that it is easy to mistake it for a virtue, whereas even when justified it remains of itself a reaction of instinct.

The spread of Communism among the masses, the grouping of oppressed minorities who aim at vindicating their rights, the egalitarian tendencies—all can be explained by this instinct. Doctor De Greeff[80] has well shown to what pessimism we are condemned if we fail to channel the ever-expanding forces of instinct by means of virtue. Vindictive justice cannot bring about a peaceful solution to the social question. Only the virtue of justice can direct us toward mutual love, on condition that it is itself animated by charity. "Justice alone," writes Pope Pius XI, "if scrupulously observed, may well remove the causes of social conflict, but by its own strength can never bring about union of minds and hearts."[81] The virtue of justice begins where instinct takes on a new "sense" by being assumed by charity. Ordinarily, the instinct of justice amounts to "discussing the injustices which others have committed against us."[82] True, this manner of action insists on respect for rights; but because by it we vindicate personal rights—which necessity may well justify—we meet with a reaction of self-defense in others. As long as they remain in this frame of mind, both parties only aggravate their differences. The virtue of justice, on the contrary, reverses the orientation of this instinct. Instead of inciting us to vindicate our rights, it leads us to respect others' rights in the very matter that forms the usual object of self-defense. It is here that we recognize its kinship with love. Love causes us to go out of ourselves in order to communicate with others' wills. The instinct of justice is, as it were, the center of our instinctive sociable being and is one of the most difficult instincts to sublimate.[83] Hence the vital role of the infused virtue of justice. On the other hand, justice cut off from charity, its true "soul," is radically powerless to carry out its function.

It might be well to point out here an especially delicate, "interior" form of Christian justice, namely, reparation.

We are not thinking of that reparation which elementary justice strictly imposes on him who damages another's property, but rather of that more profound reparation which consists in generously compensating by works of supererogation for the wrong done to the glory of God by men's offenses, whether these be sins of injustice, strictly so called, or any other sins whatsoever. Reparation looks to the integrity of God's rights. It seeks to repair—insofar as this is possible, in union with the reparation accomplished by the Redeemer Himself—not only for personal faults, but also for the failings of others, for which this soul feels somehow jointly responsible. Obviously such a form of justice is far removed from the biological equilibrium of instinct and has no true counterpart in purely natural morality. Since it involves making amends for the faults of others, reparation can only find place in a conscience already aware of its community with others in Christ. But even reparation for personal faults involves in an unusually high degree the virtue of penance, which is itself allied to justice, inasmuch as it compensates for evil done.[84]

We conclude this chapter by suggesting a definition of Christian justice. It is "the moral virtue which causes us to respect the person of our brother in Christ, at least in what concerns his rights,"[85] in view of assuring between us the minimum of relations that is necessary for union in charity.

Postscript: Charity and Realism

Some might be tempted to accuse us of a certain lack of realism in this study. How often have we not heard it said that what our generation needs more than others is insistence on the strict obligation of law, on vigorous discipline, on certain pressures that may lead men, even against their will, to the good life, in brief, measures that can save a man from himself and his anarchist tendencies. Why then talk to him of charity, when what he needs, first of all, is force? Why appeal to love when justice is still not appreciated?

It is true that we have need of force, for we are easily given over to violence; but force is, after all, violence penetrated by love. If the passage from violence to force is not accomplished under the aegis of charity, a new state of violence simply replaces the old and the battle rages anew.

It is also true that we have need of discipline and justice, of strict and vigorous laws, for we are duped by the anarchy of instincts. But what are justice and law but mediations of love introducing on the biological level an order preliminary to that of charity? We have many wise laws. What we lack is the will to respect them.

Yes, our generation has need of force and justice—but force and justice taken in their full sense, for of themselves they are without meaning. Perhaps the greatest catastrophe that has befallen our age is that it has been cut off from the very source of spirituality, which is love. Witness the divisions and the hates which today range man against man and nation against nation. What is unjust war if not a state of violence which even the mediation of justice fails to penetrate? That is why our age has a special need of love.

But yet another danger threatens our age, that of losing the sense of the "absolute" dignity and value of the human person. Already in 1937, the twenty-ninth session of the "Semaine Sociale de France" deplored how much rationalism had cut man off from his true finality by no longer considering his personal vocation, which bears witness to the presence of the spirit in him, and by making of him an object, an anonymous, abstract "means" at the service of a technique or the objectified bearer of an ideology. The same danger stalks the proletarian masses, for they are "abstracted" from their human milieu and "mechanized" in view of ever greater production. Youth, confronted with these excesses of "reason," tends to react by adopting an "irrational" attitude, scorns all that is "reasonable" and logical and willingly has recourse to violence, if only for a change. How are these forces to be channeled if not by searching, beyond the rational, the genuine attractiveness of spiritual love, which requires the rational as its necessary complement? Only love can restore the true value of the person, for only love really personalizes by reaching to the very depth of being.[86]

Again, there are those who will maintain that the time has not yet come to talk of a morality of perfection, such as our morality of charity pretends to be, for as yet the most elementary rudiments of morality are far from being generally accepted. The most exterior and natural principles, they say, must first be re-established before we can begin to talk of perfection. In the course of this study we have fixed our attention primarily on the interior pole of our being in order to discover there the sense of our moral life at its very root; however, we have also observed that even on the most exterior levels of our being we are animated by the mediations of charity. When discussing the apostolate, we recalled how necessary it is to begin by even the most exterior mediation we find in a soul whom we wish to lead toward the interiorization of charity. This "returning into one's self"—for that is what this interiorization of charity really is—at the beginning, and even for some time to come, may remain very limited, but if we are to choose a certain road, we must first know the direction of our final goal. Those for whom fear of the law is, for the moment, the most suitable mediation should know that even rigor derives ultimately from a still greater love. And we must remember that often it is not the "simple" who are most insensible to the beauty of a charity-animated morality. Moreover, at the heart of the indifferent masses we find today an ever-increasing elite whose spiritual thirst can only be quenched by the revelation of the Christian economy in all its delicacy and richness.

As for those whose vocation it is to preach this doctrine to others, must they not, as it were, interiorly intuit the sense of Christian life as charity, which provides the simple, almost unique solution to the numerous difficulties raised?

Thus a charity-animated morality does not risk being unrealistic, for it actually sounds the depths of reality and gives it its only acceptable sense, provided, of course, it is taken in all its fullness and not converted into a disincarnated morality or spirituality, or into a theory of pure love accessible only to the "perfect." Our notion of mediation safeguards us against this tempting error. Throughout this study we have at no time desired to create the impression of minimizing any of the values of an objective morality; even justice has been presented as one of the more exterior mediations of charity. We love all the more a face which reveals the interior presence of a soul. Our purpose has been to fix attention on this presence of a soul in the body of moral theology and thus prevent us from stopping at the mere surface, at the impersonal enumeration of prohibitions and precepts. Exterior precepts lose nothing of their urgency by abandoning their apparent arbitrariness in order to reveal the presence of this still more profound reality; in fact, the whole purpose of a face is, as we have repeatedly insisted, to express its real incarnate soul. And, on the other hand, because it has all the power of divine attraction, the soul of charity that underlies each law and each obligation is capable of rousing us to efforts and sacrifices, of inspiring in us courage to meet the demanding obligations of our age, of seeing them not as examples of violence to be instinctively resisted, but rather as the engaging, even if distressing, preludes of love.

General Conclusion

At the beginning of this study we posed the question: What is the relation between charity and the multiple acts of our moral life? Quite naturally we were attracted to the scholastic doctrine, especially to that of the Thomistic school which considers charity as the form of the virtues. We have tried to analyze the traditional solution, which makes the virtue of charity the queen of the virtues, with the intention of rejoining, if possible, the intuition which underlies the very technical expression of the scholastic thesis. We have attempted to formulate this more direct insight by the notion of active mediation, thus having recourse to a more existential mode of thought, which seems to take full account of the sense of moral action and of the dynamic relation between the different levels of this action. This solution seems better to translate the synthetic and fundamentally mystical insight which must have guided St. Thomas in constructing his theological masterpiece. Moreover, it has at the same time the advantage of providing a "subjective counterweight" for a form of thought which excessively favors the objective element in moral theology.

In our perspective, moral life appears as the expression of that mysterious ambivalent being that is an incarnate spirit. It has the sense of a returning into one's self. Being bipolar, it can take two possible directions: it can tend toward the "value," which is spiritual, or toward the exterior limit. This active progression toward the interiority of the spirit gives meaning to all the problems raised by the mysterious nature of our being and to the many apparent antinomies we have encountered in the course of our study.

346

We have recognized in this movement toward interiority a love for God which is at the very source and dynamic center of our being. This progress is possible only in Christ, from whom we are not adequately distinct and certainly not separated. It involves all members of Christ, even the potential ones. Our moral life is a distinct and actual continuation of the recapitulatory action of Christ on the cross. It is, then, an act of charity revealing itself in spatio-temporal multiplicity. Because it is incarnate, this interior act of charity blossoms forth in a diversity of virtues and hardens somewhat in the demands of justice and strict rights, in brief, finds for itself a whole organism of partial mediations which only serve to reveal the richness of charity on that level of our being where we are many as well as one. Thus charity appears no longer as one virtue among others, but as the soul, the spiritual "sense," of the other virtues. It must be so if it is really the created presence of the divine Spirit in us. And, in its turn, moral life reveals itself as the body of divine charity, as its manifestation in human action, as the mystery of a life inspired by the Holy Spirit. This does not mean that the moral act loses its specifically human nature, but simply that it is a specific manifestation of charity on the incarnate level of our being.

Such a position entails demanding consequences for our pastoral and apostolic work as well as for our own spiritual life itself.

Perhaps most important of all, moral doctrine now appears as more intimately related to Christian dogma and to God's unique plan of redemption. It requires, therefore, a careful study of the sources of revelation. It is the love of the Trinity, it is the intimate nature of God Himself that we find at work in human activity—under a very humble form, it is true, but ever so expressive. Our life has the sense of a progressive entry into the very Godhead, following on the steps of Jesus Christ, who is sanctifying the universe by His sacraments and leading it back to the Father even from its uttermost limits, thus preparing that eternal kingdom where charity will never fail.

This approach is, at the same time, an attempt to answer the often-repeated plea that the teaching of moral theology be adapted to the needs of our age. Such is the theme, for example, of Canon Thils's study, *Tendances actuelles en théologie morale*, in which he summarizes the results of a recent investigation conducted among moralists. In fact, our approach seems to foster a course wherein moral doctrine would be at once "Christian, ontological and sacramental (I, 1)."* It would be universal in scope and take into account even modern technical progress, for matter is here seen as a manifestation of the spirit (I, 2). It would be theological by definition, for in our perspective theological charity is the principle of the whole structure of Christian action (I, 3). Then too, our approach facilitates the presentation of moral doctrine in a more "personalist" and positive manner, for love is nothing if not personalizing; and it includes, as we have seen, all the positive contributions of revealed supernatural life: the sacraments and the visible Church (II, 1). We have already sufficiently insisted on its quality of interiority (II, 2); and since moral doctrine is to manifest life, its presentation will naturally be more organic than abstract and systematic (II, 3). Here general moral theology finds its true importance as a synthesis of the central Christian convictions, as a Christian mystique to be more technically resumed in special moral theology (II, 4).

Finally, if we have had recourse to new terms in this

* The numbers refer to the chapters and paragraphs of the French edition of Canon Thils' study.

study, it was, nevertheless, with the conviction that their content was wholly traditional. We have merely attempted to comment—in the spirit of the Church, to which we submit our work—on this first commandment, which is, after all, the only commandment: "Thou shalt love."

Notes

INTRODUCTION

1. Cicero *De officiis* I. 7. See also Aristotle *Nichomachean Ethics* v. 1, 15: "Præclarissima virtutum videtur esse justitia, et neque est Hesperus, neque Lucifer ita admirabilis." Here there is question of "general" justice which presides over the common good, the order and equilibrium of the city.
2. M. Viller, *La spiritualité des premiers siècles chrétiens* (Paris, 1930), chap. 2.
3. See A. Lamy, "Bios Angelicos," *Dieu Vivant*, 7 (1946), 52–77.
4. *Sum. th.*, 2–2, q. 23, a. 2, ad 1.
5. J. Huby, *Saint Paul, Les épîtres de la captivité* (14th ed.; Paris, 1947), p. 91; see also Eph. 3:17.
6. *De moribus ecclesiæ* xv. 25; see also *Sum. th.*, 1–2, q. 55, a. 1, ad 4; q. 62, a. 1, ad 1.
7. A. Vermeersch, s.j., "Soixante ans de théologie morale," NRT, 56 (1929), 884.
8. Cf. the restrictions of O. Schilling, "Das Prinzip der Moral," ThQ, 119 (1938), 425; cf. also *below*, p. xxviii, n. 25; p. xxxi, n.
9. *Imitation of Christ*, bk. II, chap. 12, 8.
10. Cf. L. Lochet, *Son of the Church* (Chicago, 1956), chap. 3.
11. *Epistle to the Trallians* 13. 1 (ACW, 1 [1946], 79).
12. *Epistle to the Magnesians* 1. 2 (ACW, 1 [1946], 69); cf. *Epistle to the Ephesians* 14. 1 (*loc. cit.*, p. 65).
13. *Epistle to the Corinthians* 49 (ACW, 1 [1946], 39–40).
14. Cf. J. Farges and M. Viller, s.j., "Charité," DSAM, vol. II (Paris, 1940), col. 524.
15. Polycarp *Epistle to the Philippians* 1. 1 (cf. ACW, 6 [1948], 76).

16. Ignatius of Antioch *Epistle to the Romans* 6. 1–3; 4. 2 (ACW, 1 [1946], 83, 82).

17. Cf. A. D'ALÈS, *La théologie de Saint Cyprien* (Paris, 1922), pp. 370–371.

18. Cf. T. J. BOUQUILLON, *Theologia moralis fundamentalis* (3rd ed.; Bruges, 1903), p. 76, n. 131.

19. PL, 32, 1309 ff.

20. PL, 32, 1322.

21. *In evangelia homiliæ* 27. 1; PL, 76, 1205.

22. *Liber de diligendo Deo*, PL, 182, 973; *Sermones in Canticum canticorum*, PL, 183, 785.

23. *De perfectione vitæ spiritualis*, chap. 1; cf. *Sum. th.*, 2–2, q. 184, a. 1, ad 2; cf. also, 2–2, q. 27, a. 6: "Finis omnium actionum humanarum et affectionum est dilectio Dei, per quam attingimus ultimum finem"; cf. also, J. DE GUIBERT, s.j., *The Theology of the Spiritual Life* (New York, 1953), pp. 44–60.

24. Cf. "Charité," DSAM, vol. II, col. 569–636.

25. Cf. O. SCHILLING, *art. cit.*, pp. 419–426: "Die caritas ist somit Prinzip des Sittlichen, ob man nun unter dem Prinzip Ziel und Norm oder Motiv oder man darunter die Grundkraft versteht" (p. 421).

26. Cf. I. A. ZEIGER, s.j., "De conditione theologiæ moralis hodierna," Per, 28 (1939), 183.

27. *Ibid.*, pp. 181–185.

28. Cf. Burchard (*ca.* 1010) and Gratian (*ca.* 1145).

29. Cf. J. MAUSBACH, "Die neuesten Vorschläge zur Reform der Moraltheologie und ihre Kritik," ThR, 1 (1902), col. 46.

30. Cf. Fr. TILLMANN, *Handbuch der katholischen Sittenlehre* (2nd ed.; Düsseldorf, 1940), vol. II: *Die Idee der Nachfolge Christi*, pp. 32–42.

31. A. VERMEERSCH, s.j., "Soixante ans de théologie morale," NRT, 56 (1929), 864.

32. J. MAUSBACH, *art. cit.*, col. 1–8; 41–46; notice especially the numerous articles referred to in col. 1.

33. *Ibid.*, col. 45–46.

34. A. Lehmkuhl, s.j., *Theologia moralis*, 2 vols. (Freiburg im Breisgau, 1883–1884).

35. A. Tanquerey, *Synopsis theologiæ moralis et pastoralis*, 3 vols. (Paris, 1902–1905).

36. D. M. Prümmer, o.p., *Manuale theologiæ moralis*, 3 vols. (Freiburg im Breisgau, 1915).

37. A. Vermeersch, s.j., *Theologiæ moralis principia, responsa, consilia*, 4 vols. (Bruges, 1922–1924).

38. J. Mausbach, *Katholische Moraltheologie*, 3 vols. (3rd ed.; Münster, 1927–1930).

39. O. Schilling, *Lehrbuch der Moraltheologie*, 2 vols. (Munich, 1928).

40. B. H. Merkelbach, o.p., *Summa theologiæ moralis*, 3 vols. (Paris, 1930–1932).

41. B. Häring, c.ss.r., *Das Gesetz Christi, Moraltheologie* (Freiburg im Breisgau, 1954).

42. Cf. G. Marcel, *Positions et approches concrètes du mystère ontologique* (Paris, 1949).

43. Cf. A. Marc, s.j., "Solitude et communion," Et, 228 (1936), 5.

44. Cf. G. Thibon, *Diagnostics* (Paris, 1942) and *Back to Reality* (London, 1955).

45. Cf. *idem*, "Surnaturalisme," RCIF, 19 (1939), 5.

46. Cf. J. Lacroix, "Ce qui, chez nous, menace la personne humaine," *Semaines sociales de France*, 29th session (Paris, 1937), pp. 99–122.

47. Cf. G. Thils, *Tendances actuelles en théologie morale* (Gembloux, 1940).

48. Cf. Zeiger, *art. cit.*, p. 188.

49. P. Claudel, *Feuilles de saints* (Paris, 1925), p. 69.

50. R. Le Senne, *Traité de morale générale* (2nd ed.; Paris, 1947); *Obstacle et valeur* (Paris, 1946).

51. J. Maréchal, s.j., *Le point de départ de la métaphysique*, vols. I–III (3rd ed.; Brussels, 1944); vol. IV (Brussels, 1947); vol. V (2nd ed.; Brussels, 1949).

52. Zeiger, *art. cit.*, p. 185.

53. *Sum. th.*, 1–2, q. 1, aa. 6 and 8.
54. *Sum. th.*, 1–2, q. 26, a. 1.
55. A. VERMEERSCH, S.J., *Theologia moralis*, I, n. 136.

PART I

CHARITY AND MORALITY IN ST. THOMAS

(*Historical Part*)

INTRODUCTION

1. J. E. Cardinal VAN ROEY, *De virtute caritatis quæstiones selectæ* (Mechlin, 1929), pp. 13–14.
2. PRÜMMER, *op. cit.*, I, n. 559; MERKELBACH, *op. cit.*, I, nn. 860–868; AERTNYS-DAMEN, C.SS.R., *Theologia Moralis* (Turin, 1939), p. 260, who gives a more practical treatment of this question; VERMEERSCH, *op. cit.*, I, n. 136; MAUSBACH, *op. cit.*, II, pp. 106–110, approaches the question from the angle of Scripture.

CHAPTER I. CHARITY AND THE MORAL ACT

1. *Sum. th.*, 1–2, qq. 1–5.
2. *Sum. th.*, 1, q. 77, a. 7.
3. *Sum. th.*, 1, q. 80, a. 1; q. 82, a. 1.
4. Cf. *Sum. th.*, 1, q. 77, a. 7.
5. *Sum. th.*, 1–2, q. 9, a. 1.
6. *Sum. th.*, 1, q. 48, a. 5.
7. *Sum. th.*, 1–2, q. 1, a. 1.
8. *Sum. th.*, 1–2, q. 17, a. 4; cf. also 1–2, q. 17, a. 1: "Imperare est actus rationis præsupposito tamen actu voluntatis." It is this act of the will which we consider here.
9. *Sum. th.*, 1–2, q. 17, a. 4; q. 18, a. 6, c.
10. *Sum. th.*, 1–2, q. 18, a. 6 (c., ad 1, ad 2).
11. *Sum. th.*, 1–2, q. 1, aa. 1 and 3.
12. *Sum. th.*, 1–2, q. 8, a. 2.
13. *Sum. th.*, 1–2, q. 8, a. 3; q. 12, aa. 3 and 4.
14. *Sum. th.*, 1–2, q. 12, a. 2.

15. *Sum. th.*, 1–2, q. 12, a. 3.
16. *Ibid.*
17. Cf. *infra*, p. 17.
18. *Sum. th.*, 1–2, q. 49, aa. 1 and 2; q. 55, a. 4.
19. *Sum. th.*, 1–2, q. 51, aa. 2 and 3; q. 52; q. 63, a. 2.
20. *Sum. th.*, 1–2, q. 51, a. 4.
21. *Sum. th.*, 1–2, q. 63, a. 3, ad 2.
22. *Sum. th.*, 1–2, q. 55, a. 1, ad 4.
23. *Sum. th.*, 1–2, q. 56, a. 3, ad 1.
24. For a more detailed analysis, see Cardinal VAN ROEY, *op. cit.*, from which we have taken the main elements of our exposition on the various intentions.
25. *Sum. th.*, 3, q. 64, a. 8, ad 3; cf. Cardinal VAN ROEY, *op. cit.*, p. 242, note b.
26. For a list of these various opinions, see Cardinal VAN ROEY, *op. cit.*, pp. 205–254, and *passim*.
27. Cf. *infra*, p. 45, § III.
28. *De malo*, q. 2, a. 5, ad 7.
29. *II Sent.*, d. 40, q. 1, a. 5, ad 6.
30. *II Sent.*, d. 40, q. 1, a. 5.
31. *Ibid.*
32. *De caritate*, q. unica, a. 11, ad 2.
33. *De malo*, q. 2, a. 5, obj. 11.
34. These texts are quoted in Cardinal VAN ROEY, *op. cit.*, p. 229.
35. *II Sent.*, d. 40, q. 1, a. 5, ad 6; cf. also *Sum. th.*, 1–2, q. 100, a. 10, ad 2; 2–2, q. 44, a. 4.
36. *De malo*, q. 2, a. 5, ad 7.
37. ERNST, *loc. cit.*
38. *Sum. th.*, Suppl., q. 1, a. 3.
39. *Sum. th.*, 1–2, q. 113, a. 8.
40. *Sum. th.*, 3, q. 86, a. 6, ad 1.
41. *Sum. th.*, 3, q. 86, a. 6, *sed contra*.
42. *Sum. th.*, 1–2, q. 113, a. 3; cf. Council of Trent, sess. VI, canon 4 (DB 814).
43. *Sum. th.*, 1–2, q. 113, a. 7.
44. *Ibid.*, ad 4.

45. *Ibid.*, ad. 5; cf. 1, q. 53, aa. 2 and 3.
46. Cf. *supra*, p. 18.
47. Cf. M. J. Scheeben, *The Mysteries of Christianity* (St. Louis, 1946), pp. 635–641.
48. Cf. *infra*, pp. 46–48.

Chapter II. Charity the Form of the Virtues

1. *Sum. th.*, 2–2, q. 23, a. 8, ad 1.
2. Cf. *supra*, pp. 7–9.
3. Cf. *supra*, p. 22.
4. *Sum. th.*, 1–2, q. 8, a. 1.
5. *Sum. th.*, 1–2, q. 8, a. 2.
6. *Ibid.*
7. *Sum. th.*, 1–2, q. 8, a. 3.
8. *Sum. th.*, 2–2, q. 23, a. 8.
9. Cf. *supra*, p. 6.
10. *Sum. th.*, 1–2, q. 114, a. 4, ad 1.
11. *De veritate*, q. 14, a. 5.
12. *Sum. th.*, 2–2, q. 23, a. 6.
13. *Sum. th.*, 2–2, q. 23, a. 4, ad 2; cf. a. 8, ad 1.
14. *III Sent.*, d. 27, q. 2, a. 4, sol. 3.
15. *Sum. th.*, 2–2, q. 23, a. 8, ad 1 and ad 3.
16. *Sum. th.*, 2–2, q. 23, a. 8. See also *supra*, p. 29, n.
17. *Sum. th.*, 1–2, q. 62, a. 2, ad 3.
18. *Sum. th.*, 2–2, q. 23, a. 7.
19. *Sum. th.*, 2–2, q. 23, a. 7, ad 2.
20. *De veritate*, q. 14, a. 5, ad 3 and ad 4; *III Sent.*, d. 27, q. 2, a. 4, 3.
21. *Sum. th.*, 1, q. 77, a. 7.
22. *Sum. th.*, 2–2, q. 58, a. 6, ad 4.
23. *III Sent.*, d. 27, q. 2, a. 4, sol. 2, ad 1.
24. *III Sent.*, d. 23, q. 3, a. 1, sol. 1; cf. *II Sent.*, d. 41, q. 1, a. 2; *De caritate*, q. unica, a. 3.
25. *Cursus theologicus*, tr. 19, "De caritate," disp. 7, dub. 3; tr. 16, "De merito," disp. 4, dub. 4. We are indebted to Cardinal Van Roey (*op. cit.*, pp. 46, 201) for these citations.

26. *Cursus theologicus*, tr. 16, disp. 4, dub. 2, no. 22, *sub fine;* here the authors quote *Sum. th.*, 1–2, q. 18, a. 4, ad 2.

27. *Ibid.*

28. *Cursus theologicus*, tr. 19, disp. 7, dub. 3, nn. 48, 52, and 64.

29. *Ibid.*, n. 56.

30. *Ibid.*, n. 53.

31. *Sum. th.*, 2–2, q. 23, a. 8, ad 1; cf. *supra*, p. 29.

32. *De car.*, a. 3, ad 6; cf. *De ver.*, q. 14, a. 5, ad 4: *forma exemplaris.*

33. *De ver., loc. cit.*, ad 3: "Appropinquant ad modum quo exemplar formam dicimus."

34. Cf. *supra*, p. 42.

35. *De car.*, a. 5, ad 5; *De ver.*, q. 14, a. 5, ad 4: "Id quod a caritate in fide relinquitur est intrinsecum fidei."

36. *De ver.*, q. 14, a. 5, ad 13 and a. 6, *corpus;* cf. *supra*, p. 37, n. 20.

37. *De ver.*, q. 14, a. 6, ad 1.

38. *De car.*, a. 5, ad 1.

39. *Ibid.*, a. 3, ad 4 and ad 16; *De ver.*, q. 14, a. 5, ad 1.

40. *De car.*, a. 3, ad 18.

41. *Ibid.*, a. 3, ad 9 and ad 10; cf. *supra*, pp. 38 f.

42. *Ibid.*, a. 3, ad 10 and a. 5, *corpus.*

43. *De ver.*, q. 14, a. 5, ad 3.

44. *Ibid.*, q. 14, a. 5, ad 9.

45. *Ibid.*, q. 14, a. 5, ad 3.

46. See *supra*, pp. 38 f.

47. *Sum. th.*, 1–2, q. 114, a. 4.

48. *Ibid.*, q. 114, a. 3, ad 3.

49. *Ibid.*, q. 114, a. 3.

50. *Ibid.*, q. 114, a. 4.

51. P. DE LETTER, S.J., *De ratione meriti secundum Sanctum Thomam* (Rome, 1939), pp. 105 ff.

52. *Sum. th.*, 1–2, q. 114, a. 4.

53. *IV Sent.*, d. 49, q. 1, a. 4, sol. 4.

54. *In I Cor.*, 3, lect. 2.

55. ERNST, *op. cit.*, p. 192, no. 13, and p. 216, no. 7.

Conclusion

1. P. Parente, "Il primato dell'amore e San Tommaso d'A-quino," APASTh, 10 (1945), 197–211; see also discussion, pp. 211–229.
2. For a different view of this question, see A. D. Sertil-langes in the "Foreword" to *La béatitude in Somme théologique*, ed. La revue des jeunes (Paris, 1936); A. Van Kol, s.j., *Christus' plaats in S. Thomas' Moraalsysteem* (Roermond-Maeseyck, 1947).
3. P. Rousselot, *The Intellectualism of Saint Thomas*, trans. by J. E. O'Mahony, o.f.m.cap. (New York, 1935), pp. 111 f.
4. *III Sent.*, d. 23, q. 3, a. 1, sol. 1.
5. R. Le Senne, *Obstacle et valeur*, p. 323 ff.; *idem, Introduction à la philosophie* (Paris, 1947), *passim*.

PART II

Toward a Charity-Centered Moral Theology

Chapter I.   The Moral Act as Mediation of Our Profound Spiritual Tendency

1. *De ver.*, q. 1, a. 9; q. 10, aa. 8 and 9.
2. Cf. *Sum. th.*, 1, q. 12, a. 13.
3. *In Boet. de Trinitate*, q. 6, a. 2, ad 5.
4. In the present analysis, we follow the theory of knowledge of J. Maréchal, s.j., found in the "Cinquième cahier" of his *Point de départ de la métaphysique*, and also in "Le dynamisme intellectuel dans la connaissance objective," RNP, 28 (1927), 137–165, and reprinted in *Mélanges J. Maréchal* (Brussels, 1950), I, 75–101.
5. *Sum. th.*, 1–2, q. 15, a. 1.
6. Cf. A. Tanquerey, s.s., *The Spiritual Life: A Treatise on*

Ascetical and Mystical Theology, trans. by Herman Bran-
DERIS, S.S. (Westminster, Md., 1947), n. 460.

7. *Sum. th.*, 1, q. 77, a. 2.
8. It was so defined by the Council of Vienne (DB 481) and
   the Fifth Lateran Council (DB 738). Cf. *Sum. th.*, 1, qq. 75
   and 76.
9. Cf. J. RIMAUD, S.J., "Les psychologues contre la morale,"
   Et, 263 (1949), 3–22, who treats of the matter from a psychological viewpoint.
10. *The Ascent of Mount Carmel*, bk. II, ch. 29.
11. *The Living Flame of Love*, stanza 4.
12. *Ibid.*
13. *The Living Flame of Love* (second redaction), stanza 2.
14. *The Living Flame of Love*, stanza 4.
15. *Ibid.*
16. *Ibid.*
17. Cf. *infra*, p. 104.
18. *Sum. th.*, 1–2, q. 1, a. 1.
19. Cf. *supra*, pp. 67 and 76.
20. *Sum. th.*, 2–2, q. 23, a. 2, ad 2: "Caritas est vita animæ sicut
    et anima vita corporis."
21. St. John of the Cross, *The Ascent of Mount Carmel*, bk. I,
    ch. 11.
22. *Ibid.*, bk. II, ch. 6.
23. *Ibid.*, bk. II, ch. 5.
24. *The Living Flame of Love*, stanza 1.
25. *Ibid.*
26. *Sum. th.*, 1–2, q. 63, a. 4.
27. *Contra gentiles*, 3, c. 21.
28. *Sum. th.*, 1, q. 44, a. 1, ad 1; q. 61, a. 1.
29. Cf. *supra*, p. 36.
30. *Sum. th.*, 1, q. 45, a. 3; 1–2, q. 109, a. 2, ad 2.
31. *Sum. th.*, 1, q. 105, a. 5.
32. *Sum. th.*, 1–2, q. 109, a. 9.
33. See the definition of "value" in LALANDE, *op. cit.*, pp. 1159–
    1163.
34. Cf. DB 476, 1232, 1255.

CHAPTER II. OUR PROFOUND SPIRITUAL TENDENCY IS
CHARITY-LOVE

1. Cf. *supra*, pp. 64–68.
2. *Contra gentiles*, 3, c. 17.
3. *Ibid.*, c. 20.
4. *Ibid.*, c. 19.
5. *Sum. th.*, 1–2, q. 3, a. 4.
6. *Contra gentiles*, 3, c. 25.
7. *Ibid.*, c. 37.
8. A. NYGREN, *Agapè and Eros. A Study of the Christian Idea of Love*, translated by A. G. HERBERT and P. S. WATSON, 2 vols. (London, 1932–1939). For a review of this book, see NRT, 68 (1946), 347.
9. Augustine *De civitate Dei* xiv. 28; cf. PL 41, 436.
10. Cf. ROUSSELOT, S.J., *Pour l'histoire du problème de l'amour au moyen-âge*, Paris, 1933.
11. J. ROHMER, *La finalité morale chez les théologiens de saint Augustin à Duns Scot* (Paris, 1939), pp. 111–112.
12. *Sum. th.*, 1–2, q. 26, aa. 1 and 2.
13. *Ibid.*, q. 26, a. 2.
14. *Sum. th.*, 1, q. 20, a. 1.
15. *Sum. th.*, 1–2, q. 26, a. 1. Cf. 1, q. 60, a. 1.
16. *Sum. th.*, 1, q. 20, a. 1.
17. *Ibid.*, q. 60, a. 1.
18. *Sum. th.*, 1–2, q. 26, a. 1.
19. *Sum. th.*, 1, q. 60, a. 1, *corpus* and ad 1.
20. Cf. ROHMER, *op. cit.*, p. 282.
21. *Quæstiones quodlibetales*, 21, n. 14.
22. *Ibid.*
23. A. D. SERTILLANGES, "Le libre arbitre chez saint Thomas et Henri Bergson," *La vie intellectuelle*, 49 (1937), 252–267.
24. *Ibid.*, pp. 264–265.
25. *Sum. th.*, 1, q. 83, a. 1, ad 3.
26. Cf. J. GEMMEL, S.J., "Zu einer neuen Begriffsbestimmung der menschlichen Freiheit," Schol, 12 (1937), 547–551. H. WORONIECKI, O.P., "Pour une bonne définition de la liberté

humaine," Ang, 14 (1937), 146–153. About the *libertas a necessitate* required for merit, see DB 1039, 1094.

27. *Sum. th.*, 1–2, q. 26, a. 4.
28. *Sum. th.*, 2–2, q. 27, a. 2, obj. 1.
29. *Ibid.*, q. 27, a. 2.
30. *Ibid.*
31. *Sum. th.*, 1–2, q. 3, a. 4.
32. *Ibid.*, q. 27, a. 3; *Contra gentiles*, 1, c. 91.
33. *Sum. th.*, 1–2, q. 28, a. 3.
34. *Ibid.*
35. *In III Sent.*, d. 27, q. 1, a. 1, ad 2.
36. *Ibid.*, d. 27, q. 1, a. 1, ad 4.
37. *Sum. th.*, 1–2, q. 28, a. 1, ad 2.
38. *Ibid.*, q. 28, a. 3.
39. Cf. *supra*, pp. 110 f. and *infra*, pp. 116–118.
40. *In I Sent.*, d. 10, q. 1, a. 3.
41. *Sum. th.*, 1–2, q. 26, a. 4.
42. *Ibid.*, q. 26, a. 4, ad 1.
43. *Sum. th.*, 2–2, q. 25, a. 4.
44. *Sum. th.*, 1–2, q. 26, a. 4, ad 1.
45. *Ibid.*, q. 26, a. 4.
46. *Ibid.*, q. 26, a. 4, ad 3.
47. *Ibid.*, q. 26, a. 4.
48. *Ibid.*, q. 28, a. 3.
49. *Ibid.*, q. 28, a. 3, ad 3.
50. Cf. *Sum. th.*, 2–2, q. 25, a. 4.
51. *Sum. th.*, 1–2, q. 30, a. 1.
52. *Sum. th.*, 1, q. 79, a. 3, ad 1; 1–2, q. 28, a. 3.
53. *Sum. th.*, 1, q. 60, a. 4.
54. *Quæstiones quodlibetales*, 5, a. 6.
55. ROUSSELOT, *Pour l'histoire du problème de l'amour au moyen-âge*, p. 18, n. 2. For a different interpretation, see L. B. GEIGER, O.P., *Le problème de l'amour chez saint Thomas* (Montreal, 1952).
56. *Sum. th.*, 1–2, q. 109, a. 3.
57. *Sum. th.*, 2–2, q. 26, a. 3.
58. *Sum. th.*, 1–2, q. 109, a. 3.

59. *Ibid.*, ad 1.

60. *Sum. th.*, 2–2, q. 26, a. 3, ad 2.

61. ROUSSELOT, *Pour l'histoire du problème de l'amour au moyen-âge*, p. 16.

62. Cf. *supra*, pp. 119 f.

63. *Sum. th.*, 1, q. 60, a. 5.

64. *In III Sent.*, d. 27, q. 1, a. 1, ad 4.

65. *In I Sent.*, d. 10, q. 1, a. 3.

66. Cf. G. MADINIER, *Conscience et amour* (2nd ed.; Paris, 1957), pp. 93 ff.

67. ROHMER, *La finalité morale chez les théologiens de saint Augustin à Duns Scot*, p. 283.

68. Scotus, *Opus Oxoniense*, II, d. 25, n. 2.

69. *Ibid.*, IV, d. 49, q. 6, n. 9. Cf. ROHMER, *op. cit.*, from which we take these quotations.

70. *Opus Oxon.*, IV, d. 49, q. 10, n. 2.

71. Scotus, *Quæstiones quodlibetales*, q. 21, n. 14; *Opus Oxon.*, IV, d. 49, q. 10, n. 4.

72. *Opus Oxon.*, IV, d. 49, q. 6, n. 24.

73. Cf. ROHMER, *op. cit.*, pp. 257–259, quoting *Opus Oxon.*, II, d. 6, q. 2, nn. 8 and 9.

74. *Opus Oxon.*, IV, d. 49, q. 2, n. 24.

75. ROHMER, *op. cit.*, p. 262.

76. *Opus Oxon.*, III, d. 29, q. unica, nn. 2 and 3.

77. *Ibid.*, III, d. 27, q. 1, nn. 2 and 3; III, d. 28, q. unica, nn. 2 and 3.

78. For an opposite opinion, see *Sum. th.*, 1–2, q. 109, a. 3.

79. Cf. *Opus Oxon.*, III, d. 34, q. unica, n. 17.

80. ROHMER, *op. cit.*, pp. 260–269.

81. *Opus Oxon.*, IV, d. 49, q. 6, n. 11.

82. William of Auvergne, *De virtutibus*, c. 9.

83. St. Bernard, *Sermones in Canticum canticorum*, 83, 4; PL 183, 1183.

84. Suárez, *De bonitate et malitia actuum humanorum*, d. 1, s. 2, nn. 13 and 14; Vives ed.: IV, 283.

85. ROHMER, *op. cit.*, p. 236.

86. *Ibid.*, p. 251.

87. L. B. Geiger, *op. cit.*

88. Cf. *Sum. th.*, 2–2, q. 23, a. 2, ad 1.

89. M. Blondel, *L'Action* (Paris, 1893; reprinted in 1950), p. 254.

90. *Sum. th.*, 1, q. 35, a. 2.

91. Cf. *Formes, vie et pensées,* edited by Groupe lyonnais d'études médicales, philosophiques et biologiques (Lyons, 1934); *Les rythmes et la vie,* from the same source (Lyons, 1931).

92. *Contra gentiles,* 3, c. 19.

93. H. Bergson, *The Two Sources of Morality and Religion,* trans. by R. A. Audra and C. Brereton (New York, 1935), ch. 3.

94. H. Bergson, *La pensée et le mouvant* (22nd ed.; Paris, 1946), p. 286. Obviously, man could never have suspected the existence of the Trinity nor discovered these "vestigia" without revelation.

95. Blondel, *op. cit.,* p. 256.

96. L. Vander Kerken, s.j., "Menselijke liefde en vriendschap," *Bijdragen,* 7 (1946), 179.

97. According to John Damascene *De fide orthodoxa* I. 12; PL 94, 850.

98. Vander Kerken, *art. cit.,* p. 179.

99. G. Salet, "Le mystère de la charité divine," RSR, 28 (1938), 20–21, and n. 4.

100. Cf. *infra,* pp. 281 f.

101. Cf. L. B. Gillon, o.p., "A propos de la théorie thomiste de l'amitié," Ang, 25 (1948), 3–17.

102. Cf. F. Prat, s.j., "Charité—Charité dans la Bible," DSAM, vol. II, col. 510.

103. Cf. *supra,* pp. 131 ff.

104. *Quæstiones disputatæ de virtutibus in communi,* q. unica, a. 10.

105. *Ibid.*

106. É. Mersch, s.j., *Morale et Corps Mystique* (3rd ed.; Brussels, 1949), vol. II (yet untranslated), p. 35.

107. *Sum. th.,* 2–2, q. 24, a. 1.

108. *Sum. th.*, 1, q. 20, a. 1.
109. *Sum. th.*, 2–2, q. 27, a. 2.
110. Cf. *Sum. th.*, 1, q. 77, a. 1.
111. *Sum. th.*, 2–2, q. 24, a. 1.
112. *Sum. th.*, 1–2, q. 9, a. 1.
113. On this subject, see *supra*, Part I, Chapter II.
114. Cf. *supra*, pp. 20 ff.
115. Cf. Athanasius *De synodis* 51: "en hô ta panta theopoiei-tai"; PG 26, 784; Gregory Nazianzen *Oratio XXX*; PG 36, 121.
116. MERSCH, *loc. cit.*, p. 29.
117. MERSCH, *The Theology of the Mystical Body*, trans. by C. VOLLERT, S.J. (St. Louis, 1951), p. 368.
118. Cf. *supra*, p. 89.
119. MERSCH, *The Theology of the Mystical Body*, p. 368.
120. DB 744, 804 (sub fine), 841, 818.

CHAPTER III.   THE VIRTUOUS ACT, A MEDIATION OF
CHARITY

1. *Sum. th.*, 1–2, q. 50, a. 6. Many elements of our analysis are taken from Placide DE ROTON, O.S.B., *Les habitus, leur caractère spirituel* (Paris, 1934).
2. Cf. *Contra gentiles*, 1, cc. 93–94.
3. *Contra gentiles*, 1, c. 92.
4. *Sum. th.*, 1–2, q. 49, a. 4.
5. *Sum. th.*, 1–2, q. 50, a. 5, ad 2.
6. Dom DE ROTON, *op. cit.*, p. 38.
7. *Sum. th.*, 1–2, q. 50, a. 5, ad 1 and ad 3.
8. Cf. Dom DE ROTON, *op. cit.*, p. 51, n. 1.
9. *Sum. th.*, 2–2, q. 17, a. 1; q. 81, a. 2; q. 104, a. 2.
10. Cf. *Sum. th.*, 1–2, q. 51, a. 4; VERMEERSCH, *Theologia moralis*, vol. I, n. 456; MAZELLA, *De virtutibus infusis*, nn. 30–32; SUÁREZ, *De gratia*, lib. VI, c. 8, n. 14; BILLOT, *De virtutibus infusis*, pp. 118–119, cited by VERMEERSCH.
11. VERMEERSCH, *loc. cit.*, n. 455.
12. *Sum. th.*, 3, q. 89, a. 1, ad 3.

13. *Sum. th.*, 1–2, q. 65, a. 3, ad 2 and ad 3.
14. Cf. *supra*, p. 88.
15. *De civitate Dei* xv. 22; PL 41, 467.
16. *Epistula* clxvii. 4. 15; PL 33, 739.
17. *De moribus ecclesiæ* xv. 25; PL 32, 1322. Cf. *Sum. th.*, 1–2, q. 56, a. 3, ad 1; q. 55, a. 1, ad 4.
18. Cf. *supra*, p. 92.
19. Cf. *infra*, pp. 317 ff.
20. Cf. *infra*, p. 315.
21. Cf. *De moribus ecclesiæ* xv. 25; PL 32, 1322. Cf. also G. FESSARD, S.J., *Pax nostra* (Paris, 1936), p. 137.
22. Cf. *infra*, pp. 284–288.
23. DB 476.
24. *Sum. th.*, 2–2, q. 23, a. 7.
25. *Sum. th.*, 2–2, q. 58, a. 1.
26. *Sum. th.*, 1–2, q. 51, a. 4; q. 65, a. 2.
27. Cf. O. LOTTIN, O.S.B., "La connexion des vertus avant saint Thomas," RTAM, 2 (1930), 21–45.
28. *Sum. th.*, 1–2, q. 61, aa. 3 and 4.
29. *Ibid.*, q. 61, a. 4.
30. *Ibid.*, q. 61, a. 2, ad 1.
31. *Ibid.*, q. 58, a. 4.
32. *Ibid.*, q. 58, a. 5.
33. *Sum. th.*, 2–2, q. 58, a. 6.
34. Cf. *supra*, pp. 171–173.
35. Cf. É. MERSCH, S.J., *Morale et Corps Mystique*, II, 33 f.
36. ERNST, *Über die Notwendigkeit* . . ., p. 217.
37. DB 809, 836.
38. Cf. *supra*, p. 471.
39. Cf. *supra*, 40 f.
40. Cf. *supra*, pp. 24–27.
41. Cf. *In II Sent.*, d. 40, q. 1, a. 5.
42. *Ibid.*, d. 40, q. 1, a. 5, ad 6.
43. Cf. *supra*, pp. 71 f.
44. Cf. *supra*, pp. 7 f.
45. Cf. *supra*, pp. 71 f.
46. Cf. *infra*, pp. 310 ff.; 316 ff.

47. Cf. *supra*, pp. 118 and n.; 119.
48. Cf. *infra*, pp. 240 ff.
49. BILLOT, *De gratia Christi*, q. 114, th. 20, p. 234.
50. Cf. J. DE GUIBERT, S.J., *Leçons de théologie spirituelle* (Toulouse, 1943), I, 143–145.

CONCLUSION

1. Cf. *supra*, pp. 57 f.
2. Cf. *supra*, pp. xxi–xxviii.
3. Cf. *supra*, p. 86.
4. Cf. *supra*, pp. xxxiv–xxxvi.
5. Cf. *supra*, pp. 153 f.
6. Cf. *supra*, pp. xxviii–xxxiv.
7. Cf. *supra*, pp. 93–95.
8. Cf. *infra*, pp. 216 f.

PART III

OUTLINE OF A CHARITY-CENTERED MORAL THEOLOGY
(*Practical Part*)

CHAPTER I.   FUNDAMENTAL ATTITUDES OF A CHARITY-CENTERED MORAL THEOLOGY

1. Cf. LE SENNE, *Traité de morale générale*, pp. 375–515.
2. Cf. *supra*, p. 158.
3. Rom. 6:11; Rom. 8:9–10; 2 Cor. 5:14–17; Gal. 2:11–20; Eph. 3:14–19; Phil. 1:21.
4. St. John of the Cross, *The Ascent of Mount Carmel*, bk. 2, ch. 5; *Spiritual Canticle*, st. 27; *The Living Flame of Love*, stt. 1, 3, and 4.
5. M. VILLER, S.J., "La spiritualité des premiers siècles chrétiens, chap. 2.
6. Cf. A. DURAND, *Évangile selon saint Jean* (24th ed.; Paris, 1938), p. 362; A. SUSTAR, "De caritate apud S. Joannem," VD, 28 (1950), 129 ff., 193 ff., 257 ff.; J. BELSER, *Das Evan-*

gelium des hl. Joannes (Freiburg im Breisgau, 1905), pp. 386 ff.

7. *Sum. th.*, 3, q. 48, a. 2, ad 1; see also 3, q. 19, a. 4.

8. *In III Sent.*, d. 18, a. 6, sol. 1.

9. É. MERSCH, s.j., *The Theology of the Mystical Body*, pp. 96–128.

10. Cf. *supra*, pp. 86 ff.

11. See the condemnations of Fénelon and of pure love, DB 1327–1349.

12. On the obligation to prefer others to self, see *infra*, pp. 299–303.

13. É. MERSCH, s.j., *Morality and the Mystical Body*, trans. by D. F. RYAN, s.j. (New York, 1939), pp. 97 ff., 115 ff.

14. Cf. L. LALLEMAND, *Histoire de la charité*, 5 vols., Paris, 1902–1912.

15. MERSCH, *The Theology of the Mystical Body*, p. 359.

16. *Ibid.*, p. 424.

17. Cf. *supra*, pp. 154–160.

18. Cf. Acts 2:33; Lk. 24:49; Jn. 14:26; Jn. 15:26.

19. Cf. *infra*, pp. 254 ff.

20. Cf. *infra*, pp. 257 ff.

21. DB 834.

22. Cf. F. HÜRTH, s.j., and P. M. ABELLAN, s.j., *De principiis, de virtutibus et de præceptis* (Rome, 1948), n. 660, pp. 300–301.

23. Cf. *infra*, p. 289.

24. L. RULAND, *Handbuch der praktischen Seelsorge*, III, 3–152.

25. Cf. *supra*, pp. 87 f.

26. Cf. *supra*, pp. 16 and 83.

27. *Sum. th.*, 1–2, q. 3, a. 8; 1–2, q. 5, a. 5; 1, q. 12, a. 4; *In Boet. de Trin.*, q. 6, a. 4, ad 5.

28. DB 1786, 1791, 1808.

29. Cf. K. FECKES, "Übernatürlich," LThK, 10, 354–356; H. DE LUBAC, s.j., "Remarques sur l'histoire du mot 'surnaturel,'" NRT, 61 (1934), 225–249, 350–370.

30. MERSCH, *The Theology of the Mystical Body*, pp. 455–478.

31. Aristotle *Physics* 2. 3; *Sum. th.*, 3, q. 2, a. 1; 1, q. 29, a. 1,

ad 4; 3, q. 2, a. 12; Y.-E., Masson, "Nature (état de),"
DTC, 11, 36.

32. Cf. *supra*, p. 54.
33. Mersch, *loc. cit.*, pp. 89–93.
34. Cf. *infra*, p. 337; see also A.-D. Sertillanges, o.p., *La philosophie morale de saint Thomas d'Aquin* (Paris, 1942), p. 170.
35. Cf. *infra*, pp. 320–324.
36. Cf. *supra*, pp. 182–187.
37. Mersch, *loc. cit.*, pp. 264 ff.
38. C. de Condren, *L'idée du sacerdoce et du sacrifice de Jésus-Christ*, Préface; G. Salet, s.j., *Le Christ notre vie* (Tournai, 1937), chap. 2; M. de la Taille, s.j., *The Mystery of Faith and Human Opinion Contrasted and Defined* (London, 1930), pp. 32 ff., 37, 213 ff.
39. Cf. L. Richard, p.s.s., "La rédemption, mystère d'amour," RSR, 13 (1923), 193–217, 397–418; Mersch, *The Theology of the Mystical Body*, pp. 274 ff.
40. Mersch, *Morality and the Mystical Body*, pp. 89–93.
41. *The Life of St. Teresa of Jesus*, trans. by David Lewis (Westminster, Md., 1943), p. 416.
42. Cf. *supra*, pp. 205 f.
43. F. Prat, s.j., *The Theology of St. Paul*, trans. by J. L. Stoddard (Westminster, Md., 1946), II, 469, note Y, I.
44. Cf. Pius XII on suffering and its alleviation in *Osservatore Romano*, February 25–26, 1957.
45. *Sum. th.*, 3, q. 73, a. 3.
46. *Sum. th.*, 3, q. 73, a. 3, ad 3. On the relations between charity and the Eucharist, see *La Maison Dieu*, 24 (1950). On the relations between moral life and the sacraments, see T. Steinbüchel, *Religion und Moral im Lichte personaler christlicher Existenz* (Frankfort, 1951).
47. *Sum. th.*, 3, q. 73, a. 3.
48. Cf. J.-J. Olier, *Explication des cérémonies de la grande messe*, quoted in Salet, *op. cit.*, pp. 98 ff.; de la Taille, *op. cit.*, pp. 32 f.

49. Cf. P. LIPPERT, s.j., *Die Kirche Christi* (3rd ed., Freiburg im Breisgau, 1956).
50. *Sum. th.*, 2–2, q. 104, a. 3.
51. MERSCH, *Morality and the Mystical Body*, pp. 270–285.
52. Cf. *infra*, pp. 256 ff.
53. Encyclical letter, "Haurietis aquas," AAS, 48 (1956), 311.

CHAPTER II.   PRACTICAL APPLICATIONS IN GENERAL
MORAL THEOLOGY

1. MAUSBACH, *Katholische Moraltheologie*, III, 7.
2. See, for example, GENICOT-SALSMANS, *Institutiones theologiæ moralis*, I, n. 2 (mystical theology is not mentioned); MERKELBACH, *Summa theologiæ moralis*, I, n. 4; BOUQUILLON, *Institutiones theologiæ moralis fundamentalis*, p. 6; AERTNYS-DAMEN, *Theologia moralis*, I, xvii; TANQUEREY, *The Spiritual Life*, nn. 3, 7.
3. LEHMKUHL, *Theologia moralis*, Prolegomena.
4. MAUSBACH, *op. cit.*, I, 4.
5. VITTRANT, *Théologie morale* (Paris, 1942), n. 4.
6. DE GUIBERT, *Leçons de théologie spirituelle*, I, 20–21; *idem*, *The Theology of the Spiritual Life* (New York, 1953), pp. 6 ff. (The beginning of the second paragraph of p. 7 of this latter work should read "the second opinion" instead of "the first . . .".)
7. VERMEERSCH, *Theologia moralis*, I, 7, and the encyclical *Rerum omnium perturbationem* cited there.
8. Cf. *supra*, pp. 213–216.
9. *Sum. th.*, 2–2, q. 184, a. 1.
10. Cf. *supra*, p. 67.
11. Cf. *supra*, pp. 82 f.
12. BOUQUILLON, *op. cit.*, p. 6.
13. Cf. A. PLÉ, o.p., "Pour une mystique des mystères," *Supplément de la Vie spirituelle*, 5 (1952), 394 ff.
14. DE BROGLIE, "Charité," DSAM, vol. II, coll. 675–676.
15. TANQUEREY, *op. cit.*, nn. 627–632.

16. *Sum. th.*, 2–2, q. 180, a. 3, *corpus* and ad 1; a. 7, *corpus* and ad 1; TANQUEREY, *op. cit.*, nn. 1386, 1391.
17. *The Ascent of Mount Carmel*, bk. 2, ch. 29.
18. L. DE GRANDMAISON, S.J., *Personal Religion*, trans. by A. THOROLD (London, 1929).
19. Cf. *supra*, pp. 82 f., 242.
20. But, cf. *supra*, p. 87, on "mediation" and "means."
21. VERMEERSCH, *Theologia moralis*, I, n. 2.
22. Cf. H. GODIN and Y. DANIEL, *France pays de mission?* (Paris, 1943).
23. Cf. G. GILLEMAN, S.J., "The Educator, Witness to Charity," LV, 9 (1954), 556–568.
24. A. MARC, "Solitude et communion," Et, 228 (1936), 5.
25. BERGSON, *The Two Sources of Morality and Religion*, ch. 3.
26. LE SENNE, *Traité de morale générale*, pp. 460–461.
27. *Ibid.*, p. 568.
28. *In II Sent.*, d. 39, q. 3, a. 3.
29. Cf. *infra*, pp. 263, 265.
30. TANQUEREY, *op. cit.*, nn. 353–361.
31. "Regula secundum quam inducitur aliquis ad agendum" (*Sum. th.*, 1–2, q. 90, a. 1).
32. *Sum. th.*, 1–2, q. 90, a. 1, ad 3.
33. *Ibid.*, q. 91, a. 1, ad 3.
34. *Ibid.*, q. 90, a. 1.
35. *Ibid.*, q. 17, a. 1.
36. Cf. *supra*, pp. 81–83.
37. Cf. *supra*, pp. 81–83.
38. Cf. *supra*, pp. 78–80, 84–86.
39. Cf. *infra*, pp. 265–268, 271–275.
40. Cf. J. LACROIX, *Personne et amour* (Paris, 1955), pp. 46–51.
41. Cf. *Idem*, "Ce qui, chez nous, menace la personne humaine," *Semaines sociales de France*, 29th session (Paris, 1937), pp. 99–122.
42. *Sum. th.*, 1–2, q. 95, a. 2.
43. *Ibid.*, q. 95, a. 1.
44. Cf. J. DABIN, *Théorie générale du droit*, pp. 123 ff.
45. *Ibid.*, pp. 170–190.

46. *Ibid.*, pp. 64 ff.
47. *Ibid.*, pp. 186 ff.
48. LIPPERT, *op. cit.*, part II, ch. 5.
49. MAUSBACH, *Katholische Moraltheologie*, I, 119–121.
50. M. LEDRUS, "Le problème des lois pénales," NRT, 59 (1932), 45–56.
51. LACROIX, *Personne et amour*, pp. 52–71.
52. *Sum. th.*, 1–2, q. 71, a. 6.
53. *Ibid.*, q. 72, a. 2.
54. M. DE LA TAILLE, "Le péché véniel dans la théologie de saint Thomas, d'après un livre récent," Greg, 7 (1926), 31.
55. TILLMANN, *Die Idee der Nachfolge Christi*, p. 272.
56. *Sum. th.*, 2–2, q. 156, a. 3.
57. *Sum. th.*, 1–2, q. 77, a. 4.
58. *Ibid.*, q. 88, a. 2, ad 1.
59. *De civitate Dei* xiv. 28; PL, 41, 436.
60. *Sum. th.*, 1–2, q. 84, a. 2.
61. *Ibid.*
62. *Sum. th.*, 1. q. 20, a. 1.
63. *Sum. th.*, 1–2, q. 73, a. 5.
64. TANQUEREY, *op. cit.*, n. 875.
65. *Sum. th.*, 1–2, q. 73, a. 1, ad 3.
66. *Ibid.*, q. 81, a. 1.
67. Cf. *supra*, pp. 162 ff.
68. Augustine *De moribus ecclesiæ catholicæ* i. 15. 25; PL, 32, 1322.
69. Cf. G. GILLEMAN, S.J., "L'obéissance dans notre vie divine," *Christus*, 2 (1955), 466–487.

CHAPTER III. PRACTICAL APPLICATIONS IN SPECIAL MORAL THEOLOGY

1. *Sum. th.*, 2–2, q. 81, a. 3.
2. *Ibid.*, a. 5.
3. I. MENNESSIER, O.P., *La religion* (a French translation of the *Summa theologica*), I, 320.
4. *Ibid.*

5. *Ibid.*

6. *Sum. th.*, 2–2, q. 84, a. 1.

7. *Ibid.*, q. 85, a. 4.

8. *Ibid.*, q. 88, a. 2.

9. R. Otto, *Das Heilige* (Tübingen, 1929).

10. *Sum. th.*, 2–2, q. 82, a. 1.

11. *Ibid.*, a. 2.

12. *Ibid.*, a. 3.

13. *Ibid.*, q. 80, a. unicus.

14. Mennessier, *loc. cit.*, pp. 290 ff.

15. G. Madinier, *Conscience et amour* (2nd ed.; Paris, 1947), pp. 101–102.

16. Cf. *supra*, pp. 191 ff.

17. Genicot-Salsmans, *Institutiones theologiæ moralis*, I, n. 216; cf. *Sum. th.*, 2–2, q. 26, a. 4.

18. *Ibid.*, n. 217.

19. Cf. *Sum. th.*, 2–2, q. 26, a. 7.

20. St. Ignatius Loyola, *Constitutiones societatis Jesu*, Examen generale (new ed.; Rome, 1937), ch. 4, n. 7; cf. rule 8 of the *Summary of the Constitutions*.

21. *Ibid.*

22. C. Spinas, *Les sociétés animales*, pp. 379–380, quoted in J. Lacroix, *Personne et amour*, pp. 82–83.

23. Lacroix, *op. cit.*, p. 83.

24. Vermeersch, *Theologia moralis*, II, n. 78; Genicot-Salsmans, *op. cit.*, I, n. 216.

25. *Sum. th.*, 2–2, q. 26, a. 4, ad 3.

26. Cf. F. Prat, s.j., "Charité–Charité dans la Bible," DSAM, vol. II, col. 512.

27. Cf. *infra*, pp. 315–317.

28. Cf. *supra*, pp. 259 and 330.

29. Cf. DB 236, 242, 243, 706, 707.

30. Cf. DB 481, 738.

31. Cf. *supra*, pp. 77 f. and 81.

32. Cf. *supra*, p. 118.

33. Cf. *supra*, p. 283, on the "Two Standards."

34. Cf. the address of Pope Pius XII to the Italian National

Congress of Sports and Physical Education, AAS, 44 (1952), 868–876.

35. Cf. R. CARPENTIER, S.J., Unpublished notes on moral theology, *De temperantia christiana.*

36. Cf. *supra*, p. 142.

37. At least according to Father MERSCH; cf. *Morality and the Mystical Body*, pp. 89–93.

38. Cf. P. CLAUDEL, *L'annonce faite à Marie* (Paris, 1940), p. 135.

39. Cf. *supra*, pp. 78 and 81 f.

40. Cf. *supra*, p. 254.

41. Cf. *supra*, p. 295.

42. Such is the scope of the books of Dr. R. BIOT; cf. *Santé humaine* (Paris, 1942), and *Au service de la personne humaine* (Joigny, 1934); see also A. CARREL, *Man the Unknown* (New York, 1935), especially chap. 8.

43. Cf. *infra*, p. 323.

44. Cf. *supra*, pp. 346 f.

45. A. CHRISTIAN, *Ce sacrement est grand* (Paris, 1943), pp. 78–81.

46. THIBON, *What God has Joined Together*, trans. by A. Gordon SMITH (London, 1952), p. 104.

47. *Ibid.*, pp. 101 ff.

48. E. DE GREEFF, *Notre destinée et nos instincts*, pp. 163–169.

49. Cf. *supra*, p. 318.

50. CIC 1013.

51. Pope Pius XI, "Casti Connubii," AAS, 22 (1930), 548.

52. *Ibid.*, pp. 548–549.

53. CIC 1013.

54. Cf. NRT, 67 (1945), 838–842; and the Decree of the Holy Office, April 1, 1944, AAS, 36 (1944), 103.

55. See, for example, H. DOMS, *Vom Sinn und Zweck der Ehe* (Breslau, 1935).

56. Cf. *supra*, pp. 62 ff.

57. E. BORNE, "Le rationalisme freudien et le mystère du péché," *L'homme et le péché* (Paris, 1938), pp. 78–88.

58. BORNE, *op. cit.*, pp. 61–78.

59. Psychoanalysis, which formerly fixed its attention almost exclusively on the content of repression, has, since 1918, turned to the study of the *forces* of repression. G. RICHARD, in *La psychanalyse et la morale* (Lausanne, 1946) summarizes the acquisitions of this second period which is preoccupied with the "super-ego," the "censor" referred to by E. BORNE, and the psychological factor implied in moral behavior. For a review of this book, see *Erasmus, Bulletin international de la science contemporaine*, 1 (1947), 590–593 and RT, 46 (1947), 158. See also C. ODIER, *Les deux sources, consciente et inconsciente, de la vie morale* (2nd ed.; Neuchâtel, 1947); J. C. FLÜGEL, *Man, Morals and Society* (New York, 1945); J. NUTTIN, *Psychoanalysis and Personality*, trans. by G. LAMB (New York, 1953); J. H. VANDER VELDT, O.F.M., and R. P. ODENWALD, *Psychiatry and Catholicism* (New York, 1952); V. WHITE, *God and the Unconscious* (London, 1952); G. ZILBOORG, "L'amour de Dieu et Freud," *Supplément de la Vie spirituelle*, 6 (1953), 5–30; and the special issue on "Théologie et psychologie des profondeurs," *Supplément de la Vie spirituelle*, 4 (1951), 359–467.

60. BORNE, *art. cit.*, p. 85.

61. SERTILLANGES, *La philosophie morale de saint Thomas d'Aquin*, pp. 169–170.

62. *Sum. th.*, 2–2, q. 58, a. 8; cf. *ibid.*, q. 58, a. 10.

63. E. DE GREEFF, "La structure affective de la notion de justice," TP, 5 (1943), 529. The author has resumed his study of the instinctive sentiment of justice in the first part of his book, *Les instincts de défense et de sympathie*, pp. 33–69.

64. DE GREEFF, *art. cit.*, p. 526.

65. Cf. *supra*, pp. 118 f.

66. DE GREEFF, *art. cit.*, p. 531.

67. *Idem, Notre destinée et nos instincts*, pp. 203–211.

68. *Ibid.*, pp. 195–203.

69. Cf. *supra*, pp. 162–169.

70. Cf. *supra*, pp. 267 f.

71. DABIN, *Théorie générale du droit*, pp. 257, 259.

72. Lacroix, *Personne et amour*, p. 37, note.
73. Madinier, *Conscience et amour*, p. 121, n. 1.
74. Cf. *supra*, pp. 264 ff.
75. Cf. *supra*, pp. 195 f.
76. Vermeersch, *op. cit.*, II, no. 316.
77. Sertillanges, *op. cit.*, p. 178.
78. *Sum. th.*, 2–2, q. 58, aa. 5 and 6.
79. Sertillanges, *op. cit.*, p. 177; cf. *Sum. th.*, 2–2, q. 61, a. 1, ad 5.
80. De Greeff, *Notre destinée et nos instincts*.
81. "Quadragesimo Anno," AAS, 23 (1931), 223.
82. De Greeff, *Notre destinée et nos instincts*, p. 194.
83. De Greeff, *art. cit.*, pp. 530–531.
84. *Sum. th.*, 3, q. 85, a. 3.
85. R. Carpentier, s.j., Unpublished notes on moral theology.
86. *La personne humaine en péril* (Paris, 1937).

Bibliography

ADAM, A. *The Primacy of Love.* Translated by E. C. NOONAN. Westminster, Md., 1958.

ALSZEGHY, Z., S.J. *Grundformen der Liebe.* Rome, 1946.

ALTHAUS, P. *Grundriss der Ethik.* Gütersloh, 1953.

"Amour et violence," *Études carmélitaines.* Paris, 1946.

BALDUCELLI, R. *Il concetto teologico de carità attraverso le maggiori interpretazioni patristiche e medievali de I Cor. XIII.* Rome, 1951.

BARSOTTI, D. *La révélation de l'amour.* Paris, 1957.

BENZ, K. *Die Ethik des Apostels Paulus.* ("Biblische Studien," No. 17.) Freiburg im Breisgau, 1912.

BERGSON, H. *The Two Sources of Morality and Religion.* Translated by R. A. AUDRA and C. BRERETON. New York, 1935.

BEZZINA, E. E., O.P. *De valore sociali caritatis secundum principia S. Thomæ Aquinatis.* Naples, 1952.

BILLOT, L. Card., S.J. *De gratia Christi.* 4th ed. Rome, 1928.

———. *De virtutibus infusis.* 2nd ed. Rome, 1905.

BIOT, R. *Au service de la personne humaine.* Joigny, 1934.

BIRNGRUBER, S., O.S.B. *Laienmoral. Aufstieg zum Göttlichen.* Graz, 1953.

BLIC, J. DE, S.J. "La théologie morale dans la Compagnie de Jésus," in "Jésuites," DTC, VIII, 1, col. 1069–1092.

BLONDEL, M. *L'action.* Paris, 1893 (reprinted 1950).

BROGLIE, G. DE, S.J. "Charité (essai d'une synthèse doctrinale)," DSAM, II, 1, col. 661–691.

———. "Du caractère mystérieux de notre élévation surnaturelle," NRT, 64 (1937), 337–376.

———. "De la place du surnaturel dans la philosophie de saint Thomas," RSR, 14 (1924), 193–246.

——. "Malice intrinsèque du péché et péchés heureux par leurs conséquences," RSR, 24 (1934), 302–343; 578–605; 25 (1935), 5–44.

——. "Malice intrinsèque du péché: esquisse d'une théorie des valeurs morales," RSR, 26 (1936), 46–79; 297–333.

BRUNNER, A. *Eine neue Schöpfung. Eine Beitrage zur des christlichen Lebens.* Paderborn, 1952.

CARPENTIER, R., S.J. "Conscience," DSAM, II, 1548–1575.

——. "Le sense du bien commun," NRT, 67 (1945), 34–63.

——. "Vers une morale de la charité," Greg, 34 (1953), 32–55.

CARREL, A. *Man the Unknown.* New York, 1935.

DABIN, J. *Théorie générale du droit.* Brussels, 1944.

D'ARCY, M. C., S.J. *The Mind and Heart of Love.* London, 1945.

DE CONINCK, A. *L'unité de la connaissance humaine et le fondement de sa valeur.* Louvain, 1943.

DE GREEFF, E. *Les instincts de défense et de sympathie.* Paris, 1947.

——. *Notre destinée et nos instincts.* Paris, 1945.

——. "La structure affective de la notion de justice," *Tijdschrift voor philosophie,* 5 (1943), 515–552.

DE LETTER, P., S.J. *De ratione meriti secundum Sanctum Thomam.* Rome, 1939.

DEMAN, T., O.P. "Accroissement des vertus, dans saint Thomas et dans l'École Thomiste," DSAM, I, 1, pp. 138–156.

——. *Aux origines de la théologie morale.* Paris, 1951.

DIDIER, G., S.J. *Désintéressement du chrètien. La rètribution dans la morale de saint Paul.* Paris, 1955.

DITTRICH, O. *Geschichte der Ethik.* 4 vols. Leipzig, 1923–32.

DOCKX, S. J., O.P. *Fils de Dieu par grâce.* Paris, 1948.

DUBLANCHY, E. "Charité," DTC, II, col. 2217–2266.

ERNST, J. *Die Notwendigkeit der guten Meinung.* Kempten, 1900. (Also appeared in *Theologische-praktische Monatsschrift,* 10 [1900], 768–782; 859–870.)

——. *Gottesliebe und Sittlichkeit. Neue Untersuchungen über die Notwendigkeit der guten Meinung.* Tübingen, 1907. (Also appeared in ThQ, 90 [1908], 34–88.)

——. *Über die Notwendigkeit der guten Meinung. Untersuch-ungen über die Gottesliebe als Prinzip der Sittlichkeit und Verdeinstlichkeit.* ("Strassburger Theologische Studien," No. 7, Fasc. 2 & 3.) Freiburg im Breisgau, 1905.

FALANGA, A. J. *Charity, the Form of the Virtues According to St. Thomas.* Washington, 1948.

FORD, J. C., S.J. *Contemporary Moral Theology,* I, Westminter, Md., 1958.

FUCHS, J., S.J. *Situation und Entscheidung.* Frankfort on the Main, 1952.

GEIGER, L.-B., O.P. *Le problème de l'amour chez saint Thomas d'Aquin.* Montreal, 1952.

GÉNICOT, E., S.J. and SALSMANS, J., S.J. *Institutiones theologiæ moralis.* 2 vols. 16th ed. Brussels, 1946.

GRAHAM, A., O.S.B. *The Love of God. An Essay in Analysis.* London, 1939.

"Grandes lignes de la morale du Nouveau Testament," *Lumière et vie,* no. 21 (May, 1955).

GUIBERT, J. DE, S.J. *The Theology of the Spiritual Life.* Translated by P. BARRETT, O.F.M.CAP. New York, 1953.

GUINDON, R., O.M.I. *Béatitude et théologie morale chez saint Thomas d'Aquin.* Ottawa, 1956.

GUITTON, J. *Essai sur l'amour humain.* Paris, 1948.

HÄRING, B., C.SS.R. *Das Gesetz Christi, Moraltheologie. Dargestellt für Priester und Laien.* Freiburg im Breisgau, 1954.

HARVEY, J. F., O.S.F.S. *Moral Theology of the Confessions of St. Augustine.* Washington, 1951.

HEINEN, W. *Fehlformen des Liebesstrebens in moralpsychologischer Deutung und moraltheologischer Würdigung.* Freiburg im Breisgau, 1954.

HÉRIS, CH.-V., O.P. *Le mystère de Dieu.* Paris, 1946.

——. *La spiritualité de l'amour.* Paris, 1952.

HILDEBRAND, D. VON. *Christian Ethics.* New York, 1953.

HILGENREINER, K. "Moraltheologie," *Lexikon für Theologie und Kirche,* VII, col. 319–322.

HÜRTH, F., S.J. and ABELLAN, P. M., S.J. *Notæ ad prælectiones theologiæ moralis.* Part I: *De principiis, de virtutibus et præceptis.* Rome, 1948.

JOHANN, R., S.J. *The Meaning of Love.* Westminster, Md., 1955. London, 1959.

JOHN OF THE CROSS, Saint. *Obras completas de San Juan de la Cruz.* 5 vols. Nueva edicion por el P. SILVERIO DE SANTA TERESA. Burgos, 1929–1931.

————. *The Complete Works of St. John of the Cross.* 3 vols. Translated by E. A. PEERS. 2nd ed. Westminster, Md., 1946.

KRAUS, J. *Situationsethik.* Mainz, 1956.

LA BARRE, A. DE. *La morale d'après S. Thomas et les théologiens scholastiques.* Paris, 1911.

LACROIX, J. *Personne et amour.* Lyons, n.d.

LAGRANGE, M.-J., O.P. *La morale de l'Évangile.* 3rd ed. Paris, 1932.

LALANDE, A. *Vocabulaire technique et critique de la philosophie.* 5th ed. Paris, 1947.

La loi de charité principe de vie sociale. ("Semaines sociales de France," 20th session.) Paris, 1928.

LA TAILLE, M. DE, S.J. *The Hypostatic Union and Created Actuation by Uncreated Act.* Translated by C. VOLLERT, S.J. West Baden Springs, Ind., 1952.

LECLERCQ, J. *L'enseignement de la morale chrétienne.* Paris, 1950.

LEHMKUHL, A., S.J. *Theologia moralis.* 2 vols. 12th ed. Freiburg im Breisgau, 1914.

————. "Moral Theology," *The Catholic Encyclopedia,* XIV, 601–611.

LE SENNE, R. *Introduction à la philosophie.* 2nd ed. Paris, 1947.

————. *Obstacle et valeur.* Paris, 1934.

————. *Traité de morale générale.* 2nd ed. Paris, 1947.

LOTTIN, O., O.S.B. "La connexion des vertus avant saint Thomas d'Aquin," *Recherches de théologie ancienne et médiévale,* 2 (1930), 21–53.

————. "Les éléments de la moralité des actes chez saint Thomas d'Aquin," RNP, 24 (1922), 281–313; 389–429; 25 (1923), 20–56.

——. *Morale fondamentale.* Paris and Tournai, 1954.

——. "Pour une réorganisation du traité thomiste de la moralité," *Acta congressus scholastici internationalis, Romæ, Anno Sancto 1950,* pp. 309–351.

——. *Principes de morale.* 2 vols. Louvain, 1947.

——. *Psychologie et morale aux XIIe et XIIIe siècles.* 3 vols. Louvain, 1942–1949.

LUBAC, H. DE, S.J. "Méditation sur le principe de la vie morale," *Revue apologétique,* 65 (1937), 257–266.

——. "Remarques sur l'histoire du mot 'surnaturelle,' " NRT, 61 (1934), 225–249; 350–370.

MADINIER, G. *Conscience et amour. Essai sur le "Nous."* 2nd ed. Paris, 1947.

MARCEL, G. *Being and Having.* Translated by KATHERINE FARRER. Boston, 1949.

——. *Homo viator.* Paris, 1944.

MARÉCHAL, J., S.J. *Le point de départ de la métaphysique.* Book V: *Le thomisme devant la philosophie critique.* 2nd ed. Brussels, 1949.

MASSON, Y. "Nature (Etats de)," DTC, XI, 1, col. 36–44.

MAUSBACH, J. "Die neuesten Vorschläge zur Reform der Moraltheologie und ihre Kritik," ThR, 1 (1902), col. 1–8; 41–46.

—— and ERMERKE, G. *Katholische Moraltheologie.* Vols. I and III. 9th ed. Münster in Westfalen, 1953–1954.

MÉLINE, P. *Morale familiale.* Paris, 1928.

MERKELBACH, B.-H., O.P. "Moralis theologiæ idonea methodus," *Miscellanea Vermeersch,* I (Rome, 1935), 1–16.

——. *Summa theologiæ moralis ad mentem D. Thomæ et ad normam juris novi.* 3 vols. 3rd ed. Paris, 1939.

MERSCH, É., S.J. *Morality and the Mystical Body.* Translated by D. F. RYAN, S.J. New York, 1939.

——. *The Theology of the Mystical Body.* Translated by C. VOLLERT, S.J. St. Louis, 1951.

MONCHANIN, J. "L'amitié et l'amour. De la solitude à Dieu," *Médecine et adolescence* (Lyons, 1936), pp. 290–302.

MOUROUX, A. *The Meaning of Man.* Translated by A. H. G. DOWNES. New York, 1948.

———. *Je crois en toi. Structure personelle de la foi.* Paris, 1949.

MÜLLENDORF, J., S.J. "Das übernatürliche Motiv als Bedingung der Verdienstlichkeit, nach dem hl. Thomas von Aquin," *Zeitschrift für katholische Theologie,* 17 (1893), 42–78.

———. "Das Glaubensmotiv als Bedingung der Verdienstlichkeit, nach dessen positiven Beweisen untersucht," *Zeitschrift für katholische Theologie,* 17 (1893), 496–520.

NICOLAS, J.-H., O.P. *Connaître Dieu.* Paris, 1947.

NUTTIN, J. *Psychoanalysis and Personality. A Dynamic Theory of Normal Personality.* Translated by G. LAMB. London, 1954.

NYGREN, A. *Agape and Eros. A Study of the Christian Idea of Love.* 2 vols. Translated by A. G. HERBERT and P. S. WATSON. London, 1932–1939.

OHM, T., O.S.B. *Die Liebe zu Gott in den nichtchristlichen Religionen.* Krailling vor München, 1950.

PENIDO, M. T.-L. "À propos de la procession d'amour en Dieu," ETL, 15 (1938), 338–344.

———. "Gloses sur la procession d'amour dans la Trinité," ETL, 14 (1937), 33–68.

PEPIN, A., A.A. *La charité envers Dieu.* Paris, 1952.

PÉTRÉ, H. *Caritas. Étude sur le vocabulaire latin de la charité chrétienne.* Louvain, 1948.

PRAT, F., S.J. "La charité dans la Bible," in "Charité," DSAM, II, 1, col. 508–523.

———. *The Theology of St. Paul.* 2 vols. Translated by J. L. STODDARD. London and Westminster, Md., 1945–1946.

PRÜMMER, D. M., O.P. *Manuale Theologiæ moralis secundum principia S. Thomæ Aquinatis.* 3 vols. 9th ed. Revised by E. M. MUENCH, O.P. Freiburg im Breisgau, 1940.

REGATILLO, E. F., S.J. and ZALBA, M., S.J. *Theologiæ moralis summa.* Vol. I: *Theologia moralis fundamentalis; Tractatus de virtutibus theologicis* (M. ZALBA). Madrid, 1952.

RICHARD, L., S.S. "La Rédemption, mystère d'amour," RSR, 13 (1923), 193–217; 397–418.

RIESENFELD, H. *Étude bibliographique sur la notion biblique d'Agapè*. ("Collectanea Neotestamentica," No. 5.) Uppsala, 1941.

RIVIÈRE, J. "Mérite," DTC, X, 1, col. 574–585.

ROHMER, J. *La finalité morale chez les théologiens de saint Augustin à Duns Scot*. Paris, 1939.

ROTON, P. DE, O.S.B. *Les habitus. Leur caractère spirituel*. Paris, 1934.

ROUSSELOT, P., S.J. *The Intellectualism of St. Thomas*. Translated by J. E. O'MAHONY, O.F.M.CAP. London and New York, 1935.

———. *Pour l'histoire du problème de l'amour au moyen âge*. Paris, 1933.

RULAND, L. *Handbuch der praktischen Seelsorge*. 4 vols. Munich, 1930–1936.

SALET, G., S.J. *Le Christ notre vie*. Tournai, 1937.

———. "Le mystère de la charité divine," RSR, 28 (1938), 5–30.

SCHEEBEN, M. J. *The Mysteries of Christianity*. Translated by C. VOLLERT, S.J. St. Louis, 1946.

SCHILLING, O. *Lehrbuch der Moraltheologie*. 2 vols. 2nd ed. Munich, 1928.

SCHNACKENBURG, R. *Die sittliche Botschaft des Neuen Testament*. Munich, 1954.

SCHÖLLGEN, W. *Grenzmoral. Soziale Krisis und neuer Aufbau*. Düsseldorf, 1946.

SCHOLZ, H. *Eros und Caritas. Die Platonische Liebe und die Liebe im Sinne des Christentums*. Halle, 1929.

SCHÜLKE, H. *Einführung in die christliche Ethik*. Munich, 1952.

SCOTT, C. A. *New Testament Ethics. An Introduction*. Cambridge, 1929.

SERTILLANGES, A.-D., O.P. *L'amour chrétien*. Paris, 1919.

———. *La philosophie de saint Thomas d'Aquin*. 2 vols. New ed. Paris, 1940.

———. *La philosophie morale de saint Thomas d'Aquin*. New ed. Paris, 1942.

SOUKUP, L. *Grundzüge einer Ethik der Persönlichkeit*. Graz, 1951.

SPICQ, C., O.P. *Agapè. Prolégomènes à une étude de théologie neo-testamentaire.* Louvain, 1955.

———. *Agapè dans le Nouveau Testament.* 2 vols. Paris, 1952.

———. *Vie morale et Trinité sainte.* Paris, 1957.

STAUFFER, E. "Agapaô, agapè, agapètos," in G. KITTEL's *Theologisches Wörterbuch zum Neuen Testament,* I, 20–55.

STEINBÜCHEL, T. *Religion und Moral im Lichte personaler christlicher Existenz.* Frankfort on the Main, 1951.

STELZENBERGER, J. *Moraltheologie.* Paderborn, 1953.

STEVENS, G., O.S.B. "The Disinterested Love of God According to Saint Thomas and Some of His Modern Interpreters," *The Thomist,* 16 (1953), 307–333; 497–541.

SURIN, J.-J., S.J. *Questions importantes à la vie spirituelle sur l'amour de Dieu.* Texte primitif revisé et annoté par A. POTTIER, S.J., et L. MARIES, S.J. Paris, 1930.

TANQUEREY, A., S.S. *The Spiritual Life. A Treatise on Ascetical and Mystical Theology.* Translated by H. BRANDERIS, S.S. 2nd ed. Tournai, 1932. Westminster, Md., 1945.

TAYMANS, F., S.J. *Le mystère primordial.* Brussels, 1946.

THAMIRY, E. *Fondements de la morale. Morale naturelle et morale chrétienne.* Paris, 1927.

———. *Morale individuelle.* Paris, 1935.

THIBON, G. "L'amour humain: aridités enrichissements," *Études carmélitaines,* 22, 2 (1937), 50–68.

———. *Back to Reality.* Translated by A. GORDON SMITH. London, 1955.

———. *What God Has Joined Together.* Translated by A. GORDON SMITH. London, 1952.

THILS, G. *Tendances actuelles en théologie morale.* Gembloux, 1940.

THOMAS AQUINAS, Saint. *Opera omnia.* 25 vols. Parma, 1852–1873.

———. *The "Summa Theologica" and The "Summa Contra Gentiles" of St. Thomas Aquinas.* 25 vols. Literally translated by the Fathers of the English Dominican Province. London, 1920–1929.

TILLMANN, F. *Handbuch der katholischen Sittenlehre.* With

the collaboration of T. Müncker, T. Steinbüchel and W. Schöllgen. Vol. III: *Die Idee der Nachfolge Christi.* 2nd ed. Düsseldorf, 1940. Vol. IV, 1 and 2: *Die Verwirklichung der Nachfolge Christi.* 3rd ed. Düsseldorf, 1947.

——. *Der Meister ruft. Eine Laienmoral für gläubige Christen.* Düsseldorf, 1937.

Urmanowicz, V. *De formatione virtutum a caritate.* Vilna, 1931.

Vander Kerken, L., s.j. "Menselijke liefde en vriendschap," *Bijdragen uitgegeven door de philosophische en theologische faculteiten der Noord- en Zuid-Nederlandse Jezuïeten,* 7 (1946), 161–199.

Vander Veldt, J. H., o.f.m., and Odenwald, R. P. *Psychiatry and Catholicism.* New York, 1952.

van Kol, A., s.j. *Christus' plaats in S. Thomas' Moraalsysteem.* Roermond-Maeseyck, 1947.

Van Ouverkerk, C. A. J., c.ss.r. *Caritas et ratio. Étude sur le double principe de la vie morale chrétienne d'après saint Thomas d'Aquin.* Nijmegen, 1956.

Van Roey, J.-E., Card. *De virtute caritatis. Quæstiones selectæ.* Mechlin, 1929.

Vermeersch, A., s.j. *Theologiæ moralis principia, responsa, consilia.* Vol. I: 3rd ed. Rome, 1933. Vol. II: Rome, 1937. Vol. III: Rome, 1935.

Viller, M., s.j. *La spiritualité des premiers siècles chrétiens.* Paris, 1930.

Vittrant, J.-B., s.j. *Theologie morale.* New ed. Paris, 1944.

Warnach, V. *Agapè. Die Liebe als Grundmotiv der neutestamentlichen Theologie.* Düsseldorf, 1951.

White, V., o.p. *God and the Unconscious.* London and Chicago, 1952.

Wiéner, C. *Recherches sur l'amour de Dieu dans l'Ancien Testament.* Paris, 1957.

Woroniecki, H., o.p. "La place des preceptes de charite dans l'enseignement du catéchisme," Ang, 25 (1948), 18–26.

Zeiger, I. A., s.j. "Codex Juris Canonici et Theologia Moralis," Per, 32 (1943), 326–335.

——. "De conditione Theologiæ Moralis moderna," Per, 28 (1939), 177–180.

——. "De mutua inter Theologiam Moralem et Ius Canonicum habitudine," Per, 21 (1942), 333–345.

——. "Katholische Moraltheologie heute," StZ, 134 (1938), 143–153.

Scriptural Index

Index of Saint Thomas

389

$$2^a\text{-}2^{ae}$$

Index of Authors

General Index

A

Abnegation, inherent in the love of man historically considered, 143; more complete in charity, 159

Abortion, as an objective determination contradicting the profound tendency, 80

Absolution, and return to charity, 25–27

Act ("Formed"), 29 and n.

(Human): its complexity, 7; one in its complexity, 173 f.; its *bonitas prima*, 7; description, 7; actual participation of the act of the will, 9; numerous acts of man are not, 223 n.; in the just man, it entails a personal commitment to Christ, 203.

(Interior): does not fall as such under a human legislator, 269.

(Moral): 6 ff.; ontological value of, 6 f.; implies a concept, a "determination" of the active tendency, 77 f.; is mediation of the inner tendency, 59, 86; evidence of a love, 79; charity and, 5–28; beginning of a return to oneself, 82 f.; as act-sign, 93; is the very act of virtue under another aspect of causality, 163; participation in the Eucharistic sacrifice as Christian, 232; must be connected with the sacraments, 233; the initial, 22 f., 24, and n.

Act of virtue, 30–35; mediation of charity, 161; moral act and, 163

Action, must not be opposed to divine union, nor to progressive interiorization, 251 f.; as authentic sign of true mystics (Bergson), 252

Activism, its cure in the humility of the Christian way of acting, 215 f.

Adoration, as fundamental religious attitude, 290 f.

Agapè, in God, xxiii; intratrinitarian revealed in Jesus Christ, 135; center of the Christian life, xxvii; source of grace, xxiv; pattern of life, xxv f.; in Church, xxvii; *Eros* or *Agapè*?, 101 f.

Age of reason and moral life, 24 and n.

Alms, its measure with regard to impossibility or selfishness, 300–303; its manner, 309 f.

Amusement in Christian morality, 231

Analogy of being, 163 f.

"Angelism," danger of the method of mediation?, 257 and n.

Apostolate, as mediation of charity, 247; fundamental moral attitude of the Christian and his "acting as member," 211, 247 and n.; subjective attitude of the apostle, 249 f.; means of, 249; as mediation

401

of charity, 249; obstacles to, 250; the presentation of the message as a loving gesture of God, 250 f.; medical, 315–317.

Ascetic, *see* Theology (spiritual)

Asceticism, "exteriorization" of mysticism, 243; organically connected with mysticism, 243; tinted with docility, passivity, 243 f.; to be protected from excess, 244, 288

Attrition, does it produce charity?, 25–27 and n.

Authority, morality based on, 233 f.; as a fundamental aspect of Christian morality, 233 f.

B

Baptism, as our transformation into Christ, xxvi

Beatitude, aim of all beings, 101; moral, according to Scotus, 127 f.; "physical," according to St. Thomas, 103–108; moral, according to St. Thomas, 129 f.; its formal constitutive element, 151 n.; its role in charity, 159; will it have primacy in eternity?, 151 n.; eternal, as explicit end of charity, 170

Beneficence, order of—toward neighbor, 304

Benevolence, not enough to define love, 107 f.; compared with concupiscence, 108–124; order of—toward neighbor, 304

Bishop, as center of charity, xxvii

Body, the soul as form of, 84; mediation of the soul, 71, 87; "exteriority" of the soul, 310–315; unless it is taken as an end, 310–312; in materialistic atmosphere of today, 311 f. *See also* Culture (physical)

Bonitas prima, first specification of moral act, 7, 9, 10–14, 30–32

C

Canon Law, *see* Law (of the church)

Cases of conscience, xxix f.

Casuistry, its influence on the formulation of moral theology, xxx; as seen by non-Catholics, xxx n.

Cause (formal) of moral act, first interpretation, 30 f.; second interpretation, 32 f.

Characterology, as integrated in treatise on moral conscience, 252 n.

Charity: as cause of merit, 20; in the child, 24; in the *attritus,* 25–27; influence of in the virtuous act of the just man (St. Thomas), 17, 20–27; actual implicit influence, 18–27, 31 f.; virtual influence, 18–20, 22; habitual influence, 18, 20; *see* Intention; as principle of morality compared with the imitation of Christ, 197–198 and n.; *finis operis* and intrinsic end of all moral activity, 44; form of the virtuous act, 30–35; form of the virtues, 35–45; its efficient and final causality toward all virtues, 171–174; perfective principle of the morality of the virtues, 37 f.; its promulgation in the conscience, 252 n.; "soul" of moral virtues, practical applications, 284–288; infused virtues as mediations of, 165; works of spiritual and

tendency, 81, 193 f.; of virtue, habitual "determination," 162–164, 284 f.; of the obligation, 255 f., 259; of the law, 263 f.; of human law, 265; of the juridical order, 265, 268, 276 f.; of sexuality, 317, 318 f., 320; of conjugal love, 325; of impurity, contradictory to interior life, 327; of Freudianism, 327 f.; as concerned with external goods is the province of the virtue of justice, 331 f., 333; among the virtues, is supreme in the virtue of justice, 334 f.; appears chiefly in the "presumption of law," 335; in commutative, distributive, general justice, 336 f.; *see also* Interiority.

F

Faculties, *see* Powers

Faith and charity, 37; and conceptual knowledge, 71 f.; "uninformed," 44 and n., 180 f.

Fear, servile, as initial apostolic mediation, 251

Fecundity (conjugal), *see* Ends (of marriage)

Filiation, *see* Sonship

Finality: "physical," of love, 103–108; "moral," of love, 126 ff., and the latter's metaphysical insufficiency, 130; implicit, of charity, 171–174

Finis operis of the whole Christian moral activity: love-charity, 44

"Form," moral (St. Thomas), 29–45

Formalism, in disrepute, xxxiii

Formulation of morals, methodological aim of the present work, xxxii ff., xxxv–xxxvii; and primacy of charity in moral theology, a practical problem, 191

Forum (purely exterior), the laws of in the religious state and in the perfection of the religious Rules? 260 n.; in civil society, on account of the imperfection of human order, 266 f.; are a part of the juridical order, 268 f.; their place in a charity-centered morality, 270–275, 270 n.

Freedom, *see* Liberty

Freudianism, its error about the profound tendency, 327 f.; involuntarily witness to Christian values, 329

Friendship (obligation of), not strict, yet can be felt, 261

G

Generosity, and present aspiration toward self-commitment, xxxi f.; in love according to St. Thomas, 113; as "fundamental note of the universe" (Bergson), 139; in the psychology of love, 142 f.; as object of preaching, 144; toward neighbor, as fundamental attitude of Christian morality, 195–196 and n.

Gift, in the love of man for man, 143 f.; in man's love for God, 148–150; in God-Trinity, 135 f.; between men, 142 f.; without calculation, as understood in Christ, 210 f.; how far without calculation? 211;

Infinite, in our knowledge, 63 f.

"Information" by love-charity, description, 35; necessity, 36–40; has St. Thomas' thought been changed in this matter? 42 n.; "modal quality" (Salmanticenses), 40 f.

Instincts, the mediation of is transformed into an absolute by Freudianism, 327–329; are imbued with spiritual reality in man, cannot be analysed for themselves alone, 330, *cf.* 331 f.; of justice, 331 f., 340; sexual, 320–324; and almost universal egoism, 146–147 and n.

"Instrumentality" and mediation, 87 n.

Intellect and will, reciprocal causality, 151–152 n.; two aspects of a fundamental dynamism, 75 and n., 77, 106 f., 108; in beatitude, 151–152 n.

Intention, classification of the various, 18–20; required for supernatural merit (St. Thomas' doctrine), 182 f.; frequent and explicit of charity required or advised, 183–187; "natural" is often "deficient," 185; of love is not enough to make life morally good, 79 f.

Interestedness, and love in man, 103 f., 108 f.; *see also* Love, Concupiscence

Interior (act), *see* Act (interior)

Interior life, *see* Interiority

Interiority, active progress toward giving meaning to all problems of morality, 346–348; returning into oneself, 82 f.; progressive, call to, 235; according to the three ways, 244 f.; confirmed by the doctrine of St. John of the Cross, 245 f.; is it opposed to action? 251 f.; of the virtues as overflow of charity, 288; of the law made possible by the perfection of a given milieu, 268; of charity, 157; of virtue, 284–288; of fraternal charity, 304–308; of the law, 263 f.

(And exteriority): in being, 68; founded on the nature of our incarnate spirit, 254; must not be separated but synthesized in human knowledge, 68–71; in action, 82; and consequently in morals, 242; in spiritual, ascetical and mystical theology, 243; in obligation, 254–262; in religion, 293 f.; in physical, spiritual and moral suffering, 313–315; in the obligation to perfection, 256–262; in the whole moral life, 346 f.; in the adhesion to faith, 72; in mystical experience, 72–74; and unity and dispersion of human activity, 82 f.; as derived by Bergson from the "two sources of morality," 189 n.; interiority of the spirit and rigidity of the letter of the law, xxviii; *see also* Exteriority

Intuition, an aspect of our knowledge, 60–68; dynamic and tendential, 64 f.; and interiority, 69; how far do we possess it? 90

J

Jansenism, with regard to the body, 311 f.

Jesus Christ, our grace and charity are participations in Christ as Head, 158 f.; has no human self, 198–200; as man is "finalized" on men,

205–207; the whole of Christian morality is marked by the imitation of, 204; *cf.* 197 f., 204 n.; by His filial nature, 215 f.; by His sorrowful Redemption, 224 f.; His actual humanity is not complete without Eucharist, 232; *see also* Mystical Body

Joy, Christian, xxxiii; Christian morality is morality of, 231

Judgment, implied in concept, 65

Juridical order, 267–270; exterior to moral order or inseparable from it? 267–270; exteriority of the moral order considered under its social aspect, 268; does not entirely coincide with the moral order, 265–267, 272 f.; demanded by love, 277 f.; object of justice on account of its exteriority, 334 f.; preferential object of human (civil) law, 335; presumption of the law, 335

Justice (virtue of), its praise by some ancient philosophers, xxii; as explicit end of charity-love, 169 f.; substitute for love in the field of "mine-thine" relations and of exchange and distribution of goods? 179 f.; its true nature: mediation of love, 332 f.; without love, 285; with love, 286; is it opposed to charity? 330 f.; the apparent antinomy explained, 332–337; compared with the instinct of justice, "otherness" on the animal level, 331 f.; where does it begin? 340; its object, 331; is its object opposed to the subject of? 334; the equality of less rigid where love is growing, 333 f.; interior pole of, 338; it is unjust to "stop" at justice alone, 338.
(Christian): compared with natural, 222; its nature, 337 f.; its definition, 341; examples of attitudes of, 339
(General virtue): xxii n. 1; legal, a "general" virtue, 37 f., 181; in what sense is it a social virtue? 335; *cf.* 336 and n.; commutative, distributive, general (legal), 335–337; as infused virtue, 183 f.

Justification of the sinner and charity, 26–27 and n.

K

Knowledge, affective aspect of, 74–77

L

Law, in a charity-centered morality, 253–279; as "determined" obligation or limit-obligation, 256; as interior principle of order (metaphysical sense), 262–264; doubtful, *see* Probabilism; and the liberty of God's children, 278 f.
(Eternal): 262; *see also* Trinity; natural, 219–222; *see also* Love, Virtue (acquired), Supernatural; revealed, *see* Jesus Christ, Imitation of Christ, Charity, Virtue (infused), Virtue (Christian).
(Human, civil): its imperfections, 265–267; yet it is demanded by love, its good offices, 276–278; "purely penal," better called laws of "the purely exterior forum," 273 f.; *see also* Forum; valid obliges in conscience, either directly or indirectly, 268 f.; even if a particular law is useless for an individual? 269; does not bear on

is free, 106 f.; affective union, 108; its psychological description, 110–120; love of concupiscence and love of friendship: their meaning, 114–117; both are found even in the purest love, 119, 124 f.; antinomy surmounted by communion, 153; to be found in friendship, 116, 119 f., 122 f.; metaphysical nature of, 120–124.

(Scotus): theory of the moral finality, 126–131.

(In God): 133–137; in Christ, selflessly detached from the created world, 198–200; of Jesus Christ for men, 205–209; *see also* Charity.

(Sensible): if left to itself, is always self-centered, 118, 124; is selfish after original sin, 118 f. and n.; is drawn by the happiness corresponding to it, 153 f.; sexual, 317–324; conjugal, 306 f., 325 f.; filial, patriotic, 304–307; "national," 307.

Love-charity, explanation of, 32 f., 44 f., 99; to be included in the definition of virtue, 32 f.; according to St. Jerome and St. Augustine, 36, 43; of man, greater for God than for himself, 121 f., 125 f.; overflow of divine charity, 157 f.; *see also* Love, Charity

M

Manuals of moral theology, compared with the Gospel, xxi, xxviii f., xxxi; compared with present day aspirations, xxxiii f.; with modern thought, xxxiv ff., 55 f.; and the influence of charity, 3; why they pay little attention to charity-love, 49–55, 221–224; and spiritual theology, 240–242; and the order of fraternal charity, 299–302; and present tendencies and needs, 348 f.

Marriage, its aspect of creative love, 145; its ends, 324–326; sanctified by the sacrament and by the virtue of Christian conjugal chastity, 323 f.; blossoming in the child's birth and chiefly in his education, 325 f.

Martyrdom, a Christian ideal, xxiii, xxvii; and Christian perfection, 205; virtually contained in the Christian virtue of strength, 231

Mary, fundamental aspect of dependence on in Christian morality, 214 f. and n.

Mass, actual center of the world, 227 and n.; and consecration to the Heart of Christ, 237; our Christian moral acts are continuations of, 232 f.

Mediation, the moral act as, 86; content of, 86 f.; compared with "means," 87 f., *cf.* 96; with "participation," 88; connected with the theology of the Mediator, 87; and "sign," 87; definition of according to Lalande, 87 n.; double function of, 89; connected with "mystery," 89 n., 90 n.; based on the interior tension between matter and spirit in us, 90 f.; moral expression of our "duration," 94; function of moral "value," 97; *see also* Love, Charity, Act (moral), Virtues

Mercy, essential note of Christian charity, 230 f.; works of spiritual and corporal indispensable to charity here below, 167 f.

N

Nation and fatherland, 307; *see also* Politics, Society (civil)

"Nature" as distinct from supernatural, 83, 218–224; *see also* Supernatural

"Nausea" of existentialism, has its antidote in the humility of Christian way of action, 215 f.

"Nights" (mystical), deeply interior sufferings, 314 f.

Nominalism, 12

O

Obedience (virtue of), present crisis of obedience? xxxiii; as fundamental attitude of Christian morality, 234; without love, 285; with love, 286 f.; though indispensable, yet it is second to love, 278 f.

"Object" (moral), 9 f.; "form" of moral act, 7; about "abstract" object, 10; criticism, 11–14; cannot be the "physical" object, 11; the so-called "indifferent" object, criticism, 12 ff., 50; of human acts and of virtues, two interpretations of Thomistic doctrine, 10–14, 32 f., 50–52; when reduced to its purely representative elements, 50 f.; as mediation, 93; interiorly orientated by the current of charity-love, 190

Obligation, the moral object is perceived as, 11; description of as objective moral necessity, its two forms: "limit-obligation" and "love-obligation," 254–262; to perfection, 256–258; of friendship, not strict and yet felt, 261 f.; limit-obligation in justice, 333–334 and n.; limit-obligation at its highest in commutative justice, 337

Onanism, contradicts love-charity, 176

Optimism, characteristic of Christian morality, together with realism, 231

Order (juridical), *see* Juridical order

Ordo amoris (St. Augustine), xxiv, 17, 286

Original sin, a doctrine of love explains better the consequences of, 282 f.

P

Parousia, and expectation in fraternal love, xxv n.

"Participation" of charity in the virtues, 37–40; explained by a "modal" quality (Salmanticenses), 40 f.; text of St. Thomas, 44 and n. 43; of God in created things, 63 f.; compared with mediation, 87 f.; virtues and charity, 172; *see also* Virtues

Passivity, in moral and ascetic life of Christian, 215 f.

Pastoral, *see* Apostolate, Theology (pastoral)

Patriotism, 307

"Penal" laws, *see* Forum (purely exterior)

Penalty, is individualization of a remedy to the generality of law? 269 f.; moral obligation to accept the, 273; *see also* Forum (purely exterior)

Penance (virtue of), 313; as allied to justice, 341

Perfection, measured by charity, xxvii f.; obligation to, total gift of self

Supernatural, elevation to order, as supposed in the present study, xxxviii; conceptual cognition of the, 71 f.; moral activity, 83 f.; means a higher degree of communion with God and men, 156 f.; compared with "natural" from the psychological point of view, 83 f.; from the ontological viewpoint, 218–224

Surpassing of self, as a fundamental attitude of Christian morality, 234 f.; love is, 125; the mediation urges to continuous, 241 f.; the religious state chooses it as its own law, 260

Sympathy and knowledge, 75; between children of a family, 306 f.; between citizens, 307

Synderesis, source of the "moral" object, 13 f., 32; of moral intuition, 78; discovers natural morality, 220 f.; role of in a "morality which takes the subject into account," 51 f.; does affirm the moral "value," 57 f.

T

Taxes, sometimes intentionally exaggerated by the legislator, 265 f.; when would they not oblige in conscience? 271–273

Temperance (virtue of), without love, 285; with love, 286 f.; Christian, 313

Temptation, uses the selfish tendency of nature deprived of the control of charity, 283 f.

Tendency, its decisive influence in any moral object, 13 f.; as expressed in the concept, 65 f., 75 f.; perceived in the concept, 67; cannot be reduced to its conscious aspect, 77; the profound cannot be opposed by "determination," 80; our being is a profound, 100; profound as "value" of moral life, 95; Freudianism bears witness to profound, but misinterprets it, 329 f.

Theology (moral), in what sense is it theology? 217 f.; criticism of its formulation, xxviii f., xxxiii; its possible adaptation to modern conscience, xxxiii–xxxv; methodological research, aim of the present work, xxxvi f.; its formulation too "negative," 50, cf. 231; "abstract," 50 f., 222; "minimizing," 51, 221, cf. 234; its "subjective" formulation, in what sense? 51 f.; compared with contemporary morality, 55–56 and n.; of the confessional, 50
  (Pastoral): to be integrated into moral theology, 246–253; pastoral realism of the "animation by charity," 342–345
  (Spiritual): inseparable from moral theology, 240–242

Thomism, the perspective of the present work, xxxviii, 96, 190 f.

Tradition, marks the fundamental attitude of Christian morality, 234

Tremendum and *fascinans*, aspects of the religious object, 292 f.

Trinity, model for fraternal charity, xxv; as a pattern of all created loves, 135–137; as the perfective model of our love for God, 147–150; and chiefly of our charity toward ourselves, 156 f.; of our charity toward our neighbor, 159 f.; as revealed in the Incarnation, 212; as traced in creation, 138 f.

U

Unconscious, *see* Implicit

Union, by love, 111; with oneself, 131; with God, 132; with others, 132 f.; carnal, as a mediation that must be gradually surpassed, 323 f.; *cf.* 325 f.

V

"Value," set off by mediation, 95; absolute, 95; philosophy of, xxxiv f.; *see also* Charity, Tendency (profound)

Venial sin, *see* Sin

Vigilance (virtue of), 313

Vindictiveness, as a product of the instinct of justice, 332; its influence in Communism, 340; as effect of the virtue of justice, 333 f., *cf.* 338 f.

Virtue(s), its elicited acts, 15; its "commanded" acts, 15; hierarchy of in the moral act, 34; no "true" without charity-love, 35 f.; the concrete nature of as mediation, 162–165; all summed up in love (St. Augustine), xxvii; *ordo amoris*, 17, 266; as specifically different ramifications of the fundamental dynamism, 171–174; virtues find their "sense" in charity, 178–180; their classification in subordination to charity, 180 and n.; of self-denial have priority in Christian morality, 230 f.; Christian have a special redemptive character, 231.
(Acquired): 14–16; remain after the loss of charity, 44; their exercise as dependent on love, 287; are not replaced by the exercise of charity, 177 f.; are indispensable on account of charity itself, 288; the moral without love, 285 f.; animated by love, 286 f.
(Cardinal): according to St. Augustine, 286.
(Infused): 16, 19 f.; as mediations of charity, 165; their specific effect, 165; the infused moral virtues, either denied or differently interpreted by some authors, 52; yet they are different from natural virtues, 83 f.; they are like the retinue of charity, 172 f.; relationship between infused and acquired virtues, 183 f.; how infused are exercised in the act of acquired virtues of the just man, 183 f.
(Moral): 169, 284, 288.
(Theological): they divinize our spiritual powers of action, 154

Vision (beatific), does it suppress liberty? 107; specifies "beatitude," but the "total beatitude" is more extensive than, 151 n., 152 n.; and communion, 156–158, *cf.* 151 n.; in the definition of the supernatural, 219

Vocation, personal implied in our very being, 254 f.; sexuality, perfect chastity and, 319 f.; religious, 315 f.; *see also* Counsels (evangelical)

Voluntary, *see* Intention, Act (human)

Vow, 291; its exteriority-aspect, 293 f.; a religious must beware of stopping at the exterior aspect of, 294

W

Ways (the three), division of and charity, 244 f.

Will, its proper act, 33 f., *cf.* 7 f.; a faculty concerned with the end, 6; and tending to God, 8; elevated, 34; as unifying our appetitive powers, 6, 15; its role in human acts, 7 ff., 9–14; in the acts of virtue, 15 f.; and intellect, their reciprocal causality, 152 n.; divinized by charity, 155 f.; and form of morality, 33 f.; and good will, 107 f.; *see also* Intellect, Love, Charity

Witnessing, Christian as extension and actual manifestation of divine charity, 157 f.; concrete sign of Christ's love for man, 247 f.

Works (apostolic), are they opposed to interior life? 251 f.; of mercy as apostolic mediations, 249; of charity as specific remedies to sin and temptation, 284

A NOTE ON THE TYPE

IN WHICH THIS BOOK IS SET

This book is set in Janson, a Linotype face, created from the early punches of Anton Janson, who settled in Leipzig around 1670. This type is not an historic revival, but rather a letter of fine ancestry, remodeled and brought up to date to satisfy present-day taste. It carries a feeling of being quite compact and sturdy. It has good color and displays a pleasing proportion of ascenders and descenders as compared to the height of the lower case letters. The book was set and printed by The York Composition Company, Inc., of York, and bound by Moore & Co. of Baltimore. The typography and design are by Howard N. King.

THE PRIMACY
OF
CHARITY IN MORAL
THEOLOGY

by GÉRARD GILLEMAN, S.J., *professor at
the Jesuit faculty of theology, Kurseong,
India. Translated from the second French
edition by* WILLIAM F. RYAN, S.J., *and*
ANDRÉ VACHON, S.J.

The Newman Press • 1961 • Westminster, Maryland

Second printing, 1961

Imprimi potest: T. RICHIR, S.J.
v.a. Praep. V.-Prov. Calcuttensis
August 31, 1959

Imprimatur: FERDINANDUS PÉRIER, S.J.
Archiepisc. Calcuttensis
September 7, 1959

This is a translation of *Le primat de la charité en théologie morale* published by Éditions Desclée de Brouwer, Brussels.

Library of Congress Catalog Card Number: 59-14798